CULTURES OF AGEING AND AGEISM IN INDIA

This book examines the discourses on ageing and ageism in Indian culture, politics, art, and society. It explores its representations and the anxieties and fears associated with old age.

The volume looks at ageing within the contexts of the larger discourses of gender, sexuality, nation, health, and the performance and politics of ageing. The chapters grapple with diverse issues around ageing and elder care in contemporary India, shifts in socio-economic conditions, and the breakdown of the hetero-patriarchal family. The book includes personal accounts and narratives that detail the daily experiences of ageing and living with disease, anxiety, loneliness, and loss for both elders and their friends and families. The book also explores the models of alternative networks of kinship and care that queer elders in India create in India as well as examining narratives – in society, art, sports, and popular culture that both critique and challenge stereotypical ideas about the desires, aspirations, and mental and physical capabilities of elders.

Topical and comprehensive, this book will be useful for scholars and researchers of gerontology, literature, cultural studies, popular culture, sociology, social psychology, queer studies, gender studies, social anthropology, and South Asian studies.

Paromita Chakravarti (D.Phil., Oxon.) is Professor of English and has been the Director of the School of Women's Studies, Jadavpur University, Kolkata. She teaches Renaissance drama, women's writing, sexuality, and film studies and introduced the first Master's course in Queer Studies in India (2005). She has led national and international projects on gender in textbooks, sex education, women's higher education, homeless women, HIV and women, and single women. Her books include *Women Contesting Culture* (2012),

Shakespeare and Indian Cinemas (2018), and *Asian Interventions in Global Shakespeare* (2020). Her book *Bengal and Italy: Transcultural Encounters from the Mid Nineteenth Century to the Early 21st Century* is forthcoming from Routledge.

Kaustav Bakshi is Associate Professor, Department of English, Jadavpur University. A Charles Wallace India Trust Fellow, he has worked on Sri Lankan War Literature and sexualities for his doctoral programme. An LGBTIQ+ activist, he has published in several national and international journals, such as *South Asian Review* (2012), *Postcolonial Text* (2015), *New Cinemas: Journal of Contemporary Film* (2013), *South Asian History and Culture* (2015, 2017, 2021, & 2022), *South Asian Popular Culture* (2018), and *Cultural Trends* (2023) on queer politics, literature, and culture. His latest books include *Rituparno Ghosh: Cinema, Gender, Art* (2015), *Queer Studies: Texts, Contexts, Praxis* (2019), and *Popular Cinema in Bengal: Star, Genre, Public Cultures* (2021).

CULTURES OF AGEING AND AGEISM IN INDIA

*Edited by Paromita Chakravarti
and Kaustav Bakshi*

LONDON AND NEW YORK

Designed cover image: Biswanath Datta at Gobar Guha's akhada, warming up. Photograph by Kawshik Aki, courtesy School of Cultural Texts and Records, Jadavpur University.

First published 2024
by Routledge
4 Park Square, Milton Park, Abingdon, Oxon OX14 4RN

and by Routledge
605 Third Avenue, New York, NY 10158

Routledge is an imprint of the Taylor & Francis Group, an informa business

© 2024 selection and editorial matter, Paromita Chakravarti and Kaustav Bakshi; individual chapters, the contributors

The right of Paromita Chakravarti and Kaustav Bakshi to be identified as the authors of the editorial material, and of the authors for their individual chapters, has been asserted in accordance with sections 77 and 78 of the Copyright, Designs and Patents Act 1988.

All rights reserved. No part of this book may be reprinted or reproduced or utilised in any form or by any electronic, mechanical, or other means, now known or hereafter invented, including photocopying and recording, or in any information storage or retrieval system, without permission in writing from the publishers.

Trademark notice: Product or corporate names may be trademarks or registered trademarks, and are used only for identification and explanation without intent to infringe.

British Library Cataloguing-in-Publication Data
A catalogue record for this book is available from the British Library

ISBN: 978-0-367-35229-5 (hbk)
ISBN: 978-0-367-37071-8 (pbk)
ISBN: 978-0-429-35256-0 (ebk)

DOI: 10.4324/9780429352560

Typeset in Sabon
by Deanta Global Publishing Services, Chennai, India

CONTENTS

List of Figures   *vii*
List of Contributors   *viii*
Acknowledgements   *xi*

Introduction   1
Paromita Chakravarti and Kaustav Bakshi

1 The Power of Vulnerability: Age, Activism, and the "Daadis"   13
Paromita Chakravarti

2 From Maintenance to Care-ing: The Aged in Times of
Changing Familial Geographies   33
Rukmini Sen

3 Queering Chrononormativity in India: Challenges and
Possibilities   48
Kaustav Bakshi

4 Care, Intimacy, and Shifting Power: The Ageing Body
within and without the "Family"   74
Chayanika Shah

5 Precarious Lives, Caring Networks, and Queer Ageing   88
Ranjita Biswas

vi Contents

6 Physical Cultures and the Ageing Body: The Long
Careers of Manohar Aich and Biswanath Datta   104
Sujaan Mukherjee

7 Umar Ka Lihaz: Ageism in Indian Classical Dance   126
Shantanu Majee

8 More than Memories: Aging and the Attachment to
Material Objects in Three Indian Short Stories   145
Ira Raja

9 Actor as a Time-Traveller: Politics of Performing Age
Onstage   157
Mansi Grover

10 His Master Voice: Amitabh Bachchan, Aural Stardom,
and the Ageless Baritone   177
Madhuja Mukherjee

11 "Second Childishness and Mere Oblivion": Indian Films
on Dementia and the Idea of Ageing Differently   201
Nilanjana Deb

12 Ageing, Caring, and Mortality   222
V. Geetha

13 Loneliness, Belatedness, and Care: Arriving Late Where
You No Longer Are   232
Trina Nileena Banerjee

Index   249

FIGURES

6.1	Biswanath Datta at Gobar Guha's akhada, warming up. Photograph by Kawshik Aki, courtesy School of Cultural Texts and Records, Jadavpur University	112
6.2	"The Panther on a Lion," Posed by S. Bose. Published in K.C. Sengupta and B.C. Ghosh, Muscle Control and Barbell Exercise	113
6.3	"The Living Statue," Posed by S. Bose. Published in K.C. Sengupta and B.C. Ghosh, Muscle Control and Barbell Exercise	114
10.1	The Bachchan mask in *Badla*	179
10.2	Prosthetics and aging in *Gulabo Sitabo*	180

CONTRIBUTORS

Trina Nileena Banerjee is currently Assistant Professor in Cultural Studies at the Centre for Studies in Social Sciences Calcutta. Her book *Performing Silence: Women in the Group Theatre Movement in Bengal* was published in October 2021.

Ranjita Biswas identifies as a queer feminist activist and is a member of Sappho for Equality, a collective-organization working for the rights and social justice of lesbian, bisexual, and queer cis women and transmasculine individuals. Ranjita divides her time between mental health work, research, and gender sexuality knowhow-building. Her care network consists of her queer kin, her feline companion, and her garden of greens and yellows.

Nilanjana Deb is Associate Professor in the Department of English, Jadavpur University. Her areas of research and teaching interest include postcolonial, diaspora and subaltern studies, cultures of protest, environmental humanities, and indigenous epistemologies. She has been involved in research for the development of decolonizing pedagogies in secondary and tertiary education, the study of South Asian cities, and the culture of the old Indian diaspora.

V. Geetha is a feminist historian who has written extensively on gender, labour, education, caste, and civil rights. Her published works include *Bhimrao Ramji Ambedkar and the Question of Socialism in India* (2021) and *Undoing Impunity: Speech after Sexual Violence* (2016). Currently she is Editorial Director, Tara Books, Chennai.

Contributors **ix**

Mansi Grover is working as Assistant Professor in the Department of English, College of Vocational Studies, University of Delhi. For her Ph.D., she has examined the representation of women with disabilities in Hindi Cinema since 1970. She also practices theatre and works with a Delhi-based theatre group. Her areas of interest include cultural studies, disability studies, feminist studies, age studies, film studies, and performing studies.

Shantanu Majee is an early career academician from Kolkata, currently employed as Assistant Professor in the Department of English at Techno India University, West Bengal. He received his M.Phil. and Ph.D. on Nineteenth-Century Studies from Jadavpur University. He has contributed to digital humanities and cultural informatics through his engagement as Project Fellow in the School of Cultural Texts and Records, Jadavpur University. Shantanu has also been the recipient of the Varta Publishing Grant 2021, offered by Akar Prakar Art Gallery, New Delhi.

Madhuja Mukherjee is Professor of Film Studies at Jadavpur University, India. She extends her research into art-practice and filmmaking. Recently she co-edited *Popular Cinema in Bengal* (2020) and *Industrial Networks and Cinemas of India* (2021). She is the Director of *Carnival* (No-dialogues, 2012), and her feature film, *Deep6* (Bengali), had its World Premiere at the 26th Busan International Film Festival 2021.

Sujaan Mukherjee is a researcher, writer, and translator, currently based at the Centre for Studies in Social Sciences, Calcutta, as a Mellon Foundation Postdoctoral Fellow. He completed his Ph.D. on urban spaces and colonial memory in Kolkata as a SYLFF Fellow at the Department of English, Jadavpur University. Sujaan has worked with museums in various capacities and publishes in academic journals and public platforms.

Ira Raja is Professor of English at the University of Delhi, India. Her research is concentrated on South Asia, with ageing, intimacy, care, colonialism, friendship, memory, objects, and nation states, being some areas of particular interest. Her most recent publications include the following co-edited special journal issues: "Postcolonial World Literature" (Thesis Eleven 2021) and "In the Line of Fire: The Public University in India" (*Postcolonial Studies* 2021). Ira is part of the DFG-funded RTG Minor Cosmopolitanisms located at the University of Potsdam, Germany. She is an Honorary Associate of the Department of Social Inquiry at La Trobe University, Australia.

Rukmini Sen is Professor at the School of Liberal Studies at Dr B R Ambedkar University, Delhi. She teaches and researches on sociology of law, kinship and intimacies, and feminist methodologies. Her co-edited books are *Doing*

x Contributors

Feminisms in the Academy: Identity, Institutional Pedagogy and Critical Classrooms in India and the UK (2020) and *Trust in Transaction* (2019). She has published in the *Indian Journal of Gender Studies, Economic and Political Weekly, Indian Anthropologist, Journal of Educational Planning and Administration,* and *Contemporary Voice of the Dalit.* She has been curating a blog series #16daysblogathon during the UN-recognized Violence Fortnight (Nov 25–Dec 10) in collaboration with the University of Edinburgh, Scotland, and the University of New South Wales, Australia.

Chayanika Shah is a queer feminist who has worked and written extensively on issues of the politics of population control and reproductive technologies, communalism, feminist studies of science, and sexuality and sexual rights. She has been an active member of autonomous voluntary women's and queer organizing based in Bombay and has engaged to different degrees with various movements for the rights of the marginalized.

ACKNOWLEDGEMENTS

Both the editors are grateful to the UGC-CAS III programme, Department of English, Jadavpur University, for funding the national conference, "Ageing, Ageism and Cultures" in 2016. The idea of the current anthology germinated out of the conversations and scholarly presentations at the conference.

INTRODUCTION

Paromita Chakravarti and Kaustav Bakshi

> *Old age is not a status we choose to become; it is a status that we inherit simply by the virtue of living, not dying.*
>
> – Holstein (2006: 317)

(i)

The COVID-19 pandemic saw an unprecedented burgeoning of discussions on ageing and ageism around the question of the greater susceptibility of the elderly to the virus which made a case both for the need to protect them and equally for their dispensability. One of the countries to be worst hit by the first wave, Italy struggled with the large number of older people infected by the virus and the need to make difficult choices about how or indeed whether to offer them already stretched health services. A report in *The Telegraph* from Turin, Italy (14 March 2020), quoted a doctor allegedly claiming: "[Who lives and who dies] is decided by age and by the [patient's] health conditions. This is how it is in a war." In the face of an inadequate healthcare system overwhelmed by the enormous numbers of COVID cases, senior citizens were marked out as dispensable. The *US Today* later reported (21 March 2020), "If cases continue to surge, officials might be forced to prioritize care for those with 'the best chance of success' and the 'best hope of life'," taking care to underline the fact that killing senior citizens (with unmanageable comorbidities) was certainly not the intention of the Italian government. Achille Mbembe, in a philosophical intervention on the concept of "necropolitics," had claimed in 2003, "the ultimate expression of sovereignty resides, to a large degree, in the power and the capacity to dictate who may live and who must die. Hence, to kill or to allow to live constitute the

DOI: 10.4324/9780429352560-1

limits of sovereignty, its fundamental attributes"; interestingly this applies to the COVID crisis – a warlike medical emergency that hit several countries across the globe at the beginning of 2020. In this unforeseen "state of exception," bio-power was materialized in horrific ways particularly against ageing citizens. Puar's (2017) conceptualization of the "right to maim" in the context of police atrocities against black Americans and Palestinians – debilitating and de-capacitating citizens based on their perceived value – may be used to understand the COVID emergency and the culling of the elderly. Puar talks about authoritarian logics in which a certain section of the population is "definitively unworthy of health and [are] targeted" (68–69) in relation to others who are considered worthy of health service. Under the overpowering COVID-19 waves which threatened all lives, a judgement of worth was arrived at, in which older citizens were marked out as "slated for death or slated for debilitation" (p. x). This form of ageism, although practised under exceptional circumstances, exposed the dispensability of the elderly even in "normal" times.

The term "ageism," underlining the negative stereotyping of old age, was coined by Robert N. Butler in 1968, and in 1969, it entered the Oxford English Dictionary. Butler described ageism or discrimination against older people, as analogous to racist and sexist prejudices:

> Ageism can be seen as a systematic stereotyping of and discrimination against people because they are old, just as racism and sexism accomplish this with skin color and gender … I see ageism manifested in a wide range of phenomena, on both individual and institutional levels – stereotypes and myths, outright disdain and dislike, simple subtle avoidance of contact, and discriminatory practices in housing, employment, and services of all kinds.
>
> *(qtd. in Butler 1989: 139)*

Ageism, as Butler observes, is non-normative, vis-à-vis youth, since society is largely structured on the assumption that the majority is *not* old. But it is important to note that ageing is a universal process. While ageism can be linked to racism, sexism, or homophobia, unlike the latter, it affects everybody, regardless of class, caste, race, ethnicity, and gender or sexual identity. Therefore, the "aged" cannot be an exclusive identity or demographic category.

In fact, COVID brought this home in an unprecedented way. Even as the elderly appeared to be brutally dispensable during the pandemic and the divide between old and young populations deepened, the lockdown experience also blurred the distinctions between them as active working people whose temporalities were structured by the logic of high-paced capitalist productivity which suddenly experienced a slowing down of time. Compelled to live homebound, less active, isolated existences haunted by constant anxieties about health, disease, and death, the young came to experience the texture and rhythms of the lives of retired, older people. As usual amenities and services operated at a bare minimum and people became more susceptible to sickness and death; the importance of mutual care not just for the old but for all was acutely felt. The lived experience of the pandemic necessitated a revisiting and reframing of the most dominant discursive frameworks of ageing and ageism – the ideas of elderly care and the binaristic construction of the young and the old as almost separate demographic categories.

But these experiences are yet to inform the prevalent discourse of ageing which continues to negatively stereotype the elderly who are urged to follow appropriate, decorous, and respectable ways of ageing, especially in India. For instance, in both Hindu and Buddhist theological and social texts older people are encouraged to observe austerity, practise detachment, and renounce materialistic pursuits. The ageing body is thus removed from the mainstream of life and living and is associated with disease and decay, and death. This makes it akin to the queer body which is unable to reproduce life and is thus marginalized and reviled by society and the state. The idea of active or productive ageing is rarely celebrated in India. The United Nations characterize the increasing population of the elderly as a "crisis" since "old persons cost money rather than produce income, and need care rather than provide care" (Lamb 2009: 7). Within capitalist economies, older people are therefore seen as an encumbrance unless they are profitably integrated within it as potential consumers of the medicine or cosmetic industry, of professional caregiving, or organizations promising productive ways of ageing. Unsurprisingly, therefore, the cosmetic industry has made ageing more undesirable than ever before, by launching and promoting anti-ageing creams and serums, facilitated largely by rapid advancement in nanotechnology in synthesizing retinoid/s – tretinoin, tazarotene, retinaldehyde, and retinol – which have apparently proved beneficial in arresting the effects of biological ageing.

In *No Aging in India* (1999), the medical anthropologist, Lawrence Cohen points out that studies on old age commonly begin by assuming it is a "problem." But strangely, it is only "assumed, not demonstrated." As a result, "the language of gerontology is alarmist, almost apocalyptic" (87). It is by default paternalistic, as is the practice of romanticizing old age as second childhood. They allow "older people to be treated as property, possessions or objects, not as individuals" (Spencer 2009: 11). It is extremely difficult to evade these terms; yet, modern scholarship on ageing is trying to approximate a more neutral language.

Instead of "old people" and "old age," modern scholars prefer "older people" and "later life." However, a contrary view to replacing "old" with "older" is also found in ageism studies. Toni Calasanti (2003) writes:

While "old" is socially constructed, reified and stigmatized, as are many other terms for oppressed groups, using the term "older" conveys that the old are more acceptable if we think of them as more like the middle-aged. In much the same way that many would find it ludicrous to refer to Blacks as "darker" and instead recognize the efforts to reclaim the word "Black" and imbue it with dignity, so too I use "old" to recover and instil the term with positive valuation.

(16)

"Older," one may argue, appears to be a more useful term, because, ageing, as the suffix "–ing" signifies, is a continuous process, and therefore, age is always relative. However, the controversy over the political correctness in the use of language in ageing discourses is beset with the paradox of the social and cultural construction of ageing itself. While there is a necessity to accept ageing as inevitable, nothing to be ashamed or scared of, the euphemistic language of encouragement actually ends up projecting ageing as undesirable, emphasizing the need to defer it as much as possible. Segal says: "'You are only as old as you feel', though routinely offered as jolly form of reassurance, carries its own disavowal of old age" (2013). Ironically, attempts to destigmatize ageing through affirmative rhetoric end up reinforcing the stigma.

(ii)

The COVID-19 crisis and the attendant lockdowns, considerably altered our understanding and experience of temporalities: As Antentas (2020) observes "[T]he simultaneous perception of living an unknown moment and a foretold catastrophe has been coupled. It seems to bring up-to-date atavistic fears (death, contagion, etc.) but in a hyper-technological and accelerated environment." For Levrini (2020), the pandemic deepened "the dichotomy between alienation from time and time re-appropriation through intense meditation on experiential time." The experience of COVID appeared to have accelerated ageing for all, as the immanence of death shrouded everyday existence. Mortality, debility, and disease were no longer the exclusive concerns of the elderly, the consciousness of fragile human corporeality touched everyone intimating them of an imminent apocalyptic end.

Ironically, all this was concomitant with a moment in human history, when scientists were making unprecedented advances in bio-technology and genetic engineering, which suggested possibilities of prolonging life, arresting and delaying ageing, and eventually conquering death.[1] Modern science, as Harari (2017) observes, does not think of death as "a metaphysical mystery," but as "a technical problem that we can and should solve." However, this is not a new perception. As Katz shows, the discourse of senescence can be traced back to the early developments in medical science in the late 18th and early 19th centuries, particularly in the works of Xavier Bichat (1771–1802) of the Paris School of Medicine. Bichat's tissue theory of anatomy, which claims that life of the tissue is life in miniature, can be seen as a precursor to the much talked about "telomere effect"[2] today.

Although conquering death is still an unrealizable dream, the discovery of powerful antibiotics such as teixobactin, the unprecedented advancement in the development of nano-tech immune systems, and the exciting possibility of reversing telomere attrition responsible for damaging the DNA and hastening death have considerably enhanced the possibility of human beings becoming "a-mortal," if not "immortal," as Harari claims. Modern science has been undoubtedly successful in arresting premature death if not in conquering death, augmenting life expectancy and assuring a healthier life, for at least some, who can afford to access these gifts of medicine. In this context one is reminded of Vincent's (2006) critique of bio-gerontology's preoccupation with discovering anti-ageing medicines to postpone old age:

> Constructed, even from an implicit perspective that science will cure death, old age becomes an unnecessary burden; it is a result of an unnecessary failure technically to control a biological process. Immortality sees the boundary between old age and death removed, leaving the boundary between youth and old age problematic.
>
> *(692)*

Vincent roots his argument in Foucault's observation (1973):

> The aged body became reduced to a state of degeneration where the meanings of old age and the body's deterioration seemed condemned to signify each other in perpetuity. By recreating death as a phenomenon in life, rather than of life, medical research on aging became separate from the earlier treatises that focus on the promise of longevity.
>
> *(41)*

But, the progress in technology has also expedited a shift in geological time epoch, from the Holocene to the Anthropocene epoch, when the possibilities of many more pandemics – natural or humanly engineered – are imminent. While the Anthropocene is still a "proposed" epoch in the geological time scale, and the date of the exact transition from the Holocene to the Anthropocene is still debated, what is evident is a growing awareness of the rapidly approaching end of human civilization. As Roy Scranton wrote in *The New York Times* (2013):

In the epoch of the Anthropocene, the question of individual mortality – "What does my life mean in the face of death?" – is universalized and framed in scales that boggle the imagination. What does human existence mean against 100,000 years of climate change? What does one life mean in the face of species death or the collapse of global civilization? How do we make meaningful choices in the shadow of our inevitable end?[3]

The idea of time or of eternity has been seriously challenged by the epoch of the Anthropocene. While on the one hand, bio-technology and genetic engineering are peddling hopes of defying death, and postponing ageing (as a condition of failing health in advanced years), a disturbing sense of a condensed time is looming large over the world – the synchronicity of these two contradictory discourses have in a way made ageing studies even more relevant today.

(iii)

Till date ageing studies in India has been largely focused on sociological, and demographic or bio-medical and analyses, rather than on critical and theoretical engagements with the cultures of ageing. Popular publications on ageing have inundated the market filling up the "lifestyle" sections in bookstores where the focus is on "successful" ageing. Serious academic interventions in the discourse of ageing are rare and far between. A series of enquiries into the "problems of ageing" and possible solutions have been published within the discipline of sociology, in many cases, with policy implications. For ageing citizens, *Ageing in Contemporary India* by Suhas Kumar Biswas (1987), *Understanding Greying People of India* by Arun Bali (1999), and *Health Status of the Urban Elderly: A Medico-social Study* by S. Siva Raju (2002) fall into this category. Cohen's *No Ageing in India: Alzheimer's, the Bad Family, and Other Modern Things* (2000) is one of the first serious medical anthropological enquiries into ageing in India located within the larger discourses of the nation, modernity, kinship, language, and culture. Sara Lamb has contributed significantly to the study of cultures of ageing in India in publications such as *Aging and the Indian Diaspora: Cosmopolitan Families in India and Abroad* (2009). A recent book, *Culture, Context and Aging of Older Indians: Narratives from India and Beyond* by Jagriti Gangopadhyay (2021) adopts a socio-cultural optics and takes an ethnographic approach to understand emotional, social, and psychological issues of older adults in urban India, with respect to the cultural practices that affect ageing.

This book seeks to take a different course by refusing to start with the assumption that ageing is a problem. It takes a close look at the nuanced cultures and politics of ageing locating it within larger discourses of nation, gender, sexuality and the body, time and temporality, chronology and chrononormativity, and stasis and kinesis, examining representations across genres – dance, theatre, cinema, and literature. Located across multiple disciplines the chapters in the book speak to each other in their critical engagements with normativities whether in understanding queer ageing, the ageing body, street politics of the elderly, or representations and performances of ageing in cultural texts. Although an anthology, there is a methodological parity across the chapters, in terms of their resistant, subversive stance vis-à-vis the existing discourses of ageing. The book deploys a queer-feminist method, overtly stated or not – one that "champion(s) the fluid, disruptive, transgressive, interpretivist, and local knowledges," as opposed to the "systematic, coherent, orderly, modal, normative, positivist, and generalizable" (Ghaziani and Brim 4) method often deployed by social science scholars. The chapters reveal what Paul Ricoeur calls *hermeneutics of suspicion*, which entails "expos(ing) hidden truths and draw(ing) out unflattering and counterintuitive meanings that others fail to see" (Felski 1). While Ricoeur's *hermeneutics of suspicion* held sway over humanities and social sciences since the second half of the 20th century, a recurring critique against it is that it discounts affect and emotion – particularly when it comes to literary and cultural studies – with an urgency to break away from liberal humanist methods of criticism. This book takes a middle ground – while demonstrating both a political criticality and being sensitive to affect. As ageing subjects, the researchers write with a deep awareness of the historical and cultural ramifications of being in time – ageing in time and with time – within a complex network of intersectional identities, and political and affective lives, of being and becoming.

(iv)

The 13 chapters in this volume on ageing and ageism were written or revised during the pandemic years under the shadow of the anxieties of giving and receiving care, fears of disease and death, and the contradictions of feeling responsible for and protective of the elderly while experiencing a kind of ageing and vulnerability ourselves, living in the suspended, liminal time of the lockdowns filled with watchful waiting. Although most of the chapters do not overtly mention the COVID situation, many of them are haunted by it. Six out of the 13 chapters are concerned in differing degrees with the changing cartographies of elderly care in a context of a failing hetero-patriarchal family (Rukmini Sen, Nilanjana Deb, Chayanika Shah, Ranjita Biswas, Kaustav Bakshi, Ira Raja), while the two chapters by V. Geetha and Trina Nileena Banerjee are moving personal testimonies about their memories of caring for the elderly and sick – and how the COVID experience, its stress and stasis, provoked a reconsideration of those attempts to sustain and nurture life in the face of death and oblivion. V. Geetha meditates on how the lockdown brings back the feelings of helplessness she felt when caring for an older friend suffering from Alzheimer's disease and attendant loss of memory and personhood, while Trina revisits an earlier hurried bereavement (her father's death) during the pandemic closure which allows her time to comprehend her loss and grief belatedly. Both the chapters explore the power of texts – religious, literary, cinematic – and how they helped to make sense of the traumatic rupture of the pandemic moment. These chapters set the tone for the volume in their unflinching examination of intimate experiences, their reflections on the heightened perception of temporalities in the processes of waiting, caring, and grieving and in their deployment of cultural texts to better understand intimations of mortality, disease, decay, compassion, and nurture.

Section 4, featuring the chapters of Nilanjana Deb and Ira Raja reading cinematic and literary representations of dementia and of material attachments of the ageing respectively, foregrounds the cultural focus of the volume while continuing the underlying theme of elderly care or the lack thereof. While Deb's chapter focuses on the representations of the Indian family and its norms of intergenerational care shaped by class, gender, and caste locations as well as Indian cultural and philosophical, even religious traditions, Ira's chapter shows how diverse literary narratives challenge the Indian association of ageing with renunciation and dwell on almost fetishistic attachments of elderly protagonists to particular objects which give them a sense of belonging and meaning in an uncaring world. Ira shifts the contours of the predictable narrative of older people's dependence on the young towards an almost post-human contemplation of their attachment to objects which is characterized as a "technology of self-care."

Discussions of ageing are almost over-determined, particularly in sociological contexts, by the care needs of a growing and longer lived older population and the changing roles of institutions like the family, State, community, and market in providing it. Often framed by an East-West duality these deliberations locate intergenerational kinship networks as the site of elderly care in South Asia while the West is associated with the decline of the family and the normalization of paid, commercial care (see Cohen). During COVID however, the much celebrated Indian family came under severe strain, revealing the limits of its role as a caregiving institution, particularly for the old and the ailing who became dependent on paid care, hospitals, and safe home facilities. Families were not even allowed to perform the last rites of those who died of COVID. As lockdowns forced parents and children to spend months together in claustrophobic domestic spaces, the rates of intergenerational and gender-based violence soared.

This immediate context contributes to the critical reevaluation of the accepted frameworks of elderly care which is spread across several other chapters in the volume, particularly in the section on queer ageing. Sen's examination of the growing crisis of intergenerational familial care for the ageing in a context of rapid social changes sets the tone for the section on queer ageing. The chapter analyses Indian law and state policy to show how an ageing and longer lived population, the nuclearization of the family, migration of youth, women joining the workforce and not being available as full-time carers have made the family an unviable institution of elder care. As the neoliberal state also withdraws from these responsibilities, paid care offered by the burgeoning market becomes the only option. Recognizing this, law and state policy, once critical of families which failed to take care of their elders, are increasingly recognizing the need for alternatives like old age homes.

It is in this context of failing familial support that the question of elder care for queer people becomes moot. The inadequacies of the hetero-patriarchal family, its authoritarianism and entrenched caste, class, gender, and sexuality biases were most clearly revealed in the violent rejections faced by queer persons and sex workers when they had to return to natal families after their rented apartments, hostels, and brothels shut down with the onset of the pandemic. While the viability of kinship-based support systems came under stress, people rallied around each other, performing acts of kindness and care for near strangers at great personal risk – friends, acquaintances, neighbours, attendants, and particularly those in essential public services like doctors, nurses, paramedics, social workers, and mortuary workers entrusted with the disposal of the bodies of those dying from COVID.

The chapters in the section on queer ageing are informed and intensified by these experiences of the pandemic by Shah, Bakshi, and Biswas challenge the normative temporalities structured by the reproductive logic of heteropatriarchy which governs the family and its structures of reciprocal intergenerational care. Rejected by their natal families for their sexual choices, most queer people develop alternative networks of care. All three chapters present ways in which the existing models of kinship care based on ideas of duty and responsibility could be reimagined through the elective affinities of a queer commune built by the affective and mutual care of community members and friends. In all three chapters a new and radical ethics and politics of elderly care is envisaged which is not a compulsory duty stemming from the accident of birth and blood relationship, fraught with guilt and resentment but a voluntary, affective, chosen action, shared with other carers in a creative and non-hierarchical environment. In the face of a failing paradigm of familial care, these alternative modes become relevant not just for queer people but for others too.

These chapters delink discussions of ageing and care from the intergenerational binary of old and young, parent and child, helping us to see the elderly not as a burden on future generations who are compelled by a reproductive logic to look after them but as valuable entities, esteemed and cared for by strangers, acquaintances, community members, and friends, both young and old. Beyond the narrative of decline and decay, renunciation and withdrawal, the ageing queer emerge as autonomous subjects defined by desires, sexualities, aspirations, and friendships. This leads into the section on performing age in which four chapters challenge the narrative of diminishing capacities of ageing bodies engaged in the performative cultures of dance, acting, and bodybuilding which place the highest premium on youthful vitality, power, and energy. Sujaan Mukherjee and Shantanu Majee's chapters argue for the need to revise our performance aesthetics based on the normative, pristine, and young body to enable an appreciation of the performing body not as a static product but as a process, undergoing continuous change as it moves through life. Our cultural histories and traditions provide examples of how the ageing bodies of bodybuilders and dancers may be perceived not in terms of a deficit or a falling away but in terms of a growing – in skill, experience, control, and an embodied knowledge of the craft which can be handed down by the "gurus" to less mature performers. These chapters urge us to develop ways of valuing the performing body as a work in progress which brings different kinds of skill sets into play at different stages of life.

Madhuja Mukherjee's chapter shows how the film industry has handled the changing locus of Amitabh Bachchan's stardom from his body to his voice – while his body was allowed to age on screen, his voice was rendered ageless, even turned into a deeper baritone. From the 2000s Bachchan was reinvented as an ageing hero who no longer featured in action films, choosing more offbeat stories to showcase his histrionic skills, while the aural appeal of his voice was enhanced and underlined particularly through voice-overs and dubbings. But while the age-related shifts in the performer's body should be acknowledged and valued, it is equally important to appreciate the performer's ability to represent a character of any age. Mansi Grover's dialogic chapter demonstrates how stage actors perceive the challenges of ageing up and down, performing characters which are either considerably younger or older than their own age. These discussions by practitioners which dissociate representation from the materiality of the performing body help us to perceive age as a fluid, performative category rather than as an essentialized, naturalized state which reifies and boxes us into the binaries of young and old, as separate and fixed categories.

The final chapter of the book by Paromita Chakravarti attempts to transcend this artificial divide between the young and the old by trying to envisage a new politics of ageing built on care-based solidarities. The chapter seeks to analyse the unique leadership of the "Daadis," the elderly women who with no previous experience of activism resolutely led the anti-CAA protests in various Indian cities. Their success lay in their experiences and wisdom garnered through long lives, the respect they commanded as community elders and their ability to keep a diverse group of protestors together. Exposing themselves to physical privations as they braved winter nights in open-air demonstrations, they forged a politics based not on power but on human vulnerability, iconized through their suffering, ageing bodies. The anti-CAA protest sites, dominated by women, were characterized by a network of mutual care where the younger women supported the older by tending to their physical needs, while the daadis protected them against police violence, family disapproval, and sexual harassment. The movement was represented by an assemblage of vulnerable bodies (Fineman), connected with each other across the binaries of youth and age, capacity and incapacity, and experience and immaturity through shared susceptibilities and a solidarity of mutual, non-hierarchical, non-familial care.

As societies become more and more resentful of the ageing, positioning them as enemies of youth and seeing them as dispensable (as the COVID experience showed), questioning and transcending the artificial boundaries the old and the young becomes critical. It's time to revise aesthetic norms which fetishize youth, reframe melodramatic social narratives of parental neglect by cruel children, rewrite the representations of age as decline and decay, and dismantle the power hierarchies of the old and the young. As one becomes more cognisant of their own implication in the universal ageing process and the vulnerable human body and of building empathy and care across age, cultures, economies, and politics of age, ageing, and ageism in India would demand a different kind of optics in order to be meaningfully understood. This book is a step in that direction.

Notes

1 Silicon Valley luminaries, such as the gerontologist Aubrey de Grey and the polymath and inventor Ray Kurzweil, Bill Maris, the president of Google Ventures Investment fund, and Peter Thiel, the PayPal co-founder – all guarantee the possibility of cheating death with a healthy body and a healthy bank account.
2 The attrition of telomeres damages DNAs which in turn expedite the process of ageing and eventually dying.
3 https://archive.nytimes.com/opinionator.blogs.nytimes.com/2013/11/1h0/learning-how-to-die-in-the-anthropocene/

Bibliography

Antentas, J. M. "Notes on Corona Crisis and Temporality." *Dialectical Anthropology*, 2020. doi:10.1007/s10624-020-09613-2.
Blasi, Erica. "Italians Over 80 'Will Be Left to Die' as Country Overwhelmed by Coronavirus." *The Telegraph*, 14 Mar. 2020. https://www.telegraph.co.uk/news/2020/03/14/italians-80-will-left-die-country-overwhelmed-coronavirus/.
Butler, R. N. "Dispelling Ageism: 'The Cross-Cutting Intervention'." *Annals of the American Academy of Political and Social Science*, vol. 503, 1989, pp. 138–147.

Calasanti, Toni M. "Theorizing Age Relations." *The Need for Theory: Critical Approaches to Social Gerontology for the 21st Century*, edited by S. Biggs, A. Lowenstein, and J. Hendricks. Baywood, 2003, pp. 199–218.

Cohen, Lawrence. *No Aging in India: Alzheimer's, the Bad Family, and Other Modern Things.* University of California Press, 1999.

Dunn, A. "Fact Check: Were Elderly Italians Left to Die? And is Socialized Health Care to Blame?" *US Today*, 20 Mar. 2020. https://www.usatoday.com/story/news /factcheck/2020/03/20/fact-check-were-italians-left-die-socialized-medicine -blame-coronavirus/2887743001/.

Felski, R. *The Limits of Critique.* E-book, Chicago University Press, 2015.

Fineman, Martha Albertson. "What Vulnerability Theory is and Is Not." *ScholarBlogs*, 1 Feb. 2021. https://scholarblogs.emory.edu/vulnerability/2021/02 /01/is-and-is-not/.

Ghaziani, A. and M. Brimm, editors. *Imagining Queer Methods.* E-book, NYU Press, 2019.

Harari, Y. N. *Homo Deus: A Brief History of Tomorrow.* E-book, Harper, 2017.

Lamb, Sarah. *Aging and the Indian Diaspora: Cosmopolitan Families in India and Abroad.* E-book, Indiana University Press, 2009.

Levrini, O., et al. "The Present Shock and Time Re-Appropriation in the Pandemic Era." *Science & Education*, vol. 30, no. 1, 2020, pp. 1–31. doi:10.1007/ s11191-020-00159-x.

Mbembé, J.-A. and Libby Meintjes. "Necropolitics." *Public Culture*, vol. 15. no. 1, 2003, pp. 11–40. *Project MUSE*, muse.jhu.edu/article/39984.

Puar, Jasbir. *Terrorist Assemblages: Homonationalism in Queer Times.* Duke University Press, 2007.

Scranton, Roy. "Learning How to Die in the Anthropocene." *New York Times*, 10 Nov. 2013. https://archive.nytimes.com/opinionator.blogs.nytimes.com/2013/11 /1h0/learning-how-to-die-in-the-anthropocene/.

Segal, L. *Out of Time: The Pleasures and Perils of Ageing.* E-book, Verso, 2013.

Spencer, C. "Ageism and the Law: Emerging Concepts of Housing and Health." *Advancing Substantive Equality for Older Persons through Law, Policy and Practice.* Law Commission of Ontario, Aug. 2009. https://www.lco-cdo.org/en /our-current-projects/a-framework-for-the-law-as-it-affects-older-adults/older -adults-funded-papers/ageism-and-the-law-emerging-concepts-and-practices-in -housing-and-health/.

Vincent, J. A. "Ageing Contested: Anti-Ageing Science and the Cultural Construction of Old Age." *Sociology*, vol. 40, no. 4, Aug. 2006, pp. 681–698.

1

THE POWER OF VULNERABILITY

Age, Activism, and the "Daadis"

Paromita Chakravarti

As the Western world ages and countries like India become demographically younger, it becomes imperative to ask the question whether the young or the ageing should decide the future of the world and take on its leadership. The Malalas and Greta Thunbergs are exposing the irrationality and injustice of a system where older men are still taking crucial decisions the consequences of which they would not live to experience. Yet the ancient traditions of male gerontocracy remain difficult to dislodge.

In Western political thought, elderly males have been considered to be the best suited for leadership and governance. In Plato's *Republic*, Book 4, Socrates and his companions discussing the roles of the guardians of the just state declare "it is obvious that the elder must govern, and the younger be governed" (Plato 2007, 178). Aristotle in *Nichomachean Ethics* excludes the young from the study of politics because they lack experience and act emotionally and irrationally (Aristotle 1953, 28). In *De Senectute*, Cicero recommends that the elders should be entrusted with political leadership since they have the necessary attributes:

> Those...who allege that old age is devoid of useful activity... are like those who would say that the pilot does nothing in the sailing of his ship, because, while others are climbing the masts, or running about the gangways, or working at the pumps, he sits quietly in the stern and simply holds the tiller...It is not by muscle, speed, or physical dexterity that great things are achieved, but by reflection, force of character, and judgement; in these qualities old age is usually not only not poorer, but is even richer.
>
> ...perhaps it seems to you that I who engaged in various kinds of warfare...am unemployed now that I do not go to war. And yet I direct the

DOI: 10.4324/9780429352560-2

senate as to what wars should be waged and how.... If these mental qualities [reflection, reason, judgement] were not characteristic of old men our
fathers would not have called their highest deliberative body the "senate".
(Cicero 1923)

Older men have held power in most parts of the world including tribal societies. In the west it goes back to the Greeks. Sparta was ruled by a *Gerousia*,
a council made up of members who were at least 60 years old. The Roman
Republic was governed by the *senate* a word related to the Latin *senex* ("old
man"). Gerontocratic traditions continue in contemporary times.[1]

While institutional and state power is concentrated in the hands of older
males, there is now a growing concern about the political apathy of the
youth who are indifferent to voting, joining political parties, or participating in social activism (Quintelier 2007: 165–180). A disinterested youth and
the growing elderly population have raised questions about the future of
nations. In the "ageing economies" of Europe where the majority of voters
will be 50 and above by 2030, it is possible that the region's policies will
shift towards the interests of elderly citizens. It is thus likely that pensions,
healthcare, and protection against crime will receive greater policy attention
than education, climate change, and employment which are more relevant
for the young (Winkeler 2015).

This pitting of young against the old has created a polarized discourse
which presents them as political enemies. This was seen in 2016 when older
voters were blamed for Trump's victory and the Brexit win. In *This Chair
Rocks: A Manifesto Against Ageism* Ashton Applewhite urges us to abjure
this tendency and build transgenerational solidarities since "All of us were
young, and everyone is old or future old" (Applewhite 2018).

In India politics is largely gerontocratic and the extended multigenerational family system requires subservience to the elderly. This has caused a
growing dissatisfaction among the youth who feel forever relegated to the
waiting rooms of history while elders refuse to cede power. Unlike an ageing
Europe, 50% of India's population is under 25 and more than 65% is under
35. In 2020, the average age of an Indian was 29 years, compared to 37 in
China and 48 in Japan. Yet the young country continues to be led by elderly
men who fail to represent or serve the youth. In 2014, the Indian Parliament
had just 12 MPs under 30 while the average age of an MP was above 50
(Panda 2013; Kumar 2019).

It is against this international and national context of male gerontocracy
that we would attempt to read the political emergence of the matronly older
women, affectionately referred to as the "daadis" (paternal grandmothers) as leaders of a pan-Indian protest movement against the Citizenship
Amendment Act, 2019 (CAA), passed by the Indian government on 12
December 2019. The agitation which started with primarily local women

sitting on a three-month-long public demonstration in Shaheen Bagh, a Delhi neighbourhood, was replicated by local mobilizations across India marked by the predominance and leadership of Muslim women, particularly the daadis. Homebound for most of their lives, uninitiated in politics and political activism, aliens to the public sphere, and weighed down by age-related disabilities, the daadis took control of a national movement for the right to equal citizenship of India. They brought in a different language of political protest, redefined the understanding of politics, and radicalized the notion of power and agency by marshalling their vulnerability into an idiom of resistance through a collaborative, co-dependant intergenerational collectivizing – an "assembly of bodies" which became the source of power. By examining their own words spoken in interviews given to the media and to writers, this chapter would attempt to read the daadis' protest through the framework of Vulnerability theory, looking at age not as a source of individualized masculinized gerontocratic power but as an aspect of bodily fragility which is deployed to underline the need for mutually caring solidarities. This empathetic acceptance of the universal frailty of the human condition embodied by the daadis frames the movement and attempts to redefine the ideas of equal citizenship. Going beyond mere bureaucratic documentation based on identity papers which the new Citizenship Act was asking for, the daadis asserted the need for an affective and embodied notion of belonging to the nation. The material experiences of long lives spent on Indian soil and the entwined histories of their families and the nation became stronger and more indisputable claims to citizenship than mere documentary evidence.

The CAA and the Daadis of Shaheen Bagh

The Citizenship Amendment Act (2019) amended the Citizenship Act (1955) by making migrants from the neighbouring Muslim-majority countries of Afghanistan, Bangladesh, and Pakistan who had suffered "religious persecution" or its threat in their country of origin and entered India before 31 December 2014, eligible for Indian citizenship. However, this would only be granted to persecuted religious minorities of Hindus, Sikhs, Buddhists, Jains, Parsis, or Christians and not to Muslims from these Muslim-majority countries, although some Muslim groups, such as Hazaras in Afghanistan, Rohingyas in Myanmar, Ahmadis in Pakistan, and Uyghurs in China, have historically faced persecution. Harsh Mander reads this law as clearly messaging:

> that if people of any identity except Muslim are unable to produce the required citizenship documents for the NRC, they will be accepted as refugees and given citizenship. This means that the real burden to prove that they are Indian citizens... will be on Muslims, because only they will

risk statelessness. Most Indians would find it impossible to muster the required documents to prove their citizenship, but only document-less Muslims will face the prospect of detention centres, or being stripped of all citizenship rights.

(Mander 2020: 169)

The CAA drew criticism for using religion as a citizenship criterion for the first time under a secular Indian Constitution. Concerns were expressed that while migrants or refugees from other faiths could become Indian citizens, all Muslims, even those who had lived all their lives in India, would be required to produce stringent identity proof documents:

The Indian Republic was built on guarantees of equality and non-discrimination. The creation of potentially stateless persons exclusively because of their religious identity would mark the demise of India as a secular republic

(Mander 2020: 166)

The legislation caused widespread protests. There were violent demonstrations in Assam and other northeastern states over fears that granting Indian citizenship to refugees will undermine the political, cultural, and land rights of local indigenous people. In other parts of India, protestors demanded the repeal of CAA for discriminating against Indian Muslims. The symbolic epicentre of these protests was Delhi's Shaheen Bagh and its iconic daadis – the octogenarian Bilkis with her associates, Asma Khatoon, 90, and Sarwari, 75, who led a national movement anchored by local women in which people from all communities, states, professions, ethnicities, and genders participated. Soon this neighbourhood-based model of anti-CAA protests was replicated all over the country with mostly older women in leadership – whether Mumbaibagh (Mumbai), Park Circus (Kolkata), or Ghantaghar (Lucknow).

After the CAA was passed on the 12th of December 2019 students and teachers at Jamia Milia Islamia University (JMI) took out protest rallies on 15 December in the surrounding Jamianagar neighbourhood in which large numbers of residents joined. The student leadership called off the proposed march to the Parliament at the last moment and returned to the campus. Following this, the police forcibly entered the university premises and attacked the students leading to large-scale injuries and hospitalizations. Local people, particularly women, many of whose children and grandchildren were JMI students, were outraged. They started a sit-in protest at a crossroads in Shaheen Bagh, leaving their homes to occupy a public space probably for the first time in their lives. For the daadis the attack on JMI students represented an assault on the very future of their community.

Sarwari, 75, asked:

> Who leaves the comfort of the home and hearth to sit on the road in the biting cold of Delhi? We came out because it is a do or die situation. If we keep quiet today, there is no tomorrow.
>
> *(Salam and Ausaf 2020: 82–83)*

Bilquis Bano, 82, explained why the older women made the first move:

> I have lived my life. Now, before I breathe my last, I want to make sure my children and their children stay Indians, nobody questions their citizenship. We were born in India and we will die in India. Today is not the time to sit at home. Even if I die, I want my children's future to be secure.
>
> *(Salam and Ausaf 2020: 89–90)*

Although triggered by a protective grandmotherly instinct, the daadis' movement was different from other international movements led by mothers like those in Latin America, Kashmir, Sri Lanka, or Nagaland. Not merely asking for justice for the injured students, the daadis were addressing the issues of Indian constitutionality, secularism, and citizenship. And though predominantly led by women,[2] community men and civil society members were closely involved in the movement. Muslim women have protested earlier against triple talaq, rape, or denial of alimony, but they have remained largely "women's issues." Shaheen Bagh was distinctive in being a women-led civil society movement with the daadis in the vanguard.

The visual image of a large number of frail, aged bodies braving the elements as they sat in protest against a recalcitrant state in the wintry cold drew popular sympathy and support. Yet this was an image of power, even physical robustness rather than vulnerability, as asserted by the daadis themselves. Asma Khatun, 90, said:

> I have four boys and four girls... close to forty-five grandchildren. I had pure and unadulterated food during my days. You people are consuming poison...Your generation cannot match us in strength. My bones are stronger than yours.
>
> *(Mustafa 2020: 61)*

In a gerontocratic society like India where institutional or activist leadership is mostly held by older men, older women are rarely seen leading people's movements.[3] But the daadis took naturally to their new roles since they already commanded respect as elders in the community and were listened to. Their advanced years helped to neutralize state action against them. On many occasions they negotiated with the police to ensure that protestors were not arrested. Thus instead of making them vulnerable, age provided a license and enabled the daadis to offer a protective space for others, particularly for younger women.

Shaheen Bagh represented a unique multigenerational space where women of all ages (including children) came together. While the daadis provided leadership, the younger women planned events, delivered speeches, mobilized the social media, and gave press statements. A continuum of mutual care and shared tasks marked the sit-ins where the older women who had fewer domestic responsibilities and faced less sexual threat would spend nights in the open allowing younger women to go home, while the latter ensured that the daadis were fed, wrapped up warm, and had escorts to take them to the toilet. The protest sites presented a mostly non-hierarchical, democratic model of shared leadership between the young and the old, where age did not become a vector of domination as in the masculinist, exclusionary, gerontocratic politics of parties and parliaments.

Hasina, a Mumbai-based feminist, narrated how an 80-year-old daadi had asked her why she had cut her hair short. As Hasina responded carefully thinking that the older woman disapproved of her short hair (often considered inappropriate for Indian women), the daadi removed her dupatta (veil) to mischievously reveal how she too had cropped her hair since it was more convenient now that she was busy in the movement. This incident is a testament to how the daadis' everyday lives had been changed by the protest, transforming their bodies and minds and closing the generation gap. Their role in the movement was radically different from their earlier gatekeeping positions in the family and community. Kolkata activist Sabir Ahmed said:

> within the family, grandmothers would usually restrict the mobility of younger women, scolding granddaughters for venturing out or daughters-in-laws for returning late, neglecting domestic duties or wearing western clothes – but this changed. During the movement, these same daadis encouraged younger women to come to the protests and stay the night. A new public space opened up for women creating a carnivalesque site where usual norms were temporarily suspended in a festival of democracy.
> *(Sabir Ahmed, personal communication, 22 December 2021)*

Although characterized by the familial address, "daadi," the older women in the movement stepped out of their domestic roles, homes, and communities to participate in a national struggle. Interacting with civil society, media, and administration and listening to a diverse range of people (including trans people, lesbians, sex workers, dalits, and others), they were engaging with ideas and politics that were outside their known world. But even as they learnt, grew, and changed they also helped to transform the arena of public political protest through their unique vocabularies of resistance.

New Languages of Protest

Novices in political activism the daadis forged a new language of protest which was primarily affective. Nausheen, a Kolkata activist, described the daadis' emotional investment in the movement:

> something from within them would push them, which was incomprehensible to them. They would sit at the ground all day, all evening.
>
> *(Nausheen Baba Khan, personal communication, 23 August 2021)*

Despite lacking political exposure, the daadis had lifetimes of experiences of oppression and negotiating with patriarchy. Even with little or no formal education they had native intelligence, an understanding of right and wrong derived from the business of living. Asma Khatun, 90, said, "I'm not an educated woman. My grandmother didn't allow me to pursue education.... But I have married off ten children. Life has taught me. I understand the danger to the Constitution" (Salam and Ausaf 2020: 91).

Age and unfamiliarity with politics actually worked in the daadis' favour. As ordinary women and outsiders to the political establishment, people found them easier to trust and identify with. When Asma visited the television studios for the first time, she said that though new to the media she knew how to make it work for their cause: "I have never been there... But I know... they made a video of me...I was seen on television talking against new laws. That is how the word travelled across the world. Initially, people were saying what would I do on television. Now, they have the answer" (Salam and Ausaf 2020: 92).

Even as they led the movement the daadis were also going through a continuous learning process themselves. The younger women mentored them in handling the media, raising slogans, delivering speeches, and keeping themselves abreast of the latest events. A student activist recounted how the older women of Park Circus, Kolkata, wanted to learn the correct technique of throwing their fists in the air when slogans were raised. They requested her to write out the slogans many of which they could barely understand like "lesbian *mange azadi*" (lesbians demand freedom) or "*manuvaad se azadi, pustak vaad se azadi*" (Freedom from the laws of Manu[4] and of academic texts). Unused to the language of metropolitan political protests "they were learning how to sound, act, behave like an activist" (Dipanwita Paul, personal communication, 20 February 2022) as they were performatively inducted into the appropriate gestures, speech, and demeanour of the movement.

The intergenerational cross-learning led to innovative forms of protest. On February 14, 2020, Valentine's Day, daadis joined the young women in holding heart-shaped cutouts bearing the message, "PM Modi please come to Shaheen Bagh." In the evening, the daadis sang a plaintive love song asking the prime minister to meet them and unwrapped a giant red teddy bear, a Valentine's gift for him.

As women who had lived out their lives, the daadis had no long-term political ambitions and could thus afford to be irreverent, showing little regard for political hierarchies. Unfamiliar with demagoguery, the daadis spoke with an immediacy, freshness, and authenticity which had instant appeal. The grounded common sense with which they articulated their positions resonated with the masses. They addressed powerful state leaders in familiar and familial terms, often treating them as wayward sons and grandsons who needed disciplining.

Asma made a simple appeal to the Indian Prime Minister demanding from him the same respect that he accorded to his own mother:

> The prime minister is my son's age. I'm like his mother. He should not trouble me. I've been told he goes to seek his mother's blessings on festivals... It is good. But should he treat others' mothers differently? He should think about what he has done that grandmothers who should be resting at home are on the streets fighting for their children and grandchildren.
>
> *(Salam and Ausaf 2020: 92)*

Responding to the State minister's declaration that the government would not budge, 80-year-old Noorunissa said, "I must be his mother's age. I know better" (Salam and Ausaf 2020: 86).

When it was alleged that the daadis were being bribed 500 rupees a day to demonstrate against the government, 75-year-old Sarwari reprimanded the accusers with the indignation of an insulted mother: "It is all dirty talk. Can they talk like that about their mothers? My son is into refrigeration and air conditioners. I can pay the leaders who made these allegations ₹5000. Let them ask their mothers, wives or daughters to come and sit here in the freezing cold" (Salam and Ausaf 2020: 81).

Asma answered the charge that the daadis were protesting because they were being served biriyani at the site with dignity and humour, "My son and granddaughters bring me food. I do not like biryani. But let me remind you, Modi himself went to Pakistan to eat biryani with Nawaz Sharif" (Salam and Ausaf 2020: 92).

While speaking in deceptively mundane and domestic terms, Asma also quietly scored a political point. Although the daadis' observations sounded like the remonstrance of homely grandmothers, they were astute and politically informed. By addressing senior leaders as their sons and grandsons, they were shrewdly drawing them into a kinship network. This claiming of familial access not only afforded them authority, legitimacy, and impunity but also connected them with State politicians across religious affiliations that the CAA appeared to deny. This unique use of a feminized familial language to speak about a masculine public sphere challenged the patriarchal separation of public and private arenas. It also redefined the idea of the political usually understood as public, by linking it with the personal, local, and feminine. The model of the neighbourhood protests enabled women, particularly older women with restricted mobility, to gather easily at the local sites which became extensions of their homes where domestic chores, child care, as well as political work were done. These protest sites emerged as liminal spaces between the public and the private which women could occupy and transform into the political. Could women's claiming of the semi-public space of the neighbourhood mobilizations be seen as a challenge to patriarchy? Or was it a privatization of the public sphere, an extension of the domestic into the political? Were familial norms and hierarchies recreated in these sites or was there a redefining of domestic relationships as kinswomen became political comrades? Either way a blurring of the private-public divide in the movement spaces helped to forge a new language of resistance. Social reproduction theorists like Silvia Federici have called for a political activism which takes women's lives and their social reproductive roles into account. She has pointed out how many of the "Occupy" movements have made provisions for collectivised elderly and child care, cooking and cleaning in the protest sites to ensure women's continued participation.[5] This has effectively challenged the gendered separation of roles which limits women's access to politics. When Bilquis drew on the Quran, the secular spirit of the Constitution and the struggles of national leaders to legitimize Muslim women's political activism, there appeared to be little contradiction between their religious, domestic and civic roles all of which were responses to a national crisis:

> What is important is not that I am eighty-two, but that I am here to support other women.... We too have a voice. We know how to raise it. We will not bow down... Women in our Muslim society don't step out unnecessarily. But when the need arises, we don't hold back. The Quran does not stop women from going out. If we stay at home, it is because we believe we are needed to groom our children, keep the house clean... Today, we have stepped out because the nation needs us. We have to protect our Constitution. You see so many photographs of Baba Ambedkar, Gandhiji, Maulana Azad. They made our laws...
>
> *(Salam and Ausaf 2020: 90)*

22 Paromita Chakravarti

The daadis moved easily between the authorities of Islamic patriarchy, constitutional law, and nationalist history to create a new language of women's collectivization, agency, and resistance deriving discursive legitimacy from their age, the respect they commanded in the community and the kinship networks they claimed with political leaders.

Daadis as Embodied History and Nation

In India questions of women's relationship with the nation have historically been mediated through the feminized icon of "Mother India" represented by the deified Hindu upper caste female reproductive body. The elderly Muslim daadis, of a non-reproductive age usually from poor households, were very unlike this image (Dipanwita Paul, personal communication). Yet they were associated with nationalist symbols like the tricolour, histories of anti-colonial struggles, and the constitution. Despite being traditional older women, they laid claim to the nation in terms of a constitutional modernity which went well beyond the Hinduized conceptions of Bharatmata and presented a new imaginary of Indian women's secular citizenship. Kavita Panjabi writes:

> Women's resistance... has...[brought] renewed attention to the Constitution, and it has been marked by an absence of religious and sectarian symbols... "Save the Constitution" is the rallying call that has defined conversation at all protest sites. This call testifies to the significance of the Constitution and how much we are shaped by it and why it can be used to challenge majoritarian, authoritarian governments.
>
> *(Panjabi 2020)*

Kolkata activist Nausheen spoke of a conscious decision to avoid religious or communal markers at the protest sites: "if there were no Gitas at the site, there would be no qurans either. This is a mass movement and everybody should be able to participate in it" (Nausheen Baba Khan, personal communication, 23 August 2021). While she agreed that a hijabi woman should be able to represent a secular India, she herself preferred to wear jeans as did many of the younger women from across faiths gathered at the sites: "I was determined to maintain my identity as a Muslim woman with a secular and modern approach" (Nausheen Baba Khan, personal communication, 23 August 2021). The movement was inclusive enough to have older women wearing a sari and chador (hailing from less communally polarized times) as well as middle-aged women who wore the hijab and even younger women in Western wear. Decorated with posters and festoons celebrating the plurality of Indian culture, filled with Faiz's anti-communal songs, and populated by people from various walks of life, the protest sites became microcosms of the diverse and tolerant India the protesters wanted to celebrate and the CAA appeared to threaten. The daadis became symbols of this inclusive, constitution-governed India, claiming their citizenship through shared histories, ideas, music, and emblems rather than through the CAA-mandated identity documents.

With little or no formal education, the daadis inhabited a largely oral culture which was suspicious of the demands being made by the state for bureaucratic papers. They raised the popular slogan – "*hum kagaz nahin dikhayenge*" (we will not show you papers). Asma Khatun demanded:

> Who has proof of birth in my generation?...We are here to tell the government that we are all Indians. We do not need to give any certificate to anybody. If I am not an Indian, how come I have lived here for ninety years? Which government grants visa for ninety years? This is my country. I'm not going away.
>
> *(Salam and Ausaf 2020: 92)*

Like many of the daadis born before Independence, Sarvari, 75, did not have a birth certificate. Never having gone to school, she had no academic certificates either. Her husband being dead, there were no papers to prove his ancestry. This meant, under the CAA not only was Sarvari's citizenship in doubt but also her children's (Salam and Ausaf 2020: 81).

Eighty-year-old Noorunissa pointed out that not just Muslims but the old and the poor would have trouble establishing their citizenship. Since most babies were delivered at home at that time, elders from her generation had no birth certificates while the large number of poor and illiterate Indians had no property or academic documents "How is a poor person to prove he is Indian?" (Salam and Ausaf 2020: 84)

In lieu of non-existent identity papers the daadis offered their aged bodies as corporeal testaments to lifetimes spent in the country and narrated family histories to prove unbroken residence in India. They dared legitimate Indian citizens, including the Prime Minister, to recite the names of several generations of ancestors as they could. (Salam and Ausaf 2020: 92).

Gul Bano, a protester in her 50s, asserted:

> We've been here for at least eight generations. Our ancestors are buried in this land. Why should we go to Pakistan? If we did not leave in 1947, why would we leave now? This is our country. We will live here and die here.
>
> *(Mustafa 2020: 45)*

Like Asma and Gul Bano, Shabeeran, 80, flaunted her long pedigree, giving names, years of birth even addresses of multiple generations of family members, demonstrating that despite not having the papers required by the

CAA, her claim to the land was indisputable. Evoking childhood memories Shabeeran established her family's long association with the land where they were born. The sentiments of birthright and local belonging provided an affective basis of citizenship more powerful than impersonal official documents. Stressing the familial and community solidarities developed through collective living in a neighbourhood, Shabeeran wondered if the Prime Minister about whose family little is known had any claim to the nation in the way that they did:

> Please tell us where did you play with marbles? Did you play *gulli–danda* (a game played with sticks) or (cricket)? Where are your ancestors from? We were born here, we will die here. Nobody can throw us out. I'm from Meerut. My father was among the elite of the city. After marriage, I came to Delhi. My in-laws were from Turkman Gate, gali Teliyan. Can the prime minister give us such details of his early years?
>
> *(Salam and Ausaf 2020: 94)*

Single and childless, the Prime Minister was also criticized for not having any long-term investment in the future of the country and in its youth as they did:

> The prime minister gave us a slogan of "Beti Bachao, Beti Padhao." Then brought the daughters to the road! Children who should be studying in schools and colleges are sitting on the road and protesting, but he's not affected. Why would he be? He claims he does not have a family. They ask us to move from the road, clear the place. Why? It is our home.
> We eat here, we sleep here. We are not going back until the CAA goes back.
>
> *(Salam and Ausaf 2020: 94)*

But while they made an emotional plea as grandmothers fighting for their children's futures, they also had a well-informed political agenda in exposing what they saw as the hypocrisy of the government schemes for girls' education which seemed to exclude Muslim children whose lives were jeopardized by the CAA. The above quote also asserted the daadis' claim to the protest site as an extension of their homes. By occupying local parks and cross roads, eating and sleeping there the daadis performatively acquired a stake in the public space, the "commons" which belong to every citizen of the country and from which nobody could evict them. As such the daadis' protest can be linked to the "occupy" movements all over the world and their claiming of the commons.[6] Asma pointed out, "I pray five times a day on this ground. I touch it with my forehead in every prayer. After I die, I will be buried in this land. Now the government wants us to show evidence that we belong here? I'm not going away. And I want to ensure, nobody has to go away. Only this black law has to go" (Salam and Ausaf 2020: 93).

Basing their claim to the land by virtue of everyday embodied living, the daadis were professing a corporeal, radical, and originary idea of citizenship which was material, immediate, and prior to any bureaucratically generated identity papers. Through their lived connection to the land and its history the daadis appeared to have access to a past, predating the independent Indian state, its laws and documentation protocols. Even as they asserted the Constitution they also mobilized a pre-constitutional conception of national belonging based on their roles as witness bearers to a history older than the nation. Most of the daadis had experienced the independence movement and the birth of the very India that now threatened to exclude them. They felt that a new struggle for freedom had to be launched against the CAA. Noorunissa said, "I have seen the 1947 Partition, the creation of India and Pakistan. This is like second freedom struggle... Earlier we fought the British, now we have to fight our own. But CAA has to go" (Salam and Ausaf 2020: 86).

Many of the daadis had lived through the fears of exile and homelessness evoked by the 1947 Partition which divided the Indian subcontinent along communal lines. Remembering its trauma with an intensity that the younger protesters could not gauge, the daadis were determined to prevent a second displacement which the CAA could unleash. Their refusal to budge from the protest sites expressed their resolve not to be evicted from the land that they had known as home for generations.

Reading the CAA as a move to complete the unfinished business of the Partition, Harsh Mander wrote:

> It was questions of belonging and religion-as-politics that tore India apart in 1947...But the architects of our Constitution firmly rejected this idea, and the country's first prime minister, Jawaharlal Nehru, declared, "We accept as Indian anyone who calls himself a citizen of India." By introducing the CAA, the Modi government has deliberately revived the fears, anxieties and hatreds of Partition. In effect, it endorses the two-nation theory by creating a hierarchy of citizenship based on religious faith, and excluding Muslim immigrants from this hierarchy.
>
> *(Mander 2020: 166)*

Countering the accusations of anti-nationalism levelled against Muslims, the daadis both passionately and strategically presented themselves as freedom fighters for the nation who would defend the spirit of a constitutional, secular Indian Republic against the CAA. The daadis declared that they would embrace martyrdom in this *"azadi ki doosri jung"* (second war for independence) and the protest sites rang with the popular *"azaadi"* (freedom) slogans. Asmat Jamil, who spearheaded the Park Circus protest announced, "As Gandhi had declared a struggle for *azaadi* in 1919, and the chants of freedom rent every part of this country, so we too have declared *azaadi* now – the freedom to lay claim to our own land" (Panjabi 2020).

Fiery speeches were made recounting the contributions of Indian Muslims to the making of the nation. The role played by Rokeya, Fatima Khan, Khan Abdul Ghaffar Khan, and Abdul Kalam in winning India's independence was remembered alongside that of Gandhi, Ambedkar, and Subhash Bose. The daadis saw themselves as inheritors of this legacy of sacrifice and patriotism. Asma asserted, "I have seen the British raj. I have seen the Emergency. Now I've seen 2019. The British could not break our spirit. This law also will not be able to break us. I might die here but I will not go away… If I die I become a martyr for my children, for the children of our nation" (Salam and Ausaf 2020: 93)

The daadis stressed how they were greater loyalists for choosing to live in India in 1947 despite having the option (which Hindus did not) of going to Pakistan. They hoisted the national flag at midnight on New Year's eve and sang the national anthem. By embracing national symbols, finding a place in the history of Indian nationalism, recounting their generational connection with the land, and underlining their roles as witness bearers to the moment of nation making, the daadis embodied and performed their status as legitimate Indian citizens. Instead of presenting identity documents they used their protesting bodies, affective attachments to the land, family histories, and memories of Independence and Partition to performatively occupy the political public sphere that remains inaccessible to women, particularly elderly minority women. Reporting on the Republic Day celebrations at Park Circus, Kavita Panjabi asserted:

> A republic truly comes of age when its women too claim it…When millions of women begin to insist that the state is a matter of *res publica*, a public affair, and not the private estate of rulers to decree as they please, then it marks a turning point in the history of the nation. When women take over public spaces in small towns and big cities across the country… and when they claim in unison that it is their historical rooting in the soil of Hindustan that will determine their nationality, as well as the place of their graves, then the authority of papers indeed does seem to decline.
> *(Panjabi 2020)*

The Power of Vulnerability: The "Dabang" Daadis?

Although referred to as the "dabang (dominating) daadis" whose endurance and fortitude were much admired, the undeniable physical fragility of the elderly women emerged as a distinctive feature of their leadership. Their frail bodies ranged against a powerful state became a symbol of an unequal yet resolute struggle intensifying the emotional impact of the movement. It also focused attention on how vulnerability was not synonymous with weakness or passivity and could be deployed for protest and resistance.

Martha Fineman theorizes vulnerability as an "inherent and constant" aspect of the human condition defined by changing social and bodily circumstances at different life stages (Fineman 2021; Arendt 1958: 198–199). Challenging the liberal idea of a fixed, autonomous, agential, adult, rational (male) subject at the heart of western legal and philosophical theory, she posits the conception of a vulnerable embodied being susceptible to change and dependent on relationships and institutions like the family, market, or state. Vulnerability analysis questions abstract notions of autonomy and is sited on the materiality of the human body (rather than on the rational mind) and its changing capacities and functionalities as it moves through the life cycle. Such a theoretical framework focuses on questions of health, disease, and age in subject formation and thus provides a relevant tool to read the daadis' resistance which combined physical vulnerability and moral strength, bodily dependence, and political agency.

The foregrounding of the suffering, weak, and aged body was evident in verbal and visual media portrayals of the anti-CAA protests as also in the daadis' self-representations. Noorunissa spoke poignantly of the hardships of sleeping in the open in a Delhi winter:

> at night also, when some of the younger women go home, we sleep on the rugs spread on the floor. When it rains also, we do not move back. Come what may, we have to face it. Nothing is gained sitting at home. You too have come here to talk to me because I am at the protest. If I were sitting at home, you wouldn't have known who is Noorun Nisa. Now the world knows.
>
> *(Salam and Ausaf 2020: 85)*

The daadis located their identity and credibility as leaders on their ability to endure physical hardships. Sarwari asserted in a Learesque tone, "We did not move from here when icy winds were blowing, when we were told that the temperature had fallen to 2 degrees Celsius. We will not move till the black law is repealed" (Salam and Ausaf 2020: 81).

The bodily privations of elderly women acquired an iconic status, visibly representing and performing the destitution, homelessness, and statelessness that the CAA threatened to unleash on many. Although spearheaded by Muslim women, the anti-CAA protests drew in the civil society at large underlining the imminent dangers it posed not just to Indian Muslims but to all Indians under a repressive law.[7]

Fineman frames vulnerability not as an attribute of particular individuals or groups which can be mobilized as an identity category requiring protection or anti-discriminatory measures but as a human condition universally experienced in varying degrees at particular life stages because of physical, psychological, socio-economic, or political changes. Although the daadis' frailties were in focus, all protesters' bodies were marked by multiple susceptibilities to police action, sexual assault, or exposure.[8] Yet these vulnerable bodies were creating what Fineman terms "resilience" through solidarities and mutual care (Fineman 2021).[9] This could be compared to Arendt's conception of power created when an "assembly of bodies" appears in a public space and engages in concerted speech and action for a shared political goal (Arendt 1958: 198–199). A depressed minority neighbourhood, Shaheen Bagh, was thus transformed into a "polis," a space of assembly of vulnerable bodies for political action. Bilquis Bano stressed the common objective which transforms individual bodily sufferings into resources of resistance – "One of my daughters-in-law tells me every day that if I fall sick, I should call her…But I tell her, am I special? Have I landed from the skies? I have to be here with all these women…they have families too. Many have small children" (Salam and Ausaf 2020: 89).

Rejecting the comfort of homes and families the daadis embraced adversities to create a political community. Physical togetherness, shared food, and protest alleviated bodily fatigue. Noorunissa says, "Yes, I do get tired. We all get tired. But then we tell each other, either sit here with thousands of other sisters with tea flowing all the time, samosas coming for all… Or else, prepare to sit in that jail [detention centre] where there will be no comfort, no family member. Who would like to die like that? Even if we die here, we will be called martyrs" (Salam and Ausaf 2020: 87).

Judith Butler's reading of Arendt's "assembly of bodies" frames individual bodies as defined and enabled by their relationships with and dependence on others (Butler 2020). Performance, Disability, and Vulnerability studies have demonstrated how all bodily actions need to be supported by other humans, institutions, and structures. Fineman, Butler, and others have critiqued masculinist and individualist ideas of agency and autonomy which characterize humans as acting on and mastering their environment rather than being acted upon. Vulnerability can be seen as an openness and responsiveness to other bodies through an understanding of interdependence.

The physical exposure and bodily risks faced by the anti-CAA protesters heightened the experience of vulnerability and the need for mutual care adumbrating how "only a supported life can persist as life" (Butler 2020, 212). By deliberately baring their bodies to the elements, police power, and state violence the daadis (and others) were "demonstrating it [their vulnerability] but also demonstrating with it" (Butler 2020, 212). Their corporeal suffering was an assertion of the persistence of the frail body against repression, enabled by networks of support. Analysing refugee demonstrations in Europe, Butler contends that despite being shorn of political agency and reduced to the substance of the biological body, to characterize the protestors as Agamben's "bare life" would be to ignore the power of vulnerability. Threatened with a similar possibility of statelessness, the anti-CAA protesters' theatrical foregrounding of their suffering bodies (as both instrument and argument for their demands) affirmed their will to persist and their refusal to disappear as the State wanted them to. By obstinately and spectacularly displaying themselves in the public site these bodies declared "'I will not disappear so easily,' or, 'My disappearance will leave a vibrant trace from which resistance will grow'" (Butler 2020, 215), and thus performatively rejected the CAA's mandate. The protester's body "acts as its own *deixis*, a pointing to, or enacting of, the body that implies its situation: *this* body, *these* bodies; *these* are the ones exposed to violence, resisting disappearance. These bodies exist still, which is to say that they persist under conditions in which their very power to persist is systematically undermined" (Butler 2020, 216).

This "embodied persistence" of the body ensures that it leaves a mark, is documented and thereby resists erasure through detention, deportation or death. While the anti-CAA protesters were refusing to show identity documents, they were also demanding that their lives, family histories, and contributions to the nation be registered, counted, and remembered. Amir Aziz's poem, "*sab yaad rakha jayega*" (all will be remembered), pledged that people's suffering and struggles would be remembered despite attempts to silence dissident voices, obliterate opposition, and rewrite the history of the Indian secular republic by altering its Constitution (Arendt 1958: 192).[10] As witnesses to and custodians of the nation's inclusive and diverse past, the daadis' recollections of long lives spent in a syncretic Indian culture provided a bulwark against the relentless endeavours to generate amnesia. Their persistent memories materialized through their persistent bodies surviving against all odds became texts of an endangered history bearing proof of their citizenship as also of the spirit of a nation which was fast disappearing. Marked by pain and age the daadis' vulnerable bodies also underlined the need for a reciprocally caring community that the secular civic spaces of the protest sites represented. By locating their bodies in and sustaining them through the social and political relationships with other citizens, the daadis challenged the law which was questioning their status as Indians. Not seeking to overcome their vulnerability the daadis marshalled it as an instrument of protest and power. Both affected and active, their exposed bodies represented not bare life but an assertion of citizens' persistence against persecution, demonstrating how vulnerability enables resistance and works with it. They not so much opposed the State since that would require them to counter its idiom of violence and repression, they rather resisted it through

30 Paromita Chakravarti

a different language of physical susceptibility. Their protest indicated possibilities for challenging the politics of domination and coercion with an alternative imaginary of vulnerability iconized through the daadis' aged and failing bodies (Butler 2020, 221).

Analysing the politics of vulnerability Butler evokes Gandhi's *satyagraha* a form of moral resistance which refused to answer violence with violence, mobilizing the power of truth instead to face a repressive colonial regime with the frail body of a barely clothed, often fasting, elderly man. Not merely a counter to violence, nor synonymous with weakness or passivity, Gandhian non-violence like vulnerability is "a way of living in the body and of persisting, precisely under conditions that attack the very conditions of persistence" which is "manifest in solidarity alliances of resistance" (Butler 2020; Mander 2020).[11]

But while the daadis' deployment of the vulnerable body for protest has Gandhian elements, it is also distinctive. Ordinary women from marginal communities with no experience of public life, the daadis had almost accidentally found themselves at the helm of a movement. They were referred to through a familial term since their individual names carried no political significance. Gandhi's leadership on the other hand depended largely on his personal charisma, his stature as an internationally respected public figure who became the face of India's anti-colonial struggle. Revered as the "Father of the Nation," Gandhi remained largely within the individualist, gerontocratic tradition of leadership which the daadis questioned through their anonymous, collective, affective, and mutually supportive solidarities. Their braving of the elements to "feel what wretches feel" (Shakespeare, 2008, 3.4.35), manifesting the vulnerability of "unaccomodated man" in their shivering bodies, resonates more with Lear on the heath. Like him they gather around them other vulnerable bodies of the poor, homeless, and the disinherited with whom they form alliances of mutual sustenance and resistance. The daadis' leadership demonstrated that instead of shoring up gerontocratic power, age could project bodily vulnerability as a basis for a new political articulation based not on domination, strength and autonomy but on the need for dependence and care. The elderly daadis' protest thus pointed towards the need to rethink ideas of power which undergird existing paradigms of political activism as well as to reevaluate the interactions of age, gender, and leadership in movements.

Notes

1 The last two presidents of the USA, Trump and Biden, are both in their 70s. Communist polities like Cuba and China are led by older men. Fidel Castro retired from Cuban premiership at 82, to be replaced by his 89-year-old brother Raul Castro. Mao Zedong ruled China till he died at 82. Theocratic states such as Iran, Saudi Arabia, and the Vatican have also been led by male elders.

2 Women were at the helm of the anti-CAA movement perhaps because they were the worst affected by the amendment which requires all citizens to produce birth and school certificates and property documents which the majority of poor and illiterate Indian women were unlikely to have, even less so than their male counterparts. Since women leave natal homes and change names after marriage, many of their identity papers are misplaced or require changes. Out of the 19 lakh people excluded from the National Register for Citizens for not having proper documents, a large majority were women.
3 Some exceptions are provided by the Meira Paibis of Manipur who are peace-keepers and community leaders or the Mothers in Nagaland and Kashmir who mobilize themselves to demand the return of "disappeared" sons during insurgency and state repression.
4 Manu's laws refer to *Manusmriti*, a Hindu code of social, gender, and caste norms which are often cited with great authority, although they have doubtful textual authenticity.
5 See Silvia Federici's talk"Gender and Democracy in the Neoliberal Agenda: Feminist Politics, Past and Present" delivered on 13.05.2013 at the 6th Subversive Festival on https://youtu.be/enpTFJsswWM?si=Tr6Akk1U1RVKk01u.
6 See Silvia Federici, "Feminism and the politics of the common in an era of primitive accumulation", in *Revolution at Point Zero: Housework, Reproduction, and Feminist Struggle*, PM Press, New York, 2012, pp 138-148.
7 There were instances of Hindus adopting Muslim identity markers like the skull cap or hijab to empathize and share the socio-political vulnerability of their fellow protesters. See Mander 2020, pp. 170–1.
8 An infant died tragically at Shaheen Bagh which led to a debate on consent and political protest. Similar issues were raised when middle school students in Bidar, Karnataka staged a play criticizing the CAA leading to sedition charges being levelled against the school management. Thus the question of age and activism was discussed from the other end too.
9 Fineman does not see vulnerability as antithetical to agency, which can be socially produced as what she calls "resilience" through resources and relationships available to individuals.
10 Arendt underlines the need for recording and bearing witness for political action to have its full meaning. As holders of memory and of bodies which need to be remembered and narrativized the daadis' protest needs to be documented for it to become a meaningful political action.
11 Mander also described the anti-CAA protests as Gandhian particularly for their secular character.

References

Applewhite, Ashton. "How Old People Become Political Enemies of the Young." *The Guardian*, 23 Dec. 2018. https://www.theguardian.com/commentisfree /2018/dec/23/old-people-enemies-young-generational-compact.

Arendt, Hannah. *The Human Condition.* University of Chicago Press, 1958.

Aristotle. *The Ethics of Aristotle: The Nicomachean Ethics.* Translated by J. A. K. Thomson. Penguin, 1953.

Butler, Judith. *The Force of Nonviolence.* Verso Books, 2020.

Cicero. *Cato maior de senectute.* Translated by Loeb Classical Library, 1923. http:// penelope.uchicago.edu/Thayer/e/roman/texts/cicero/cato_maior_de_senectute/ text*.html.

Federici, Silvia. "Gender and Democracy in the Neoliberal Agenda: Feminist Politics, Past and Present" talk delivered at the 6th Subversive Festival on 13.05.2013. https://youtu.be/enpTFJsswWM?si=Tr6Akk1U1RVKk01u

Federici, Sivia. "Feminism and the politics of the common in an era of primitive accumulation". *Revolution at Point Zero: Housework, Reproduction, and Feminist Struggle*, PM Press 2012, pp 138–148.

Fineman, Martha Albertson. "What Vulnerability Theory Is and Is Not." *ScholarBlogs*, 1 Feb. 2021. https://scholarblogs.emory.edu/vulnerability/2021/02/01/is-and-is-not/.

Kumar, Sanjay. "Young Country, Old Leaders: While Politics Engages Large Numbers of Youth, It Does Not Serve Their Interests." *The Times of India*, 15 Oct. 2019. https://timesofindia.indiatimes.com/blogs/toi-edit-page/young-country-old-leaders-while-politics-engages-large-numbers-of-youth-it-does-not-serve-their-interests/.

Mander, Harsh. "Mahatma Gandhi Would Have Approved." *Shaheen Bagh and the Idea of India: Writings on a Movement for Justice, Liberty and Equality*, edited by Seema Mustafa. Speaking Tiger, 2020, pp. 166–174.

Mustafa, Seema, editor. *Shaheen Bagh and the Idea of India: Writings on a Movement for Justice, Liberty and Equality*. Speaking Tiger, 2020.

Panda, Ankit. "Indian Gerontocracy: Why Are Indian Leaders so Old?". *The Diplomat*, 24 Dec. 2013. https://thediplomat.com/2013/12/indian-geronotocracy-why-are-indian-leaders-so-old/.

Panjabi, Kavita. "Women at Kolkata's Park Circus Prove the Indian Republic Has Come of Age." *The Wire*, 27 Jan. 2020. https://thewire.in/women/kolkata-park-circus-women-protest-caa.

Plato. *The Republic*. Translated by D. Lee. Penguin, 2007.

Quintelier, Ellen. "Differences in Political Participation Between Young and Old People." *Contemporary Politics*, vol. 13, no. 2, 2007, pp. 165–180.

Shakespeare, William. *King Lear*. Edited by Grace Ioppolo. W. W. Norton & Company, 2008.

Us Salam, Ziya and Usma Ausaf, editors. *Shaheenbagh: From a Protest to a Movement*. Bloomsbury, 2020.

Winkeler, Hernan. "How Will Ageing Populations Affect Politics." *World Economic Forum*, 18 June 2015. https://www.weforum.org/agenda/2015/06/how-will-ageing-populations-affect-politics/.

2

FROM MAINTENANCE TO CARE-ING

The Aged in Times of Changing Familial Geographies

Rukmini Sen

From Caring to Becoming the Recipient of Care: Changes in Age and Its Roles

As a daughter of ageing/aged parents, the interest in this issue stems from deeply personal as well as sociological roots, locating the discourse around ageing within the changing familial networks and how that impacts the aged. As far as my grandparents were concerned, I witnessed their decay and death, but not so much a process of ageing, while the ageing of parents has been a process to encounter, negotiate, and come to terms with. This went simultaneously with the process of ageing of a residential apartment in South Kolkata (where I spent my childhood, adolescence, and also a part of adulthood before moving to another city). These were the early days of multi-storied buildings in South Kolkata constructed in place of big individual/family-owned bungalows. Bengali middle-class heterosexual families, where the husband was the only earning member without any exception, and with an average of two school-going children among the 34 households in this building, determined the composition of the residents of this apartment. By the end of the 2000s, most of the sons of these families were settled outside of Kolkata or India with jobs. There was regular death of the original flat-owners (except for one or two all ownership rested with men and the wives were nominees), and those who survived rarely had their children (those belonging to my generation) living with their mothers/parents. The celebration of *Durga puja* became the time for children to *return* to their homes/apartments/cities. This transformation and the ageing of an apartment complex in South Kolkata can be seen in the background of the ageing of the city of Kolkata. Based on the five-year age group analysis of the 2011

DOI: 10.4324/9780429352560-3

Census, Kolkata with 11.76% has the highest 60 plus population among the four metropolitan cities in India. There is also a shift from family/community services to professional services, in the care of the elderly thereby leading to an emergence of "business" of caring for the "left behind" elderly population. This industry is based on the philosophy that children are supposed to take care; in their absence, someone else, a stranger or an institution, is providing those services. Also a demographic shift and decreasing fertility rates are evident in Kolkata – increased elderly population and lessening of the children population. Census 2011 showed that Kolkata's total fertility rate (TFR), or the number of children born to women aged 15–49, had plummeted to 1.2 – the lowest among all districts in India. In this same report, the West Bengal government claims that 9% of Kolkata's population is currently aged 60 and above. Clearly, these numbers and some attention that the newspapers have given towards the concerns of the elderly warrant a more systematic and critical engagement with ageing and elderly care in Indian sociology.

While engaging with ageing, I would like to start with a Bengali song that was the first, *natural* thought that engulfed me as I started thinking about the ideas for this chapter: "Tini bridhha holen" (Translation: The one who has grown old provided shelter as many trees with shading canopies do ... however, age breathes heavy in the leaves and the trunks of the tree in its older age ... leaving me behind, my loved one age). This song by Suman Chattopadhay (later Kabir Suman) released in 1993 has deeply impacted me and my changing relationship with ageing parents. As a daughter of ageing/aged parents, I thought of my father while hearing this song again, for the purposes of this chapter. While the aged grandparent was given to me, naturally aged in her early 60s when I was born, the ageing parent was a process to be confronted – for which I was ill-prepared. It took me a couple of years to reconcile with the fact that he is no longer the father that I grew up with; he is sometimes still the person that I learnt a lot from. I have been trying to understand what it means to observe ageing and feel helpless in trying to create a care environment, while at the same time being conscious about striking a balance between care and indignity, discouraging consent and believing that the aged can make one's own decision. So when Baba jokingly announced a couple of years ago that "now I only have guardians around me," I wondered what it would mean for a dominant patriarch of the household and extended family to feel the paradigmatic shift from "naturally" being the protector, whose function was to care and protect (in both material and non-material forms), to becoming the recipient of care. Undoubtedly these are gendered experiences and reactions to receiving care or becoming dependant which vary between men and women. As Segal (2012) says, for those in need of care, there are often deep levels of shame, guilt, and resentment if they find themselves in situations of extreme dependence on partners or children, when they may feel simply a burden on those very people whose well-being was always dearest to them. It is important to acknowledge that ageing is not about growing old, it is also about shifting or shrinking roles as a person.

Aged, Elderly, Senior Citizen: Categories and Meanings

Within the discipline of sociology and social anthropology, ageing has not found a lot of focus for two reasons according to Turner (1989). In the post-Malthusian moment, sociological research was more about the over-crowding of urban space and the threat of infectious diseases, and not about ageing and population decline in Britain. On the other hand, classical sociology became theoretically and morally distant from both Darwinistic theory and eugenics, emphasizing instead the importance of values and culture in the explanation of human action and social organization. Despite that, it is important to trace a classical and contemporary sociological review of conceptualizations around ageing.

Max Weber while talking about the three forms of authority has a classification of traditional authority which is legitimized by the sanctity of tradition. The ability and right to rule are passed down, often through heredity. It does not change over time, does not facilitate social change, tends to be irrational and inconsistent, and perpetuates the status quo. In fact, Weber believes that the creation of new laws opposite traditional norms is deemed impossible. Traditional authority is typically embodied in feudalism or patrimonialism. The dominant individual could be a priest, clan leader, family head, or some other patriarch, or the dominant elite might govern. Different types of traditional authority might be (i) gerontocracy or rule by elders and (ii) patriarchalism where positions are inherited. Patriarchalism means the authority of the father, the husband, the senior of the house, the rule of the master and patron over bondsmen, serfs, and freedmen; of the lord over the domestic servants and household officials; of the prince over house- and court-officials, nobles of office, clients, and vassals; and of the patrimonial lord and sovereign prince over the "subjects" (Gerth and Mills, p. 296). Anthropological studies have also talked about the importance of age in connection with the attainment of wisdom, knowledge (of ceremonies, ancestors), and experience which has the potential of attaining leadership roles. For Parsons (in Turner: 595), the two primary illustrations of ascriptive criteria in social stratification systems were sex and age. While Parsons acknowledged age grading as an important feature of status (especially in the USA where early retirement often leads to extreme isolation of the aged), he also argued that given the emphasis on activism in the USA, the importance of ascriptive components in the stratification system would be eventually eroded. Political questions on old age have been raised consistently in the

36 Rukmini Sen

USA. In the Presidential address of the American Philosophical Association after proposing that philosophers, although have engaged with the fear, anxiety, and inevitability of death, have however been uncomfortable discussing ageing. The address suggested,

> *we, the oldies, are very expensive ... we are mostly unemployed and assumed by those whose opinions count to be unemployable. We are unproductive. Some of us live off pensions and annuities; others (not everybody) have social security which, we are reminded daily, is running out of funds. We have a disproportionate number of medical problems, many chronic and severe. Some of us need part-time caregivers; some need round-the-clock institutional care. Who is responsible for us? Who is supposed to provide for housing and pay our medical bills? Who is to keep us from dying boredom? Our children? But what if we have no children or if our children are supporting their children and finding it hard to make ends meet? Should wage-earning taxpayers foot the bill? Why should they get stuck with having to subsidize us?*
>
> *(Mothersill 1999: 13)*

In our cultures in India and other parts of South Asia, from political leadership to decision-making within the family, gender and age have dominated authority. What is important to foreground in contemporary urban contexts is that there seems to be a paradox between this traditional authority of the aged in the family/community and the changing familial structures and kinds making the aged lonely, uncared for, as well as humiliated. Respecting the aged co-exists with treating them with indignity. Neil Thompson (1998) argues that the frequently used term "the elderly" is in itself an example of dehumanization in so far as it presents a diverse group of people with ages spanning several decades as if they were a homogeneous group and describes them by that supposedly shared characteristic, rather than as people in their own right, depersonalizing them in the process. Sociologist A. M. Shah (1998) draws attention towards the social reality of sons not staying in parental homes due to the changes in occupational structure. He additionally argues that the increase in the marriage age of women leads to troubles in adjustment with parents-in-law thereby causing tensions and finally segregation from matrimonial homes. While these are deeply problematic hetero-patriarchal explanations, Shah is an Indian sociologist who talks about the need for maintenance, household grants, and homes for the aged to tackle the changing geographies of urban households and neighbourhoods. Sarah Lamb, an anthropologist who has been consistently working on ageing over the last two decades, in one of her earlier essays argued that age is a crucial dimension of personhood. Late life is an unusually revealing period of myriad transformations, during which many of the dilemmas and properties of cultural understandings of personhood become highlighted. Especially in a society such as India where persons are believed to be constituted via networks of substantial emotional ties, it makes no sense to look only at how these ties are formed; we must also consider how they are loosened and taken apart (1997: 296). The dominant economic narrative around old age is represented through the assessment of the National Family Health Survey (NHFS) data of 1992 and 1993. Though the survey was not specially designed to elicit information from the elderly members of the households, the kind of information available from the details of each of the members of the household provides some insights into the living arrangements of the elderly (Rajan and Kumar 2003: 78). As a majority of the current elderly in India, as per this survey, is illiterate, their living conditions depended upon their co-residence with children or the ability of the elderly to work beyond the official designated retirement. More elderly women (3.49%) live alone compared to men (1.42%). In other words, only 6% of the elderly in India are living in a household where their immediate kinship is not present. Another 6% of the elderly are living with their spouses alone, possibly due to the displacement or migration of their children. Almost half of the elderly (54.4%) live with their spouses, own children, and grandchildren (ibid 79). Through her ethnography in a village in West Bengal, Lamb concluded that retirees displayed their greater detachment from family centres as well by moving beyond the confines of household space: spending more of their days at others' houses chatting, playing cards, and drinking tea; resting on the cool platforms of temples; loitering at shops or on roadsides; and simply watching people come and go – behaviours that are considered appropriate for them but that among younger persons would be criticized as defections from duty (1997: 287). Age as an authority marker, elderly as a liability and dependent, or possibilities of leisure in retirement seem to be the conceptual transformations that we see in this literature.

In the Indian Constitution, under the Directive Principles of State Policy old age is considered as "undeserved want" and categorized with sickness, disablement, and unemployment and ensured public assistance. In 1973, Section 125 Criminal Procedure Code (CrPC) added the provision of monthly allowance if it was reported that a person was neglecting or refusing to maintain his "helpless' parents." A Law Commission recommendation in 1989 as well as 1996 suggested that the calculation of the monthly allowance may take into account not just food, shelter, and clothing but emergencies arising out of sickness, accidents, and physical disability. Very clearly the manner in which there is infantilization of old age and parents needing maintenance suggests the undermining of their personhood. That is, to treat older people like children (the section on maintenance in Section 125 CrPC brings together separated destitute wife, children, and parents in the same category) both reflect and reinforce their vulnerable, but unproductive status in society. It is important to remember as Turner argues retirement and ageing rather than simply being "natural" processes are bound up with struggles between labour and capital. Since retirement is an important aspect of industrial relations, some writers adopting a Marxist perspective have tried to suggest that the elderly worker rather than being retired should be regarded as having been abandoned, because he or she can no longer provide effective or efficient economic service to capital (Turner 1989: 599).

The National Policy for Older Persons 1999, proposed by the Ministry of Social Justice and Empowerment, was announced since 1999 was the International Year of Older Persons. The Policy, while recognizing the demographic transformations in India, suggesting 21% of the Indian population in 2050 will be elderly, determines the need and importance for a separate policy and plan of action for this category of people in India. There are key areas in which the policy says that this section will not live unprotected, ignored, or marginalized, and government intervention will be ensured in providing financial security, healthcare, shelter, and welfare services. The policy explains the importance of family in the following way:

> *Family is the most cherished social institution in India and the most vital nonformal social security for the old. Most older persons stay with one or more of their children, particularly when independent living is no longer feasible. It is for them the most preferred living arrangement and also the most emotionally satisfying. It is important that the familial support system continues to be functional and the ability of the family to discharge its caring responsibilities is strengthened through support services Programmes will be developed to promote family values, sensitise the young on the necessity and desirability of intergenerational bonding and continuity and the desirability of meeting filial obligations. Values of caring and sharing need to be reinforced.*
>
> *(1999: 8 and 9)*

This pronouncement of the policy is in congruence with the NFHS report assessment that has been mentioned above in this section. Twelve years later came the second policy, National Policy for Senior Citizens 2011, but in between the two policies the legislation on Senior Citizens was promulgated in 2007 (the next section will discuss this briefly). The policy stated that all those of 60 years and above are senior citizens. In principle the policy valued an age integrated society. It would endeavour to strengthen integration between generations, facilitate interaction between the old and the young, and strengthen bonds between different age groups. The policy focused on the promotion of the concept of "Ageing in Place" or ageing in own home, housing, income security and homecare services, old age pension and access to healthcare insurance schemes, and other programmes and services to facilitate and sustain dignity in old age. The thrust of the policy would be preventive rather than cure. The objective of the policy was to consider institutional care as the last resort. It recognized that care of senior citizens has to remain vested in the family which would partner the community, government, and the private sector. Although the policy still talked about the family and the need to age with members of the family, the tone was very different from the 1999 policy that had announced the cherished value of the family as the vital social security for the elderly. In 2011, there was no separate section on family or familial values, rather an institution along with private entities to care of the aged. This rearrangement of focus seems to be in consonance with my personal experiences of the transformation in familial geographies in the South Kolkata apartment and also the increase in elderly population and a private industry growing around its care as detailed in the first section of this chapter.

The major change between the two policies is also with respect to the marking of an age determining senior citizens. Since the aged experience ageing as a form of discrimination which negates or conflicts with their universalistic rights as citizens, the aged become clients of the state in order to enforce their social entitlements. In so far as the state, as it were, accepts their legitimate right to political client-ship, we may refer to "state-administered status groups," which are constituted by the state's response to citizenship claims. While this argument made by Turner may hold true in the context of Britain and many other countries of the Western world, in South Asian cultures the state, even when they construct the senior citizen category, has expectations from and directives to the family about maintaining people above 60. Age plays an important factor not only as a sociological basis of stratification but as legal determinism as well. Much debate exists in India about the exact age of the child in various labour-related legislations, although below 18 is what or who a child is since Juvenile Justice Act 2000. The age of marriage for girls is fixed at 18, and 21 for boys; the age of voting is directly connected with embarking on adulthood which is 18; while the age of consensual sex has also increased to 18 (from 16) in 2013. From the early legal measures for old age (either in the Constitution or Criminal Procedure Code), the elderly were detached from a specific age, and when the change to the terminology of senior citizen happened in India through the Maintenance and Welfare of Parents and Senior Citizens Act 2007, there was an age determining "senior" status of the citizen – above 60. This has interconnections with retirement age, which although varies across professions still is between 58 and 65 years. Within the juridical framework the terminological changes have been destitute parents, older persons, and senior citizens. There clearly is a shift from the condition of the aged to the age of the person and the need to attach a token of dignity with the latter.

In Search of Shelter: New Meanings of the "Home"

According to the 2007 Act, maintenance of parents (biological or adoptive father or mother) and senior citizens (anyone above the age of 60) includes provision for food, clothing, residence, medical attendance, and treatment; while welfare indicates provision for food, healthcare, recreation centres, and other amenities. This legislation proposed that a parent and/or senior citizen (or someone/some organization authorized by the parent/senior citizen) needs to make an application to a Maintenance Tribunal if he is unable to maintain oneself from his own property against one or more of his children (who is not a minor) or a relative of the senior citizen who will be the legal heir of his property after death. Family, as an institution operates in the most informal manner and yet, the law, while conceiving of how a 'normal life' could be led by a parent/senior citizen, formal processes of making application, etc., are laid. Are the principles of maintenance of parents/senior citizens same as that of "maintaining" a separated wife? Moreover, there are two interconnected prerequisites, having a property and having a child or a legal heir (relative) to whom the property will be transferred, before an application can be made. Close connections between kinship relations and property relations have been constantly established and critiqued by feminist anthropologists like Gayle Rubin, and the principal basis of this legislation remains the perpetuation of that co-relation. This Act prescribes the establishment of old age homes and leaves it to the respective State governments to create their rules/schemes for its construction and management and is accessed by those senior citizens who are "indigent." It is interesting to see how in this brief section from the 2007 Act, the category parent does not find mention. This legislation in some places talks about parents and senior citizens together, while in other parts these two categories are separated. One wonders whether there is an underlying assumption that the parent will not need the old age home but a senior citizen will thereby suggest that the parent has a child/children, while the childless senior citizen needs shelter through the old age home.

"Therefore, my address is the old age home...": This song by Nachiketa composed in 1999, however melodramatic and taking a stigmatizing position about those who are sent to old age homes, captures the shift from elderly as the protector to old age being a liability, a transformation that is evidenced also in the sociological juridical shifts around ageing as seen earlier. From being the shelter to searching for shelter – I look at the two songs of Suman and Nachiketa composed in the early 1990s and late 1990s as the shifts that were taking place or being envisaged in the Bengali upper-caste middle-class households as a marker of the shifts. While not a liability, the need for elderly parents to stay separate from professionally successful sons as a rule since the 1970s, in foreign firms in Calcutta, gets discussed in one of Ray's films of the Calcutta Trilogy. In Satyajit Ray's *Seemabaddho* (Company Limited, 1971), the parents of the protagonist, Shyamalendu, working as a company director of a British fan manufacturing company, do not stay with their son. Rather, they cannot. For, the company rules do not allow that. Through Dolon's dialogue the viewer comes to know that although Shyamalendu wanted to fight this rule, his father had voluntarily consented to this rule, considering the future of his son. There is an evident awkwardness when Shyamalendu's parents visit their manager son's house in the middle of a party – a binary gets constructed between cocktails, racing, and fashion parlours on the one hand and the nostalgia surrounding a life in Patna that the parents remember and miss. There is a twofold injury suggested – it is not just the creation of a separate household, but the uprooting from a completely different life that the parents were familiar with. On the other hand, in another of Ray's films *Mahanagar* (The Big City, 1963), where the "joint" family structure exists in a partition-affected family, the retired father/father-in-law repeatedly considers his wife and himself burden on their son and their earning daughter-in-law. Although the elderly population are considered productively unnecessary and an economic burden (that's the reason for they being included along with the sick, disabled, and unemployed in the Constitution), in a country like India the joint family principle has for long supported them and even valued their presence either as providing advice or as caregivers of the grandchildren in situations where the husband and the wife jointly earn a living.

The idea and the reality of old age homes arrive in our contexts as a result of negotiating with the emotions of being uncared for, rejected, or treated as a burden. Older people may occasionally choose to go to old age homes; but in most cases they are forced to go, which involves a loss of dignity and self-respect. Rarely has the old age home emerged as an alternative community through which new forms of companionship can be explored after a certain age.

While Ray's movies bring in the ageing and rejection of the erstwhile patriarch, the one who has lost the Weberian authority that age gave, later films have a different depiction with women's voices and silences of negotiating with ageing. Experiences of ageing and expectations around the process are gendered. Aparna Sen's directorial debut *36 Chowringhee Lane* (1981) through the characterization of the Anglo-Indian school teacher Mrs Stoneham may prove relevant in this context of being alone and feeling the need for care from a younger generation. While talking about ageing and the elderly the need to conceptualize care and companionship from the same or different generation is extremely essential. While on the one hand, Chowringhee Lane had Stoneham's brother residing in an old age home, where the residents were awaiting death; on the other hand, Stoneham did find the elusive promise of companionship from the younger generation, although to lose it harshly in the end, and to come face to face with her loneliness. Interestingly, the film ends with Stoneham, the boring Shakespeare teacher, reciting lines from *King Lear*, a profound play on ageing and ageism, as much as trusting "wrong" people in old age and left lonely. The lines are: "Pray, do not mock me. I am a very foolish fond old man, Fourscore and upward, not an hour more nor less. And to deal plainly I fear I am not in my perfect mind. Me thinks I should know you, and know this man."

In another movie, Jhinuk's [one of the leading protagonists of Rituparno Ghosh's film *Dahan* (Crossfire, 1997)] grandmother voluntarily relocates to a home for the aged, saying that it is important for her to create her own space. She also talks about how with some friend dying in that home, everyone else remains in fear about "whose turn would be next," a similar metaphor felt in Sen's film. The grandmother is the most independent woman in the movie, whose decision to stay by herself in an old age home does not go down well with the generation younger to her. However, at times it could also be liberating for elderly women receiving *seva* from staffs and nurses in institutional care, rather than to serve a household (Sarah Lamb 2007). This creation of one's own space that Jhinuk's *thammi* expresses in this film is not the most common way of imagining elderhood, and certainly very different from the Nachiketa song on old age homes.

There are a number of ways in which old age homes, which Sarah Lamb calls elderly abode, define themselves "a life away from the din of family, spent in solitary religious practices," others consider this as a site to pursue the *vanaprasthaasrama*, which is the third and "forest-dwelling" phase of the Hindu householder's life. Other descriptions are "to serve and honour the old people living here. You see, they are all revered people living here." From being the creator and the protector of the home (in the sense of household/family) to being abandoned in the home (in the sense of old age home) – it's a paradigmatic shift that needs us to understand that while domesticity, privacy, and comfort, through the concepts of the home and of the family, were the principal achievements of the bourgeois age, parents and children living together in one dwelling became the core of this ideology. The evolution of home, in a sense, separated the family and its private life from the larger community. Home/family is indeed a place of intimacy, but in privileging the intimacy of close kin it has made the outside world cold and friendless and made it harder to sustain relations of security and trust except with kin, as Michelle Barrett (1982) wrote, caring, sharing, and loving would be more widespread if the biological family did not claim them for its own.

There has also been a new kind of judicial response with respect to the already assumed relation between parents and children. Judgements saying:

Where the house is self-acquired by the parents, son whether married or not has no legal right to live in that house and can live in that house only at the mercy of the parents up to time the parents allow. Merely because the parents have allowed him to live in the house so long as his relations with the parents were cordial does not mean that the parents have to bear the burden throughout his life (Delhi High Court judgment 2016). *Or, any person of ordinary prudence would have adopted the same course and would not have given anything to the ungrateful children from his or her share in the property. Neither of them (two sons) bothered to look after the parents in their old age.*

(Supreme Court judgment 2016)

Removing any misgiving about the claim of a share in the joint family property, the Supreme Court held that the parents have every right to deny the share to the negligent children who simply do not take care of them in old age when they need their help the most but are virtually left in the lurch. Further, the Bombay High Court in a 2016 judgement had affirmed that a married woman too is responsible for maintaining the parents. Now, even the daughter-in-law and son-in-law of senior citizens would be responsible for taking care of them. Moving to amend the Maintenance and Welfare of Parents and Senior Citizens Act, the government has expanded the ambit of social security for the elderly by making distant relatives responsible for their upkeep, increasing fine and imprisonment for abandoning parents, and doing away with the financial cap of Rs 10,000 for maintenance of parents.

Undoubtedly, there are cultural, legislative, and everyday ways in which the neo-liberal urban, middle-class Indian families are confronting and confronted by their own transformations and therefore the ways in which roles, functions, and the site itself are going through flux. For instance, to turn to popular culture once again: the Hindi movie *Piku* (Shoojit Sircar directed, 2015) depicts an independent career woman living with and taking care of her elderly father – the pressures, vulnerabilities, and the satisfaction in this care-ing being the crux of the film. An Axis Bank commercial first broadcast in 2018 shows a mother proposing that her son and his future wife should take a separate/different home. The son's question *aapse dur* (away from you) is answered by the mother *ghar aas paas hi lena* (let the location be near to mine).

What are the ways in which setting up a separate home or being left in an old age home (Nachiketa's song) can be looked at? Should it be looked at as abandonment by kin members (sons/daughters) or a chance to form and maintain new relationships (through the shared realities of residents in an old age home) within and outside of the kinship boundaries? Is the presence of the idea of old age home in a 2007 Indian legislation or the above-mentioned judgements, the "grim" reality that faces the elderly population as much as a social reality within the neo-liberal times, indicating loss and separation from always already familiar familial landscapes?

Towards Care: A Discourse Beyond Security

My concluding arguments are around contemporary discussions within the policy, movement, and market landscape constructing or analysing ageism and elderly care. Discussions around social security and ageing in India have occupied some academic space such as in the works of Meena Gopal (2006) and Arvind Joshi (2011). Both point out the limitations of the state's policy framework around the aged, specifically ageing women. I want to suggest that there is an urgent need to take the discussion to the register of care. The amount of time and energy that was spent in engaging with sexual violence or labour by the women's movements was not given to either old age or disability. If there was a connection between productivity and entitlement that the state made, ironically campaign spaces made similar co-relations, and thus care and companionship-based discourses were unfortunately missing. Care in contemporary times is given by people who may not have the "disposition of care" in their personal aims but do have a structural "practice" of care, pointing towards the alarming increase in middle-class Indian households of stranger/professional caregivers, most of whom are women, caring (for) the sick, elderly, and disabled. Is it necessary that the women's movement or disability rights movement reflect and build bridges between care and care-ing (Sen 2018)? The reason why this reflection is needed is because unless that happens the discourse on ageing will only be constructed through ill-researched government policies, paternalistic laws, or judgements, as we have seen in the earlier sections of this chapter. While putting care central to the discussion, I am borrowing from Veena Das' formulation that "pain may be seen as the possibility of a new relationship, the beginning of a language game rather than its end" (Das 1995), and arguing whether care can potentially create a new language within the political spaces of the movement(s). Das further talks about the embracing of relation that brings about a relief in suffering, since the latter is based partially on the experience of isolation: "[p]ain and disease disrupt communion with the natural and the social world…" There is therefore a twofold set of questions here: how to create a discourse around care and how to also talk about the caregiver, which then leads us to ask who is the caregiver to the elderly in the changing familial geography? With the shift from family/community services to professional services, there is an emergence of business of caring targeting the "left behind" elderly population. The absence of social security measures to address the emergent elderly population, delimiting laws for old age homes for senior citizens, and no sustained civil society initiatives to make the elderly a group worth talking about, politically and in the transformed familial landscape, the market has entered into this gap. This is an industry based on the philosophy that children were supposed to take care; in their absence – mainly because of jobs that take them to other cities, within and outside India – someone else, a stranger from an institution is providing those services. One such service centre in Kolkata writes on their website, we understand that "*Care means more than just a directory of providers - doctors, physios, nurses. It is also about arranging 'One-Stop' Care platform.*" One of their services is Managed Elder Care, through which they provide intellectual companionship. The manager visits the elderly and helps them re-discover their hobbies, converses on various topics, and stimulates their minds. Most elders accomplish more when they simply have someone they trust and lean on. This is based on the need that "they have found that many elderly people don't necessarily need a lot of help, but would sometimes like a companion to support them during various activities: someone they can chat and discuss things with, at home or out-and-about." An entire economy around "consumptive labour" with the availability of consumer products (Joseph 2002) gets built around the elderly. The business of caregiving therefore is not merely about changes in family geographies, but once emerges, it is facilitated in sustaining these changes by providing market-driven "caregiving." Buying or availing the services of this industry is definitely determined by one's class, caste, and gender locations. Similarly the Axis Bank introduced "Senior Privilege Account" for senior citizens and also emphasizes locations of privilege in order to receive care or ensure care in old age. Companionship or creation of alternative sustainable communities clearly is not the objective of this care industry also.

The experiences of loss and separation together with a desire for companionship dominate the everyday lives of the ageing landscape. The policies around maintenance of the elderly or the market-driven medical care industry fail to address any of these complex living processes where how to live the life remaining still needs to be an important question even though the aged may be forced to ask how to wait for death? The character of Dr Alice Howland, in the movie *Still Alice* (2015), an Alzheimer-affected elderly woman academic says,

> *I am not suffering. I am struggling, struggling to be a part of things, to stay connected to who I once was. So live in the moment I tell myself. It's really all I can do. Live in the moment…I have, uh, good days and I have bad days. On my good days, I can, you know, almost pass for a normal person. But on my bad days, I feel like I can't find myself. I've always been so defined by my intellect, my language, my articulation and now sometimes I can see the words hanging in front of me and I can't reach them and I don't know who I am and I don't know what I'm going to lose next.*

Segal (2012) writes in her last chapter that embracing survival is always as painful as it is pleasurable. As we try to encounter the rhythms of life and death in the process of ageing, it is important to start conversing in what contexts will "we" (my generation) be ageing – how shall we talk about caring in situations of singleness, childless adults, and non-married cohabiting adults and create communities of companionships? Unless we move from the juridical discourse of maintenance, which is where the chapter begun through provisions in Criminal Procedure Code or statutes passed by the Parliament as well as the political economy framing of private care service providers, which the chapter is referring to at the end, to a more everyday living discourse on care and companionship within and outside kinship networks and with multiple meanings of home for the elderly, the sociological ability to comprehensively engage with ageing will be limited.

Bibliography

Barrett, Michel and Mary McIntosh. *The Anti-Social Family*. Verso, 1982.

Basu, Manish. "Falling Total Fertility Rate in Kolkata Sets Alarm Bells Ringing." 2014. https://www.livemint.com/Politics/9jV7AFSSMgeCrJqyPgNwFI/Falling-total-fertility-rate-in-Kolkata-sets-alarm-bells-rin.html. Accessed 20 Jun. 2022.

Gopal, Meena. "Gender, Ageing and Social Security." *Economic and Political Weekly*, vol. 41, no. 42, 21 Oct. 2006, pp. 21–27.

Joshi, Arvind. "Globalisation and Ageing in India." *The International Journal of Social Quality*, vol. 1, no. 1, 2011, pp. 33–44.

Lamb, Sarah. "Aging, Gender and Widowhood: Perspectives from Rural West Bengal." *Contributions to Indian Sociology*, 1 Oct. 1999. https://doi.org/10.1177/006996679903300303.

———. *Aging and the Indian Diaspora: Cosmopolitan Families in India and Abroad*. Indiana University Press, 2009.

Maintenance and Welfare of Senior Citizens Act, 2007.

Mitra, Ipshita. "36 Chowringhee Lane, Revisited: Aparna Sen's Ever-Relevant Tale That Merged Life, Death, and Shakespeare." 2019. https://www.firstpost.com/entertainment/36-chowringhee-lane-revisited-aparna-sens-ever-relevant-tale-that-merged-life-death-and-shakespeare-7164081.html. Accessed 30 Jun. 2022.

Mothersill, Mary. "Old Age." *Proceedings and Addresses of the American Philosophical Association*, vol. 73, no. 2, Nov. 1999, pp. 7, 9–23. American Philosophical Association. https://doi.org/10.2307/3131085.

Pal, Chandrima. "Old Is Gold: How Kolkata's Greying Population Is Feeding a New Kind of Business." 2016. https://scroll.in/article/802543/old-is-gold-how-kolkatas-greying-population-is-feeding-a-new-kind-of-business. Accessed 15 Jun. 2022.

Rajan, Irudaya S. and Kumar Sanjay. "Living Arrangements among the Elderly." *Economic and Political Weekly*, vol. 38, no. 01, 04 Jan. 2003, pp. 3731–3740.

Rubin, Gayle. "The Traffic in Women: Notes on the Political Economy of Sex." *Toward an Anthropology of Women*, edited by Rayna R. Reiter. Monthly Review Press, 1975, pp. 157–210.

Segal, Lynne. *Out of Time: Pleasures and Perils of Ageing.* Verso, 2012.

Sen, Rukmini. "Still My-Self? or the Loss of the Self." 2016. https://cafedissensus.com/2016/08/14/still-my-self-or-the-loss-of-the-self/. Accessed 20 Jun. 2022.

———. "Re-imagining Kinship in Disability Specific Domesticity: Legal Understanding of Care and Companionship." *Mapping Disability Studies in South Asia*, edited by Anita Ghai. Sage Publications, 2018, pp. 401–412.

Sen, Saibal. "Kolkata Is Ageing Faster Than Other Metros." 2015. https://timesofindia.indiatimes.com/city/kolkata/Kolkata-is-ageing-faster-than-other-metros/articleshow/49546289.cms. Accessed 15 Jun. 2022.

Shah, A. M. *The Family inn India: Critical Essays.* Orient Blackswan, 1998.

Sharma, Nidhi. "Daughter-in-Law and Son-in-Law Too Would Be Responsible for the Care of the Old." 2018. https://economictimes.indiatimes.com/news/politics-and-nation/daughter-in-law-son-in-law-too-would-be-responsible-for-care-of-old/articleshow/63756469.cms?from=mdr. Accessed 30 Jun. 2022.

Thompson, Neil. "The Ontology of Ageing." *The British Journal of Social Work*, vol. 28, no. 5, Oct. 1998, pp. 695–707. https://www.jstor.org/stable/23714858.

Turner, Bryan S. "Ageing, Status Politics and Sociological Theory." *The British Journal of Sociology*, vol. 40, no. 4, Dec. 1989, pp. 588–606. https://doi.org/10.2307/590890.

3
QUEERING CHRONONORMATIVITY IN INDIA

Challenges and Possibilities

Kaustav Bakshi

Any discussion on queer ageing cannot but begin with the question of chrononormativity or how it is undone in the process of ageing queerly; time being understood largely through the lens of heteronormative life and modes of living, queer ageing or ageing queerly could be remarkably subversive, occasioning discomfort and inviting social censure. Judith (Jack) Halberstam (2005) while reimagining the concept of time queerly (with the melancholic reminder of the HIV-AIDS crisis that "compressed" life and "annihilated" time for millions of queer individuals) writes:

> Queer subcultures produce alternative temporalities by allowing their participants to believe that their futures can be imagined according to logics that lie outside of those paradigmatic markers of life experience-namely, birth, marriage, reproduction, and death.
>
> *(2)*

In other words, queer lives disrupt chrononormativity, while constantly struggling to exist in resistance to it. But, if queer futures are to be imagined outside the pre-set timeline of a chrononormative life, are there many options to choose from? If not so much when one is relatively younger, this becomes a pressing question as one ages in a predominantly heteronormative society. In India, where the LGBTIQ+ movement is comparatively recent, queer-affirmative lives are rare and far in-between to guarantee a pattern and model of queer liveability, outside the paradigmatic timeline charted by Halberstam, particularly as one ages.

It is important to note that the original radicalism of the queer movement, by the time it arrived in India and spread through the social media, is

DOI: 10.4324/9780429352560-4

almost dead, with a predominant inclination to approximate homonormative ways of life. Elizabeth Freeman in *Time Binds: Queer Temporalities, Queer Histories* (2010) casts a nostalgic glance at a more revolutionary past, while being sceptical of a rewind to that in the future. While it is now possible to imagine, "each 'queer youth' as having a future as a queer adult and/or a future in which he or she might move among gay, bi, or straight identities (or abandon them), or between or beyond genders," there is also a discomfort that there is an urgency to adopt the "state-sponsored narratives of belonging and becoming" (xv). In other words, queer lives are becoming more chrononormative than ever, for, in all these years, no desirable model of a non-chrononormative life has become available as a successful model.

In India the challenges of thinking outside the chrononormative pattern are more intense. Closely related to this is the question of ethical ageing: what does it mean to age ethically outside the chrononormative expectation of society? In the Indian context, the idea of an ethical-moral life is remarkably different from how it is understood within Western cultures, dominated by Christian values. As I shall argue, that discourses of feminist ethics which challenge hetero-patriarchal notions of ethics and value could be conducive in reimagining an ethical life of queer ageing individuals. Within a society, dominated by an idea of chrononormatively progressive life, starting with celibacy and ending with asceticism, integrating queer ageing respectfully demands refurbishment of the understanding of the ethics of ageing in general. This, in turn, could open interesting conversations on what "queer temporality" means within the discourses of ageing and ageism.

Beginning with the question – "Where are the older queers in India?", this chapter will move on to addressing more pressing philosophical questions of what ageing queerly could eventually mean within the ethical framework of "appropriate" ageing. The chapter will end with an in-depth examination of the workings of Seenagers, an initiative catering to queer men above 50 years of age, and examine if such an initiative can divert the clock of queer ageing towards an imaginable queer future, not immersed in melancholia and loneliness, in opposition to the commonplace perception of queer lives.

Where Are the Older Queers in India?

[1]

In India, the LGBTIQ+ community is generally perceived as young, though, ironically, those who actually worked towards inaugurating and organizing the queer movement in the late 1980s and early 1990s, leading to the reading down of Sec. 377 of the Indian Penal Code on 6 September 2018 are no longer young. While some of them have gone down in the queer folklore of India, a majority of the older queer population is largely invisible, almost to the extent that it appears as if queer identities only emerged with the politicization of sexuality in the public sphere and the subsequent construction of the marginalized and oppressed sexual citizen subject vis-à-vis the evocation of IPC 377 as the major legal obstacle to realizing a queer life to its fullest. It took almost 24 years, since the first petition was submitted by AIDS Bhedbhav Virodhi Andolan (ABVA) at the Delhi High Court, for the Supreme Court of India to declare IPC 377 unconstitutional. There is no census report to determine the precise statistics of how many queer people aged during these 24 years, how many died, and how many never came out to identify as queer.

In this context, one may recall a scene from Tarun Mansukhani's film, *Dostana/Friendship* (2008): Mrs. Melwani, the middle-aged aunt of the female protagonist, on discovering that their young tenants are a gay couple, exclaims that in her times, men were men, and they only romanced women. By "her times," she means her youthful days, when, she believes, queer men were non-existent, a view the film, tactlessly, does not contradict or clarify. In a way, Mrs. Melwani is right: there was no visibility of queer folks back then, as it is now. Or, for that matter, queerness was not understood the way it is understood currently. Unfortunately, queer people, who definitely existed in "Mrs. Melwani's times" are still quite invisible.

In India, the realization of living within a "queer temporality" is very recent. 1991 may be considered an inaugural moment of queer temporality in India when ABVA published *Less than Gay: A Citizens' Report on the Status of Homosexuality in India* which launched an affirmative discourse on homosexuality and the unconstitutionality of IPC 377 which picked up momentum as the decade progressed, culminating in the Friendship Walk in Kolkata – a little simulation of the Pride March – in 1999. This was facilitated by another event in 1994 – a watershed moment in India's queer temporality – when ABVA filed the first petition challenging the constitutionality of IPC 377 at the Delhi High Court, to reverse prison authorities' ban on condom distribution, amid the high risk of inmates contracting HIV, given sexual intercourse among men was rampant in prisons. The queer social and political landscape underwent a paradigm shift with these two events in particular providing the fulcrum of transition. The visibility question of older queer people needs to be understood in connection to this paradigm shift.

John D'Emilio's seminal essay, "Capitalism and Gay Identity" is useful in this context. D'Emilio argues that gay identity first emerged at the turn of the 19th century, consequent to industrialization and urbanization, when people moved away from agrarian-based familial units and kinship ties, and led a more independent sexual life at urban centres. The emergence of the free market further enabled large-scale gay visibility (although queer individuals were always in touch with each other at any given point in history). The movement from wage labour to new modes of consumer capitalism which may be described in terms of "consumptive labour" and not in traditional Marxist terms of "productive labour" (see Joseph) also had substantial bearing on the consolidation of queer identities. Alluding to this essay, Eng writes:

> In the age of queer liberalism, homosexual identity is increasingly produced as a supplement to late capitalism. Queer family and kinship emerge in the historical context – indeed, as an effect – of this new ordering of political economy and the governance of social and biological life. To resituate D'Emilio's insights in our current moment, queer family and kinship increasingly emerge as an affective social unit, now absorbed into what Lauren Berlant ... has called the "intimate public sphere"
>
> *(43).*

Here Eng is specifically speaking of an American queer history – particularly, the volatile, revolutionary decades of the 1960s and the 1970s which inaugurated a queer temporality like never before, and the changes that happened thereafter culminating in the reclamation of the term "queer" at the New York City Pride March in 1990. Because of rapid globalization – in which India eventually became a willing participant with the liberalization of its economy in 1991 – the cultural lag between the West and India was erased into a simultaneity, contingent upon the revolution in information technology that enabled a much faster both-way cultural traffic. The inaugural moment of queer temporality in India "coincided neatly (and not coincidentally)," as Naisargi Dave says (10), with these significant transformations in India's economic policies.[1]

The visibility of (relatively younger) queer bodies and queer intimacies increased almost exponentially since the liberalization – particularly, with the easy access to the internet and smartphones in the past decade (see Jeffrey & Doron) – to an extent of overshadowing, even erasing, queer lives – clandestine, unorganized, and largely apolitical – that existed previously without much awareness of what it meant to inhabit and embody sexuality tags such as L, G, B, T, I, etc., even though some local terms referring to sexual practices or preferences, if not identities – *kothi*, *dupli*, *chapati*, etc. – were available to some. To a certain degree, this explains the near absence of older queer people – in the age bracket of (or older than) *Dostana*'s Mrs. Melwani – in the action field of queer politics and the public domain in "her times" as well as at the current moment.

Kolkata-based, LGBTIQ+ activist, Pawan Dhall asks, "If you are not on [Facebook] do you not exist?" (132). It is a rhetorical question which is very important in the context of the invisibilization of older queer individuals. It is undeniable that online absence is almost equivalent to non-existence today. Clueless of the whereabouts of numerous queer people who wrote

52 Kaustav Bakshi

to Counsel Club[2] in the 1990s – people who are much older now – Dhall wonders that they have either withdrawn into isolation or into the security of social norms, for none of them are "seen" anymore. One reason behind this invisibility could be physical and mental degeneration that accompany the process of ageing. For instance, if not particularly mentally agile and cognitively functioning, older queer individuals may not have the quickness of mind to learn operating the internet and find access to social media to take an active part in the changing season of queer politics in India much of which has now shifted online.

Yet, interestingly those to whom today's queer youth owe much of their freedom – whatever little has been achieved in the last four decades – Ashok Row Kavi (1947–), Manvendra Singh Gohil (1965–), Sunil Gupta (1953–), Navtej Singh Johar (1959–), Ruth Vanita (1955–), Malobika and Akanksha, Giti Thadani, Pawan Dhall, and so many others – are no longer young, as mentioned above. Many have left the mortal world: Bhupen Khakhar (1934–2003), Saleem Kidwai (1951–2021), Bentu Singh (1964–2013), Riyad Wadia (1967–2003), and Mona Ahmed (1937–2017) to name a few. Two names, which often recur in LGBTIHQ+ history of India – Dominique D'Souza (1960–1992) and Siddharth Gautam (1964–1992) who played a seminal role in initiating a dialogue with the state to de-stigmatize HIV-AIDS victims – died rather young. Generally, there was scarcely any visibility of rights-demanding, rainbow-flag wielding queer citizens in the public domain (except for *hijra*s, not yet politically organized into a collective and brought within the purview of the protection of transgender persons' rights until the NALSA judgement in 2014) even 20 years ago which also explains the invisibility of ageing queer individuals or for that matter any desirable model of ageing queerly today.

The magnitude of invisibility in those times can be gauged if one takes a quick look at the letters sent to Giti Thadani's Sakhi, Delhi, and Pawan Dhall's Counsel Club, Kolkata, founded in 1991 and 1993, respectively. A certain Anuja, then 35 years of age, wrote to Sakhi in 1991 from Allahabad that there were a very few lesbians in her town; they were not sure of each other. She wanted Sakhi to put her in touch with some "lesbian sisters." Another Ms Bhan, then 21, wrote in 1992 from Jammu that she knew only one other lesbian person and she was reaching out to them in desperation (see Dave, 33–60). Anuja would be 67 and Ms Bhan 52, if they are still alive. Ruth Vanita (67) speaking to Project Bolo, recalls the 1980s, when meeting another lesbian person was a matter of luck, and how, even when they developed romantic feelings for each other, they did not have a language to identify that relationship. A letter received by Counsel Club on 18 September 1995 echoes this general lack of community or even for that matter *that one other queer person*. It said, "I am a lonely boy of 24 years of age. I am gay. I have no friends with whom I can share my joys or sorrows of my life. Our society is very rigid. I did not see any hope in my life till I found your magazine (*Pravartak*)" (see Baset). The writer of this letter would be 52 today if he is still alive. These lives, and so many more as one can speculate, have gone undocumented.

[2]

The paradigm shift – which happened slowly over a decade if not more – clearly did not facilitate queer visibility as much. While it inaugurated a new avenue for the queer population to find visibility and representation in public discourses, it did not make life easier in any way at the beginning at least. Living a (homo)sexually non-conforming life before HIV was detected in India (sometimes around 1986) and after ABVA filed a petition at the Delhi High Court challenging the constitutionality of IPC 377, in the context of the possibility of the surge of HIV-infected prisoners in Tihar Jail in the absence of condoms (1994), was not the same. While a spectrum of identity categories, comforting for some, confusing for others, emerged in the public sphere, the "homosexual" – "queer" was still a lesser known term – entered the public consciousness through two registers – the "pathological" (individuals who engage in "unnatural" sexual intercourse and are a threat to society as the most vulnerable carrier of HIV) and the "illegitimate" (individuals who could be punished under IPC 377). Those who had lived queer lives without labels, and without the fatal threat of contracting the virus, and perhaps even without the knowledge of the existence of IPC 377, away from society's disapproving gaze, were suddenly exposed: on the one hand as a pathological aberration and, on the other hand, a criminal who deserved disciplining.

Let's take the example of the raid on an international development agency, Bharosa Trust, providing technical support for the promotion of male sexual and reproductive health and information on prevention of HIV-AIDS in Lucknow on 7 July 2001. LGBTIQ+ activist Arif Jafar (53+) who ran the trust was arrested and kept in police custody for 47 days. Referring to a time prior to the emergence of the "homosexual" as a bio-medical category, Jafar says how passing as "straight" and avoiding social inspection was much easier (for cis-gender gay men): "The lack of labels helped us escape scrutiny. We could hold hands in public and people would think of us as friends" (see Dhrubo Jyoti and Ratnam).

LGBTIQ+ activism paradoxically exposed a partially invisible community – with homoeroticism being veiled under the garb of approved homosociality in many cases – to state and social vigilance, in a classic real-life substantiation of Foucault's observation, in *Discipline and Punish*, that how "the constitution of the individual as a describable, analyzable object … in order to maintain him in his individual features, in his particular evolution, in his own aptitudes and abilities," brings him under the "gaze of a permanent corpus of knowledge" (190), which occasioned disciplining of that individual to the extent of punishing him brutally. The raid on the Lucknow-based Bharosa Trust run by Jafar, and his subsequent imprisonment, is a case in point.

Therefore, one can speculate that the sudden transition from complete invisibility to being put under the spotlight was not comfortable for many, for it spawned newer challenges of negotiating one's existence in a predominantly heteronormative nation-state, leaning towards recognizing the queer as a troubled and traumatized population in want of protection under international pressure. When one wonders "Where are the ageing queers?", it needs to be acknowledged that for a sizeable number of older queer people, after a certain age, having lived life in a certain way for the most part, being seen as "queer" could be disconcerting. The discourse surrounding the evocation of IPC 377 and its eventual repeal, paradoxically, reinforced the bio-power of the state to make legible those who so far lived a relatively clandestine life, constituting them as a particular category of sexual citizen subject – a certain "sexuality type" – to the disenchantment of those – particularly cis-gender queers – who have lived the greater part of their lives without being labelled and, therefore, scrutinized for being sexually non-conforming.

The LGBTIHQ+ movement in India and the eventual reading down of IPC 377 have, therefore, been both empowering and disempowering, depending upon several factors specific to individuals – class, caste, religion, gender (trans-/inter-/cis-), marital status, family, and location. The near absence of older queer individuals in the public domain can be partially attributed to this irresolvable paradox.[3]

Straight-washing, Death by an Epidemic, and Class Matters

Referring to an AIIMS doctor who killed herself on discovering her husband, also a doctor, was gay, Sandip Roy says: "I was shocked because he was a doctor in 2015 who wasn't able to not get married, and then, his wife kills herself because she can't think about divorce" (Dhall 121). What shocks Roy is the time of the incident – 2015 – when presumably Indians were more accepting of non-heteronormative sexual identities. Clearly they are not. Queer people getting married and entering heterosexual family life is an open secret since time immemorial, and even after the reading down of Sec. 377 of the IPC in 2018, queer Indians are still getting married with the opposite sex and, in many cases, in the presence of their queer friends, and sharing pictures of their wedding on social media. Shocking it may be, but getting married, notwithstanding one's sexuality, is such an important coming-of-age activity for Indians – and anywhere in the world – that nobody questions it. When one wonders, "Where are the ageing queers?" one definitive answer to that could be a sizeable number of them have been "straight-washed" through marriage, raising a family and living a normative life (in many cases dual lives, if circumstances allow them). Back then – even 20 years ago – because of the lack of available models of queer intimacies in the public sphere – namely, friendship, romance, or coupledom – the fear of being left alone to fend for oneself was paramount in queer individuals – a fear leading many to opt for heterosexual marriage which apparently guaranteed companionship and security in old age. This tactic of getting straight-washed, voluntarily or under familial persuasion, for a more secure life, is still a readymade solution, even when models of queer intimacies are relatively more easily available, for queer people in India still cannot foresee or even imagine an optimistic "queer" future.

The familial and peer pressure of getting married, voluntarily getting married to avoid social scrutiny, and then the angst of leading a dual life have caused many suicides, and even murders. There is no record of these queer deaths, as queer deaths are often not recognized as "queer." Besides that, the HIV-AIDS epidemic, which became a concern in India around 1986 (according to the National Portal of India), became a major threat, before the government could be moved into taking action by social activist groups – one being the ABVA – into forming the National AIDS Control Programme (NACP-I) in 1992. A number of queer individuals – the exact count is not known – contracted the virus, primarily because of the lack of awareness at that time, and lost their lives. One queer person who has gone down in history is Dominique D'Souza, Goa's patient zero of the virus, who contracted it in 1989, and died within three years. However, he played a significant role in legally challenging the quarantine in which he was put on being discovered to be positive and, together with a friend, founded Positive People – an NGO to extend assistance to HIV-AIDS infected people and de-stigmatize it – only a month before he passed away. Had he been alive today, an openly out gay man back then, he would have been 63 years old. While D'Souza has been immortalized by a novel and a film, there are several others who lost their lives and, their deaths, again, were never recognized as queer deaths. As Sara Ahmed (2014) writes:

> Simply put, queer lives have to be recognised as lives in order to be grieved. In a way, it is not that queer lives exist as "ungrievable loss", but that queer losses cannot "be admitted" as forms of loss in the first place, as queer lives are not recognised as lives "to be lost" ... Given that queer becomes read as a form of "non-life" – with the death implied by being seen as non-reproductive – then queers are perhaps even already dead and cannot die.

(156)

If the queers are already dead and cannot die, understandably the visibility of queer deaths will be negligible. In the literature available in the domain of HIV-AIDS prevention measures and awareness-building, one frequently comes across categories such as *kothi*s (feminine men who are passive recipient in sexual intercourse with men), MSMs (a developmental, and not an identitarian category, created in the 1990s by epidemiologists to study the spread of STDs among men who have sex with men, regardless of how they self-identify), and transgenders (mostly engaged in *khajra* or sex work) as the most susceptible. It is difficult to speculate how many queer individuals had their lives cut short in their prime by this deadly virus – just as suicide and murder have ended many queer lives. Like D'Souza, several of them could have been alive today, had it not been for HIV or societal rejection. While talking about older queer population today, it is important to recall all those deaths caused by HIV or suicide or murder, for each of these became less threatening with the progress of time: while HIV is less deadly today than it was 20 years ago – thanks to preventive and remedial measures discovered along the way, societal acceptance of LGBTIHQ+ individuals is relatively more today. Therefore, in making sense of queer temporalities vis-à-vis queer ageing, the progressive waning of these two major threats to life and well-being demands consideration.

Those who are identified as older today, based on their age, have lived a relatively invisible life in their prime. Even when the LGBTIQ+ movement began gaining roots in India, in the late 1980s and early 1990s, queer-affirmative discourse was not available to many. In its rudimentary stage, the movement was predominantly metro-centric and pioneered mostly by the English-educated elite, many of whom fought the cause from diasporic locations. If any information was available in the public domain regarding this, it was mostly circulated by the English language press,[4] if at all, restricting the access of a vast majority of queer population to it. In the beginning, most, if not all, LGBTIHQ+ activists had a certain degree of privilege in terms of class, caste, education, and location, unavailable to most of the queer citizens at that time, and even today. In fact, even with the legal constitution of the sexual citizen subject – first by evoking IPC 377 and later through a reading down of the penal code – could not ubiquitously integrate everyone, who felt they were "different," into the movement.

Firstly, sexual citizenship, as David Evans has argued, is intimately linked with privatized and capitalist citizenship built on the practices of consumption. Not only class and access to the means of consumption, caste, education, location, and most importantly age also matter in one's ability to derive maximum benefit from being identified as a sexual citizen subject with a certain set of rights. Sandip Roy in an interview with Pawan Dhall, while speaking about arriving on the activism scene accidentally, says: " … in the early 90s if someone had told me that to be fully involved in these kinds of issues I would need to work with hijras, for instance, I would freak out!" (Dhall 121). Roy is referring to the elitist dominance and studied distance maintained (from *hijra*s in particular) within the LGBTIQ+ community back then, which has, fortunately, become more intersectional today. This also underscores the invisibility of a sizeable queer population which did not have the privileges of and means to fully living out their lives.

The long and short of it is that older queers are and may remain invisible for quite some time now – until about the time the current generation of queers – the millennials and the Gen-Z, for instance – ages.

Challenges of Queering Chrononormativity in India

In India, since ageing, in strictly chrononormative precepts, is often associated with renunciation and asceticism – the last of the four *ashramas* or sequential stages of life – *Brahmacharya, Grihasthya, Vanaprasthya*, and *Sannyas* – charted in the *Ashrama Upanishad*, the *Vaikhanasa Dharmasutra*, and the later *Dharmashastra*. The mandate of asceticism, abstinence, and austerity as a way of life has been prescribed, not just in the ancient Hindu *shastras* but in several philosophical discourses across centuries – religious or secular. In delineating how *aphrodisia* has been intensely problematized in philosophical writings, Foucault, in *The Care of the Self*, enlists a gamut of philosophers who recommend sexual austerity as a desirable means to a proper end – a way of being which separates and valorizes an individual as superior to "the throngs" (40). Therefore, ageing and queerness – queerness being popularly understood only in terms of "sexual deviancy" in acts of sexual intimacy – do not seem to go hand in hand – in a way misaligned with each other, given the ageing subject is expected to abstain from any form of sexual practices or expressions. It is highly probable that even the slightest departure from the expectation of ethical ageing is dissed as licentious, as suggested by the research conducted by Quam and Whitford (1992) in the context of the US. In fact, the concupiscent older man has repeatedly appeared a villainous or comic stereotype in literature and cinema across the globe.

As one probes deeper into the various aspects of queer ageing, one is faced with a few issues: first, to "come out" as an ageing queer person to oneself and to society at large, at the risk of exposing oneself to moral judgement; and second, to reconstruct the perceived notions of the ethical ageing subject – who is also queer – in opposition to several discriminating forces and moral precepts of chrononormative ageing. The magnitude and nuances of these issues of ageing queerly, outside chrononormative expectations, not only in opposition to the hegemonic structure of heteronormativity but also within the LGBTIQ+ community in India predominantly imagined as young are intriguing.

58 Kaustav Bakshi

Ageing is a social construct (Green 1993; Katz 1996), notwithstanding its biological inevitability – the fact that it is an inescapable part of life. Just as the "homosexual" emerged as a pathological category in the late 19th century, the ageing body too acquired a negative signification, when 19th century science "re-conceptualized death as an internal phenomenon of the body" (Vincent 2006: 682). The ageing body has been recurrently constructed as a *problem* within discourses of bio-gerontology since then. Elaine Showalter (2013) in her introduction to Lynne Segal's book *Out of Time* brings out the perceived undesirability of ageing through a striking analogy between ageing, obesity, and queerness:

> Like being fat, being old also has its own kind of secret closet. The late literary critic and gay theorist Eve Sedgwick gave a famous conference talk in which she came out as fat, and described her fat dream of entering a closet full of luscious clothes, all in her size, and then seeing that their label was a pink triangle... There are a hundred ways to deny, defy, or avoid the fact of ageing, from strenuous exercise and cosmetic surgery to relentless workaholism and maniacal activity.
>
> *(1)*

Breaking out of this closet is not easy. For, old age brings with it the anxiety of being less desirable, and therefore, this insane obsession with looking younger. For ageing, single queer people, in particular, it is a bigger challenge, given they often have to deal with bitter rejection on dating sites, notwithstanding the fact that ageing people are sexually desirable to many. Even if romance arrives, sometimes, it comes with a heavy penalty to be paid later – of being financially blackmailed, conned, and even murdered. Cat-fishing is rampant on gay dating sites in India, where older men, particularly those who are well-established, are targeted very often. Anupam Joya Sharma and Malavika A. Subramanyam (2020) come to the conclusion in an ethnographic research on gay ageing that:

> Almost all the participants ... claimed that they became "unattractive" and failed to meet certain norms expected in online dating spaces like Grindr which idealized young age and bodies ... Such reports suggest that the ageist discourse in Grindr neglects a wide section of the population, rendering them invisible and creating a sense of isolation. The unresponsiveness, rejection, and abuse that the respondents faced stressed them to a large extent.
>
> *(n.pag.)*

Therefore, coming out as queer and aged is not very easy, as ageing men are faced with a double challenge – the disapproving gaze of heteronormative policing as well as rejection from the community for being undesirable. More than anything else, what appears challenging is to understand what makes for ethical ageing despite of or by the virtue (or "the vice") of being queer.

Rethinking the Ethics of Ageing Queerly

To begin with, the construction of the ethical queer ageing subject has to first of all debunk the stereotypes of the "good homosexual" and the "bad homosexual," as Siedman (2001) makes the distinction – the "good homosexual" is the one who eagerly approximates and endorses heteronormativity by being in a committed monogamous relationship, as opposed to the "bad homosexual" who has a sexually active life with multiple partners, exhibits their sexuality throwing to the winds precepts of appropriate social behaviour, and refuses to conform. The stereotype of the "bad homosexual" invites a greater censure from moralists, particularly since the AIDS epidemic became a major threat to life and longevity, since the 1980s when it began to wrought havoc in the United States. As mentioned earlier, since ageing is burdened with a renunciation of desire – physical or material – for the queer subject – more for those looked upon as "bad" – ageing *appropriately* is a greater struggle.

Foucault's formulation of "technologies of self" claims that individual lives are never quite complete and finished – that in order to function socially individuals must somehow work on themselves to turn themselves into subjects. The notion of "technologies" offers the scope for an analysis of the sites whereby certain effects on old age are brought about. As Foucault puts it: "both meanings [of control and self-conscience] suggest a form of power which subjugates and makes subject to" (1982: 212). Repeatedly, Foucault has claimed that it is not asceticism but a (homosexual) *askesis* which is needed in order to invent "a manner of being that is still improbable." *Askesis*, as opposed to asceticism, involves care of the self, leading to a self-mastery and self-transformation – "an exercise of oneself in the activity of thought" (*Use of Pleasure*, 8). Foucault's *askesis* is not how it has evolved within Christian discourses of asceticism (or even within Vedic dictates on old age), predominantly – meaning self-denial or self-renunciation – but as it was understood in ancient Greece – an exercise in perfecting oneself through relentless physical and spiritual/philosophical training. Foucault's philosophical *askesis*, as Edward McGushin observes, "is a kind of release from oneself, but one which does not exactly renounce the self or mortify it. To the contrary, for Foucault, *askesis* results in a subtle transformation" (xiii). Intimately associated with this subtle transformation is the care of the self, which is not merely a feeling or attitude but an ensemble of practices, involving actively taking care not only of oneself but also of others. In *The Care of the Self*, Foucault writes:

60 Kaustav Bakshi

> As for the definition of the work that must be carried out on oneself, it too undergoes, in the cultivation of the self, a certain modification: through the exercises of abstinence and control that constitute the required *askesis*, the place allotted to self-knowledge becomes more important. The task of testing oneself, examining oneself, monitoring oneself in a series of clearly defined exercises, makes the question of truth – the truth concerning what one is, what one does, and what one is capable of doing – central to the formation of the ethical subject.
>
> *(67–68)*

In so doing, the notion of the ethical ageing subject can be revamped by reviewing and recasting sexual ethics in a different mould. Just before the passage quoted above, Foucault writes:

> Sexual pleasure as an ethical substance continues to be governed by relations of force – the force against which one must struggle and over which the subject is expected to establish his domination. But in this game of violence, excess, rebellion, and combat, the accent is placed more and more readily on the weakness of the individual, on his frailty, on his need to flee, to escape, to protect and shelter himself. Sexual ethics requires, still and always, that the individual conform to a certain art of living which defines the aesthetic and ethical criteria of existence.
>
> *(67)*

Generally, the idea of what constitutes an ethical life within the LGBTIQ+ community is an extremely complex one, notwithstanding age, but becoming more convoluted with age. The ageing queer subject finds themselves in a double-bind: on the one hand, they have to deal with endless moralizing against their sexuality, and on the other hand, to complicate things even further, constant reminders on age-appropriate behaviour.

The construction of the ethical ageing queer subject that threatens and jeopardizes chrononormativity requires a different value system, a different set of moral standard of judgement (if at all), opposing what is understood as ethical within the hetero-patriarchal framework of society. A good starting point could be the feminist debunking of what constitutes feminine virtue as prescribed by hetero-patriarchy: such as praising women for being chaste and virtuous and creating ethical-moral standards of "goodness" based on the woman's perseverance to maintain her chastity and virtue. Feminist ethicists are committed, before everything else, to the elimination of women's subordination – and that of any other oppressed person – in all of its manifestations. They challenge power and inequality, before raising questions about good and evil, care and justice, etc. The ageing queer subject too needs to exercise their ethics in questioning the moral precepts and proprieties of ageing (in other words, the virtue of ageing appropriately) and their social devaluation with inordinate power and value being invested in youth.

M. Daly (1978, 1984) holds that what is actually good for women is indeed what patriarchy identifies as evil for women, namely, becoming her own person. Following Daly, lesbian ethicists, such as Sarah Lucia Hoagland, in *Lesbian Ethics* (1989), state that women must replace the questions "Am I good?" and "Is this good?" with the question "Does this contribute to my self-creation, freedom, and liberation?" This, to an extent, resonates with what Foucault emphasizes on in his discussion of *askesis*. From the perspective of traditional western ethics, Hoagland's question is not the *right* question to ask. But, ethics, as one must concede, is not an individualistic quest; moral value is not innate to one's self or external to it. On the contrary, moral value emerges from what Hoagland terms "lesbian context," or "an energy field capable of resisting oppression." A lesbian approach to ethics is about lesbians challenging any form of oppression and refusing to take part in anything other than egalitarian relationships. Hall, in "Is there a queer ethics?" (2000) makes it clear that for queer theorists, the approach to ethics cannot follow from how ethics is traditionally understood. Quoting from Seyla Benhabib's *Situating the Self* (1992) where, Benhabib stresses that ethical models should be reflexive, pluralist, and tolerant of all ways of life compatible with the framework of universal rights and justice, Hall writes:

> In ways from which queer theoreticians could learn much, Benhabib and other postmodern ethicists define ethics in explicit ways as an aggressive practice of questioning and self-questioning, a repudiation of the validity of universal maxims and reliance upon unilateral power, but an allowance of limits on the self and its enactments of desire and autonomy.
>
> *(475)*

He goes on to say that "moral labour" remains the biggest challenge for queer theorists since the times Oscar Wilde made his own tentative moves against heteronormativity. Jeffery Weeks, also quoted by Hall, makes the point that the more one dares debunk norms, the more one becomes "unfree" in undermining the real autonomy of the self. Responding to Hall, Allen writes in the same essay:

> The real problem with ethics, I would argue, lies here. No matter how relativistic or postmodern it is, the dream of any ethics is that it is transcendental. Driven, if only implicitly, by modal operators like, *ought* and *should*, even an ethics that argues merely for the necessity of working out the best way of balancing one's autonomy with responsibility to the other nonetheless suggests that everyone should always do that.
>
> *(484)*

62 Kaustav Bakshi

For the ageing queer subject, therefore, ethical idea of living a proper life, cannot be imposed from outside, though the question of responsibility towards the other needs an overhaul in this context. Coming out as queer and old would, therefore, involve deflating hetero and chrononormative ethics centred on the "ought" and "should" which may not apply for a liveable queer life outside the normative. In the previous segment, in analysing the absence of ageing queer individuals in the public domain, straight-washing – that is, heterosexual marriage – is identified as one of the reasons. If not for all, for many Indians, marrying is a social duty, a responsibility to make their parents happy – in other words, the emphasis is more on taking care of other people's happiness over and above oneself. Something one "should" or "ought" to do. But in so doing, each of them ends up violating a basic ethical duty – sacrificing one's duty towards oneself – that is, their right to be happy in their own way. In this very act of getting married, one ethical responsibility is embraced at the expense of other ethical responsibilities – another of which being the mandate of being truthful to one's partner in marriage.

A reconciliation between queerness' resistance to the precepts of the natural and the normal and the idea of ethics is perhaps best realized in Levinas' declaration in "Ethics of the Infinite": "Ethics is … against nature because it forbids the murderousness of my natural will to put my own existence first" (190). In India, and in any other postcolonial nations, where the draconian law, projecting homosexuality as "against the order of nature," has oppressed queer citizens for centuries, Levinas' idea of ethics would make more sense. Putting one's own self first may sound selfish by ethical standards; it need not be so, in the context of queer ageing or in any other context actually. Prioritizing the self could be the starting point, if not the end point, of ethical queer ageing, as long as it does not harm others. On the other hand, following the thesis of *Advaita Vedānta* – one of the primary sources of the Indian philosophy of the Self (or *ātman*) – eventually, *moksha* is achieved through the transcendence of the material Self, and merging into the *Brahman* (the real Self), whereby the person or empirical self dissolves as an illusory (*maya*) projection of consciousness. In this thesis, the nature of the material Self – for example, what it identifies as – is ultimately immaterial. Working back from here, it is important to note that the question of ethical living (ageing) is not contingent on the worldly identity and there is no one correct way of being ethical.

Absence of Queer Model/s of Ageing

Even when queerness and ethics are caught in a contentious relationship, and reconciliation appears difficult, if not impossible, the question of ageing happily looms large over the community. This is precisely because till date, there has not been a powerful and discernible alternative model of liveability – not even *hijra* households – that could contest heterosexual monogamous (or even polygamous) marriage and replace it. The *hijra* household, despite providing an alternative model of kinship and liveability, is remarkably hierarchical and oppressive, as recorded by several insiders (see *I am Vidya*). Since there is no reliable model, and may not be any in the near future, queer individuals, rather than inventing alternative models, are willingly submitting to the indomitable power of marriage, at the risk of getting co-opted into chrononormativity. Not all of them, though. But, irrefutably, there is a general perception and belief that legalization of same-sex marriage in India is the ultimate "equality" goal to achieve for the LGBTIHQ+ community (the only sanctified and sanctioned model of family, companionship, and most importantly, the means for availing maximum benefits offered by the state, with advancing age and attendant physical degeneration).

Ageing and marriage are very closely related, and in Indian families, if someone ever refuses to tie the knot, close relatives, friends, and well-wishers, while singing paeans to marriage, often deploy, when all other pleas and implorations are exhausted, the ultimate weapon of invoking the fear of loneliness in old age or of dying alone uncared for: "Who's going to look after you in your old age?" Anyone who has refrained from marrying encounters this question a million times in their life, at least as long as they appear marriageable. This apparently rhetorical question is based on some flawed assumptions: first, it assumes that the marriage is going to last forever; second, the couple will die at the same time, so that they could look after each other till the very end; third, the marriage will beget children who will look after their parents, if and when they are incapable of taking care of each other; and fourth, the children will be loving and dutiful enough to take care of ageing parents. While all these assumptions may have proved to be true in several cases, in equal number of cases, they may have just remained assumptions. Therefore, there is no assured warranty that marriage could help alleviate the plight of ageing, even though advocates of marriage claim it to be so.

But didn't radical queer politics have always challenged the very institution of marriage, although there is a scramble for the same at the current moment in India? While on the one hand, there is a deep sense of deprivation on being denied the equal rights of getting married, and therefore, a perpetual anxiety of being forced to age alone within the LGBTIHQ+ community, on the other hand, there is a discomforting wariness about celebrating the right to marry as the most desirable end of the community's combat for state recognition and equal rights. While projecting marriage as the legitimate end of their collective agonism, advocate Saptarshi Mandal (2021) highlights what the LGBTIHQ+ community often tends to overlook:

The right to marry not only means obtaining legal recognition for one's relationship, but entails entering a complex of laws that determine each aspect of the relationship. If the current laws exacerbate misery in heterosexual married life, either by preventing people from easily ending their unhappy marriages or by intensifying economic inequality and power imbalance between spouses, then these issues will be faced by married queer couples as well. If heterosexual interfaith couples face difficulties in using the SMA, [sic] so would queer couples, whether interfaith or not.

(n.pag.)

Mandal proposes encountering "the politics of family law reform in India" and goes on to argue that it was time Indian queer citizens, rather than pushing the law to aid same-sex marriages, pondered over the kind of family or kinship model, beyond the one sanctioned by the legal institution of marriage, they actually desired. On 19 July 2020, in an online session with Arundhati Katju and Menaka Guruswamy titled "The Battle for Equal Rights for the LGBTQ+ Community," gay activist Ashok Row Kavi points out that given that by the end of 2025, India will have 2.8 crores senior citizens, there will be "a considerable number of gay men who haven't been able to find partners" and questions "how are we going to look after them?" As such, he says that we "have to look ahead, beyond same-sex marriage." If neither the models of the *hijra* household nor marriage could be ideal models of queer ageing and liveability, is there an alternative? Row suggests looking at "Buddy systems."

"Buddy System": A Possible Model of Ageing Queerly?

In an oft-cited interview of Michel Foucault entitled, "Friendship as a way of life" (1981), the philosopher, responding to the question, "Can you say that desire and pleasure, and the relationships one can have, are dependent on one's age?", says:

> two young men meeting in the street, seducing each other with a look, grabbing each other's asses and getting each other off in a quarter of an hour. There you have a kind of neat image of homosexuality without any possibility of generating unease, and for two reasons: it responds to a reassuring canon of beauty, and it cancels everything that can be troubling in affection, tenderness, friendship, fidelity, camaraderie, and companionship, things that our rather sanitized society can't allow a place for without fearing the formation of new alliances and the tying together of unforeseen lines of force. I think that's what makes homosexuality "disturbing": the *homosexual mode of life, much more than the sexual act itself.* To imagine a sexual act that doesn't conform to law or nature is

not what disturbs people. But that individuals are beginning to love one another – there's the problem.

(emphasis added)

The perception of homosexual relationality as temporal and prurient is approved and maligned at the same time. Approved, because it does not threaten the inviolability and iterative reproduction of the hetero-patriarchal model of marriage and sexuality understood in binary terms; maligned, because that way homosexuality, perceived as a bawdy "act" and nothing more, could be safely kept outside social registers of affective human relations. This hetero-patriarchal fear of a sustainable homosexual relationality within an affective model could be one reason behind the absence of queer models of ageing happily.

In popular culture, the queerness of the homosexual is particularly apparent in the image of the ageing homosexual who, forsaking marriage and parenthood, is often portrayed as lonely and despairing. But, is it only despair and loneliness that is left, in the absence of socially approved models of liveability? In this context, I would like to turn to "The Lotus Eater" (1935; pub. 1940) – a short story by the English author, William Somerset Maugham (1897–1964). Written at a time when homophobia was rampant in England, and sexual censorship was the order of the day, this story, though not overtly queer, when read through a queer optics provides an interesting perspective on a possible queer model of ageing. It is public knowledge now, thanks to Maugham's biographer Ted Morgan that the story is based on Maugham's close friend and sexual partner John Ellingham Brooks (1863–1929), a pianist and a classical scholar who had escaped to Capri, along with numerous other homosexual Englishmen, following the trial of Oscar Wilde in 1895. However, the story itself has barely any resemblance to that of Brooks who Maugham often visited. The story goes like this: Once his wife dies, Wilson, the protagonist, leaves everything behind and immerses himself in the gay abandon (pun intended) of Capri planning to commit suicide at the end of the 25th year, when all his savings would be exhausted. He miserably fails in his attempt and is eventually reduced to a pitiable older man, frail, partly out of his mind and emotionally vacuous. However, his death, which happens on a stunning moonlit night of Capri – the beauty of which had initially made him abandon his life as a banker and set up home here – seems like a boon, an escape from the life of misery he has been thrust into. Maugham ends the story with a flourish – "Perhaps, he died of the beauty of the sight" (87). The story's queer currency and aesthetics are subterranean, carefully closeted in the way the narrative navigates itself through symbols, allusions, and metaphors recognizable only to the well-informed.

Whosoever is aware of Capri's reputation as a haunt of homosexual men and women would immediately recognize the queer drift in Maugham's story, without even having access to the author's biography. Rilke and Norman Douglas were in love with Capri; so were Oscar Wilde, Henry James, Truman Capote, Tennessee Williams, Christopher Isherwood, Gore Vidal, and Graham Greene, to name a few. It was a regular getaway for lesbians as well. As Stephen Spender says in his introduction to *The Temple*, one great attraction of Europe to the Englishmen and Americans was the availability of "sex," not to mention high-quality liquor (Spender x). Capri had turned into a homosexual haven, owing to the efforts of the German industrialist Friedrich Alfred Krupp and the French poet and real-estate heir Jacques d'Adelswärd-Fersen, both millionaires. Notably, the latter built a palace next to that of the ruined palace of Tiberius. In the hyper-luxury of the palace, d'Adelswärd-Fersen invited innumerable boys from outside and often indulged in elaborate orgies (see Hone).

Fascinating as Wilson's choice as it may sound, the blueprint Wilson draws out for himself fails miserably as mentioned above, raising profound existential questions about life, death and the absurdity of human life in general. If the existential message be kept aside for a moment, one probable way out, as Wilson's choice suggests, could be, saving enough, enough to serve one's needs till one dies, and giving oneself up to the pleasures of Capri, a well-known gay asylum of Western Europe or some such place. The story seems to warn against such whimsicality (read, queerness) and risk-taking – more like challenging life itself – but, it is in this risk-taking Wilson's queerness comes out most compellingly. For, it is about challenging chrononormativity, arresting time to serve oneself, and giving oneself up to indolence and enjoyment of beauty opposed to the capitalist demand of industriousness as long as one is capable of. The penalty Wilson pays is not so much for his sexuality but more because of his daring to resist time and abandon himself into perpetual leisure as he gets on in age. This story succinctly upholds the challenges of thinking outside the chrononormative box, underlining the impossibility of queering time.

But, in real life, John Ellingham Brooks who was the inspiration behind the story did not encounter a similar fate. As is evident from the story, Maugham's biography, and also from several accounts of Capri that exist in queer writings, most of these men on self-imposed exile, survived through, what Ravi calls, a "buddy system." Can friendship really be a way of life, then? This story seems to suggest that. This "system" provides a counteractive response to chrononormative diktats. In other words, the very choice of entering into this system underscores a political disposition which does not only challenge chrononormativity, but also homonormative alternatives which queers seem to adopt unquestioningly at the current moment. On another level, queer friendships and the community solidarity forged through nurturing friendships for long could also instigate social justice activism, as a recent anthology, *Friendship as Social Justice Activism* from South Asia claims. In the introductory note, the editors write:

> Friendship is believed to be something common, yet something familiar, banal, or even mundane, it is almost taken for granted and overlooked as an inescapable, recognizable truth of life. Friendship evokes something about the other, relationality with the other, a process that is forged perhaps throughout one's lifetime, involving modalities of awareness, of unlearning with self and others – acknowledgement of which is merely the first step – and pain and loss as part of its temporality, and hence the desire to endure, almost obsessively.
>
> *(4)*

This is true of all friendships, but of queer friendships in particular, because forging such friendships is necessary for community building of the socially "misfits," fighting for social justice and demanding equal rights. The editors go on to say, "Capitalism, racism, sexism, ableism and ageism, all collude in selling romantic attachment as the scarce and penultimate brass ring of life" (5), while friendships are never invested with such a currency. So, the "buddy system" which Row underlines as a possible way to counter existing heteronormative models of togetherness, companionship, and liveability requires more visibility. In the next section, I shall focus on one such initiative – Seenagers – a Mumbai-based initiative for gay men above 50 years of age which brings in its *modus operandi* the spirit of social justice activism, although it is not explicitly stated anywhere.

Seenagers: A "Buddy System" in Action in India

Founded in 2017, Seenagers GupShup group is an initiative, and not an organization, to provide a support system to ageing gay, bisexual, and asexual cis-gender men of India. The "Mission" of this initiative is spelled out on its official page in these terms:

> A large number of gay men in India are married to women, mostly due to societal pressures. These men face many challenges such as leading a double life, suppressing their sexuality, and fear of being outed to their family. Gay men, who are not married, have challenges such as loneliness, discrimination by society, and lack of physical and emotional support. Seenagers aims to create an inclusive space for these gay, bisexual, asexual men to express themselves and build new friendships to tackle loneliness. We hope to create a large enough community that supports itself and helps people lead a fulfilling and happy life.
>
> *(n.pag.)*

The initiative has brought under its wings several queer cis-gender men, 50 and above, in the last five years, among which around 9 members responded to a few questions I had emailed them through one of the founding members, Dr. P.R. Dandekar. The responses are far too less to be analysed scientifically for making sense of how Seenagers as an initiative is standing in as an alternative kinship system for these older queer men, but the responses are important because many of them confirmed the issues older queer men are perceived to deal with, given homophobia and ageism are still rampant in India. The interviews revealed that some of them feel discriminated against even within the LGBTIHQ+ community because of their age, some have encountered rejections on dating sites, while some of them have been victims of conning by younger gay or posing-to-be-gay men. For some, Seenagers provides a safe platform to come out and socialize and reach out for help in times of emergency. When asked "Do you feel that you could have a more secure and easier life as a queer person if you were younger today?", 68% of the interviewees responded in the affirmative. Simultaneously, an equal number of them felt that legalization of same-sex marriage could not alleviate the problems of ageing queerly and chose "meaningful friendships, compared to romance, marriage or civil partnership" as a vehicle for a happy life.[5]

This "support" comes in multiple forms – creating safe space for socializing, organizing inter-generational interactive sessions, providing expert advice on management of finances and properties, providing guidance on averting abuse and possibilities of getting conned through dating apps and social media platforms, providing assistance in healthcare and in recognizing one's rights to one's body, etc. In pre-pandemic times, physical meetings were frequent, most of which have shifted online since the middle of 2020. These meetings, as one can glean from the minutes, which have been regularly made available publicly, underscore Seenagers' agenda of tutoring its members on minimizing risks as one grows older alone or with a partner: in my reading of these minutes, I observe that there is an endeavour of imbibing in the members a sense of the importance of self-care. The sessions on management of finances, bequeathing of property through the creation of a will, and addressing mental health issues seem to prepare the members for exercising self-care in the absence of another person – a designated partner or any other family member – in order to ease life. For example, in cases of extreme physical or mental health issues, one may not be in a position to take care of oneself; but, making one aware of conscientious planning to obviate distressful situation in the times of need – one being planning one's finances in such a way so as to have sufficient savings to ensure care and support in times of major health crises – is one of the most important lessons in self-care that is absolutely necessary. Apart from that, sessions are conducted to make ageing gay men aware of their right to their own body, the right to passive euthanasia, and the concept of a "good death" – the legality and the ethics surrounding it. On 29 October 2017, Dr. Roop Gursahani convened a session on the creation of a "Living Will" – a document which clearly charts out about how one's body should be treated when one is alive but can no longer see what is happening to them or articulate what you want – taking the attendants through a clause-by-clause understanding of their right to their own body, mostly in the absence of a biological family, in a medical context. This is again a form of self-care which the members are made aware of, given dying may not always come with dignity, particularly when one is without a partner or a biological family.

Seenagers seems to be addressing those particular worries and anxieties which plague ageing queer citizens of India, living outside the normative models and looking for a more secure future. While one important agenda of Seenagers is to create a space for safe socializing, companionship and bonding, it also seems to redefine the mechanism of care: while care is something which is expected from others – a partner or maybe a hired professional, care is also about becoming self-sufficient in order to eliminate the necessity of being cared for to an extent. Seenagers in its agenda to bring more and more ageing queer men under its wings investigates the formation of a community which plays an important role in visibilizing queer friendships. Friendship between two men or between two women, as mentioned earlier, often gets straight-washed, and in many cases rightly so. But, to insert a queer currency into a narrative of friendship and togetherness enabled by an initiative such as Seenagers is absolutely important for allowing a model of liveability to emerge for other queer citizens to follow.

Friendships are never considered as an equal alternative to marriage or having a biological family; the reason being friendship is not bound by law. A lawsuit cannot be filed against a friend who abandons; therefore, considering friends as companions or caregivers is looked upon with suspicion and rarely valorized as a sustainable kinship model. But, in India, particularly in Gujarat a legal friendship contract, by the name of Maitri Karar (similar to Nata Pratha practised in parts of Madhya Pradesh and Rajasthan) has existed for centuries, which gives legal recognition to the friendship between a man and a woman, one of whom could be married. In modern terms, Maitri Karar could be interpreted as a legal license to live together. Queer individuals have often used Maitri Karar to legalize their romantic relationships (see Khandekar). However, one can also argue that friendships which may not be erotic and/or romantic may work precisely because there are no legal bindings on them. Such friendships could actually be more genuine, for they function without the pressure of compulsion. What Seenagers is suggesting is to expand this network of friendship, where real-life friends, virtual acquaintances, and erotic partners everyone can come together to create a sense of companionship. The protection – if one is concerned about

70 Kaustav Bakshi

that – is that if one friendship sours, there is a community of other friends (or even just like-minded people) to fall back on.

While such an alliance could be encouraging and aspirational for queer folks apprehensive of ageing alone, it also engenders a few challenges, given that homophobia is still rampant, notwithstanding whether Sec. 377 of the IPC has been decriminalized or not. The emergence of such an alliance of ageing queer men, beyond the fleeting need of satisfying sexual appetite, could be deeply unsettling to those who could so far safely dismiss homosexuality as a perversion of youth, which would disappear with age, or endure homosexuality as long as it was delimited to a mere sexual act, as Foucault said, sans emotions or a sustained coalition-building over time, distinct from a single day's event such as a Pride Parade – the most visible form of queer cultural and political camaraderie in India.

Coda

This chapter was an attempt to map queer ageing in India, with some obvious limitations. The issues raised in this chapter are debatable and can open up further conversations based on lived experiences of being queer and older in India. However, it may be important to bring to fruition alternative forms of liveability and companionship challenging the predominantly oppressive model of marriage, a goal which the LGBTIQ+ community has its eye firmly set on. The remarkable invisibility of older queer individuals though rationalized early in the chapter actually remains the most important site to be explored further. This would require an intense ethnographic approach, which can only be accomplished through development of deep friendship and trust. Because of the non-existence of any census report identifying the indefinitely large spectrum of non-normative sexualities, the task will be daunting. Nonetheless, this chapter, I assume, will act as a stepping stone to throw more light on the hitherto unexplored blind spots of what it means to age queerly in India.

Notes

1 However, as Aniruddha Dutta challenging, what she calls the "metronormativity" (that is, the formation of support groups and collectives was urban-centric and all progressive developments had a global-to-local or urban-to-rural flow) shows that even earlier transgender women, in particular, had formed functional collectives in peri-urban and rural areas, though those were relatively not so well-known.

2 The Counsel Club, a peer-to-peer support group, operated between 1993 and 2002 in Kolkata.

3 For instance, from my own experience I can say that even 10 years ago, when I declared I would not marry, my relatives speculated that it was a whim which would pass with maturity, or that I was so traumatized by a failed romantic relationship with a woman that I had become anti-marriage, or that I was too

cerebral to get into something as physical and material like marriage and raising a family, etc. But, recently, they began speculating about my sexuality, and the family grapevine was abuzz with the rumour of the possibility of me being gay, which I later confirmed. While for me confirming the speculation was not an issue, it is not easy for everyone.
4 To cite an example: the Counsel Club ran a support column on the pages of *The Statesman*, an English daily published from Kolkata, in the 1990s.
5 Perhaps this choice is conditioned by the rampant failure of heterosexual marriages one is witnessing today. Although India boasts of high success in sustaining marriages, with statistics showing only 1 out of 100 marriages dissolve legally in the country, in the last few years, the divorce rate has increased significantly. The Advocate Khoj law library (2021) reveals, "A survey states that over the past four years, the divorce rate in Delhi, the capital city of India has almost doubled and is projected to be 12000 in the year 2008. In 2006, Bangalore, the IT hub of India it was recorded that 1,246 cases of divorce were filed in the court that pertain to the IT sector exclusively. It has been estimated Mumbai has shot up to 4,138 in 2007 while cities that are acknowledged for their cultural richness and social values like Kolkata and Chennai, are no less behind. Agro based states like Punjab and Haryana are now seeing an increase of 150% of divorce rate since the last decade. Kerala, known to be the most literate state has experienced an increase of divorce rate by 350% in the last 10 years" (see, Anon. "Divorce Rate in India").

Bibliography

Anon. "Divorce Rate in India." *AdvocateKhoj.* https://www.advocatekhoj.com/library/lawareas/divorceinindia/9.php?Title=Divorce%20rate%20in%20India. Accessed 17 Sept. 2022.

Ahmed, Sara. *Cultural Politics of Emotion.* Edinburgh University Press, 2014.

Banerjea, Niharika, et al. *Friendship as Social Justice Activism.* Sea Boating, 2018.

Baset, Zaid. "Missives of Loneliness." *Varta*, 2013. https://varta2013.blogspot.com/2013/11/missives-of-loneliness.html?zx=f516e7091c26dc6.

Benhabib, Seyla. *Situating the Self: Gender, Community, and Postmodernism in Contemporary Ethics.* Routledge, 1992.

Daly, M. *Gyn/Ecology: The Metaethics of Radical Feminism.* Beacon Press, 1978.

———. *Pure Lust: Elemental Feminist Philosophy.* Beacon Press, 1984.

Dave, Naisargi N. *Queer Activism in India.* Duke University Press, 2012.

D'Emilio, John. "Capitalism and Gay Identity." *The Lesbian and Gay Studies Reader*, edited by Henry Abelove et al. Routledge, 1993, pp. 467–476.

Dhall, Pawan. *Out of Line and Offline.* Seagull Books, 2020.

Dhar, S. "Swipe and Scam: The Dark Side of Gay Dating Apps." *The Times of India.* http://timesofindia.indiatimes.com/india/swipe-and-scam-the-dark-side-of-gay-dating-apps/articleshow/74652948.cms. Accessed 15 Jan. 2022.

Dhrubo, Jyoti and Dhamini Ratnam. "The Way We Were." *Hindustan Times*, 1 Feb. 2020. https://www.hindustantimes.com/more-lifestyle/the-way-we-were/story-3ZcKC2adsX6UIJ568c3TVL.html.

Eng, David L. "Freedom and the Racialization of Intimacy: Lawrence v. Texas and the Emergence of Queer Liberalism." *A Companion to LGBTQ Studies*, edited by G. E. Haggerty and M. McGarry. Blackwell, 2007, pp. 38–59.

Evans, David. *Sexual Citizenship: The Material Construction of Sexualities.* Routledge, 2013.

Foucault, Michel. "The Subject of Power." *Michel Foucault: Beyond Structuralism and Hermeneutics*, edited by H. Dreyfus and P. Rabinow. Harvester, 1982.

———. *The History of Sexuality: Uses of Pleasure* (Vol. 2). Translated by Robert Hurley. Vintage Books, 1985.

———. *The History of Sexuality: Care of the Self* (Vol. 3). Translated by Robert Hurley. Pantheon Books, 1986.

———. *Discipline and Punish: The Birth of the Prison* (2nd ed.). Translated by Alan Sheridan. Vintage Books, 1995.

———. "Friendship as a Way of Life." *Ethics: Subjectivity and Truth*, translated by John Johnston and edited by. Paul Rabinow. The New Press, 1997, pp. 135–140.

Freeman, Elizabeth. *Time Binds: Queer Temporalities, Queer Histories*. Duke University Press, 2010.

Green, B. S. *Gerontology and the Construction of Old Age*. Aldine de Gruyter, 1993.

Halberstam, Judith. *In a Queer Time and Place: Transgender Bodies, Subcultural Lives*. NYU Press, 2005.

Hoagland, Sarah Lucia. *Lesbian Ethics: Toward New Value*. Institute of Lesbian Studies, 1988.

Hone, Michael. *Capri: A Homosexual Paradise*. CreateSpace Independent Publishing Platform, 2016.

Jeffrey, Robin and Assa Doron. *The Great Indian Phone Book: How Cheap Mobile Phones Change Business, Politics and Daily Life*. C. Hurst & Co. Ltd., 2013.

Joseph, Miranda. *Against the Romance of the Community*. University of Minnesota Press, 2002, pp. 43–44.

Katz, S. *Disciplining Old Age: The Formation of Gerontological Knowledge*. University Press of Virginia, 1996.

Khandekar, O. "Same-Sex Couples in India Are Using a Gujarati Practice to Get 'Married'." *Mintlounge*. http://lifestyle.livemint.com/news/talking-point/same-sex-couples-in-india-are-using-a-gujarati-practice-to-get-married-111601876888126.html. Accessed 10 Sept. 2021.

Levinas, Immanuel. "Ethics of the Infinite." *States of Mind: Dialogues with Contemporary Thinkers*, edited by Richard Kearney. New York University Press, 1995, pp. 177–199.

Living Smile, Vidya. *I am Vidya*. Rupa, 2014.

Mandal, Saptarshi. "Redefining the Same-Sex Marriage Question." *The India Forum*, 10 Sept. 2021. https://www.theindiaforum.in/article/redefining-same-sex-marriage.

Maugham, Somerset. "The Lotus Eater." *Modern Prose: Stories, Essays and Sketches*, edited by Michael Thrope. Oxford University Press, 1973, pp. 72–87. Print.

McGushin, Edward F. *Foucault's Askesis: An Introduction to the Philosophical Life*. Northwestern University Press, 2007.

Quam, J. K. and G. S. Whitford. "Adaptation and Age-Related Expectations of Older Gay and Lesbian Adults." *The Gerontologist*, no. 3, June 1992, pp. 367–374. doi:10.1093/geront/32.3.367.

Seenagers. "The Battle for Equal Rights for the LGBTQ+ Community." *Facebook*, 19 July 2020.

———. "Home." http://www.hpqi.org/seenagers. Accessed 17 Sept. 2021.

Segal, L. *Out of Time: The Pleasures and Perils of Ageing*. Verso, 2013.

Seidman, Steven. "From Identity to Queer Politics: Shifts in the Social Logic of Normative Heterosexuality in Contemporary America." *Social Thought and Research*, Apr. 2001, The University of Kansas. doi:10.17161/str.1808.5178.

Sharma, Anupam Joya and Malavika A. Subramanyam. "Psychological Wellbeing of Middle-Aged and Older Queer Men in India: A Mixed-Methods Approach."*PLoS One*, no. 3, Mar. 2020, p. e0229893. Edited by Geilson Lima Santana, Public Library of Science (PLoS). doi:10.1371/journal.pone.0229893.

Spender, Stephen. "Introduction." *The Temple*, edited by Stephen Spender. Grove Press, 1988, pp. ix–xiii.

Vanita, Ruth. "Project Bolo- Ruth Vanita." *YouTube*, 6 Nov. 2011. https://www .youtube.com/watch?v=CUe-AwrJdVA

Vincent, J. A. "Ageing Contested: Anti-ageing Science and the Cultural Construction of Old Age." *Sociology*, vol. 40, no. 4, Aug. 2006, pp. 681–698.

4

CARE, INTIMACY, AND SHIFTING POWER

The Ageing Body within and without the "Family"

Chayanika Shah

I write this at a time when I have officially (by the standards of the country and laws that I need to abide by) turned an age that they term senior. Ok let me not hedge around. In the eyes of the State and society as well, I am old. So while this quote by Terry Pratchett, "inside every old person is a young person wondering what happened,"[1] makes sense to me, I also find myself agreeing with Margaret Atwood when she says, "everyone else my age is an adult, whereas I am merely in disguise."[2] And I say this not to be trite but also to emphasize that age and ageing have different connotations in different contexts.

As a queer person who does not have a marriage and family with children and grandchildren already there or on the way, my sense of my age is slightly unhinged. As a person who voluntarily retired from a full-time job because I had the privilege of class and no responsibility of thinking of anyone's future but my own, and as someone who continues to work many hours, I have sidestepped the forced retirement from familiar work. Moving around with friends whose mothers (and I dare say soon grandmothers) are my age and younger (something made possible due to my choices in life) has its funny moments as I empathize with their woes about their "ageing parents"!

Many of these choices are definitely linked to my social location and the privileges that I have of birth and access to stability in this society. But these are also linked to the fact that I have chosen to lead a "queer" life whose contours are often unclear and hazy but come into sharp focus in some situations like the above. Being out of the system helps focus on and evaluate what is often taken as the normal way to be in intimacies and in situations of care and nurture. At the same time, I am by no means completely out of the system as well, since I am connected to my fairly normative birth family

DOI: 10.4324/9780429352560-5

and do need to abide by some of those rules. So there is a dissonance of sorts because of the queerness but also an immersion in the reality of care taking of parents in a completely normative setup.

I use this location as I write this chapter analysing this sociological context of growing old and ageing with a specific emphasis on the intimate. Through this analysis I wish to critique the heteronormative family, an institution that is becoming critical to care and ageing in the present times of neoliberal, non-welfarist, political economies. I particularly wish to interrogate the parent–child relationship within this context as that is where the power balance of gender and age transforms through one's lifetime. Concern, care, and control operate in tandem in ways that maintain the patriarchal power of the institution, undermining the choice of the individual in need of care.

The chapter also discusses other frames and ways of nurture and care beyond the known familial structures. There are several stories of ageing of those who, for different reasons, do not rely on the blood (or marital) family as their support base. I use these to illustrate and highlight the different ways in which some people live and the ways in which they find support and care. Bringing these real lived experiences to light is important because it loosens the hegemonic hold of the notion of the normative family on all discussions about age, care, nurture, and intimacy and pushes us to look for other more humane solutions.

Contextualizing Ageing

Dictionary meanings of ageing clearly say that ageing means "becoming older and less healthy or efficient"[3] or a more benign "relating to getting older or used to describe a thing or a person who is getting older."[4] So there is a sense of getting older, a relative term meaning that there is a time when the person or thing is not old or indicating that they are old but just getting older. The allusion to becoming "less efficient" and "less healthy" than what they were also means that there is some standard of these that exists. Obviously then there have to be meanings to ageing that are contextualized in the socio-economic cultural milieu.

Time is a dimension in which we just move in one direction. There is no reversal. Chronological time hence is something uniformly experienced by all. If age were just a number marking a person's relationship with time, then that is uniform for everyone. The trouble is that this does not remain merely a number. Time on a body gets marked in clear biological ways – as an initial process of growing from childhood to adulthood and then ageing further to become old. The body is not just a biological entity; it survives in a social milieu. Hence, each body has its own unique ways of responding to these changes as per the other locations of class, caste, religion, gender, and ability.

76 Chayanika Shah

There are individual differences within these broad locations too and so there is a unique relationship that each individual has with their own material body. It is within this that the signals of ageing of the body are read and analysed. Often the body indicates age through explicit experience of its wear and tear and even surprises the self that "sees itself in disguise." So there is also a psychological sense of age as well which is mostly a personal perception, making ageing a very intimate thing.

In society, however, such individuality does not work. And so there is a clear social sense of who is of what age by the social standards set for it. A social understanding of ageing, hence, uses location markers set by society to understand these biological processes and passages of time. And finally in consonance with this, there are standards set by the State that determine, by chronological age, when a body is young (infant, child, adolescent, teenager), when it is adult, and when it is a senior body, and when is it super senior. These numbers are arrived at depending on the life expectancy figures and also keeping in mind the needs of the society at that time.[5]

In some sense the Collins dictionary meaning of ageing gives us a further clue what ageing means in a social context. When a person is less healthy and efficient, they are not socially productive and useful and also demand care because they start getting less healthy. Thereby they become citizens who give less and take more from society. Their needs and their contributions shift. So a person is said to be old when they stop doing productive labour, also marked by the State as the age of superannuation and retirement. This age also shifts as per the job market and the economics of pension funds.

The Normative Family

The landscape for speaking of ageing vis-à-vis the different institutions and mechanisms in society is fairly large. In this chapter the focus will be on the connection between family and ageing, that is, the sphere of the personal, the space of the intimate, where the actual nurture and care happens, both while growing up and when growing old. The family of birth is a critical institution as far as society and the State go. It is made such that all care and nurture needs of the individual are taken care of within it. This is where children are brought up and nurtured to become productive adults and then these adults look after those that nurtured them when they become less productive and need care. This system of familial care is fine-tuned over generations and different forms of families have reorganized themselves so that this is maintained. Hence this is a critical institution as far as society and the State go.

The family is conceived through an ideal heteronormative marriage which preserves caste, community, and religious purities. Patrilineality is the norm and so is patrilocality. This means that the woman enters not only a marriage but another family. In doing this she gets displaced, figuratively and metaphorically, as she leaves her natal family behind. This is critical to the organization of care, property, and wealth. In an overweeningly patriarchal society it also means that in the textbook imagination of the family, house work is the responsibility of the woman, and paid work outside or managing familial resources and owning them is the man's job. Since society is very diverse and practices vary across caste, class, religion, and region, there may be many variations of this in different parts of the country. The imagination of the family as conceived by the independent State, however, pretty much follows this understanding and in some form or the other most mainstreamed communities have fallen into some similar system.

The axes of gender and age are the primary axes along which power within a family gets aligned. Gender is a given hierarchy in a patriarchal world but is made much worse by patrilocality in a predominantly agricultural economy where resources are held by the larger family. Added to this is the inbuilt hierarchy of age that is added through necessarily having the woman younger than the man. So the woman in the couple does not have real control. The only power she acquires is sometimes as an older married woman whose husband is still alive and who is a mother of sons.

Crucial to this conception of the family is the fact that the marriage is necessarily followed by birth of children. The children belong to the paternal family, caste, and community.[6] They are hence necessary for furthering the population of the caste and community and for passing on the private property, if any. But they are also needed for maintenance of the care cycle and that is what we shall focus on here. Every new born in the marriage is looked after, grows up as a child, is educated, trained, made an adult and then this adult starts another family through marriage which looks after its own children but is also responsible for the care of those that started the initial family. Between marriage and blood relations (only through marriage), there is a neat system of organizing lives of people as per their age.

The markers of when a person is seen as a child, or as an adult who can be on their own, or ready to start another family of their own, that is to marry and reproduce, and when someone can then be entitled to being recognized as old and demanding of care, is almost a fractal-like re-creation of the original – maybe different in scale but similar in structure. This happens in a way that the next-generation child becomes an adult and starts their own life as the previous generation parent retires and becomes 'old' as per the chronological and social understanding of ageing. This co-ordination is essential for the system to be maintained as a whole. The external society marked by the hierarchies of class, caste, religion, gender, and other such, influences the internal and the more intimate sphere and deciphers the shifting balance of age and power therein. There is no common age for each of

78 Chayanika Shah

these happenings across all families but the cycle is similar and essential for political and socio-cultural economies to survive.

Parent–Child Relationship[7]

As the family with children (preferably sons) is society's way of organizing human lives, children are critical to human existence. And yet there is very little that we speak of the parent–child relationship. Age as an axis of hierarchy is built into this relationship. Traditionally primary power is with the father, and this also gets influenced by the control over resources that he may have. When resources are shared and passed on from generation to generation of men, it is difficult to get out of the cycle of power. When there is nothing to pass on and this happens in large populations marginalized because of caste, and class as well as religion, it is the caste and community pride that is passed on, especially for those that are higher in the hierarchy. These too keep the equation intact between the father and son. Even when there is no real power, the facade of the senior patriarch is maintained because that is how notions of gender and age are perpetuated and inculcated within the family.

The relationship of the son with the mother is more complex because resource control goes from the father to the son and with it her economic and other dependence often shifts to the son. In that case then gender plays an interesting role in controlling and changing the power of age. Gender also plays a crucial role in the parent-daughter relationship. Interestingly, till very recently the understanding was that on getting married the daughter's relationship with her parents and natal family became formal if not broken off completely. Once given in marriage her claim over the natal family was also controlled by the family she was married into. In this imagination where marriage is compulsory, the only daughter who has connections with her parents is the rare unmarried daughter. Instead of having rights she often seems to be at the mercy of the rest of the household as it evolves and does not usually gain control with age.

This system as described above is a generalization and may not replicate exactly in the same manner, but the principles of the system are maintained in most families and have been replaced with other ways of being only in the rarest of situations. This family is the space that provides all care – not only material needs but also physical and emotional. Belonging to this system is hence almost a requisite for everyone since without it there is no mode of care – an essential component of all people's full age graph. It is also the primary bond that seems to connect every person to other human beings and is almost essential for a sense of safety and belonging to the individual. All other connections of friendships and other affections that cannot fit into this mould are seen as of less value and are never considered equivalent to what this system provides.

As much as the parent–child bond is about caring for each other, it is also a bond of material need and control. The higher the family is in the social hierarchy of society, the more it strives to maintain the normativity. When there is a lot, the child also does not want to leave and gets absorbed within the existing system. In fact, the sons almost carry the responsibility of building the family wealth further. Most sons are happy to inherit the familial charge. Those who do not become the black sheep; those who have very little try to hold on to any prestige and power that may come from their social locations other than class as they learn to survive in the world.

The Cracks in the Wall

In this overall picture of the family, there are many cracks that can be seen. Some have always been there and others are being made visible and coming into existence now. Caste and patriarchy combine with class in particular ways when it comes to the marginalized. The above normative of course comes from a dominant caste patriarchal tradition. But there are others that too need mention.

Spread across the country there are pockets in which there exist communities that follow matrilineal traditions. Some of these also intersect with patriarchy in a strange way to uphold a few practices and subvert some others. So while the woman has property in her name, the male in her natal family, her brother, seems to look after it. This of course shifts the relationship of parents (read mothers) with daughters and also the equation of the couple but does not really invert the system. In tribal communities all across the region, there are many ways of living where the resources are more shared, family ties are not as rigid and children much more independent from the parents. The different equation with property changes some of the ways of care and nurture. There is much to learn from the ways in which these communities live, and this needs to be done soon as we are facing a scenario where there is depletion of these cultures and traditions as they get influenced by the dominant mainstream.

In this chapter, however, I continue with looking at this specific exploration of ageing and the family from two very different locations. One of these is through seeing the situation of a growing population of older people in the nuclear middle class urban family. From the dynamics between these otherwise able-bodied ageing parents and their able-bodied children (who may be seniors themselves), I draw upon the connections between care, intimacy, power, and control. There is a changing dynamic of care and intimacy as property relations also change with both generations being economically independent of each other. The second location I would like to explore is that of the queer subject who is often denied these family ties – in being rejected by the family that they were brought up in and in not being allowed to create a family of their own by society and law. I look at how intimacy and care and ageing work within the spaces that this queer subject creates and thereby learn the lessons that can be drawn from these marginal locations – this usually being the best place from where to look at the normative centre.

Care, Intimacy, Power, and Control

With changing economic realities and more urbanized and globalized living, a certain section of people is caught in a conundrum of change. This is the urban upwardly mobile middle class family. Here children are being helped by family members to move out of the family, especially for education and better job prospects. Among the women it is already the second or third generation that has got higher education and now women are ready to leave home for education and work even before marriage. Living patterns in these households have changed and so have aspirations and ways of interaction. Patriarchy operates in different ways and has survived often through extracting more allegiance from the women of this class.

Migration of men for employment is not a new thing. They, however, often left their parents in the care of an extended family and also at times in the care of their own wives. Working-class people have been doing this for years. The family left behind is supported by the larger community in the village or the town. The recent migration is from urban locations to metropolitan cities or to foreign lands where even citizenship is sought. The nuclear nature of the family does not allow for building of community in the same way. Often jobs make it impossible to be settled enough to be around extended families and their support.

Besides this, women from dominant caste and upper class backgrounds are seeking formal employment outside the house. Sometimes it is for making ends meet so that there is enough for all dependants to survive and at other times it is an urge to do something different. But it is always accompanied by a sense of freedom and an access to public life hitherto denied to them. Women from this class and caste stepping out of the home for gainful employment have not changed the dynamics of housework within the family members. Either older and/or single women who are unmarried, widowed, or dependent are called in to step in. And if that is not available then this domestic labour is shifted to women from marginalized classes and castes. So labour remains gendered, just that some women are free of it because other women have taken it over as employment, often with bad working conditions, poor pay, and not enough respect. The young, the old, and the disabled in the families of these women are in turn deprived of the care. Thus showing that who gets what kind of care is in itself a gender, caste, and class issue.

Inheritance from families is essentially the opportunities that these families provide through education and many other avenues for individual growth that help children become economically independent. At the same time economic dependence of these parents on their children has decreased over generations. If they do not have chronic illness, they stay on their own for longer periods of time. In the last century, as it is life expectancy has gone up considerably even in India. From somewhere around the mid-20s at the beginning of the twentieth century, India now has a life expectancy around almost 70. This figure improved from about 35 to 60 in independent India itself.[8] Not only has the average life span increased; this also means that we have a large population of the "aged" who need care. Obviously the age span for the section of people that we are looking at is even higher than the national average.

This means that very often in these upper middle class families we now have senior "children" looking after their "super senior" parents without the support and help of the extended family and community. There are new patterns of care taking. These families have been nuclear and face less assertion of power from the extended family. The women are more independent and so familial relationships, though still patriarchal and in control of the age and gender hierarchies, tend to be differently played out at a day-to-day level. In this changed family scene, responsibility of care of older family members is also changing.

We see more parents being looked after directly by their own children and not by the spouse of their son. Daughters are more independent to be able to do so even if married. So all daughters, whether single or married, are taking on the care of parents in more ways than before. And so are some sons, usually the unmarried man or the gay man. This is a new situation. In the earlier arrangement finally the nitty-gritty care was taken by the spouse of the son. The relationship was in any case marked with the other inequalities of the institution of marriage. In this case it is the person who has had a much longer and direct relationship with the parent who is responsible. And this is where we see a clear reversal of care roles and dependencies as ageing happens.

In this new equation between the parent and the child there are many complications. There is a baggage that both parties carry of the past. Familiarity does not automatically mean that affection is the only sentiment that underlies the relationship. It is difficult to break out of older patterns because no one has been taught to do so. In most Indian families it is an acknowledged fact that "Children remain children for the parents."[9] Parents, used to being independent all their life and in control of their lives and those of others, slowly start losing control, and this transition is not easy. For the "children" looking after their parents, seeing them not in control is also not easy either. Further this new role of suddenly getting the power over those that were always seen as powerful can also create a dissonance.

It is from these new scenarios of care taking that we may understand the limits of this model of care. I speak here from my experience and from that of many others who are around my age. Most of them are non-masculine and are taking care of their parents.

We find ourselves in a fix as we see ourselves suggesting ways of behaviour that we resented as younger people. "Do not go out at night, it is not safe for you." "You are too old to stay by yourself." "Let me take care of your finances. You are getting flustered and not able to do it properly." Statements we have fought and struggled against not very long ago. The truth is these things do not happen in any sequential manner. While we may ask our parent to not step out at night, they too suddenly discover the careless ways in which we lead our lives and say the same! The trouble is that in familial intimacies we often exercise control over the one we provide care for, thinking of it as concern. And yet the one at the receiving end – be it the child or parent or whoever – sees it for what it is, as power. The question that remains is how do you take care and negotiate the power.

Concern that takes away autonomy is a familiar thing. We have all seen it in different situations. It retains dependencies of all kinds. And this is true not only in case of age differentials but true for every situation where someone needs care and whose life is more or less dependent on the caregiver. It is only recently that we are hearing of disability being defined as a continuum and also of dealing with it through encouraging independence and integration in the disability movements. Both these ways of handling require us to alter our normative ways of extending help and assistance. The world as it is constructed is difficult for all people to navigate at some point in their life. So the disabled, the young or the old, the chronically ill, or the caregiver in any of these situations – all of them feel excluded from gaining full access to everything in society because of the way it is structured for a certain "normal." Integration of all within spaces and making it possible for more autonomy to most people are what should propel us to think of care taking differently, of structuring the world differently. Unless this is done there is the perpetual conundrum in the best of situations – of the care taker risking their autonomy in making sure that the person they care for has it.

Maybe there are lessons to be learnt from the parenting of parents and extended to the parenting of children and vice versa. Maybe it is also time to relook at this whole parent–child relationship as well. The relationship of blood is the only one that is permanent and there is no way to really get out of it other than abandonment. It is also the only relation where there is no choice made by either party. The mother–child relationship in particular is venerated much more than any other probably because of this. There is an assumption that in this relation there can be no ill will. There will always be the good of the child that the parent holds and the reverse is expected as well. In reality it is the certainty of care through the life cycle that this belief ensures. And, it is this compulsory character that makes people give in to power in that intimacy rather than provide for true care.

If we listen to children's narratives, we also see how the parent asserts power with withdrawal of affection and at times of even basic care. Girl children have faced it in many households where they were not wanted. And boys have faced it the minute they transgress the prevalent boundaries of masculinity or are unable to meet the expectations of their parents. We see this repeated in the reverse when children are made to take care of older parents. Stories of violence against older relatives are not new. The cycle of violence continues to operate. There is urgent need to think of other ways of doing this.

Maybe we need to find other less compulsory ways and urgently. The State at the moment in its neoliberal capitalist best is in fact promoting the family as much as possible because it is also doing away with any semblance of social security that might have been there. It is in the interest of capital and power that those who cannot afford paid help figure their own ways of looking after each other through familial or community connections and the rest join the market for it. The right-wing nationalist government is also interested in the purity of caste and community and religion. And so it will surely be encouraging of the "right" kind of family as well. The answers then can probably come only from those who have found other ways of being as they were excluded from their natal families, and whose own intimacies have not been recognized.

Queer Intimacies

The only well-known and visible queer community is the hijra community. For years they have existed and supported their members through their tough times and in their perilous lives. Over generations it has become a matrilineal system although the lineage is defined by choice. There is no relationship of blood. It is probably one of the oldest communities that people join out of choice. They are not born in it. And yet they have been there as an oasis for many transwomen and others who have been violated and assaulted by blood family for being who they are. Unrecognized and outside the pale of law, they have developed their own mechanisms of care of the new arrivals, the younger hijra as well as the ageing hijra. The point is not about whether it is the ideal to be emulated. But it is important enough to pay attention to and learn from as they are organized mainly by choice – of family and of identity.

The other queer communities are new and yet to really consolidate as lives so far have been invisible and hidden, lived in shadows and in loneliness. So far the violence and alienation that people feel is so intense that most that are trying to form these communities through organizing political and social space are actually dealing more with death as a young people's issue and have not really paid much attention to ageing queer people. HIV has taken a toll on some but so have other illnesses resulting from precarious living conditions. Hate and violence in society also lead to murders by others and by self. So, old age is not really part of the discussion other than very recent attempts at setting up old age homes and making social groups for people above 50 and so on.[10]

Also queerness itself is being defined very differently by different people. The upper class urban social scene is fairly ageist like any other mainstream understanding of desire. In these spaces there seems to be an imagination of the queer subject as the homonational good tax-paying citizen with their right to marry the person of the right caste and religion, have children through modern technology, and carry on the pure lineage in adherence to the natal family norms. Essentially, lead the monogamous married life and get full acceptance from the natal family. In so doing they follow all norms to live up to the parental magnanimity of acceptance and thereby overcompensate for their different desire. In this severely heteronormative world and society such a need has to be seen as valid too, especially for those that have been denied it thus far. So while I do not challenge this choice, I do think that the possibility of new ways shall not come from them.

It is those who, irrespective of their own specific desire, are willing to challenge norms of society that we look towards to see how new caring patterns can emerge: those, who do not think that all relationships have to be monogamous or long term and try living polygamously making their rules as they go along; those who are not in relationships at all because that is how they cherish their lives or make committed intimacies independent of sexual desire; those who are single by choice or because they have not found anyone to share their life with or are so because a commitment they made did not last and are not looking but are also not averse; those who care for many young people with full responsibility without actually being parents; and even those who adopt children with many others and bring to parenting the joys of shared concern but also do not see these children as their investment for an old age.

Each of these is a lived reality as much in the same-sex desiring world and the gender non-conforming and trans people's world as it is elsewhere in the straight world too. It gets identified as the queer universe because the absence of the option of marriage so far makes it easier to speak of multiple ways of being there. We need to listen, observe, and live differently to find more ways of caring and looking after those that require care. They could be young, disabled, with chronic illness or the aged. Blood and marriage cannot be the only frames as these are frames of compulsion and not having a choice in the matter is not the best way to construct care.

Then there are some other models that are being tried in different countries. One is the example of the "time bank" where people care for strangers, use technology to get in touch, and volunteer time to others in lieu of earning care hours for oneself, thus making the whole exercise reciprocal and yet not mutual.[11] Maybe this is the best way to go. Taking away from the parent and the child cycle where care is reciprocal but also mutual, where care at one point is being returned back at another after a full life of intimacy in between where affection is assumed and power ignored. The lack of mutuality is what probably helps make the bank more successful and less cloistered and geared to? The need for return is definitely there, but it need not be from the same people.

Conclusion

As an ageing person I look with apprehension at my choices in life. As I see older friends and family members around me, I find us paying very little thought to our tangible options as we start needing care. As we joked once that if we do not start talking about it now, we shall fade away in our solitary individual bourgeois lives. This chapter is an attempt at trying to unravel some of the problematic strands of the system that exists. The purpose is not to find individual solutions but to understand available systems and the pitfalls within it.

No relationship other than the parent–child seems to have this perfectly mutual exchange of care separated by time and different needs. At one point it is a growing body being taken care of by an adult being, and at the other end, it is an ageing body looking after an even more ageing person. The in-between years stay as memories, on these bodies and these interactions. So long as this care was mediated through surrogate children, meaning the wives of the sons, a lot of the problems were attributed to the fact that the relationship was finally only a legal and not an affective one as it exists between a child and its biological parent.

In certain families now when children are primary care takers of their parents, one realizes that power is not only because of the fact that the caregiver is a daughter-in-law. It is the power of age and the years of intimacy woven in a tapestry of expectations and demands. There is no easy equation and probably this mutually exchanged model of care itself seems to be a problem. It pushes people to have children and it pushes children to stay within the norms acceptable to parents. Technically it ought to make parents reorient to their children later, but then the years of independence and power come in the way of both parties and what we have is not always a happy situation. Over and above this, all care in this framework is control in the name of concern and safety – again not a happy option. It becomes the means to perpetuate and maintain power that is inbuilt into the system.

In its mutuality it demands allegiance for life and thereby a maintenance of the public facade of the institution.

Those that do not or cannot show allegiance drop out of this model. As family structures change and care is paid, another form of inequality is generated, where power is clearly aligned with the one who is making the payment and getting the care. What we need is a transferring model of care – such a model would enable people to gather credit for at least the time they spent by looking after some people not necessarily connected to oneself. Can there be ways to bank care so that we get at least as much as we have given but in a larger structure not connected by birth or marriage? Also, it is important to have a transfer model which is not necessarily mutual. I give someone care and someone else gives me the same but not the same person. This frees the care from a direct mutual structure of power of one over the other as much as possible.

In a world full of transactions maybe this non-transactional exchange of care, a transferring of care, is something that we need to work towards.

Notes

1 Terry Pratchett, *Moving Pictures: (Discworld Novel 10)*, Random House, 2009
2 Margaret Atwood, *Cat's eye*, Doubleday, 1989
3 Collins English Dictionary at https://www.collinsdictionary.com/dictionary/english/ageing (accessed as on 18 September 2019)
4 Cambridge English Dictionary at https://dictionary.cambridge.org/dictionary/english/ageing (accessed as on 18 September 2019)
5 One of the indicators for this is the way in which retirement age keeps shifting between 58 and 65 across different sectors and over time periods. As life expectancy increases, this age is shifted up and a balance is sought by increasing the number of productive years and decreasing the number of years for which pension is paid while maintaining the job market for new incumbents.
6 Uma Chakravarti discusses the patriarchal way in which marriages across castes maintain the hierarchy of caste showing thereby the intricate ways in which caste, gender, and sexuality are connected in her paper. Uma Chakravarti, 'Conceptualising Brahminical Patriarchy in Early India: Gender, Caste, Class and State', *Economic and Political Weekly*, vol. 28, no. 14, April 3, 1993, pp 579–585.
7 As I write I realize that I am forced to use parent and child as the only way in which the relationship can be described. There are no other words. So either it has to be gendered and son/daughter or it has to be parent and child.
8 The reasons for these are multiple. Critical among these are better medical facilities and better sanitation and hygiene leading to control of infant mortality thus increasing survival for children and better survival from illness for adults as well.
9 As I write this chapter I am struggling with the use of child and children for senior adults but not finding any word other than the equally bad "offspring."
10 One example could be the Mumbai-based Seenagers GupShup group which is the only existing initiative to provide a support system to ageing gay, bisexual, and asexual cis-gender men of India.

11 This practice is prevalent in Switzerland and to some extent in the UK, where comparatively younger people take care of senior citizens who are living alone without a biological family.

References

Atwood, Margaret. *Cat's Eye*. Doubleday, 1989.

Chakravarti, Uma. "Conceptualising Brahminical Patriarchy in Early India: Gender, Caste, Class and State." *Economic and Political Weekly*, vol. 28, no. 14, 3 Apr. 1993, pp. 579–585.

Pratchett, Terry. *Moving Pictures: (Discworld Novel 10)*. Random House, 2009.

5
PRECARIOUS LIVES, CARING NETWORKS, AND QUEER AGEING[1]

Ranjita Biswas

Introduction

A casual conversation among five friends cum co-travellers turned serious on a lazy windy morning in a faraway island in Greece. The year was 2016. The name of the island is significant – Lesbos – the birthplace of lesbian poetry, the land of Sappho, Greek poet of the 6th century BC. The conversation revolved around ageing, singleness, and queer politics. The five participants were all queer or lesbian-identified, gender non-conforming cis women presently in partnerships/relationships with gender non-conforming cis women in varied living arrangements. Three of us were in our 50s, and two in our 40s, all members of a queer feminist activist group, *Sappho for Equality*, working for the rights and social justice of lesbian, bisexual, queer women, and transmasculine persons in the eastern part of India, as well as, part of the larger sexuality rights movement in the country.

A couple of us shared concrete plans to get into an oldage home at some opportune moment in life. Some of us spoke of our dream of building a single women's commune where queer-identified women[2] would spend their hypermature days. Of course we debated and ranted about "gate keeping" and the norms of entry to the commune, if at all. Notwithstanding the intricacies of that debate, two thoughts took hold of us. The first was a conviction: we were not looking to our natal/marital families for sustenance even if we were surrounded by loving daughters, nephews, nieces, and cousins. We were quite certain that we would spend the latter part of our lives, whatever its duration and substance, in the midst of like-minded, like-spirited, and like-missioned people. The second was a question: Do we buy care or do we build care? Buying care appeared an easier and less complicated choice

DOI: 10.4324/9780429352560-6

given our socio-economic profile – saving up and investing in a good oldage home or if one wished to stay "independent" then save up enough for the medical bills and paid caregiving. But then, given our political zeal, buying care seemed a less challenging option. Building care was where we seemed to arrive.[3] Our hopelessly political beings refused to give up on the dream of what we called a queer[4] commune – a collective living arrangement where members live in a kinship forged outside and beyond filial ties and with the intention of sharing resources and responsibilities. In other words, we envisioned our ageing to be in a living arrangement made possible through queer care practices that does not rely on intergenerational kinships[5] but builds itself up on affective relationalities.

The queer community has had to grapple with the common perception that they are doomed to lives of loneliness and despair in their old age by virtue of falling (staying) outside the "safety" net of heteronormative marriage, family, and kinship. In this context, making a digression from the age-old question, "What does ageing do to queer lives?" let us ask, what does queer lives do to ageing? This piece is an attempt to talk of queer living as a starting point to imagine different ethics of care and affective relationalities that suggests an alternative to given structures of aged care practices, not just for queer lives, but, and also, for heterosexual lives.

Heterosexual Kinships and Queer Friendships

The heterosexual family, espoused universally as the seat of care, especially in old age, is held in place through the institution of marriage. Marriage is perhaps one of the oldest institutions that has expanded, fractured, negotiated, and survived. Whether in polygamy or in monogamy, marriage has spawned innumerable structural inequalities, and yet its significance as the epitome of conjugality has persisted. Socially, marriage has had a long shelf life in that it has been seen as the hallmark of commitment and loyalty. Apparently the greatest promise of marriage is certified companionship and guaranteed aged care. Marriage and its by-product, the progeny, come with the undertaking that there will be unquestioned support and care in old age. This dream is cushioned by various social and legal mechanisms[6] put in place to uphold the institution of heterosexual marriage. And takers of this promise/dream are almost *all*. People of all colour and creed, of all genders and sexualities, of all ages and kinships have, time and again, vouched for marriage irrespective of whether they enjoy the opportunity of participation.[7]

For those of us who have chosen to stay outside marriage, our friends and intimate others form our lifeline; we fall back on our pool of intimacies in any kind of exigency – from financial to emotional – rather than depend on familial resources. This is not to suggest that natal families are necessarily or generically homonegative/transnegative and dismissive of their queer kinfolks. There are sets of very empathic, supportive, and loving relatives who are queer friendly and who have been major support for the community as well. Neither am I suggesting that heteronormative heterosexual people do not value friendships nor that all of them have happy conflict-free family lives by virtue of being normative. Besides, friends per se cannot be seen as the repository of care and nurturance; friends, queer identified or otherwise, can also be hopelessly homo/transphobic, self-centred, indifferent, etc. In other words, there are contradictions and contrary narratives on both sides. Some of us are lucky to have a mix of families and friends on our radar and are able to garner help from either or both sides in case of emergencies and crises. However, the structure that propels heterosexual family kinship makes no room for the unmarried and therefore unmarked lesbian cis woman. The figure of the non-conforming woman spells disruption for the smooth workings of a familial kinship that thrives on the sexual and social exchange of female marked bodies – an exchange that serves to hold together the reins/reigns of not just reproductive heterosexism but also caste, class, and communal hierarchies.[8] The "single-woman" tag serves to locate the lesbian woman as always already outside the economics of heterosexual marriage and social legibility. Our associations with our families are mostly premised on an invisibilization of our intimate romantic others – sometimes a complete invisibility and sometimes camouflaged as "best friends." Even if we are accepted by our heterosexual natal families "despite" our different life choices and ideologies, our love remains marginalized, waiting on the threshold of familial domesticity (sometimes forever). Having said this, I would also reiterate that not all of us harbour the aspiration for our queer loves to be absorbed within familial kinship as we recognize the pitfalls of being included and appropriated. However, what is important to note here is the lack of acknowledgement of an intimacy and a relationality that potentially resists the performative[9] structures of heteronormative heterosexual domesticity.

Given the elaborate trappings of the conventional heterosexual heteronormative kinship networks woven around marriage and domesticity, being "left out" of, or choosing to stay outside of, such oppressive dispositions of power provide the stimulus and opportunity to queer lives and queer lifeworlds to explore and expand the contours of intimacies, relationalities, and care kinships in creative ways. Contrary to common perceptions that such lives entail a struggle for companionship and care in their present times, and more so, in their old age, living on the margins, living in potential "singlehood" has had a few tangible effects. Queer people foster care and solidarity in friendships, allies, and communities much more than in blood kinships. Our queer loves and queer livings have brought us close to affective relationalities and collaborative care beyond heteronormative family kinship. It has also made possible to envision a queering of aged care practices. In other words, this writing is not only about finding-founding spaces of aged care for queer-identified people but also attempts in crafting alternatives to present notions of elderly care that remain steeped in heterosexist life markers of birth, marriage, reproduction, and death. Such linear understandings of progression create hierarchies of eligibility thereby imposing limits on the social organization of care in ageing, a fact also reflected in state policies and institutions.

The question is whether this is a simple family vs. friend spat where friends shall emerge winners, our families of choice, as our framilies?[10] The answer is not simple. Let us then pause to talk of friendships in lieu of friends. Foucault in his piece, *Friendship as a Way of Life*, talks of deflecting the focus from seeking the essence of identity in one's sexual desire to seeing what that desire can open up in terms of relationship possibilities. Hinting at an ethics and "aesthetics of existence" (Kingston 2009: 16), Foucault sees homosexuality as not just "a form of desire but something desirable" (1994: 136). He asks, "What relationships through homosexuality, can be established, invented, multiplied, and modulated?" (ibid, 135). Drawing on the example of marriage as the institution that normalizes and guides erotic relationships between man and woman, Foucault argues that homosexual relationships are that much more difficult in a milieu where social conventions encourage non-affective relationships and foreclose any possibilities of friendship between men. He argues that homosexuality is this state of "desire in uneasiness" where "[T]hey have to invent, from A to Z, a relationship that is still formless." Friendship then becomes "the sum of everything through which they can give each other pleasure" (ibid, 136). Mark Kingston (2009) draws our attention to this propensity of homosexual culture to generate relational openness and social experimentation. Any romantic relationship that locates itself outside the heterosexual couple has to fashion a new language of intimacy and communication. The marginal space of homosexuality that nurtures freedom from the normalizing effects of power gives scope for collaborative creation of new friendships. Kingston further argues against the traditional understanding of friendship based on similarity and sharing of values that precludes spontaneity and creativity. Instead, he draws attention to Foucault's call for reimagining friendship as a collaborative effort at building new subjectivities and relationships outside social norms. He writes, "It is a concept of friendship that privileges experimentation over traditional, institutional or racial bonds. It also privileges heterogeneity over homogeneity, in that it anticipates the creation of many different relationships based on the various preferences of their participants" (ibid, 7).

Sasha Roseneil sees friendship as a way to reconceptualize the ethics of care that remains embedded in relations of inequality, oppression, and exploitation. She also urges us to understand the salience of friendship in

92 Ranjita Biswas

queer lives in order to explore its relevance to heterosexual lives as well. She contends that friends are an important pillar in any social organization of care (2004:410–411).

> Friendship is a significantly different relationship from that of mothering, lacking controlling institutions and firm cultural expectations and conventions...a relationship (at least ideally) between equals, based in mutuality and reciprocity, to which the partners come of their own free will, not out of need, and which requires a firm sense of the separateness of the parties.
>
> *(ibid, 414)*

Reckoning friendships appears to be of greater significance in contemporary times than ever before, she argues. Emerging processes of individualization, changing power relations in families including that of gender, and visibilities of different sexual couplings have eroded the significance of the heterosexual conjugality as the unit of intimacy, companionship, and shared confidentialities (ibid, 411–412). Caring relationships in the queer communities[11] have also contributed greatly in changing the overall cartography of intimacy beyond the sexual and the familial (King andCronin 2013: 114).

Changes in the understanding and living of intimacies have unsettled the imagination of monogamous couplehood that held sway over most romantic liaisons whether or not it was practised in real life. Educational and employment aspirations have resulted in individuals across age, gender, and sexual identity living separately from their families. Youngsters migrating to distant cities for education or work engage in cohabitational living and shared domesticity and depend on non-familial support networks for emergency care and sustenance. In such situations, it is not uncommon to find house mates, neighbours, and work mates forming the intimate circle and weaving a protective web of emotional, spiritual, and material welfare. In times of crises they are the main caregivers and fall-back coterie. Such lived realities have led to a blurring of the divide constructed between homosexual and heterosexual ways of life[12] in ways that speak of a radical reimagining of intimacies and relationalities.

Sexual Indiscipline and Affective Relationalities

Notwithstanding the pragmatics of daily living of intimacies, mono-normative romantic love appears to be a strongly desired culmination for every aspiration of a "true relationship," be it heterosexual or otherwise. Inheritance, property, progeny, and obligatory care are some of the motivations for monoamory/monogamy, more so in specific socio-economic groups. In contradistinction to this stands polyamory which is one form of consensual non-monoamory where all people involved openly agree to have more than one concurrent sexual and/or romantic partner is said to be a challenge to monogamy/monoamory – marked by competition, jealousy, and insecurity. Polyamory which is one of the most popular forms of consensual non-monogamy entered the Oxford English Dictionary in 2006. It is sought to be distinguished from other forms like swinging relationships or open relationships. It is also different from polygamy which is the practice of having more than one husband or wife at the same time. Polyamory is advocated as the true recognition of human desire highlighted by self-reflexivity, autonomy, and negotiating propensity (Barker et al. 2013:193). It is seen as personally and politically liberating.[13]

Barker et al. offer us an alternative understanding of polyamory that talks of shifting from many lovers to many loves. Giving a queer twist to polyamory by taking it beyond the realm of romance and sex, they propose many loves that could range from self to the planet. They suggest a "shifting from individualised understandings of (non-) monogamy toward a loving awareness of our embodied and ecological interdependence" (2013:191). Their intention is clear – to disturb the given hierarchies between different loves and relationships. Such ways of intimacy are named by them relationship anarchy, polytical, or relationshipqueer (ibid). Not seeking to decentre love and romance, Barker et al. see loving openness in all relationships as a way to fight the contemporary culture of growing isolation, enmity, and hate collectively and creatively (ibid, 203–204).

A self-declared heterosexual heteronormative friend despairing at having to deal with first his wife's discovery of her lesbianism and then his daughter's polyamorous sexlife used the terminology, "sexual indiscipline," to hint at the disruptive energies of non-heteronormative love on his life. I borrow his terminology to argue that indeed, queerness grows wings in resisting the disciplining of sexuality and gender and if I may add of kinship too. On the one hand, queer people are scorned for breeding sexual "anarchy" – lesbianism, gayness, bisexuality, pansexuality, kinkiness, asexuality, polyamory, and the list goes on. On the other hand, the queer community is largely credited for spearheading fluidity in sexual practices and inspiring experimentation and subsequent changes in heterosexual ways of relating (Giddens 1992).[14] However, queer lives de facto are not stories of resistance. While intimacies have changed forms to blur boundaries and become fluid, they have also reinforced stereotypes and created sharply polarized camps. Members of the queer community are often seen to be aspiring to heteronormative ideals of behaviour, identity, and relationships, and not all of them are known to question heteronormativity in creative ways. "Sexual indiscipline" of queer lives (that extra-institutional moment), the refusal to succumb to the disciplining of institutions and "the regimes of the normal" (Michael Warner 1999), provides us with that creative crack to rethink relationships and kinships and offers a different imagination of care.

I would like to use the notion of sexual indiscipline to arrive at a multiplicity of relationships and care networks. I use the terminology "affective relationalities" to indicate possibilities of bondings emerging through a critical opening up of coupledom. This is not to argue that polysexuality will have to be practised in order to experience affective relationalities and perform collaborative care. Many of us are comfortable in and choose a monoamorous relationship, and such aspirations and practices are by all means justified. However, my contention is that even in a monogamous/monoamorous relationship there is the possibility to move away from the symbolics of couplehood with its accompanying sense of entitlement, exclusivity, and obligated allegiance. Being in a romantic sexual partnership does not preclude the possibility of affective relationalities and collaborative care. I would argue that instead of dividing up our lived intimacies into hierarchies of romance, family, friendship, etc. (in that order), based on the activities shared within the ambit of the relationship, we could be open to treating each one as unique and different with infinite possibilities for affective exchange – what Foucault would call "polymorphic varied and individually modulated relationships" (1994:139).

Care Work: Differences That Matter

Care is performed by various forms of workers: paid professionals, paid non-professionals, volunteers, and unpaid domestic caregivers (James 1992:489). Most familial care work is unremunerated, unacknowledged, and unreciprocated compared to paid professional skilled and non-professional unskilled labour.[15] Ideologies of care normalize caregiving as one person's responsibility only, be it the family (most often the woman), the intimate partner, or the offspring.[16]Care work in the heteronormative heterosexual family is structured largely on the exploitation of woman's physical, sexual, and emotional labour. Women are the default caregivers, "on a 24 hour, 'on call' responsibility" (James 1992:490). Whether in the natal or the marital unit, they are the unpaid labourers of love who toil relentlessly to provide care (both catering to the daily needs, as well as, any nursing work required), and caring becomes an integral part of their intimate world. For women unpaid domestic care work can be either in addition to paid work outside home or even prioritized over paid work such that she will have to organize her outside employment around her domestic responsibilities, even abrogate it if necessary. Moreover, receiving care within the familial structure is hierarchical and fractured along lines of not only age and gender but also who contributes to the family expenses, who is able-bodied or able-minded, who is single, who is ill – all these and many more become qualifiers for receiving care. For instance, the elderly man of the house is more eligible to receive care than the elderly woman or the able-bodied employed son is more cared for than the disabled brother who is dependent on the family income.[17]The hazards of care work across generations are defined by duty, responsibility on the part of the carer, and entitlement and coercion on the part of the receiver. Care work or caring involves both physical labour and emotional labour.[18]Caregiving needs skill, attentiveness, and perseverance; it is not just the knowledge of how to body sponge and dress the wound but also taking out the litter in the morning or putting the leftovers in the fridge at night. Care work can be tedious and at times uninspiring as well, be it in exchange of money or otherwise, be it for strangers, parents, siblings, friends, or intimate others.[19]

A couple of years back, I had the opportunity to experience care from my circle of friends during a period of post-surgery convalescence. Standing on the threshold of "middle age," this brief experience of receiving and accepting care brought me straight up to some questions related to ageing and care practices. How would I like my future (aged) care to be organized? How do we, as queer feminists, weave our web of care that runs across filial and non-filial associations and is sustained through affective relationalities? On the one hand, there was my natal family with its assurance of warmth, a well-ordered, functioning structure ensuring basic food and care, and on the other hand, my single unit household where my queer clan would have greater access, but there would be a greater need to self-arrange material resources. I decided in favour of the latter as my nest for post-operative recovery. I did not require paid care since I was mostly mobile and my regular domestic worker agreed to extend her hours to help me out withsome of my needs. Some of us, who believed we were part of an intimate collective, got together to draw up a roster of caregiving. We consciously kept the task of daily care spread out among friends with whom I would feel comfortable physically and emotionally. Choosing that small group of friends-as-caregivers was the tricky and exciting part. The person with whom I am in a romantic sexual relation was an important part of that group but was never seen as the sole caregiver. My romantic sexual relation/partner fulfilled some very necessary needs during that period but not all of them. This was for no lack on her part; rather, there were different needs that I expressed to different sets of caregivers. I felt happy to be hugged, mollycoddled, dressed, bathed, fed, and babbled to but with different people. With some I was comfortable in close carnal proximity that post-operative care often entailed; with some I equally enjoyed the tea and *jhalmuri*[20] that accompanied the evening visits. All of these sustained me as did some long-distance phone calls and messages. My domestic help who has been my surrogate home-maker for long years also became part of this affective relational network much beyond her professional brief.

At the end of all this caregiving, I found myself more exhausted than rested. Sitting down to ponder I realized that the work of care is not unidirectional. I was equally taking care of my caregivers who came over to nurse me and give me company. I was making sure that the fridge remained always filled; I was planning sleeping spots for each when the group got large. I was arranging breakfast for them before they left for office.[21]I was even planning and negotiating the time slots for my caregivers according to mutual convenience and affective states. In effect I never felt lonely or uncared for. I was reminded of an oft-repeated non-question: "*bayas hole ke dekhbe toke*" (who will look after you in your old age?). My natal family members, who have often been curious, interfering, and condescending exactly on this account, never having any faith in my own ability to fend for myself, took a step back and for a change watched, doubtingly at first, and then joined into the loop tentatively with their measured contribution to this care work which I was of course not averse to receive.

The experience provided a sneak peek into how I would like to build care around me –what I would like to do and not do with people around me and have them do and not do to me in ordinary as well as extraordinary times, now and in times of ageing. It involved innumerable conversations, negotiations, and exchanges of thoughts, needs, affects, and learnings around care work. These were not friends whom I took for granted; I neither chose my friends as substitute for my family or my romantic relationships, nor did I see my friends as my family. With some I had already a tenacious bond, with some the bond strengthened during the course of those 30 days. Receiving care did entail dependence, subservience, and a surrender of personal boundaries. These 30 days of convalescence involved me assuming responsibility and admitting vulnerability, all at the same time. It was an affective bond where carer and care receiver were mutually responsive to each other's needs and limits. This is also not to suggest that this form of care work is always going to be without conflict or cacophony. There were (and bound to be) disagreements, differences, and dissonances surrounding the care work as well as the relationalities that make the care possible. Such conflicts and dissonances could affect the work of care as well. Facing those moments of cacophony and engaging dissonances rather than taking care for granted is what queer care practices.

In contrast to heteronormative care practices that remain rooted in blood and kinship ties, queer[22] care practices can be seen as a collaborative project between shared lives nurtured and lived through affective relationalities. Collaborative care through affective relationalities is possible where collaboration is not a contract – a neoliberal good – neither is it treated as biological essentialism as in mother-child care work. Here collaboration is an active, dynamic practice of coming together selectively and through a process of sensitization and politicization. This collaborative care kinship is not a relationship based on a commerce (give and take, reciprocal) of exchange but a politics of exchange – power sharing, non-hierarchical and dialogic.[23] Collaboration is not between people who are like-minded, alike, and equal but between those who are open to embracing differences. Embracing difference is the radical framework of non-hierarchical, reflexive, communicative collaboration, the norms of which would include a "speaking with"[24] (not a one-to-one reciprocity) and an evaluation of dialogue and a networking. Care here is not imagined in terms of an equal exchange – "you take care of me and I take care of you" – rather care branches out in different directions, not following any predetermined direction but moving out nevertheless and forming knots of affective exchanges and collaborative care at different junctures. A transformation in subjectivity that favours rhizomatic[25] (multiple non-hierarchical interconnected) living over a treelike (vertical linear hierarchical) relationality can help map out collaborative care in different directions and practices. Collaborative care thus becomes a dynamic process that emerges out of affective exchanges that needs to animate the realm of care in our daily living of interpersonal bonds as well as in times of infirmity and old age.

Queering Aged Care Practices

When it comes to aged care practices, there are different socio-political factors that shape experiences of ageing. On the one hand, age signifies a position of power, sense of entitlement, and sometimes a license to exploitation. On the other hand, ageing denotes infirmity, dependence, and marginalization. The anxiety around ageing is mainly fed by assumptions about failing health, truncated roles, and dwindling companionship. Such stereotypes create prejudices about the ability of the elderly to be independent, productive, and nurturing. Indications of dependence, frailty, or senility cause them to be labelled, discriminated, and disregarded. Contrary to the belief that elderly people require care and nursing, the elderly have also been engaged in taking care of younger generations and providing financially as well. Giving and receiving care, however, is a socio-cultural privilege. Ageing does not treat everyone equally. Not everybody can arrange for care in ageing, for themselves or their dear ones.

The state on its part dodges its responsibilities towards the welfare of its citizens, especially the elderly population, by merely extending financial assistance that is insufficient, unequally distributed and mostly difficult to access. There are no other policies to bolster care and support in times of ageing such as facilities for residential care and assisted living.[26] The family as an institution is entrusted with the care of all elderly, feeble, or disabled members without taking into account the viability or willingness of such families to provide. This is further complicated by the fact that aged people

98 Ranjita Biswas

often take it as their entitlement to be looked after by family members using it as an instrument of oppression and manipulation, and family members too are negligent, abusive, and exploitative towards dependent elderly members.

The need to be cared for in ageing and infirmity comes as a possibility for all – queer people, single folks, married heterosexual heteronormative, and even non-normative heterosexual couples all could be requiring care in varying degrees. There is no infallible mechanism to ensure care even if one swears by heteronormativity or remains surrounded by a train of relatives. Care cannot become the assured dividend to be collected in posterity by investing in marriage (and progeny) in youth. Aged care practices will need to be built collaboratively with affective relationalities that defy the logic of conjugality and blood kinship. Living in perpetual polyamory, in rhizomatic clusters and knots, these relationalities can be imagined to find root in both, families and communities, not through any necessary lineage of entitlements but in being gingerly woven through care and justice.

I do not think of ageing as that time when I shall especially need someone to take care of me. I do not think of ageing for I do not believe I can control future time in such definitive ways. I am happy to have a network of affective relationalities that manages to sustain itself each new day through mutual and collective bouts of conflictual and collaborative care. We are still experimenting with the idea of queer commune living whereby the idea is not to live in a commune (a fixed place) with shared properties, resources, or interests. Not that we are averse to the idea of shared spaces and resources. Some of us have practised that at different junctures experimentally and lastingly. However, to live and care rhizomatically we think a single shared space is limiting in its imagination and reach. Commune living is for us lives shared not necessarily in reciprocity but also in solidarity and solitude.

Conclusion

This perspective on collaborative care is partial, from an undoubtedly privileged position that I occupy socio-economically, culturally, and politically. The idea is not to propose any model for aged care practices; that would constrain possibilities of diverse practices of affective relational living and collaborative care. There are a multitude of practices and living arrangements that speak of varied forms of care.I remain aware of the need to learn from spaces and relationalities that exist or are being constantly forged about whom I am uninformed.[27]

This piece also does not talk of the many challenges to queer care kinships. In a time when homosexuality has been decriminalized and more and more queer couples/community folks are gearing themselves up for marriage and adoption rights, there lurks the risk of falling into the set stereotypes of heteronormative family kinship with its oppressive and unequal relations that have for long rendered care work gendered, obligatory, and emotionally draining. The state's role in safeguarding the ideology of the heterosexual family kinship poses a primary challenge to alternative living arrangements and reimagining care. Be it upholding the birth family as the only family of a gender non-conforming child or be it the snatching away of the right to self-determination of gender by making surgical transition mandatory in the newly passed, the Transgender Persons (Protection of Rights) Act 2019,[28] the state obscures the demand for the recognition of alternative lives and living arrangements. Both state and non-state actors still frown upon non-conjugal households and domestic partnerships. While we have been able to expand our understanding beyond marriage to acknowledge relationships (only heterosexual) lived "in the nature of marriage," we have still not been able to accept relationships not-lived-in-the-nature-of-marriage as equally valid. Capitalism, on the other hand, has done its bit to strike at the increasingly expanding demand for individualized and specialized care that comes with a good price tag. From huggies to hug buddies,[29] market steps in with the promise of packaged comfort as well as emotions that appears to be quantified and delivered at your doorstep. Some of these promise comfort and community living in old age (with spouses and friends) in a controlled simulation of "life that had once been"![30]

Today, when a competitive market-driven neoliberal culture encourages individual rights and freedom of choice over community associations, it is a challenge to build collaborative care, but all the more imperative to do so.The state cannot be absolved of its responsibilities either. A good tentative beginning in this direction would be to lobby for changes in laws governing family entitlements, marriage, divorce, adoption, and inheritance. Recognizing multiple genders and sexualities, granting singleness a viable social, legal status, and making marriage as only one of the many living arrangementsaresome of the otherimportant directions to take.

Notes

1 I would like to express love and solidarity for my bunch of affective relationalities who have made this writing possible by being part of my life and thought processes. Taking names is a fruitless exercise as the list is endless and keeps mutating every day. To Professor Shefali Moitra, I remain, as ever, indebted.

2 Here the term "queer" is used as an umbrella concept to include cis and trans women of all shades of sexuality who are not in a thriving relation with cis men! There are really no deep ideologies behind this, just some self-devised queer attempts to strike out hetero-patriarchy.

3 This is not to create any definitive binary between paid and unpaid care work simply because no such binary is possible. Buying care is not just about paid care work and includes the planning, organizing, and putting into place a viable and sustainable system of care. Similarly, when one talks of building care, it would include paid care work as well but not solely dependent on it.

4 In this context it would be pertinent to remind ourselves that in common parlance the term queer is used as a noun (a group of queers), an adjective (a queer person), as well as a verb (queering relationships). For the purposes of this writing, the term has been used both as an adjective, to denote an identity (more as a generic group), and as a verb –as the act of persistent questioning norms and rendering absurd or incongruent that which is familiar and standard in discussions on sexuality, gender, and intimacy specifically, but also more generally. Hopefully, the context of use shall make the meaning significantly apparent.

5 The heteronormative structure of aged care practices depend on intergenerational relationships between ageing parents, siblings, adult children, grandchildren, and great grandchildren lived in a certain reciprocity that benefits each of them. When I talk of queer aged care practices and queer communes, there is no expectation of such vertical intergenerational care; rather the care network is spread out horizontally and rhizomatically. Each relationship in this care web gets built and nurtured through affective bondings and collaborative care.

6 In India a law was enacted in 2007 that requires adult children to maintain and care for their parents – biological, adoptive, or step. The Maintenance and Welfare of Parents and Senior Citizens Act, 2007, besides providing protection to life and property of such persons, allows people above 60 years of age to claim maintenance from their legal heirs if they are unable to care for themselves.

7 In India, marriage is still the privilege of heterosexual people as of now; the law clearly states marriage can happen between man and woman only. However, in recent times, the definition of who is man or a woman has undergone more liberal interpretations to include transgender people as well, but only after surgical transition. In many instances transgender persons have registered their marriages (either to cisgender or transgender partners) under the existing laws such as the Special Marriage Act, having put forward their identities as the binary man/woman as the case may be. Law, however, denies same-gender couples marriage rights. Following the decriminalization of homosexuality in 2018, members of the queer community have raised their hopes of soon acquiring the right to marry, just like heterosexual couples. On the one hand, critiques of marriage have revealed the institution as redundant, oppressive, and heteropatriarchal, and on the other hand, more and more non-heterosexual people aspire to the ideology of a "married normal." This piece, however, does not intend to delve into the debate on marriage equality rights for the queer community. That necessitates another writing altogether.

8 The discussion on how heterosexual marriage and kinship uphold the exchange of women which is again based on social hierarchies of class caste and religion is beyond the scope of the present chapter. However a good starting point for such discussions could be Gayle Rubin's article, "Traffic in Women: Notes on the 'Political Economy' of Sex," in Rayna R. Reiter (ed.), *Toward an Anthropology of Women* (1975).

9 Judith Butler uses performativity to argue how social norms are naturalized and reinforced through repeated acts (not necessarily conscious) of performance. She writes, "Hegemonic heterosexuality is itself a constant and repeated effort to imitate its own idealizations. That it must repeat this imitation, that it sets up pathologizing practices and normalizing sciences in order to produce and consecrate its own claim on originality and propriety, suggests that heterosexual performativity is beset by an anxiety that it can never fully overcome, that its effort to become its own idealizations can never be finally or fully achieved, and that it is constantly haunted by that domain of sexual possibility that must be excluded for heterosexualized gender to produce itself" (1993, 125).

10 Framily is a word that has emerged from the blending of family and friend. It signifies a family of choice made up of close friends and partners who become important affective relations and support networks. This is said to be an important feature of queer communities who tend to build their intimate networks outside the heterosexual conjugal family unit. "Families of choice" is a concept made popular by the book, *Families We Choose: Lesbians, Gays, Kinship* (1991) by Kath Weston.

11 At least one part of it can be traced back to the time when people were losing one friend every week (if not more) to the HIV/AIDS epidemic and the need to care for those afflicted emerged as the foreground for imagining creative ways of imagining intimate relationships beyond the couple and the blood family.

12 While monogamous couplehood is said to define the essence of heterosexual romance, homosexual people have been historically described as promiscuous, engaging in multiple relationships, not respecting boundaries of sexual and non-sexual intimacies, etc. Sometimes, such norms and counter norms get enforced within communities as evidence of one's belongingness leading to monogamous heterosexuality and non-monogamous homosexuality becoming markers of respectability and authenticity. However, defying all logic of linearity, there have been movements in all directions when it comes to shifts in the understanding of intimacy. Queer community folks have shown a propensity to invest in committed married, monogamous, reproductive life while more and more heterosexual people are choosing to live outside married institutional couplehood.

13 Polyamory, however, has had its own critiques. Some of these have questioned its tendency to mimic mono-normativity, and some point out rules and norms that govern the relations in polyamory laying out a moral hierarchy between polyamory and other forms of non-monogamy.

14 Queer identified people have also been criticized for miming heterosexual norms of romance and kinship and thereby reinforcing heteropatriarchy in specific ways.

15 This article does not uphold paid work in comparison to unpaid work but for the time being refrains from discussing the maladies that afflict the sphere of paid work.

16 Paid care givers are usually seen as an option only in the absence of close kin. The compulsions of care work have often led to diverse relational dynamics from paid care workers becoming family to families becoming estranged.

17 The gender non-conforming member is completely left out of this economics of care and is mostly neglected unless they perform the role of the primary bread earner. Even then, they receive very little respect and care. However, in many instances, transgender persons are the ones who bear the burden of care work of elderly parents as their cisgender siblings are busy tending their "normal heterosexual domesticities."

18 The term emotional labour was originally coined by sociologist Arlie Hochschild in the 1983 book, *The Managed Heart: Commercialization of Human Feeling*. Most times this is the kind of labour one has to take on in certain professions that involve direct interaction with clients, customers, and service seekers. It also entails regulating and managing your emotions so as to not let the person concerned know. In contrast to the physical labour of care work, emotional labour remains invisibilized but an important component of care work in situations of caring for family and friends.

19 A number of initiatives have come up that provide services to carers including advice on how to care, how to take care of self, and how to prevent burnout. There are also self-support groups and communities of carers.

20 Puffed rice mixed with spices, oil, and savouries – a Bengali comfort food.

102 Ranjita Biswas

21 I do concede that I was fortunate to have been in a physical and mental state to acknowledge and reciprocate the care I received. In many cases care is given in conditions of more serious infirmity where the receiver is not even in a state of acknowledging the care received, leave alone consider returning it. This is not to suggest that every instance of care needs to be appreciated or reciprocated by the receiver. In fact, the idea is to engage both reciprocally and rhizomatically.
22 Here queer is used not to denote care practised by queer identified people. It is used to qualify care practices that deviate and thereby question and recreate traditional understandings of care.
23 I am grateful to Professor Shefali Moitra for triggering my thoughts in this direction.
24 Shefali Moitra (2002, 89–100) talks of "speaking with…" as a mode of communication that challenges the "speaking to…" mode of communication. In "speaking to…," which can be compared to the turn-by-turn ball game, a hierarchical power play operates where the authorship of the speaker shifts with a shift in the power position. The "speaking with… mode, on the other hand, is premised on the principle that when both parties have a partial understanding of the events they encounter …they can enter into communication with an open mind" (92). The "speaking with…" mode takes into account the irreducible plurality of perspectives between subjects and pays attention to the narratives and thought worlds of those on the margins with the desire to co-construct knowledge.
25 An example of rhizome is ginger which is known to grow in multiple directions and has no linear structure that can denote a top or bottom, unlike a root tree. French philosophers, Gilles Deleuze and Felix Guattari (1980) in their book, *A Thousand Plateaus*, have used the notion of rhizome to argue against dualist categorization of knowledge and to stress the multiplicity and heterogeneity of learning.
26 A study by the Confederation of Indian Industries (CII), Senior Care Industry Report India 2018, has predicted a threefold rise in the population of senior citizens in India by 2050. The report highlights the need for infrastructure and services for this section of the population in view of the current gap between supply and demand in this sector.
27 A case in point would be the hijra communities which often become the family of choice for many a transgender child and adult who face discrimination and abandonment by families of birth. The community has its own kinship system based on mutual care and nurturance (Revathi and Geetha 2010; Semmalar 2014; Revathi 2016).
28 http://socialjustice.nic.in/writereaddata/UploadFile/TG%20bill%20gazette.pdf
29 Hug buddies or professionals cuddlers provide a no-strings-attached service of physical closeness and warmth that is said to reduce anxiety, stress, loneliness, etc. leading to mental and emotional well-being. As one tag line goes: "you can't buy love but you can rent a cuddle buddy."
30 Urban India is fast catching up to the idea of retirement communities and senior living arrangements. The change in terminology attempts to move away from the traditional stigma of "old age homes" that spelt compulsion, abandonment by children, loneliness and neglect. There appears to be a choice, a voluntarism, convenience, and pleasure in such arrangements that have independent and assisted living options as well as Continued Care Retirement Communities.

References

Barker, Meg et al. "Polyamorous Intimacies: From One Love to Many Loves and Back Again." *Mapping Intimacies*, edited by T. Sanger and Y. Taylor. Palgrave Macmillan, 2013, pp 109–208.

Butler, Judith. *Bodies that Matter: On the Discursive Limits of "Sex."* Routledge, 1993.

Foucault, Michel. "Friendship as A Way of Life." *Ethics Subjectivity and Truth*, edited by PaulRabinow and translated by RobertHurley et al. The New Press, 1994.

Giddens, Anthony. *The Transformation of Intimacy: Sexuality, Love and Eroticism in Modern Societies.* Stanford University Press, 1992.

James, Nicky. "Care = Organisation + Physical Labour + Emotional Labour." *Sociology of Health & Illness*, vol. 14, no. 4, 1992, pp 488–509.

King, A. and A.Cronin. "Queering Care in Later Life: The Lived Experiences and Intimacies of Older Lesbian, Gay and Bisexual Adults." *Mapping Intimacies*, edited by T.Sanger and Y.Taylor. Palgrave Macmillan, 2013, pp 112–129.

Kingston, Mark. "Subversive Friendships: Foucault on Homosexuality and Social Experimentation." *Foucault Studies*, no. 7, Sep. 2009, pp. 7–17.

Moitra, Shefali. *Feminist Thought: Androcentrism, Communication & Objectivity.* Munshiram Manoharlal Publishers Pvt. Ltd., Centre of Advanced Study in Philosophy, Jadavpur University, 2002.

Revathi, A.*The Truth about Me.* Translated by V.Geetha. Penguin, 2010.

Revathi, A. and NandiniMurali. *A Life in Trans Activism.* Zubaan, 2016.

Roseneil, Sasha. "Why we should Care about Friends: An Argument for Queering the Care Imaginary." *Social Policy Social Policy & Society*, vol. 3, no. 4, 2004, pp. 409–419. doi:10.1017/S1474746404002039.

Semmalar, Gee Imaan. "Unpacking Solidarities of the Oppressed: Notes on Trans Struggles in India." *Women's Studie Quarterly*, vol. 42, no. 3/4, 2014, pp. 286–291. www.jstor.org/stable/24365012. Accessed 17 Jan. 2020.

Warner, Michael. *The Trouble with Normal: Sex, Politics, and the Ethics of Queer Life.* The Free Press, 1999.

6

PHYSICAL CULTURES AND THE AGEING BODY

The Long Careers of Manohar Aich and Biswanath Datta

Sujaan Mukherjee

Introduction

The ageing human body is frequently associated with a gradual decrement of physical functionality, framed within narratives of bodily decline.[1,2] To speak of it in the context of practising the physical cultures might seem like a contradiction in terms. In most cases, the physicality of the ageing body is considered within discourses of medicine and health, and physical exercise of any sort in old age is usually seen as a means of slowing down the inevitable process of decline. In recent years some scholars have tried to shift focus away from this reductive approach, "to encompass the diverse and situated positions of older adults within a physical culture," as Cassandra Phoenix puts it (2017: 179). She delineates the range of disciplines such as "social gerontology, sociology of sport, geography and health sciences" (ibid, 179) that have grappled with this tricky combination.

The present chapter looks at two male figures from the world of physical cultures, both from Bengal: Manohar Aich (1912–2016), who won a Mr. Universe title in 1952, and many laurels since, and the wrestler, Biswanath Datta (1929–2020), who won awards at the state level and was the last practising pupil of the renowned wrestler and physical culturist Jyotindra Charan "Gobar" Guha (1892–1972). Both Aich and Datta were active till a very late age, practising and guiding protégés in their chosen fields. The two traditions this chapter considers, i.e. bodybuilding and *kusti*, are fundamentally different. The form of bodybuilding Manohar Aich practised was (re)invented in the late-19th century as a popular spectacle. The question of aesthetics of the male body, therefore, becomes central, although physical strength and muscle control play important roles, as we shall see later. Kusti,

DOI: 10.4324/9780429352560-7

on the other hand, is premised on the exchanges with another individual in bodily contact within the same field of contest, where superiority must be proven through a combination of strength, skill, balance, and understanding of the opponent's weakness and strength. Like most other forms of physical cultures, bodybuilding and kusti require profound commitment from their practitioners, both physically and mentally.

When narratives of ageing are heavily biased against viewing the elderly as exercising agency or as capable of deriving pleasure from physical activities, the careers of people such as Aich and Datta can offer "counterstories" "through which," as Phoenix says, "social actors might develop these "resistant" identities as they age" (ibid, 181). In doing so, however, one must be careful to avoid possible misreadings, whereby such narratives devalue the choices and situations of elderly individuals who have not pushed their physique to such lengths. Emmanuelle Tulle and Cassandra Phoenix disclaimer holds true for such counterstories: "while it is important to identify what lessons might be learned from these people's experiences, care must be taken not to fall into the trap of position them as heroes of ageing" (Tulle and Phoenix 2015, introduction).

Historians of Bengal's physical cultures have traditionally focused on the decades between 1860 and 1930, i.e. within the framework of colonial rule and a nationalist response to it. As John Rosselli points out, a tradition was invented by the Bengali upper middle class, predominantly Hindu *savarna* and upper class, about a revival of the physical cultures as they internalized and reacted against the colonial stereotype of the feeble and timid Bengali. He observed that this narrative ignored traditions that did exist, such as Muslim wrestlers in Bengal or stick and knife-fighters, many of whom were Dalits (Rosselli 1980: 121). Regrettably, the subaltern narratives that were lost in the process prove nearly impossible to recover except through oral histories and stray allusions in music or literature, leaving historians to analyse documented histories and archival remnants. The nationalist response has received scholarly attention from scholars like Indira Chowdhury (2001) and Mrinalini Sinha (1995), who provide nuanced readings in the contexts of nationality and gender, and more recently from Abhijit Gupta (2012), whose biographical essay on Gobar Guha offers part of the historical context of this chapter.

My intention, however, is to go venture beyond the historical narratives or biography to suggest that studying the careers of two ageing male physical culturists can offer fresh theoretical perspectives on the aesthetics of the male form and on embodied knowledge. The distinction between these two stems from the two traditions under study: body building, as represented by Manohar Aich, and kusti as represented by Biswanath Datta. The former is seen in the context of an international interest in the aesthetics of the male body in the wake of Eugen Sandow's meteoric rise in popular culture but with a view to expand the field in order to understand where the ageing body fits within it. The latter is studied through a combination of phenomenological theorization and my own practice in the martial arts. It draws inspiration from the method of Loic Wacquant, a student of Pierre Bourdieu, who had sought to "open the 'black box' of the puglistic habitus by disclosing the production and assembly of the cognitive categories" (Wacquant 2013: 27), as well as the lines of inquiry set out by Merleau-Ponty (2002) and used productively by theories of performing arts later to bring philosophy into dialogue with practice. The section attempts to understand the specific questions an ageing practitioner can help formulate regarding embodied knowledge.

Apart from the anthropological work done by Joseph S. Alter, who trained in kusti, efforts to understand the physical cultures as embodied practice are rare. In the recent past, Rudraneil Sengupta's *Enter the Dangal* (2016) has come close to offering a compromise between the more objective ethnographic method and Wacquant's proposed model of fusing "object and method of inquiry" in the habitus. The method Sengupta deploys may be considered "immersive ethnography," where a deeply sympathetic model is developed not only in the manner of gathering information but in its representation. The logic of the micro-narratives is not exoticized or presented with a sense of wonder to the presumed unfamiliarity of its readership.

The sections on Manohar Aich are based on (a) archival research conducted with the help of the National Amateur Body-Building Association, (b) health magazines available at the British Library, and (c) interviews available on YouTube. Manohar Aich's son, Bishnu Manohar Aich, also provided valuable input. Existing literature on Aich is scant and often unreliable. The sections on Biswanath Datta are based on interviews with him conducted as part of the Physical Cultures of Bengal project at the School of Cultural Texts and Records, and personal observation of his practice at the *akhada* off Beadon Street.

By Way of a Biography: Manohar Aich

Following Manohar Aich's death on 5 June 2016 (two days after Mohamed Ali), news media across the world carried obituaries that fondly recalled the "pocket Hercules" and his incredible feats. Aich was 104 years old, but the remarkable thing was that he had performed till he was above 90. Many of the obituaries carried photographs from the prime of his career. These are black-and-white photographs taken around the time of his triumphs on the world stage in 1952. They show a man, about 40 at the time and at the height of his abilities, flexing muscles in front of the cameras (Pandya 2016). Others featured more recent photographs of the bodybuilder: an elderly man with a shaved head, standing 4 feet 11 inches. He wears an orange t-shirt, sleeves rolled up to his shoulder. With the gymnasium in the background, Aich holds the front double biceps for the camera with a nonchalant expression on his face (BBC 2016).

Manohar Aich was born in 1912 in Comilla district of Bengal, in present-day Bangladesh. By most accounts, he was born into a humble family, and following his father's sickness that prevented him from earning the family's keep, the teenage Manohar took to performing feats of strength in nearby villages. Aich is said to have been spotted by P.C. Sorcar in Dhaka, and this marked the beginning of a short but productive partnership, where the magician and the physical culturists teamed up to showcase their spectacular talents. Retracing Aich's early career is a challenging proposition, given that most extant interviews were conducted fairly late in his life when his memory shows signs of fading. Different accounts, therefore, offer different versions, but some of the salient facts are as follows.

In 1940 Aich joined the Indian Air Force (yet to be given its "Royal" status following their service during World War II), and around 1942 found himself court-martialed for physically assaulting an Officer. Most reports seem to suggest Aich had hit a British Officer, provoked when the latter "made an offensive comment against India" (Pandya 2016). In an interview held in 2000, however, Manohar Aich seems not to disagree with the interviewer who asks why he had assaulted Air Marshall Subroto Mukherjee. Aich responded saying that there was a hierarchy among Officers and Non-officers, and some altercation between the two had provoked Aich to lash out (Aich 2000). The truth of this will probably elude us, but it is not unlikely that hagiographic tendencies among biographers have added a post-colonial touch to Aich's response in the Indian Air Force. Aich is said to have continued his practice while in jail, only to be released at the time of India's independence in 1947.

In 1950 Aich won the Mr. Hercules of India title and by 1951 he was ready to run for the title of Mr. Universe in the Short Class category. Aich did not win the first time round. The award went to another Indian, Manotosh Ray. Aich stayed on in England, where he worked in the British Railways to sustain himself. In 1952 Aich appeared on the Mr. Universe stage for the second time. He clinched the first prize in the Professional Short Class category, becoming the second Indian to accomplish this feat. By this time he had earned his moniker, the "pocket Hercules." In March 1952 he gave a series of performances across the United Kingdom. Aich was a name known well enough to attract crowds in Sunderland and Aberdeen. The recorded instances give us Manohar Aich at Seaburn Hall in Sunderland offering a show of "strength and yoga" on 15 March, and in Aberdeen on 22 March. In Sunderland he had for company the Mr. and Miss North Britain, and performed alongside weight-lifting displays and women's "keep-fit." Tickets were priced at £2 ("Sunderland Pair and Pick of the Month" 12 March

108 Sujaan Mukherjee

1952). The *Sunderland Daily Echo and Shipping Gazette* described Aich's presence as "one of the afternoon's high-spots" ("Sunderland Pair and Pick of the Month" 17 March 1952).

In Aberdeen, however, Aich was also participating in a competitive capacity. The *Aberdeen Evening Express* announced in anticipation that the "biggest attraction" "will be the appearance of Manohar Aich of Calcutta as a contestant in the world strand-puling championships" ("They Will Pull Their Weight" 19 March 1952). A new world record was set by Aich. The *Express* reports on 24 March that:

> A new strand-pulling world record was set up during the Soprts [sic] Cavalcade show in the Music Hall, Aberdeen, on Saturday, by Monahar Aich, the Indian pocket Hercules, who reached 315 lb in the back pull.
> *("Records Made at Sports Cavalcade" 24 March 1952)*

In 1955 Aich participated again and came third and in 1960 ranked fourth. Many laurels followed, but around 1988, Aich tried to make a come-back in the bodybuilding championships in Ahmedabad. He was denied a competitive opportunity and he received "shabby treatment" after being told he would be allowed to demonstrate in non-competitive capacity. It was important to prove himself at the national level before he could be selected for the international Mr. Universe contest, but this was not to be for the septuagenarian (Singh 1988: 36–37). An article that appeared in *Sportsworld* in 1997, traced the later career of Aich, who supposedly went from playing percussions to support his wife's *kirtan* performances in the interest of making a living to performing feats of strength and displays of muscles at circuses. Aich started a gym, "Studio-de-physique," where he trained young men and women. His last performance is supposed to have been at the age of 89, although for cameras Aich continued to flex his muscles till his very last days.

By Way of a Biography: Biswanath Datta

The first time I entered Gobar Guha's *akhada* with the hope of interviewing Biswanath Datta, I had, patronizingly, expected the elderly man to make at most a token appearance in the ring. Biswanath-*babu*, as we started calling him soon, stripped down to his *langot*, or the traditional red loin-cloth worn by wrestlers, did his rigorous warm-up routine, and once the younger students had performed the ritual cleansing of the akhada, got into the ring to lead a group of men aged between 18 and 35. In the hours that followed our research team, led by Deeptanil Ray and Nikhilesh Bhattacharya, witnessed an octogenarian engage in grapples with several students, instructing them

Physical Cultures and the Ageing Body **109**

on the finer points of each hold or grip. He performed a headstand, unheeding some onlookers who requested him to desist. Datta exited the akhada at the designated time, washed the soil off him, changed into a tracksuit, and started talking to us as if the last two hours were all in a day's work – which was probably true in his case.[3]

He told us that he was born in Chattogram in 1929, where he completed his primary schooling. His father had moved to Calcutta in search of greener pastures and stayed in a mess. In 1944 Datta's father's struggle with asthma worsened, prompting their family to move to Calcutta for additional support. Shortly after their arrival, Datta's father decided to take the sport-loving teenager to Gobar Guha's renowned akhada. Every time Datta tells the story, he relives the moment of his entry into a world that would change his life. "It was a Friday," he recalls. "Ustad-ji [Guha] was sitting there, being massaged by Durgapada Saha, who was Bhim Bhabani's [Bhabendra Mohan Saha (1890–1922)][4] younger brother." Part of the reason for bringing the young Biswanath to the akhada may have been to offer a disciplined structure that may not always have been available in schools. Guha asked Datta to join the very next day. His father hesitated. Guha immediately recognized the awkwardness and said, "Of course. Tomorrow is a Saturday. You believe in these things. Why doesn't he come in on Sunday?"

The disciplinary regime was unyielding, as Datta recalls. The trainees would be woken up at 4.30 a.m. with a prod of Ustad-ji's stick. They would bathe, and training would begin immediately thereafter. The index finger held up straight would mean a hundred *baithaks*. Half-bent meant 75, and fully bent would mean 50. Datta would do a thousand baithaks in a span of ten minutes under the strict supervision of Gobar Guha. The 250–300 *dands* were kept for the afternoons. Datta was not allowed to enter the ring during his first five or six months at the akhada. But the teacher's vision was so clear, that within a year of joining, Datta had already won his first All Bengal title. He won the title again in 1946 and was selected for a national-level match to represent Bengal. Frustratingly, Guha vetoed his participation saying the quick rise would go to his head.

In 1946, Biswanath Datta lost his father. On hearing the news, Guha visited the grieving family and told the oldest of the siblings that all rites and rituals were his responsibility. Datta was not to be engaged in these matters and his practice was to continue uninterrupted. Following India's independence and the partition, the large family moved to a house, where 19 individuals had to squeeze into three rooms. Datta took up a job as a typist for a short while before finding an opening for himself at the Customs Office in 1948. The same year he came third in the All India competition, which meant that a spot in the Olympic team would elude him. "Ustad-ji told everyone about that final 15-minute bout that I fought. He was so proud of it. It was probably my best performance," Datta recalls, beaming. In 1956 he

110 Sujaan Mukherjee

was posted at Outram Ghat, where he made friends with one Leslie Claudius (1927–2012), whose sporting spirit Datta thought very highly of. "He never lost his cool with anyone. *'Aisa kahe karta hai'* [why must you do this?] is all he would ask, no matter what his opponents did…" He continued, "We became close friends. In the afternoons, we'd meet and he'd ask, 'Datta, are you ready?' I'd say, 'Yes, Sir.' He had a scooter. We'd sit on the scooter, and drink."[5]

It was largely thanks to Biswanath Datta that Gobar Guha's historic akhada succeeded in keeping alive a traditional form of wrestling up until 2017. Until the age of 88, Datta continued his practice. He passed away in September 2020.

Bodybuilding and the Aesthetics of the Ageing Male Body

Given that bodybuilding as a spectacle sport is largely a Western tradition, it would not be too far-fetched to ask if there exists such a thing as an aesthetics of the ageing male body in Western art. Bodybuilding traditionally drew inspiration from and sought to imitate ancient Greco-Roman statues, which were held to be expressions of the male body in its most perfect form. Eugen Sandow, arguably the most iconic bodybuilder in the late-nineteenth and early-twentieth centuries, photographed himself imitating statues of the Farnese Hercules, the Discobolus, and the Dying Gladiator (Wyke 1999: 358). As Kate Nichols notes, Sandow had himself:

> photographed in these poses, and these images widely disseminated in postcards within his publications. Each edition of *Sandow's Magazine of Physical Culture* (1897–1907) opened with a photograph of a classical (or classicizing) sculpture.
>
> *(Nichols 2015: 223)*

In the classical statues, art sought to define the human form in its state of perfection, and the likes of Sandow sought, in turn, to imitate the statues. Things came full circle when in an attempt to preserve "the most perfect specimen of physical culture" of the day, the Natural History Department of the British Museum made a plaster cast of Sandow, making him hold his exact position for 15 minutes, each muscle flexed without the slightest twitch. Happy though he was to serve as the perfect specimen, Sandow confessed he would never go through again it for any amount of money (Freeborn 2014).

As Jean-Pierre Vernant noted in his classic study, *Mortals and Immortals*, the distinction between divine and mortal bodies in classical Greek thought hinged on the question of mutability (Vernant 1991: 29). Not only was the divine body unnecessary – the gods can see, hear, smell, move, and even fight

Physical Cultures and the Ageing Body **111**

without their organs and limbs – it was also preserved immortally in the moment of its perfection. Sculptures that tried to represent male beauty usually favoured youth, hoping to capture and crystallize that pristine moment, when the body is impeccable. Perhaps because of its close aesthetic allegiance to classical statuary, representations of bodybuilding have largely focused on defining static moments, when the human body is in perfect shape, although in competitive bodybuilding displays of control over one's muscles play a key role. The body, therefore, is usually not viewed as a process, and since the definition of perfection is fixed in a non-relative manner in terms of aesthetic "objectivity," the bodily perfection aspired to is regarded with respect to a particular age range.

In *Sandow, the Magnificent*, David L. Chapman offers an account of an encounter between Sandow's younger contemporary, Earle E. Liederman, and the "ageing" master.

> Sandow...flicked his bicep, making it jump and flutter just as he had done on stage in the old days. But alas, his body had not completely escaped the ravages of time, for Liederman noticed that his tricep seemed a little slack. He added that "The skin was not firm, nor were the minor muscles or ligaments in clear definition".
>
> *(Chapman 2006: 182)*

So far any dedicated regime for the elderly by Sandow has escaped attention. This may be owing in part to the fact that Sandow's rhetoric often hinged on the project of building a stronger nation. Women were included, although very limited in the roles (primarily for the purpose of reproduction and health), and children were strongly encouraged to take part in the fitness regimes from an early age. Sandow did, however, photograph himself at various times in his life and presented them sequentially. The last available photograph is one of Sandow as a 52-year-old, featured as a strategically positioned nude (Sandow 1919, prelims).

Eugen Sandow visited India between October 1904 and June 1905, and in that time captured the imagination like few celebrities could. Carey Watt writes that most of Sandow's Calcutta shows were held at the Theatre Royal, with "two special appearances 'for natives'" at the Corinthian Theatre in Dharmatala. "The tour created a physical culture 'craze' in the parts of India that Sandow visited," continues Watt (2017: 6). Sandow became a household name in Bengal. In 1930, Keshub Chandra Sen Gupta and Bishnu Charan Ghosh published a slim volume titled *Barbell Exercise and Muscle Control*, inspired by the sustained wave of enthusiasm. The introduction was written by "Capt. J.N. Banerjee, Bar-at-Law" (Sen Gupta and Ghosh 1930, prelims). A photograph of Banerjee, which appears before the authors' photographs appear, shows him a muscular, well-built man, at the age of 70.

FIGURE 6.1 Biswanath Datta at Gobar Guha's akhada, warming up. Photograph by Kawshik Aki, courtesy School of Cultural Texts and Records, Jadavpur University.

None of the posed photographs show older men, but the vogue of imitating classical statuary or posing with marble models is seen. Figures 6.2 and 6.3 show one S. Bose posing as "The Panther on a Lion," where he sits on a cowering marble lion, and "The Living Statue," where he bends over a marble statue of a woman (ibid). Right at the end, however, an advertisement appears for "Ghosh's Gymnasium" on 4 Gurpar Road, which invites both "Young and old," assuring them that, "there is a different exercise for each of you" (ibid, end advertisement). Can these be taken as markers of a change in perceptions of the body and of old age, where focus shifts from imitating aesthetic perfection to a more relative understanding of the changing body?

In international bodybuilding, the aesthetics of the male body were undergoing changes. In 1954 W.A. Pallum wrote in an article titled "The Change in Physique" that appeared in *Health and Strength*:

> From the point of view of massive muscularity, it can right away be said that, apart from a few professionally performing strong men, the physique champions of yesteryear would compare unfavourably with "moderns"... As to symmetry and definition, that's another matter entirely; *the present has nothing on the past in this direction.*
>
> *(Pallum 1945: 32) [Author's emphasis]*

FIGURE 6.2   "The Panther on a Lion," Posed by S. Bose. Published in K.C. Sengupta and B.C. Ghosh, Muscle Control and Barbell Exercise.

Internationally, as amateur bodybuilding assumed greater formality, the preferred styles of posing were also changing, as photographs appearing in *Health and Strength* in the 1950s suggest. There was even some recognition of the possibility of exercise in old age. In an article titled "How Old Is Too Old?" that appeared in *Health and Strength* in 1952 (the year Aich won his Mr. Universe title), Ron Chifney wrote,

114 Sujaan Mukherjee

FIGURE 6.3 "The Living Statue," Posed by S. Bose. Published in K.C. Sengupta and B.C. Ghosh, *Muscle Control and Barbell Exercise*.

I have heard it said that a man should participate in sport until he is thirty years of age, take part in politics until forty and then from forty to seventy reflect on his wasted years...If a man is extremely pleased to be doing the type of training he undertakes, then let him perform until he is ninety.

(Chifney 1952: 14)

Perhaps Aich, who featured on the cover of this issue, read the article and took it to heart. Aich practised well into his 90s, and, according to his son, Bishnu Manohar Aich, he performed on stage for the final time when he was about 92. While articles such as Chifney's admitted the possibility of pleasure being derived from exercise by the elderly, it appears largely as a private pursuit for one's own personal pleasure. Phoenix speaks of the "pleasures of physicality in relation to the ageing body" in terms of how it constitutes a challenge to "foreclosing assumptions about what the ageing body can and should do, produce, and represent" (Phoenix 2017: 182). Putting it on display, for public consumption is another matter altogether, and one that has to do with combatting the ageing body's state of deprived cultural capital, as Emmanuelle Tulle notes (Tulle 2012: 3).

Perhaps in order to understand the appeal of the images of an ageing Manohar Aich that circulated through television interviews, photographs in print and digital media, and on advertisement hoardings for Dulal's *talmishri* (date-palm candy), their reception requires breaking down. As 1997 article said of Aich, "At the slightest pretext, he loves to flex his muscles" ("A Day in the Life" 1997: 55) and this remained true till the end. On the one hand, the body put on display may be regarded in terms of what it lacks in comparison to images from an earlier phase in his career. His skin is wrinkled, his muscles have lost their tightness and much of their linear clarity, and even Aich's charming smile from yesteryears has disappeared. All in all, it is an image that powerfully conveys the need for greater effort to put on a show. On the other hand, if we choose to perceive the ageing body on its own terms (without falling into the aforementioned trap of positioning him as a "hero of ageing"), Aich's offers an example of what Tulle says in "elite active agers" forces "us to reconsider the upper limit of what can be achieved" (Tulle 2008: 343). As a spectator, these two ways of interpreting the spectacle are not mutually exclusive. When Aich put his ageing body on display, the fact of his age was inescapable. Yet it held the promise of the body's ability to withstand the usual effects of ageing, and perhaps gave hope by gesturing towards possibilities. Placing Aich as an endorser of date-palm candy was certainly a means of conveying to its elderly consumers the benefits of the product in old age, offering a promise of physical strength and beauty.

Embodied Knowledge, the Body as Archive, and Embodied Time

Biswanath Datta continued to practise and train generations of aspiring wrestlers well into his 80s. While the previous section dealt with the aesthetics of the ageing male body, the current section considers questions that the practice of an ageing wrestler enables us to formulate. Some of these questions are founded on the work of phenomenologists who, following

116 Sujaan Mukherjee

Merleau-Ponty's (2002) line of inquiry, have deployed ideas about embodied habit and knowledge acquisition, particularly through studies of practitioners of dance and physical cultures (Moe 2005; Purser 2017). Datta's example, however, encourages us to probe in directions that have received relatively little attention: firstly, by taking into account the inter-subjective nature of knowledge formation (and exchange) in kusti, and, secondly, by considering the ageing physical culturist as both practitioner and teacher, who transmits their embodied knowledge to others. Although it took Western metaphysics a long time to attempt a reconciliation of the Cartesian mind/body dualism, practitioners (in the widest sense of the term) must have known, if not in so many words, that our bodies are capable of acquiring and producing knowledge; indeed, that it is unusual if not impossible to find an instance where either works in pure isolation.

Asked to write an introduction to Birendranath Basu's *Bharatiyakusti o taharshiksha* [A manual of Indian wrestling] (1934), Biswanath Datta's teacher Gobar Guha had found it difficult to wholeheartedly endorse the manuscript that had been placed at his disposal. He reminded readers that there is a vast difference between learning music from your master, instrument in hand, and learning by looking at the detailed sheets of musical notation. Training in kusti requires the combination of many skills, he went on, among which are the ability to read and respond to the opponent's movements, and coordination between mind and body. He concedes later that these arguments do not render the book useless. For those who have had some experience training with an ustad, the book could come in handy as a mnemonic, so that students who do not have access to akhadas can practise some grips by looking at the book (Guha in Basu 1934: 10–11). The author was aware of the limitations of his project, despite the use of photographs to illustrate the grips, which were explained in simple language. He was also conscious of the problematic compulsion to verbalize a form that is seen by its practitioners fundamentally as physical, embodied knowledge. Basu confessed that there was some confusion when it came to naming the grips:

> I have learnt through my interactions with *pehlwans* that even though they are knowledgeable about the grips, they are often not as knowledgeable about their names…When an expert wrestler is asked to name a grip, if they happen not to know it, they make up some name for it on the spot for fear of appearing unknowledgeable.
>
> *(Basu 1934: 6)*

It is not surprising, then, that while proposing the body as a primary mode of being in and perceiving the world, Merleau-Ponty drew on examples of embodied knowledge and the acquisition of "habits" that reconstitute the "corporeal schema" (Merleau-Ponty 2002: 164). He argued that for a skilled typist it is not enough to "know the place of each letter among the keys" or to have "acquired a conditioned reflex for each one" (ibid, 166). The body "has its world, or understands its worlds, without having to make use of my 'symbolic' or 'objectifying function'" (ibid, 162) and responds before a conscious mind can to words formed in one's own mind or dictated by someone else. He concludes:

> If habit is neither a form of knowledge nor an involuntary action, what then is it? It is knowledge in the hands, which is forthcoming only when bodily effort is made, and cannot be formulated in detachment from that effort.
>
> *(ibid, 164)*

The philosophical implications of the proposition have been productively brought into dialogue with practice by scholars in recent years in the context of dance and physical cultures. For example, in an ethnographic study of contemporary dancers in the United Kingdom, Aimie Purser points to the repeated use of phrases like "getting it into the body" to explain the "shift from rule-following to flexible intuitive engagement" (Purser 2017: 6) with movements and techniques. She uses Merleau-Ponty's idea of "sedimentation" of habits into the corporeal schema through repetition to arrive at a diachronic understanding of the acquisition of embodied knowledge by practitioners, and the emergence of intuition (ibid, 9). Purser expands on these ideas by drawing attention to the "inter-corporeal" nature of this knowledge formation, where she considers how dancers prefer choreographers to "make the work on their [dancers'] bodies" (ibid, 10), rather than inhabit movements designed in abstract or with another body.

Further extending the idea of embodied knowledge, Bryan Hogeveen reflects on his practice of Brazilian Jiu-jitsu, where the acquisition of habit takes place through sustained, direct contact with a sparring partner:

> During our training sessions I am able to feel and sense the nuances of her movements as she manoeuvres to sweep, submit and control my body. I have assimilated the silent lessons taught by her body.
>
> *(Hogeveen 2014: 89)*

The slippage between the non-dualist first-person subject "I" and the corporeal "other" notwithstanding, the quoted passage gestures towards a significant aspect of inter-subjective habit formation in martial arts. There are two categories of partners that a practitioner is likely to encounter: a relatively friendly one during training with whom there is a relationship of trust, and an agonistic one at tournaments. The specific "silent lessons" acquired through inter-subjective practice must be generalized by the wrestler if they

118 Sujaan Mukherjee

are to prepare for unexpected opponents. In this, they are aided by their teachers who, by virtue of their experience, embody much larger archives of knowledge and techniques that can be transmitted to the younger trainees.

Sedimentation, as Merleau-Ponty (Merleau-Ponty 2002: 150) understands it, offers a useful way of thinking about the acquisition of embodied knowledge across time. However, since his examples focus on individuals engaged in learning skills, it stops short of exploring the implications a dialogic, inter-subjective practice can hold. If, when thinking of wrestling or a martial art, we consider each practitioner to acquire "silent lessons" from their many encounters, and if we agree that these accumulate over time, then the corporeal schema becomes a rich archive that has assimilated aspects of many an individual's practices – successfully or not is another matter – to produce an embodied archive. This idea has been explored in dance. Contemporary dancer, Claire Vionnet writes:

> The dancing body…is dancing with the shadows of all the other bodies (s)he met, danced with and touched. All these bodies left traces on his/her dancing skills. The dancing body embodies all past stories shared with others. Therefore, I will argue that the body is a living archive, still in movement, continually in transformation into new forms of being.
>
> *(Vionnet 2018)*

But when we consider the ageing practitioner as a teacher, are we confronted by a frustrating paradox? Does the relative decline in physical ability make it difficult to convey to trainees the embodied knowledge acquired over time? I would argue that the point is not to focus on the limitations by privileging the youthful body but to think of the ways in which the ageing practitioner negotiates or re-assembles their corporeal schema in order to adapt. The suggestions I put forth are based on my limited experience in martial arts practice (Aikido in particular). I formulate them more as open-ended questions, inviting further discussion particularly from ageing practitioners, who can speak from experience.

During my Aikido training, I had started noticing an unexpected bodily change that came about with practice. The school of Aikido practised at the Academy of Aikido, India, and its satellite dojo at Jadavpur University led by Sensei Deeptanil Ray believes in minimal verbal communication during class. Unlike kusti, which has an agonistic element, Aikido encourages "practitioners to 'blend' and 'harmonize' their movement and *ki* ('life force') with the ki of their attacker" (Gordon 2019: 89). This means that through collaboration with the *uke* (one who initiates the attack and receives the technique), one moves towards a non-verbal and embodied awareness of their being in the world, in a spirit of non-competition. Practising a technique repeatedly and over a period of time helped to "get it into the body," to the extent that the movement required less deliberate or conscious effort. But alongside this acquisition of a habit, for me, the bodily experience of time changed. As the conscious mind-body was freed from the task of executing the move, it allowed for greater proprioceptive and inter-subjective awareness even while performing a technique in isolation or combination, which leads me to speculate that there is a dilation of what I would call "embodied time."[6] While terms like "quicker reflex" are used to describe a shortened interval between stimulus and response, I suggest embodied time to describe the experience of inhabiting that moment as a bodily consciousness, where the practitioner perceives the self and the partner, analyses the possibilities with reference to existing embodied knowledge, and reacts to it prenoetically (Gallagher 2006: 142).

While some ageing practitioners are able to retain a high level of athleticism, bodily strength, and agility, others may need to adapt and adopt a style more economic physically. This seems to be true particularly in East Asian martial arts. Practising under the supervision of Marcella Paviot Kyoshi (b. 1957) as part of a week-long seminar at the Academy of Aikido, India's dojo in Kolkata, we noticed how seamlessly she was able to re-channel her uke's energy to produce motions that were fluid and utterly in her control: the words used most often by participants to describe her were "effortless" and "graceful." What stood out in her practice (and of others of similar seniority) was how during the exchanges, she seemed to control time, inhabiting the extended moment with far greater ease and higher awareness than the uke. Unlike Aikido, kusti relies more on muscular strength, even if the importance of balance, timing, and intuition (developed through practice) are comparable. Therefore, practitioners of kusti are unlikely to visually appear as effortless at any point in their careers. However, watching an 80-something Biswanath Datta practising in the akhada with young trainees from the vantage point of a participant (albeit in a different form), seemed to suggest a similar control over time. Coupled with the embodied archive that he drew on, this allowed him to not only read but apparently anticipate his opponent's moves and respond to them accordingly. With failing physical strength, even if he was unable to respond successfully, his embodied cues would usually suffice to gesture towards what the reaction could be. The point is not to romanticize this ability by claiming it is a sufficient replacement for the inevitable decline in physical capital in old age but to appreciate this late style as a reorientation of one's corporeal schema to adapt to bodily changes and capitalize on embodied knowledge. The other common feature of both the practitioners I have mentioned – one that they share with iconic representations of ageing masters in popular culture, such as Yoda in *Star Wars*, Pai-Mei in *Kill Bill*, and Shifu in *Kung-fu Panda* – is their inimitable sense of humour and mischief (Figure 6.1).

120 Sujaan Mukherjee

Ageing performers and athletes, who continue to play to audiences, are often able to master a skill that is specific to their years of experience and expertise: it is to develop a different aesthetic of performance, where the body in its comparatively limited capacity is able through controlled physical exertion to gesture towards the knowledge that their habitus still carries. One thinks of Pt. Ravi Shankar playing a truncated sitar at the age of 92 to a packed house at Netaji Indoor Stadium in Kolkata, or an 87-year-old Girija Devi singing her *thumri* to a winter audience in the premises of Jaykrishna Library (Uttarpara, West Bengal) in 2016, or Biswanath Datta demonstrating how to pin down a young man in the akhada earth, whose touch and smell his bones have known for the last 60 odd years. These are not the "perfect" performances of their youth, but a different idiom, appreciable in and of itself, and perhaps only perceivable in old age.

Conclusion

In *Cashel Byron's Profession* George Bernard Shaw's eponymous pugilist protagonist criticizes a painting of St. George and the dragon on the grounds that the hero is depicted in a posture that betrays too much effort. The fighter is almost off-balance and would fall at "one touch of a child's finger" (Shaw 1886: ch. 6). He criticizes it on grounds of aesthetics and efficiency: "nothing can be what you might call artistically done if it's done with an effort...The more effort you make, the less effect you produce" (ibid, ch. 6). The aesthetics of effortlessness has not received much critical attention. According to Barbara Montero, the idea of effortlessness in movement goes at least as far back as Baldassare Castiglione's (1528) formulation of *sprezzatura*, or carefully practised nonchalance that gives the appearance of effortlessness in a courtier's bearing (Montero 2011: 67). She traces the idea through Henri Bergson and Herbert Spencer, suggesting that what appears as effortless to a spectator is a combination of our proprioceptive admiration of a performer before us as well as the acknowledgement of a fitness surplus that enables the athlete or dancer to not only execute their moves but to do so with an appearance of ease (ibid, 77).

In order to understand this receptive category, it might be productive to draw a distinction between the mimetic and non-mimetic arts. In the mimetic arts and in dance, as Montero suggests, the preference for the aesthetic of effortlessness has been questioned in recent years, where contemporary artists often aim at producing "provocative, powerful, shocking, or insightful" works (ibid, 68). One of the underlying features shared by art that is often described as "effortless" is the ability, through super-abundance of skill, to efface the apparent process of production. In writing, this could be traced back to the theories of inspiration, which as M.H. Abrams in his classic study described the process of composition as "sudden, effortless,

Physical Cultures and the Ageing Body **121**

and unanticipated" (Abrams 1953: 189). John Keats, whose Romantic image held him as an example of the effortless poet, may have been able to tell us more on this based on his twin pursuits as poet and boxer. Whether it is labour in the mind or in the body, the ideology of bourgeois art felt more comfortable keeping it out of sight.

While in the mimetic arts the construct of effortless composition and performance has been critically re-evaluated, effortlessness in sport is still praised. Among elite sports stars, Roger Federer, Usain Bolt, Nadia Comaneci, and Lionel Messi are names frequently associated with effortless performance (De Jonge 2017; Hyde 2012; Amdur 1976; Bull 2016). But aside from that players with less successful careers are also often described as effortless. Cristiano Ronaldo or Rafael Nadal, for instance, rarely receive this particular word of praise. A *Guardian* article from 2015 compared the two tennis players: "Nadal, almost defying the slo-mo, was the quick-stepping boxer, all tightly sprung energy; the Swiss was a ballet dancer, the very picture of floating, effortless menace" (Mitchell 2015). Aesthetic judgement in sport is subjective, and without taking sides, the distinction between the two can be drawn without being too reductive.

In trying to write about ageing sportspersons, applying categories that are specific to a particular aesthetic of physical ability is pointless. The visible need to put in great effort rarely finds a consumer, and as a result, we have what Tulle calls a deprivation of "cultural capital" for the ageing body in sport (Tulle 2008: 3). The question remains, can we profitably study ageing bodies going beyond the sense of surprise that comes with perceiving ageing bodies in these active capacities, where they must emphatically move away from portraying this seemingly attractive trait of effortlessness? Cultures of viewing that consider ageing bodies with the expectations that define a particular sport can take us in two directions: first, to perceive a lack when judged by standards set for younger athletes, and/or, second, a patronizing acceptance of their continued practice. In comparing practitioners from these two fields, the intention of this chapter is not to write a cohesive narrative of either sport but to offer productive methods of reading the ageing individual actively engaged in what is broadly termed cultures of the body. It is to draw attention to a critical shift in perspective that is called for here: the ageing body appears to be deficient or lacking when its performance in a field of sport or physical activity is judged from the point of view of the field of practice. In fact, to be more specific, they appear lacking only when we judge with the end product – be it the spectacle or the efficiency – in mind. Understanding such "untimely" practices from the perspective of gerontology opens up the field not for exploring potentialities of the ageing body and allows us to reexamine and analyse the categories we commonly use for our appreciation of the physical cultures.

122 Sujaan Mukherjee

Notes

1 Part of the research for this chapter was conducted as part of the "Physical Cultures of Bengal" project at the School of Cultural Texts and Records, Jadavpur University.
2 The author would like to thank Si Sweeney at the National Amateur Body-Building Association, Rudraneil Sengupta, Biswanath and Debdipra Datta, and Bishnu Manohar Aich for their help with the research. I thank Professors Supriya Chaudhuri and Abhijit Gupta for introducing me to the field of physical culture research in Bengal; Deeptanil Ray, who, unbeknownst to him, taught me the value of an embodied methodology while researching the physical cultures; Vikrant Dadawala for helping me get hold of articles I could not otherwise have accessed; and Srijaa Kundu for valuable feedback about embodied knowledge and intuition. The SYLFF Research Abroad scholarship awarded for my doctoral work enabled me to access the British Library and archives in the UK for this chapter.
3 Biswanath Datta interviewed by Deeptanil Ray, Nikhilesh Bhattachara, and Sujaan Mukherjee (2014), for "Physical Cultures of Bengal" project, available at https://youtu.be/ryse-qE6R_U. The full-length interviews are available at the School of Cultural Texts and Records, Jadavpur University.
4 See Abhijit Gupta, "Man Who Lifted Elephants," *The Telegraph*, 18 July 2010.
5 Biswanath Datta interviewed by Nikhilesh Bhattacharya and Sujaan Mukherjee (2016) for "Physical Cultures of Bengal" project. The full-length interviews are available at the School of Cultural Texts and Records, Jadavpur University.
6 The term is used in neuroscience, drawing on Edmund Husserl (1928) or William James (1980) to understand the bodily experience of consciousness through time. See Wittmann (2014).

References

"A Day in the Life of Manohar Aich." *Sportsworld*, vol. 17, no. 34, Jan–Feb. 1997, pp. 54–57.
"Manohar Aich: Top Indian Bodybuilder Dies, Aged 104." *BBC News*, 6 Jun. 2016. www.bbc.co.uk/news/world-asia-india-36457508. Photograph sourced from AFP.
"Records Made at Sports Cavalcade." *Aberdeen Evening Press*, 24 Mar. 1952, p. 9.
"Sunderland Pair: The Pick of the Month." *Sunderland Daily Echo and Shipping Gazette*, 12 Mar. 1952, p. 2.
"Sunderland Pair: The Pick of the Month." *Sunderland Daily Echo and Shipping Gazette*, 17 Mar. 1952, p. 6.
"They Will Pull Their Weight – And a Bit More." *Aberdeen Evening Express*, 19 Mar. 1952, p. 8.
Abrams, M. H. *The Mirror and the Lamp: Romantic Theory and the Critical Tradition.* Oxford University Press, 1953.
Aich, M. "Mukhomukhi Manohar Aich [Face-to-face with Manohar Aich]." *Doordarshan*, Interview with Sayantan Das Adhikari, 2000. https://youtu.be/-EUWLar1S3M. Accessed 4 May 2018.
Amdur, N. "The Measure of Greatness." *The New York Times*, 25 Jul. 1976. https://www.nytimes.com/1976/07/25/archives/the-measure-of-greatness-nadia-comaneci-fearless-and-tireless.html. Accessed 20 Jun. 2019.

Basu, B. *Bharatiyakusti o tar shiksha [A* Manual *of Indian* Wrestling*].* Introduction by Gobar Guha. Rabindranath Basu, 1934.

Bull, J. J. "Ballon d'Or: Lionel Messi is Untouchable in Race to Be Named World's Best." *The Telegraph (UK),* 9 Jan. 2016. https://www.telegraph.co.uk/sport/football/players/lionel-messi/12086863/Why-Lionel-Messi-is-back-to-his-best-and-worthy-winner-of-fifth-Ballon-dOr.html. Accessed 20 Jun. 2019.

Chapman, D. L. *Sandow the Magnificent: Eugen Sandow and the Beginnings of Bodybuilding.* University of Illinois Press, 2006.

Chifney, R. "How Old is Too Old?" *Health & Strength,* vol. 81, 18 Sep. 1952, pp. 14–17.

Chowdhury, I. *The Frail Hero and Virile History: Gender and the Politics of Culture in Colonial Bengal.* Oxford University Press, 2001.

De Jonge, P. "How Roger Federer Upgraded His Game." *The New York Times,* 24 Aug. 2017. https://www.nytimes.com/interactive/2017/08/24/magazine/usopen-federer-nadal-backhand-wonder-year.html. Accessed 20 Jun. 2019.

Freeborn, A. "Specimen of the Month #10: Eugen Sandow, the 'Perfect Man'." *Natural History Museum,* 30 Aug. 2014. http://www.nhm.ac.uk/natureplus/blogs/behind-the-scenes/2014/08/30/specimen-of-the-month-10-perfect-man-eugen-sandow. Accessed 20 Sep. 2017.

Gallgher, S. *How the Body Shapes the Mind.* Clarendon Press. 2006.

Gordon, Michael A. *Aikido as Transformative and Embodied Pedagogy: Teacher as Healer.* Cham: Palgrave Macmillan, 2019.

Gupta, A. "Man Who Lifted Elephants." *The Telegraph,* 18 Jul. 2010. https://www.telegraphindia.com/west-bengal/man-who-lifted-elephants/cid/1272354. Accessed 18 Jun. 2018.

———. "Cultures of the Body in Colonial Bengal: The Career of Gobar Guha." *The International Journal of the History of Sport,* vol. 28, no. 12, 2012, pp. 1687–1700. doi:10.1080/09523367.2012.714931.

Hogeveen, Bryan. '"It is About Your Body Recognizing the Move and Automatically Doing It": Merleau-Ponty, Habit and Brazilian Jiu-Jitsu. In *Fighting Scholars: Habitus and Ethnographies of Martial Arts and Combat Sports.* Edited by Raul Sanchez Garcia and Dale C. Spencer. London: Anthem Press, 2014. 79–94.

Hyde, M. "Usain Bolt's Effortless Cool Makes Us All Yearn to Be Like Him." *The Guardian,* 6 Aug. 2012. https://www.theguardian.com/sport/2012/aug/06/usain-bolt-effortless-cool. Accessed 20 Jun. 2019.

Merleau-Ponty, Maurice. Phenomenology of Perception. Translated by Colin Smith. London: Routledge, 2002.

Mitchell, K. "Rafael Nadal in Warrior Mentality for Wimbledon." *The Guardian,* 26 Jun. 2015. https://www.theguardian.com/sport/2015/jun/26/rafael-nadal-wimbledon-2015-injuries-beautiful. Accessed 20 Jun. 2019.

Moe, V.F. "A Philosophical Critique of Classical Cognitivism in Sport: From Information Processing to Bodily Background Knowledge." *Journal of Philosophy of Sport,* vol. 32, 2017, pp. 155–183.

Montero, B. G. "Effortless Bodily Movement." *Philosophical Topics,* vol. 39, no. 1, Spring 2011, pp. 67–79.

Nichols, K. *Greece and Rome at the Crystal Palace: Classical Sculpture and Modern Britain, 1854–1936.* Oxford University Press, 2015.

Pallum, W. A. "The Change of Physique." *Health & Strength,* vol. 83, 13 May 1945, pp. 31–35.

Pandya, H. "Manohar Aich: The Father of Indian Bodybuilding." *Outlook*, 12 Jun. 2016. https://www.outlookindia.com/website/story/manohar-aich-the-father-of-indian-bodybuilding/296960.

Phoenix, C. "Ageing Bodies." *Routledge Handbook of Physical Culture Studies*, edited by M. L. Silk, D. L. Andrews, and H. Thorpe. Routledge, 2017, pp. 179–188.

Purser, Aimie. ""Getting it into the Body": Understanding Skill Acquisition through Merleau-Ponty and the Embodied Practice of Dance." *Qualitative Research in Sport, Exercise and Health*, vol. 10(1), 2015, pp. 1–15. DOI: 10.1080/2159676X.2017.1377756.

Rosselli, J. "The Self-Image of Effeteness: Physical Education and Nationalism in Nineteenth-century Bengal." *Past and Present*, vol. 8, Feb. 1980, pp. 123–148.

Sandow, E. *Life is Movement: The Physical Reconstruction and Regeneration of the People*. The Family Encyclopaedia of Health, 1919.

Sen Gupta, K. C. and B. C. Ghosh. *Barbell Exercise and Muscle Control*. Published by the Authors, 1930.

Sengupta, R. *Enter the Dangal: Travels through India's Wrestling Landscape*. E-book, Collins, 2016.

Shaw, G. B. *Cashel Byron's Profession*. Gutenberg, 1886. http://www.gutenberg.org/files/5872/5872-h/5872-h.htm.

Singh, P. "The Muscleman." *The Illustrated Weekly of India*, 10 Jul. 1988, pp. 36–37.

Sinha, M. *Colonial Masculinity: The 'Manly Englishman' and the 'Effeminate Bengali' in the Late Nineteenth Century*. Manchester University Press, 1995.

Tulle, E. "Acting Your Age? Sports Science and the Ageing Body." *Journal of Aging Studies*, vol. 22, 2008, pp. 340–347.

———. "The Ageing Body and the Ontology of Ageing: Athletic Competence in Later Life." *Body & Society*, vol. 14, no. 3, Jan. 2012, pp. 1–19. doi:10.1177/1357034X08093570.

Tulle, E. and C. Phoenix. *Physical Activity and Sport in Later Life: Critical Perspectives*. E-book, Palgrave Macmillan, 2015.

Vernant, J. "Mortals and Immortals: The Body of the Divine." *Mortals and Immortals: Collected Essays*, edited by Froma I. Zeitlin and translated by Anne M. Wilson. Princeton University Press, 1991, pp. 27–49.

Vionnet, C. "The Dancing Body as Living Archive." Art, Materiality and Representation Conference. Royal Anthropological Institute at the British Museum, London, 1–3 Jun. 2018. https://www.clairevionnet.com/lecture-performance. Accessed 19 Apr. 2022.

Wacquant, L. "Habitus as Topic and Tool: Reflections on Becoming a Prizefighter." *Fighting Scholars: Habitus and Ethnographies of Martial Arts and Combat Sports*, edited by P. S. Garcia and D. C. Spencer. Anthem Press, 2013, pp. 19–31.

Watt, C. A. "Cultural Exchange, Appropriation and Physical Culture: Strongman Eugen Sandow in Colonial India, 1904–1905." *The International Journal of the History of Sport*, vol. 33, no. 6, 2016, pp. 1921–1942. https://doi.org/10.1080/09523367.2017.1283306.

Wittmann, M. "Embodied Time: The Experience of Time, the Body, and the Self." *Subjective Time: The Philosophy, Psychology, and Neuroscience of Temporality*, edited by V. Arstila and D. Lloyd. MIT Press, 2014, pp. 507–523.

Wyke, M. "Herculean Muscle!: The Classicizing Rhetoric of Bodybuilding." *Constructions of the Classical Body*, edited by J. I. Porter. University of Michigan Press, 1999, pp. 355–380.

7

UMAR KA LIHAZ

Ageism in Indian Classical Dance

Shantanu Majee

Time is the life force of Indian Classical Music and Dance. It thrives on the here and now of existence. *Taal* in the Indian tradition embraces this dimension of time in music. Such understanding of *taal* is often interpreted as a momentarily temporal structure to the free-flowing progression of musical notes. Aesthetic discourses in India would draw in a comparison of *taal* with the banks of a river; it is the terrain that holds up a shape wherein the flow is moulded. A learner of Indian Classical Music and Dance would persevere to internalize the cycles of rhythm and pace first and then learn to control the intricacies independently. The mnemonic of the *taal* may be put to use thereafter as a creative architecture for rhythmic improvisation in music. In such endeavour, thus, the Indian Classical Dancer aspires to the perfect posture which exposes, as Kapila Vatsyayan points out, "a moment of arrested time in limited space."[1]

On the other hand, as in life, similarly in the arts, age is constantly measured as a function of time. However, if we are to reflect on our experience either in life or through arts, we find that it is more the contrary where our understanding of time is grounded in age. In Indian Classical Dance too, age gives time a measure of reality. There is no denial to the fact that our very concept of time ages and is subject to an ageing process. This is made evident more so in the field of Indian Classical Dance, wherein age is a necessary qualification to perform professionally. The *rasika* or the aesthete may appreciate the physical prowess of the young talent but they are usually not ready to accept the content of the performance seriously until performers have aged enough. Advanced years may offer one freedom, self-assurance, and room to explore as an artist but at the same time it conditions the shape and order of the body to cast its influence on the craft itself. Moreover,

DOI: 10.4324/9780429352560-8

ageing has always been associated with both physical decline and social marginalization, and hence theories of ageing have consequently focused on later life stages when issues of bodily control, dependence, and frailty become prominent. This problem is further aggravated when dancers face early retirement with little education or training in areas outside their discipline, due to the all-consuming intensity of their early training in dance. In addition, dancers reaching retirement age have to constantly give themselves into negotiating social and institutional constraints and opportunities within what can be described as an age-hostile society, and at a time when their non-dancer peers are in mid-career.

It is a truth well established that dancers in the Indian Classical Tradition are engaged in an art form that is an aesthetic as well as an athletic practice, a practice in which the ageing of the body impacts the subjectivity of the dancer and their future in dance much earlier than in many other careers. There appears to be both an idealization of dancers' bodies and, conversely, an intensification and acceleration of ageing for these dancers which those in less body-based professions may not confront until much later. This intensification of ageing experienced by dancers highlights the social constraints impinging on their social recognition and cultural valorization, which are culturally naturalized and kept, at best, hidden.

Ageing, therefore, presents itself as a typical disruption in the craft of an Indian classical dancer. Such an understanding does not only come from encountering the body of work that performers exhibit in the concert circuit but also stems deep within the literature from which these performers traditionally seek their validation. The most sought-after reference would be the oft-quoted *Natya Shastra*, an ancient encyclopaedic treatise on arts that seems to have influenced all classical forms of performing arts belonging to the Indian tradition. Though the work is attributed to the legendary figure of Bharata Muni, there is little doubt that this work is the codification of a vast amount of extant knowledge, and the exposition of a long and well-established tradition in the practice of performing arts. *Natya* implies both acting and dancing in this treatise to such an extent that across the text, acting, dancing, and music are treated as one indivisible activity. However, things become complicated with classification of qualities that one is to expect of a female performer, as mentioned in the version edited by Pushpendra Kumar:

> Women who have physical beauty, good qualities, generosity, feminine charm, patience and good manners, and who possess soft, sweet and charming voice, and varying notes in her throat, and who are experts in the representation of Passion (*hela*), and Feeling (*bhava*), know well of representation of the Temperament (*sattva*), have sweetness of manners, are skilled in playing musical instruments, have a knowledge of notes, *Tala* and *Yati*, and are associated with the master [for the] dramatic

128 Shantanu Majee

art, clever, skilled in acting, capable of using reasoning positive and negative (*uhapoha*), and have *youthful age with beauty*, are known as actresses(*natakiya*).(emphasis added)

(2006: 1436)

Even if one is to underestimate the "women who have physical beauty" as having relative interpretations, the notion of "youthful age" is clearly explicit. Most seasoned practitioners in the contemporary concert scenario would interpret "youthfulness" as a state of mind at the point of performance, which would then offer them the artistic licence of upholding that which ought to be strictly traditional in spite of their "coming of age." Nevertheless, though ageing is generally to be viewed as a phenomenon of decline in this respect, there is an aspect to it that holds more promise than present reality may reveal; it opens up the relationship between wisdom and ageing. The text edited by Pushpendra Kumar is brutally direct in its mention of the old dames though:

Women who know the manner of departed kings, and have been honoured by them, and who know the character of all [the members of the harem] are said to be old dames (*vriddha*).

(2006: 1439)

The problem with such an idea is that it fails to address wisdom as a complex, multi-faceted construct, having too little to do with age. Moreover, it fails to establish any association with the representational aspects of performance studies in such cases. Recent researches in the behavioural sciences and neuroscience literature have proved age to have no relation with wisdom-related knowledge and judgement.[2] In the light of such discovery, the commonly held equation between performance and age has been remarkably problematized.

The notion is further mystified with the reading of other ancient treatises such as the *Abhinaya Darpana* and the *Sangeetaratnakara* where dance is divided into three distinct categories, namely *natya*, *nritya*, and *nritta*. *Natya* here corresponds to drama, *nritya* to gesticulation when it is performed to the words sung in a musical melody, and *nritta* is a demonstration of rhythm through the graceful movement of the body. Though all these aspects use postures and gestures of the human body as their medium, the ultimate objective is to spring up the sentiment of the mind, *rasa*. Performers often give into the fetishization of knowledge in this respect by equating it to the accumulative experience of the passing years, being completely oblivious of the fact that every phenomenon has its age. Robert Pogue Harrison (2014), who is the Rosina Pierotti Professor in Italian Literature in the Department of French & Italian at Stanford University, reflecting on the philosophy and phenomenology of age in a monologue on his radio show had commented:

> Think of the phenomenon of looking up at the sky . . . he saw the blue sky when he was a 7-year old boy, it was an experience of making a covenant with the cosmos, when he was in his 20's it was about abstractions, and now at 60 it is an experience of a dome he knows he will not inhabit much longer. The sky itself is (perhaps) ageless, but its agelessness appears different as the spectator ages. Every phenomenon is intimately bound up with the age of the perceiver or apprehender-a grandfather and his grandson looking at a redwood tree do not see same phenomenon or experience the same meaning.

The obvious implications may be explained with the help of an analogy concerning the performance of a *Javali* "Samayanide." *Javalis* are love poems usually performed towards the end of a Bharatanatyam performance. The verbal imagery in these compositions has immense potential for being rendered kinetically. The piece under consideration crystallizes a moment of lovecharacterized by such overwhelming sway of intensity that it aspires to transcend all civil inhibitions. Interestingly, when the middle-aged performer Priyadarshini Govind (1965–) performs this piece composed by Patnam SubramaniaIyer (1845–1902), the *nayika* becomes a living embodiment of the *parakiya-rasa*, the erotic feelings one has towards a paramour. However, when the same piece is performed by the octogenarian Prof. C. V. Chandrasekhar (1935–), it is interpreted as a prayer text, summoning the Lord to enter into the heart of the devotee. Besides the obvious gender binary which operates in shaping the codification of aesthetics in such matters, the understanding of the normative concept of age and ageing, I believe, plays a vital role in analysing such choice. In contrast to Govind's erotic treatment of the piece, there exists a certain conceptual frigidity in Chandrasekhar's rendition of the song, which is further problematized by his "exceptional" physical proficiency, rarely expected by society from a man in his 80s. It is also possible to link Chandrashekhar's performance to the "four *ashramas*" wherein the octogenarian self automatically places him beyond the erotic and the material, and, squarely within the realm of the spiritual, associated with "sannyasa." In both the cases, however, the performers successfully play to the gallery, dancing to the tune.

It is a general assumption, hence, that with growing age, performers move from physically more demanding components of dance to components which allow them to come to terms with the ageing body. Some classically trained dancers may also believe that the use of stage presence informed by maturity at this stage of their career is more important than performing multiple pirouettes and other feats of virtuosity associated with younger bodies. Classically trained dancers are also often keenly aware of prevailing social codes for appropriate self-presentation in performance, allied with a concern to protect their own self from ridicule in a culture of ageism in which youth and gendered sexuality are conflated. They manage this by developing strategies, as we may locate in the case of the Kathak Queen Sitara Devi (1920–2014).

Born around the festival of Dhanteras, she was known as *Dhanno* to her family. It was not until 1931 that she would evolve as the shining Sitara when Rabindranath Tagore, Sarojini Naidu, and Cowasji Jehangir would encounter her solo Kathak performance at Atiya Begum Palace in Mumbai. Though there hardly exists any video record of her early performances in concerts, one can fairly imagine her prowess from her stint in Indian cinema. People remembered her for films like *Roti* (1942) and *Najma*(1943),where her dances and the songs – *Sanjana Sanjh Bhayi Aan Milo* from the former and *Haule Haule Ulfat Mein Rakhna Kadam* from the latter – were the highlights of the film. She also choreographed dance numbers and sometimes performed in them herself right through the 1950s such as the snakedance in *Anjali*(1957) or the Holi dance in *Mother India* (1957). These performances are uniformly characterized by the complete control over her body, exhibiting extreme dexterity in her postures and gestures. The highpoint of her Kathak recitals would have been her synchronized fast footwork, *tatkar*, and sweeping spin, *chakkar*. However, as the popular columnist Sumana Ramanan recounts, in her later years, she took to *abhinaya*, the art of expression in Indian aesthetics:

> Instantly recognisable by her huge red bindi and hair left open, Sitara Devi would often turn up at the annual Swami Haridas Sangeet Sammelan in Mumbai to watch younger dancers. She did that again earlier this year, and also gave an impromptu performance. She could not do footwork, for which kathak is famous and which was her forte. But refusing to let age get in the way, she presented a ghazal sitting in a chair, restricting herself to abhinaya, the art of facial expressions, and hand movements.
>
> *(Sumana Ramanan 2014)*

In one of her most popular items from the late performances, she danced to a *bhajan* composed by the Vaishnava poet, Tulsidas (1511–1623) – *Thumak Chalata Rama Chandra*. This particular piece glorifies the juvenile stunts of the Hindu deity, Rama. In such cases, it is usual among performers to shift between the role of the young Rama and his mother, Kaushalya, in graceful maturity while demonstrating *abhinaya*. However, Sitara always chose to stick to the persona of the aged mother whenever she had to indulge in this performative narration. She would strictly interpret the song from the point of view of a *nayika* whose soul is completely immersed in the overwhelming flow of the *vatsalya rasa* – the sentiment that is born out of parental affection. Such interpretation would allow her to not only be in line with the lived realities of her aged body but would also enhance and satiate the expectations that the members of the audience might have from a dancer at her "age."

However, to problematize the issue further in her case, we will have to read into the hints that Ramanan provides in her article. Sitara's public appearances have always been exuberant in terms of the costume, jewellery, and make-up she chose to wear for such occasions. The signature style statement, which Ramanan speaks of, did not only mark her as to be distinctly different when in a mixed crowd but also served as a throwback to her glorious past. As her inner circle of friends and well-wishers would confirm, a visit to her Mumbai apartment would never be complete without her ardent exhibition of the resplendent costumes that she wore during her stage performances. She would urge visitors to stay back for a screening of either song and dance sequences from the magnanimous 1960 epic historical drama *Mughal-e-Azam*, which was directed by her second husband K. Asif (1922–1971), or the 1955 classic *Jhanak Jhanak Payal Baje*, in which her nephew Gopi Krishna (1935–1994) played the male lead. This constant bracketing of the present seeking shelter in the past, in her case, is a testimony of the hard trudge that dancers in our society have to endure. With sheer dearth of dance philanthropists for elderly dancers, performers often succumb to the perils of ageist behaviour.

Sitara's strategy of conforming to *abhinaya* as her late style seems to be popular with most other dancers performing in her tradition. The few video recordings that have survived of the celebrated dancers from the Lucknow *Gharana* of Kathak would reaffirm such occurrence. Whether it is Kathak Samrat Shambhu Maharaj (1910–1970) or his brother Lachhu Maharaj (1907–1978), most practitioners of Kathak would perform *Kabitangi Bol* or dance to a *Thumri* in their senior years. Interestingly, Lacchu Maharaj would often appear on the stage with his young disciples such as Padma Sharma, show a piece or two, and then settle down beside the artist accompanying in tabla. Let us not forget that he is the man responsible for choreographing the celebrated dance sequences in Bombay Cinema classics such as *Mughal-e-Azam*(1960) and *Pakeezah*(1972). Subsequently, on account of such reputation, members of the audience would surely await his appearance on the stage. But in addition to that, his daunting presence bore testimony to the authority that his experiential learning and the social reception of his age gave him and it must have been interesting to note the ways in which he exerted the same to establish control over the bodily movement of the young disciple. The intention behind every single move is expected to be his, the execution hers. It is but a well-established convention that the young artist must have her *talim* of the ancient from the old master. However, where creativity is celebrated as the prerogative of youth, unfortunately ageing is made synonymous with a decrement in the capacity for generating and accepting innovations. *Rasikas* will surely remember such asynchronous dancepartners on stage like Odissi exponents Kelucharan Mohapatra (1926–2004) and Sanjukta Panigrahi (1944–1997) as well as Kathak virtuosos Birju Maharaj (1938–) and Saswati Sen (1953–), or for that instance, Kuchipudi dancing couple Raja Reddy (1943–) and Radha Reddy (1955–). In all such instances, the sheer presence of the respective dancing duo on the stage must have borne the promise of new insight into issues concerning age and gender.

The case of Odissi may provide some insight. The institutionalization of Odissi as a form of classical dance in post-independence India was a project led by an all-male group of dancers who went on to form "Jayantika." As Kelubabu's disciple and biographer Ileana Citaristi (1968–) would confirm, associates included Kali Charan Patnaik (1897–1978), Pankaj Charan Das (1919–2003), Kelucharan Mahapatra (1926–2004), Deba Prasad Das (1932–1986), Mayadhar Raut (1930–), Buda Chowdhury, Dayanidhi Das (–1979), D. N. Patnaik (1933–), and Raghunath Dutta(1933–)with Loknath Mishra (1921–2009)as the chairman of the initiative. In order to promote a common vision of the dance-form to the global audience, "Jayantika" was consolidated in 1957 to lay down guidelines for future generations of Odissi dancers. Interestingly though, the first line of star performers, whether Indrani Rahman(1930–1999) or Sanjukta Mishra (later Panigrahi) (1944–1997)and Kumkum Das (later Mohanty) (1946–), were all female protégée. Such representation of the *guru–chela* or teacher–performer relationship is a case in point. The young female performers would not only dance to the musical scores composed by the elderly male *Guru* but often the performance itself would be classified as a dedicatory act – a salutation towards the male god Jagannath, the male *Guru*, and the audience, mostly male in the early days. In addition, true to traditional values, it would be accepted that it is the *Guru* who is dancing through his disciples and the performer was to mirror the cultural heritage received through her discipleship.

Kelubabu's life as a performer itself provides a brilliant portrait of the artist as an "old" man. Not much is retained in the public consciousness of his early performances in Annapurna Theatre at Cuttack in the 1940s when Laxmipriya and Kelucharan Mahapatra performed in the style called *Odia Naach*. His lasting image is that which does not date back before the 1980s, when he started to reappear on stage as a solo performer, best known for virtuosic performances of *abhinaya*, especially the *ashtapadis* of Jayadeva's *Geeta Govinda* in which he effortlessly delineated the state of Radha.

Kelubabu's soft lines and supple gestures allowed him to put the advanced years to his benefit and he would often use it masterfully on the stage. In a 2001 performance for the Parampara Series at New Delhi, he initiated his recital with a prayer to Lord Jagannath, *Dinabandhu Ehi Ali Sri Chamure*, wherein the devotee expressedhis desire to always be near his deity. Skilfully playing with his agency on the stage, he would often place his hand on the shoulder of the Jagannath idol placed on the stage to convey the devoted intimacy between the worshipper and the worshipped. Then he would break away from the text of the song to elaborate on the mention of *Rangacharan*, the lotus feet, with an annotation from the tales of Ramayana. He would instantaneously take up the persona of the old boatman, *Kewat*, who is to ferry Rama, Sita, and Lakshmana across the Ganges during their exile. An ardent devotee of Rama, the boatman is remembered for his innocent faith which he portrayed by washing the Lord's feet.

The immediate next performance for the day was a sensual evocation of the rite of love – *Kuru Yadunandana*. This *ashtapadi*from *Geeta Govinda* is an affirmation of sensuality at its best and went on to be remembered as one of Kelubabu's most popular choreographies. In the sixth couplet of this piece, Radha urges Krishna to deck up her hair and comes up with a catalogue of embellishments for the petite tresses at the hairline and the beautiful mass of hair which fell about her. Further, the hair is likened to the *chamar*, fly-whisk, and *dhwaja*, flag, of Kamadeva, the god of love and desire in Hindu mythology. During his maiden appearances in the 1980s, Kelucharan was perhaps still a little insecure about the public's reaction to his bald head, and therefore wore a black wig which made him look "younger." However, once he had come to terms with his own body, as a man with little hair on his head, he had no difficulties in showing the lustrous shape of Radha's hair in absence of the wig. His craftsmanship allowed him enough expertise to offer a bodily vision which takes away from his body as a dancer.

Many may argue that the young dancer is more conscious of the public image whereas the master has experience enough to feel free. However, Kelubabu's disciple and renowned artist Sharon Lowen opined:

Decades ago, I was stung by a comment by a "friend-emy" who said my dance was appreciated because I was beautiful. Besides not believing then that I was any more attractive than any other, I understood this to mean that the quality of my artistic expression was irrelevant –very depressing! From that day forward I looked forward to the time when I was aged and my dance would be respected for artistry alone. Later I had my doubts as to whether an older female dancer was as valued as a male, in that, when you see a balding man evoke a young maiden, he clearly has surmounted the limitations of sex and age and it is much appreciated. However, when you see a woman with age lines on her face and no waistline portraying a heroine in love, it is perhaps more' difficult to separate the artist from images of your grandmother whom you'd rather not think of in terms of *shringara rasa*.

(personal communication, June 21, 2020)

Consequentially, let us not forget that one of the most compelling features of ageing policy has been a growth of interest in gerontological research into how older people and the ageing process are socially perceived and understood, and one of the recurrent themes of this research is that, while ageing is a biological phenomenon, it is always meaningfully interpreted within a social context.

Researchers from social gerontology, sociology, philosophy, and anthropology have been able to establish the fact that ageing is not simply biological and uniform in its effects; rather, it has been argued that humans age at different rates and experience ageing differently. These differences in ageing are not individual idiosyncrasies that are independent of the culture in which we live. Rather, as social constructionists contend, the experience of ageing in humans is historically and culturally specific, as are the meanings others attribute to it. A social constructionist account of ageing is therefore useful in understanding how we are "aged" by culture as much as by biology, and how we are categorized as aged, gendered, classed entities, and so on. This account of ageing, as discussed earlier, also allows us to appreciate that the onset of ageing is not only biologically set but also culturally monitored. Let us look at the case of two different performers, who, let's say, are roughly of the same age in their lifetime at the point of consideration but historically belong to different worlds.

Mallika Sarabhai (1954–) is a noted Kuchipudi and Bharatanatyam classical dancer and activist in her 60s. She is known for her views on societal education and women's empowerment, and ways in which she incorporates such concerns in her work in the capacity of a "communicator." Her performances, till date, are a marker of her practice which is based on rigour and dailiness, and her *padams* and *tillanas* bear a stamp of strenuous efforts. She has also received great appreciation forperforming with her son, Revanta Sarabhai (1984–). Together, in their recitals, they address contemporary issues such as same-sex love and inter-community relationships, inducing optimism in a hostile world. For instance, a *padam* entitled *Tavaro*, performed by Mallika Sarabhai, is a personal favourite. In Bharatanatyam, a *padam* typically showcases the dancer's emotive skills, allowing for multiple interpretations of the lines in the song-text. Framing the piece in a contemporary context, the performance enquires – "How can love ever be wrong?" – reflecting on the prejudice and intolerance that is all around us. Though the padam typically begins with a moving portrayal of filial love, it connects the emotion with the love that a woman may hold for another woman. It questions the heteronormative society's handling of the same with disdain and violence. However, the piece is highly evocative in linking this episode with the intervention that the world seeks in the love that exists between a woman and a man –through the concept of gotra or lineage, the traps of religious idolatry, and the malpractice of colourism. The final twist, however, is accomplished in revisiting and reviving the paradigmatic love story of Radha and Krishna by interpreting it as an age gap relationship, with the female partner being elder in this case. The narrator in the song-text promulgates – "You were in a cradle, when Radha loved you/ She a woman at her bloom, you a mere boy."

In more recent productions of Darpana Academy of Performing Arts led by Mallika Sarabhai,like the Mother River, the world premiere of which was conducted at the newly renovated Natarani theatre at Ahmedabad on Sep 21, 2018, female dancers played drums with the male dancer, breaking away from "tradition." However, when performing in more "solemn" ceremonies, she chooses to portray *nayikas* such as Draupadi, at the prime of beauty and grace. While reviewing such portrayals, people are often influenced bythe pre-conceived popular reception of such figures in performing arts and hence, often fall short of peeling off the layers of such a performance. The rasika may be easily attracted to see the representation of youth on stage dazzled with energy but it exerts a deeper demand to experience how a dancer fills the life experiences into abhinaya. Mallika Sarabhai recollects:

> Amma used to always say that you can never be a Bharatanatyam dancer unless you have experienced true and painful heartbreak. So much in dancing is about longing and loss, the search for the Supreme, whoever or whatever they might be for each of us. That pain needs certain age to be experienced. I find ten and fifteen year olds mimicking despair and anguish, quite disturbing. An older dancer needs to continue much more physical work to remain an evocative carrier of the experiences of life.
> *(personal communication, August 3, 2021)*

However, by the time the ace filmmaker Satyajit Ray (1921–1992) was working on his 33-minute documentary titled *Bala* (1976), the legend herself, Tanjore Balasaraswati (1918–1984), was 58 years old. Ray believed that by this age, Balasaraswati has passed beyond her prime as a performer and went on to state, "Bala filmed at 58 was better than Bala not being filmed at all."[3] Conforming to the director's vision, then, the central piece of this documentary appears to be Balasarawati performing the famous composition by the Kannada dialectician Vyasatirtha (1460–1539), *Krishna Nee Begane Baaro*, curiously staged along a beach, where she takes up the persona of Krishna's adoptive mother, Yashoda. This moving image of Balasaraswati, almost losing herself to a devotional trance in this sequence, suits perfectly with the social reception of the age bracket that Ray makes a passing reference to,

136 Shantanu Majee

in the comment quoted previously. Manoeuvring of that kind employs itself in such subtle manners that this central piece almost overshadows the final segment of the film which showcases Balasaraswati's solo performance of a *padavarnam*. Historically speaking, Balasaraswati's oeuvre had always been characterized bya curious mixture of *natya* and *nritta*. A regular recital for her would begin with *Alarippu*, the invocation, normally followed by a *Jatiswaram*, which would provide plenty of scope for pure dancing as in this case, movement is entirely controlled by the rhythm. The centrepiece of the recital would be a *Varnam*. It is usually a love lyric which is interspersed with rhythmic motifs. Once the *Varnam* has been performed, the *Padams* and the *Javalis* play themselves out. These, as suggested previously, are purely lyrical dances with a predominance of dramatic representation. However, the performance must return to pure dance before it can end itself and so the final act would have been a *Tillana*. In a now famous speech at the Tamil Isai Sangam, Madras, she compared the structure of a dance recital and its contents to the spaces within a temple and their respective hierarchy of divinity:

> The Bharatnatyam recital is structured like a great temple: we enter through the *gopuram* (outer hall) in *Alarippu*, cross the *ardhamandapam* (half-way hall) in *Jatiswaram*, then the *mandapa* (great hall) in *Sabdam*, and enter the holy precinct of the deity in the *Varnam*... In dancing to the *padams*, one experiences the containment, cool and quiet of entering the sanctum from its external precinct. The expanse and the brilliance of the outer corridors disappear in the dark inner sanctum and the rhythmic virtuosities of the *varnam* yield to the soul-stirring music and *abhinaya* of that padam. Dancing the *padam* is akin to the juncture when the cascading lights of worship are withdrawn and the drumbeats die down to the simple and solemn chanting of sacred verses in the closeness of god. Then the *Tillana* breaks into movement like the final burning of camphor accompanied by a measure of din and bustle. In conclusion, the devotee takes to his heart the god he has so far glorified outside and the dancer completes the traditional order by dancing to a simple devotional verse.
>
> *(Lakshmi Vishwanathan 2008: 150–151)*

Unfortunately, Ray's vision fails to encapsulate such diversity in an artist who resisted from tailoring her craft to suit the tastes of all and sundry. However, Bala's own understanding of her audience was marked with an ageist disdain as "she believed no one in the modern world could fully comprehend the profundity of her art."[4]

The choice of the central piece in Ray's documentary, steeped in *vatsalya* rasa, also pays no heed to Balasaraswati's lifelong struggle in establishing the depiction of *shringara* rasa in Bharatanatyam. From the demise of

Dasiattam or Sadir dance in the first decades of the last century to the transformation of the Devadasi Abolition Bill into an act in 1947, the reinvention of Bharatanatyam has often referred to the infamous stand-off between Rukmini Devi Arundale (1904–1986) and Balasaraswati on appropriate dance content and gesture befitting the modern audience that has been sublimated into an argument between *bhakti* and *shringara*. Though it is not necessary to pit one against the other, Ray's prioritizing the former to the latter subscribes to an ageist review of her works and delimits the scope of her artistic purview.

In the case of both, Sarabhai and Balasaraswati, the issue of ageing in the mature female Indian classical dancer may be juxtaposed with a number of other themes: their dancing becoming more "layered" with maturity and informed by life experience, and the perception of ageing as a "good thing" for a dancer because, in such case, maturity, creativity, and activism (rather than reiterating and reproducing existing structures) go hand in hand. Age also confirms some to establish a break with traditional ways of moving in order to discover new forms of expression. In the context of the Indian tradition, where dance is less of a spectacle, and more of an individual dancer's pursuit, to the expression of a voice, a counter-discourse to patriarchal power relations in which "women," "people of color," and older people – particularly older women – are for the most part marginalized, the dance-platform also evolves as a site for subversion of gender stereotypes.

Nevertheless, artists may often use age as a ploy while choosing which items to play for a particular audience or rather which not to play. Let me recall an anecdote. On a wintry evening in the mid-1990s, the *Tabla* virtuoso Kishan Maharaj in his 70s was performing at the Bhuwalka Award Ceremony in Kolkata. He was onthe verge of completing his recital with the 16-beat *Teental*, when a connoisseur among the members of the audience pleaded, "*Tanik Pancham Sawari to sunaye dijo, Maharaj*" [Amuse us with a rendition of the 15-beat cycle named Pancham Sawari, Sir] to which he replied, "*Bhaiya, umar ka lihaz to karo!*" [Allow some respite on account of my age]. That did not restrain him, though, to finish off his recital with a brilliant *Ganesh Paran* which also calls for remarkable physical strength and control!

Interestingly, in the arena of Indian Classical Dance, male performers have had an interesting legacy. For many, a male dancer is an unpleasant experience; just less attractive than the voluptuous danseuse. Echoing the concerns of Amritlal Parekh, the autocratic father in Dattani's *Dance Like a Man* (1989), one might say: "A woman in a man's world may be considered as being progressive. But a man in a woman's world is pathetic."[5] An examination of such attitudes towards the male dancer would reveal that what is at stake is the development of modern, middle-class attitudes towards the male body and the expressive aspects of male social behaviour. This

138 Shantanu Majee

might also serve to be an entry point to investigate the socially produced parameters of and on male behaviour as expressed in representations of masculinity in Indian Classical Dance. The various facets of this issue, however, differ across various traditions of Indian Classical Dance. In Odissi and Kathak, perhaps, there are as many male dancers as females. However, Bharatanatyam suffers from a lopsided sex ratio, in spite of the revelatory remarks that distinguished critic Ashish Mohan Khokar has to share:

> The gurus were all males. The musicians were all males and the mainstream dancers then were all males too, mostly. The first generation I'm talking about: Gurus like Meenakshi Sundaram Pillai, Muthukumaran Pillai, the two giants who trained nearly 90% of first gen of iconic BN names like Ram Gopal, US Krishna Rao, Nala Najan, Bhaskar Roy Chowdhury, Chitrasena... add Kathakali gurus, all males, who taught Uday Shankar, Gopinath, Anand Shivram, Yog Sunder, Gopalkrishna... In Odishi, the four pillars, all males: Adiguru Pankaj Charan Das, Kelucharan Mohapatra, Deba Prasad Das and Mayadhar Raut. In Manipuri, Amobi Singh, Atombi Singh and Bipin Singh (though he was an outcast in Manipur and taught mostly well-off girls of Mumbai like the Jhaveri sisters and later to many in Kolkata). Kathak: all males...and many Maharajas and Ganganis, in and out of Jaipur and Lucknow but let's say meeting grounds were Delhi and Bombay - Achchan, Shambhu, Lachhu and then Birju, Kundanlal, Madanlal, Sundarlal Gangani. Have I forgotten any mainstream form? Of yes, the virile men of Andhra doing Kuchipudi: the Sastrys, the Satyams and the Pasumarthys. Add Nataraja Ramakrishna and we are back to square one: Nataraja!
>
> *(Ashish Mohan Khokar 2014)*

The issue is further problematized when one attempts to understand gender difference relationally and situationally. What gendered identity, then, the male dancer puts up while delineating the bodily experiences of a female character? Are the emotions perceived to be gendered too? If the male body is culturally taken to be the norm against which female anatomical and temperamental traits are judged, then what happens to the biology of gender difference when the male body assumes a female form?

Unfortunately, this chapter will not be able to provide an adequate response to such queries but there is no denial to the fact that the professional space has not only limitations but also certain liberties. The professional stage allows certain subversive acts to the male performer which may bring in criticism if replicated in the greater world beyond the stage but it is a fact that the continuous embodiment of the other in the professional field, imparts to the aged male body certain proficiency where the body becomes its own archive. The dancer's body is not a prosthesis of the performer's self like a musical instrument is to a musician – it is that self-in-expression embodied. So when the septuagenarian Kathak Guru Birju Maharaj takes up the persona of an abhisarika, one who secretly goes out to seek the lover, it may establish counter-narratives to hegemonic gender–ageist discourses and provides alternative readings of what an "older" male dancer can be and do. Art has certainly more to itself than inappropriate bodies, or how else may one define a 70-year-old Odissi exponent Kelucharan Mohapatra hop and dance to depict the gait of Radha with such rapture, but all art must be represented through the body? This is where the need arises to read instances not under the design of a general scheme but in their particularities.

There is a lot of criticism on art that has surfaced in art itself and an acknowledgement of the same may contemporarize the traditional. Such an endeavour has the potential to reflexively revise the contemporary, as opposed to a linear, fixed, and prescriptive traditionalist approach that is projected to be seamlessly flowing from antiquity to modernity. New age artists such as Navtej Singh Johar (1959–) have been examining the idea of the body in time and ways in which the expressions that find a voice on the stage speak of the sensory responses of the body as it grows and changes.

> I don't see dance gendered at all. I think dance has been polarised between being moral-immoral, male-female, modern-traditional ... and they are all bogus binaries. So for me the question doesn't even enter my mind. It allows you the freedom to be man, woman – very erotic woman, very erotic man – animal, snake, wind...it's all the same. And I think that should be the focus. That is the focus.
>
> *(Navtej Johar 2013)*

During a personal communication conducted in July 2020, Navtej stressed the need foremotional maturity in the practice of Indian Classical Arts. He also mentioned that at times young dancers may feel acutely image-conscious which an established performer need not worry about and hence feels free to express one's mind. He referred to the brilliant career of the veteran danseuse Vyjayanthimala Bali (1936–), who has been a disciple of Vazhuvoor Ramiah Pillai, K. P. Kittappa Pillai, and K. N. Dhandayuthapani Pillai. Vyjayanthimala hashad the privilege of working with *nattuvanars*, expert musicians who accompanied the devadasi dance in the capacity of a dance-master, music conductor, and vocal percussionist. Her training enabled her to extend the practice of her art professionally as long as to her 80s and to such great heights that in a response to her public performance in 2019, a tweet message read: "That she would take up the challenge of performing the most elaborate number in a Bharatanatyam sequence is admirable. More power to Vyjayanthimalaji and boo to ageism."[6] In a recent interview, Vyjayanthimala herself clarified the rigour of her training:

140 Shantanu Majee

> We didn't leave out a single detail. In the Thaiyya Thai set, we practised all 10. We had 72 adavus. The adavu foundation with araimandi, the muzhumandi to araimandi movement, straight elbows without sagging, all were important. I was a good student and Guru Kittappa was happy with me. I would not sit down or drink water during practice. I would dance in front of the mirror to get it right. Adavusutham and angasutham were most important. Laya also — the salangai and the talam had to go together, the mridangam would follow the feet.
>
> *(Vyjayanthimala Bali 2020)*

Acquaintances confirm that there's still no break in active dancing and golfing in Vyjayanthimala's daily routine to ensure the spring in her step.

Navtej's own appearance with his well-groomed beard and brawny figure on stage has raised much public attention. However, he has consistently involved his dance background to inform his yoga practice which has enhanced his ability to centre his attention on his body, which is now in its 60s.

> I am convinced that each little part of the body has both an autonomous drive or initiative, which we need to honor, and might also have a "story" to tell. A story that can be told and fulfilled through shapes, sounds, and movement-textures. Also, dance has given me the capacity to engage and evoke imagery. Dance poetics has taught me to liberally free-associate, thus my teaching and practice is rife with imagery, which then translates to language and word-imagery. To me, linguistics and yoga are inextricably intertwined! It is not a passive practice of believing and following, but truly a practice of organizing, articulating, and absorbing thought. Therefore it is a practice of body, breath, and speech.
>
> *(Navtej Johar 2019)*

Such understanding was brilliantly portrayed in Navtej's January 2017 performance at Kolkata in celebration of 200 years of Presidency College, where he chose to perform *Meenakshi Me Mudam Dehi*, a celebrated composition by Muthuswami Dikshithar (1775–1835). The agile body of a dancer enabled Navtej to break into a spontaneous footwork at one point while elaborating on the silence and stillness in the performance. Aptly justified as a symbolism to represent the notion of eternal bliss which the aforementioned composition elaborates on, such variation well executed by Navtej's well-toned and long-limbed body added subtlety as well as intensity to his recital.

Navtej in his own journey has drawn much inspiration from the silver-haired danseuse-feminist Chandralekha (1928–2006) who interpreted dance through yoga for the exploration of a tradition of body language. Such context further intensifies the concept of age being relative and consolidates the idea of age establishing a direct propensity towards the lived reality of an individual body:

> Industrial society surges ahead, reducing the human body to a mechanical appendage. It is almost as if various components in the body are being slowly phased out to be replaced by mechanical gadgets – "the dreamt of metallisation of man" – as Walter Benjamin quotes Fascist philosopher Filippo Marinretti as having said. Under capitalism, people live at a distance from their own bodies. This is as much an indication of the alienation of man from himself as from his labour, besides being a direct impediment to praxis. Neutralise their physicality, and the system need have no fear of any potentially revolutionary class. The idea of active, physical intervention gets progressively replaced by passive verbalism. A brief survey of the material foundations of Indian dance forms will give some insights into our present predicament, where the divide between idea and action is continuously widening. All primary Indian dance forms, originating in primitive and tribal societies, are solidly linked with work activity. They are intimately related to functions of daily life – like food-gathering, hunting, fishing, cultivating and harvesting. Tribal dances are particularly distinguished by their sources in rituals, gymnastics and martial arts. Dancing, in these early communities, was a means of expression as well as a method of building up energy circuits within the body and aligning with the rhythm of the universe.
>
> *(Chandralekha 1979)*

Chandralekha's entire life has been governed by coming to terms with the memory of the body as her productions have valiantly confronted the rigid binary of youth and age by making people learn "how to be and not just appear."[7] In her celebrated essay *Who Are These Age-Old Female Figures?* Chandralekha herself elaborates on the iconography of the female in cultural studies wherein the idea of the ageing body is found to be more ritualized than real. RustomBharuchapicks up this thread while concluding her sensitive book on the danseuse by imparting an important lesson on the importance of embracing immediacy as a natural state:

> Many years ago, while being driven through a secluded part of Rajasthan, she saw a woman running against the sky, her red skirt sharply etched against the sand, billowing with the sheer flow of her movement. As Chandra drove past, she turned around to have a better look at this radiantly youthful woman only to realise that she was old and wrinkled and running against the sky.
>
> "At that moment", Chandra says, "I made a promise to myself that I would be like her".
>
> *(Bharucha 1995: 384)*

142 Shantanu Majee

It is important perhaps, then, to propose new ways of interpreting the circuitous paths that such energies may take rather than conforming to an "age"-old discourse. Let me conclude by appreciating one such endeavour that drew much attention in a Bharatanatyam recital held recently at the Rasika Ranjana Sabha in Kolkata, wherein much-acclaimed performer Rama Vaidyanathan (1968–) presented a Sanskrit version culled out of *Guru Granth Sahib* that spoke of ten stages in human life where desire plays a prominent role. Aptly titled *Jeeva Dashavastha* (i.e. The Ten Stages of Human Life), the piece charts the phases in which various forms of desire may manifest itself through the human body between infancy and death. Strikingly enough, the phases do not attempt to locate themselves atcertain years of age but rather retain their fluidity with the promise of appearing or withdrawing anytime in life. Such openness calls for a wider understanding of age with new promises for classical arts in altered times.

Acknowledgement

Amlan Das Gupta, Jadavpur University, Kolkata; Ananya Chatterjea, University of Minnesota, Minnesota; Aniruddha Knight, Chennai; Bhavana Reddy, Los Angeles, California; Charulatha Banerjee, Kolkata; Kalidas Swaminathan, New Delhi; Lekha Mukhopadhyay, Jogamaya Devi College, Kolkata; Mallika Sarabhai, Ahmedabad; Monami Nandy, Kolkata; Navtej Johar, New Delhi; Nilanjana Gupta, Jadavpur University, Kolkata; P. Mukunda Kumar, Visva Bharati, Shantiniketan; Pallabi Chakravorty, Swarthmore College, Philadelphia; Rahi Soren, Jadavpur University, Kolkata; Rita Ganguly, New Delhi; Sharon Lowen, New Delhi; Shriyana Krishna, Varanasi; Subikash Mukherjee, Kolkata; Sukanya Rahman, Orrs Island, Maine; Sunil Kothari, New Delhi; Sushree Chakraborty, Jogamaya Devi College, Kolkata; Urmila Bhirdikar, Shiv Nadar University, Greater Noida; Vandana Alase Hazra, Kolkata; Vikram Iyengar, Kolkata; Vishal Krishna, Varanasi.

Notes

1 Kapila Vatsyayan, *Indian Classical Dance*, 13.
2 Ursula M. Staudinger in her 1999 essay reviews the study of wisdom with regard to the relationship between age and wisdom.
3 British journalist and film historian Phil Hall, mostly remembered for his Bootleg Files column and as the author of *The History of Independent Cinema* (2009), has written on Satyajit Ray's *Bala* (1976). He confirms specific observations in this regard made by Ray's biographer Andrew Robinson. Douglas M. Knight Jr. also mentions it in *Balasaraswati:Her Art & Life* (2011).
4 Lakshmi Vishwanathan, *Women of Pride: The Devadasi Heritage*, 151.
5 Mahesh Dattani, *Dance Like a Man*, 50.

6 Smita Prakash, who made this tweet, has been the News Editor at Asian News International (ANI) and the India Correspondent for Channel News Asia, a Singapore-based broadcaster.
7 Rustom Bharucha, *Chandralekha: Woman Dance Resistance*, 333.

Bibliography

Anon. "The Bootleg Files: Bala." *Filmthreat*, 18 May 2012. filmthreat.com/uncat egorized/the-bootleg-files-bala/.

Bali, Vyjayanthimala. "The Araimandi Debate in Bharatanatyam." Interview by Rupa Srikanth, *The Hindu*, 23 Jul. 2020. www.thehindu.com/entertainment/ dance/the-araimandi-debate-in-bharatanatyam/article32173863.ece.

Banerji, Anurima. *Dancing Odissi: Paratopic Performances of Gender and State.* Seagull Books, 2019.

Bharucha, Rustom. *Chandralekha: Woman Dance Resistance.* Indus, 1995.

Blumenthal-Barby, J. S. "How Old Are You? Philosophy of Age and Its Relevance for Bioethics." *Bioethics*, 24 Jun. 2014. www.bioethics.net/2014/06/how-old-are -you-philosophy-of-age-and-its-relevance-for-bioethics/.

Chakravorty, Pallabi, and NilanjanaGupta. *Dance Matters Too: Markets, Memories, Identities.* Routledge, 2018.

Chandralekha. "The Militant Origins of Indian Dance." The Wire, 9 Dec. 2018. thewire.in/the-arts/the-militant-origins-of-indian-dance.

———. "Who Are These Age-Old Female Figures?" *The Wire*, 6 Dec. 2020. thewi re.in/women/who-are-these-age-old-female-figures.

Citaristi, Ileana. *The Making of a Guru – KelucharanMohapatra: His Life and Times.* Manohar Books, 2015.

Dattani, Mahesh. *Dance Like a Man.*Penguin Books, 2006.

Johar, Navtej. "Dance Has Been Polarised... All Bogus Binaries." *PURUSH: The Global Dancing Male*, 21 Dec. 2013. purush2013.blogspot.com/2013/12/a-q uickie-with-navtej-singh-johar.html.

———. "Marrying. Dance and Yoga." Interview by HollyMakimaa. *The Crazy Wisdom Community Journal*, 1 Jan. 2019. www.crazywisdomjournal.com/ featuredstories/2019/1/1/marrying-dance-and-yoga-an-interview-with-navtej -johar.

Khokar, Ashish Mohan. "Purush: Male Moves Through the Century." *Narthaki*, 9 Jan. 2014. www.narthaki.com/info/tdhc/tdhc36.html.

Knight Jr., M. Douglas. *Balasaraswati: Her Art & Life.* Westland, 2011.

Kumar, Pushpendra, editor. *Natyashashtra of Bharatamuni.* New Bharatiya Book Corporation, 2006.

Menon, Narayana. *Balasaraswati.* Inter-National Cultural Centre, 1963.

Rahman, Sukanya. *Dancing in the Family: The Extraordinary Story of the First Family of Indian Dance.* Speaking Tiger, 2019.

Ramanan, Sumana. "Sitara Devi, Kathak Dancer Who Lived Life on Her Own Terms, Dies at 94." *Scroll*, 26 Nov. 2014. scroll.in/article/691711/sitara-devi-kat hak-dancer-who-lived-life-on-her-own-terms-dies-at-94.

Schwaiger, Elisabeth. *Ageing, Gender, Embodiment and Dance: Finding a Balance.* Palgrave Macmillan, 2012.

@smitaprakash. "That She Would Take Up the Challenge of Performing the Most Elaborate Number in a Bharatanatyam Sequence is Admirable. More Power to

Vyjayanthimalaji and Boo to Ageism." *Twitter*, 26 Dec. 2019. twitter.com/smitaprakash/status/1210054917773086720. 11.30 AM.

Staudinger, Ursula M. "Older and Wiser? Integrating Results on the Relationship between Age and Wisdom-Related Performance." *International Journal of Behavioral Development*, vol. 23, no. 3, 1999, pp. 641–664.

Vatsyayan, Kapila. *Indian Classical Dance*. Publications Division, Ministry of Information & Broadcasting, Government of India, 1974.

Vishwanathan, Lakshmi. *Women of Pride: The Devadasi Heritage*. Roli Books, 2008.

8

MORE THAN MEMORIES

Aging and the Attachment to Material Objects in Three Indian Short Stories

Ira Raja

Scholarly engagement with attachment to material possessions in late life in India remains scarce. This chapter strives to compensate for this neglect by offering close readings of three short stories, one each from Urdu, Telugu, and English, in which dominant cultural norms that call for detachment and withdrawal from the material world in late life are challenged through a foregrounding of intense relationships that older people form with particular objects and possessions.[1] The chapter also pursues an implicit engagement with existing research in social gerontology where the role objects play in facilitating connections with the past is acknowledged without adequate recognition of their function in the lived present. (See Coleman and Wiles 2020; Christine Nord 2013; Keefer et al. 2012.) Roles and meanings attached to cherished objects, I will argue, can change radically over the life course, depending on individuals and the circumstances in which they find themselves, in ways that are not always intended or anticipated by individual subjects.

While the objects in all of the three stories discussed in my essay – be it the pillow in Ismat Chughtai's "Tiny's Granny," the armchair in Tulasi Chaganti's "Sunstroke," or the ancestral *haveli*[2] in Chaman Nahal's "The Womb" – at some level compensate for the instability and thinning out of human relationships in old age, they are also never *just* compensatory. The pillow, the armchair, and the haveli may be redolent of memories from the past but that does not mean their significance is unyielding and fixed in time. The same objects, that is to say, can mean very different things over the life course, with new contexts and circumstances contributing to the meaning-giving process in ways that exceed human intention. Indeed, one of the basic insights of recent work in material culture studies has been the idea that

DOI: 10.4324/9780429352560-9

146 Ira Raja

objects have "social lives" of their own (Appadurai 1986). They may begin their journey through the world as commodities, defined primarily in terms of their monetary or exchange value, but once the economic exchange has taken place, they can become decommodified by the meaning that is invested in them by individuals who are themselves defined in terms of age, class, and gender (Woodward 2007: 29–30, 99–100, 102). Even though it is human beings who do the interpreting, the impetus for meaning is not always human in origin. Useful to this discussion is the concept of "affordance," which suggests that physical items lend themselves to certain kinds of interaction with humans: "An affordance is not bestowed upon an object by a need of an observer and his act of perceiving it. The object offers what it does because it is [physically] what it is" (J.J. Gibson, 139 [1979] quoted in Chapman 2006: 109). Far from simply absorbing meanings imposed on them from above, as the stories I will discuss show, cherished possessions, and other memorabilia as "reminiscentia," (i.e., as inducers of reminiscence) accrue meanings in the course of their interactions with people (Sherman 1991), their capacity for offering concrete and visible stimulation to the remembrance of things past useful in providing "symbolic support" for people's sense of individual continuity over the life course (Hepworth 2000: 73), and helping foster an imaginative identification with significant others who may have passed on (Turkle 2007: 8; Buse and Twigg 2014: 21; Hepworth 2000: 75). Circumstances can potentially play an important role in this process, contriving to afford new and hitherto unforeseen possibilities for objects to play a catalytic role in self-discovery and meaning-making. Developments in material culture studies in particular, have encouraged an understanding of the potentially creative, liberatory, constructive, expressive, and emotional relations people can share with material objects (Woodward 2007: 55). Even the most mundane forms of consumption and the most ordinary of individual consumers, from this perspective, have the capacity for cultural construction that brings inanimate objects to life (Woodward 2007: 109, 15), in a relationship characterized by mutuality and co-dependence (Chapman 2006: 208). To the extent that they help the elderly protagonists negotiate their strong attachment to the transient world, objects are valuable not just as the site of intense feeling but also as the means of managing that intensity.

In what follows, I look more closely by turns at a trio of stories, one in English and the other two translated into English from two different Indian languages, Telugu and Urdu, for the powerful ways in which each foregrounds a post-humanist perspective in which objects are conceived as "lively," agential, and responsible for meanings that at first glance seem to derive solely from the interpretive gaze of the subject. The significance of ordinary household items, I hope to show, emerges in their interface with people, in what is a graphic testimony to the dynamic interdependence between them.

Violent Objects in Ismat Chughtai's "Tiny's Granny"

Ismat Chughtai's "Tiny's Granny" (1954) is the story of a nameless, homeless old woman who can no longer support herself by doing odd jobs in the neighbourhood where she has lived her whole life (Chughtai 2010, 115–125). Even the destitute Granny, however, has one valued possession – her pillow. Packed mostly with other people's rubbish, discards, trinkets of little or no value, the pillow however also embodies a "material convoy" of possessions, accumulated over the life course, that honour important events, emotions, and relationships in the old woman's life (Buse and Twigg 2014: 20): her mother's kajal-box, her daughter Bismillah's dried navel string, a knob of turmeric in its sachet from her granddaughter's first birthday, and so on. The pillow accompanies Granny wherever she goes, until a monkey walks away with it one day, and in front of Granny's eyes starts to tear through its many layers:

> [The monkey] proceeded with the greatest enjoyment to peel the manifold skins off an onion—those same coverings over which Granny had pored with her weak and watering eyes, trying to hold them together with stitching. As every fresh cover came off Granny's hysterical wailing grew louder. And now the last covering was off, and the monkey began bit by bit to throw down the contents.
>
> *(Chughtai 2010: 123)*

The neighbourhood wakes up the following morning to discover the old woman has died. It was as though "Granny's life was in the pillow, and the monkey had torn the enchanted pillow with his teeth and thrust a red-hot iron bar into Granny's heart" (Chughtai 2010: 124).

For a destitute woman who lacks access to spaces that are genuinely private, Granny's pillow fulfils a number of roles in life. As a container of the sum of her material possessions, it affords Granny a sense of continuity over time, and being the only private object that she can claim, it also functions as, not the *symbol* of a home so much as the home itself (Buse and Twigg 2014; 19). But the significance of the pillow, and the various objects that it contains, is clearly surplus to the meaning-making capacity of the old woman. There is something about the shape and texture of the pillow that makes it possible for Granny to invest it with deep meaning. While the pillow's secret, private and enclosed character as emblematic of a vaginal, womblike space that others are barred from entering without permission, goes a long way in explaining the fatal consequences that the pillow's violation has for the old woman (Buse and Twigg 2014: 14, 16), what must also be clear is that this meaning can only emerge in the course of the pillow's unique interaction with the old woman, in a process that is mutually transformative.

148 Ira Raja

Not only is the significance attached to objects in excess of human intention, but it is also not necessarily stable across time and space. As "Tiny's Granny" ably demonstrates, objects can mean very different things over the course of their social trajectory. Thus, while the touch, texture, and smell of "memory objects," such as those carried in Granny's pillow, "can have a strong affective dimension, evoking past roles and aspects of the self" (Buse and Twigg 2014: 15), they are in her old age shrunk to the constricted space of the pillow. Many of these may have at one time been treasured for their biographical associations, signifying important events, people and relationships in Granny's life, but their functional value in the present is apparently limited, as they now lie in an indistinguishable heap alongside other people's discards and knick-knacks that Granny has pinched unnoticed from them. This grab bag of objects, all of which invoke some memory or the other, are now stitched away, inaccessible as "tactile or visual stimulus" for memories of the past (Buse and Twigg 2014: 21). By the same token, other people's discards have come to acquire significance for Granny over and above their original or functional value: As fillers for the pillow these objects now comprise an indispensable extension of Granny's embodied self, their tangible presence standing in for the reassuring solidity of a home in which their discrete status as memory objects is no longer critical.

"Tiny's Granny" pays particularly close attention to the socio-economic context in and against which relationships people share with objects finally unfold. While Granny's very life seems to reside in her bundle of things, in foregrounding her forced, as against voluntary dispossession, the story highlights the destitute old woman's inability to protect herself. Traits that would be sympathetically framed in gerontological theory as attempts to preserve the self by retrieving lost objects, roles, and attachments in her case are ridiculed by society, if not quite criminalized. This shock of having exposed, what Granny thought legitimized her claim to interiority and selfhood, continuity, and home, as stolen goods, is momentous enough to kill her. Relationships between people and their material possessions, the story shows, may be forged in the intimacy of hearts and minds but when forced to reckon with the world outside, such relationships can prove as fragile and ephemeral as the world they were originally meant to help negotiate.

If the meanings of sundry objects in Granny's pillow change radically over the course of her life and in ways that are not always intended or anticipated by her, they are also directed towards ends that are focused on an engagement with the present much more so than a memorialization of the past. Finally, the fact that it is actual physical contact with the discrete objects that kills Granny, once the layered encasings of the pillow that had protected her from the sight and touch of its contents are torn open, shows how objects which are prominently seen to offer continuity with the past are also capable of causing acute disruption. Indeed, it is the contact with the materiality of the physical objects, as they spill out of the pillow where they had laid safely hidden beneath the many layers of fabric, that Granny finds so intrusive; their exposure to the light of day shredding to bits her imagined relationship with the only community she has ever known.

Anchoring the Self in Tulasi Chaganti's "Sunstroke"

The old man in Tulasi Chaganti's Telugu short story, "Sunstroke" (1977), also finds himself deeply attached to an inanimate object – his dear old *Narasaraopeta* armchair. Although he is not materially impoverished, the old man still feels acutely about the absence of deference and care from his adult son, with whom he has come to live after his retirement from service. In much of North India, this gesture goes by the name of *"seva"* (Lamb 2000: 59–66). The lack of seva from one's children can render old people powerless in ways that may not be as readily apparent as material poverty but which are not any the less real for it. It is in this context that we are invited to read this particular old man's powerful attachment to his armchair which he had bought with his first salary many years ago. Personified as a friend and companion, the chair allows the old man to retrieve and sustain his subjective identity over time and changing circumstances as "an honest person." Although the satisfactions of such a narrative are at one level private, for it to sustain the old man's sense of self this narrative needs to be endorsed by those around him. Unfortunately, for the old man, this does not happen. Not pleased with the old-fashioned armchair occupying their front room, the old man's son replaces it with a flashy piece of furniture he has received as bribe from a client who has benefited from his dishonesty. In the absence of any textual references to traditional institutions in which one might locate one's identity and selfhood, such as family, work, and organized religion, which have historically played the role of providing continuity and coherence to people's lives in old age (Kenyon et al. 1999: 53), the armchair appears to be the old man's only link to his past and a source of some symbolic support for a sense of continuous and uninterrupted selfhood over the vagaries of time. It presents for him the only means he has of avoiding a fragmented, splintered life course in the world (Hepworth 2000: 73). Unsurprisingly, then, the callous rejection of the old man's armchair as a source of shame for the upwardly mobile son and daughter-in-law so radically disrupts his sense of self that he simply collapses and dies on the spot. Although the story ends with a reference to the rumour, by no means implausible, that it was from all the roaming around under the hot sun that afternoon that the old man suffered a sunstroke and died, the reader has reason to believe that it was the shock of his chair (and by extension, he himself) being rejected that had killed him. Far from anchoring a stable sense of self across time, the old man's attachment to his armchair becomes symptomatic of an anxiety about

150 Ira Raja

a selfhood that is not anchored in a network of familial relationships which observe the normative hierarchy in Indian families of parents over children.

Many of the themes prominent in "Tiny's Granny" reappear in "Sunstroke." After he retired from service and prepared to move in with his son, the old man let go of all his possessions acquired over a lifetime, except for his beloved armchair. He had wanted such a chair since he was a young boy but it was only after he got his first salary that he could actually go out and buy one for himself (Chaganti 2010: 110). Clearly, the armchair connects him equally with his childhood desires as also his capacity as a self-made man to fulfil them. The armchair is then an invaluable link to the past, spanning a series of associations going back to the beginning of his life. Left without a home to call his own, it is to his armchair that the old man turns when looking to rest. Like the pillow in "Tiny's Granny," the armchair is not a symbol of home so much as the thing itself: the only place he has left that is truly his own and one that makes him feel at rest. But as quickly becomes apparent, in the context of his son's house, the chair's role as a place of rest or refuge can no longer be taken for granted. Cast by the younger couple as ugly and old-fashioned, the chair's right to space in the front room is contested by more trendy and aspirational pieces of furniture, such as the sofa-set. The old man who had always taken great pride in his armchair now starts to invest newer shades of meaning to it, shades that deepen in significance in the light of his newer surroundings, increasingly furnished by dishonest means. From being a commodity he had purchased in the market, the chair now comes to stand for the old man's moral rectitude. Made out of wood, it can claim an organicity that gives the "shifty" sofa-cum-bed a run for its money. The unbending wooden solidity of the armchair offers a neat contrast to the flashy, fashionable, and expensive sofa-cum-bed which comes to stand for a moral flexibility that is characteristic of the son himself, who had gone against his father's hope and expectation that he would "swim against the tide rather than drift along the current along with the rest" (Chaganti 2010: 112). In claiming the armchair as an extension of his very self, the old man is also making a distinction between the values he stands for from those of his son. His attachment to this cherished object now no longer stands merely for a connection with a remote past; it also helps him define his identity in the lived present, in contradistinction to that of his son and daughter-in-law: "I bought this [chair] with my sweat and blood. Yes, this creature on this chair never accepted a bribe ... I won't stay here and nor will my chair" (Chaganti 2010: 114). As the armchair undergoes a change in status from being a place of rest from which to reflect placidly on the distant past to instead become a badge of honour won in the battle between morality and immorality, the reader is invited to reflect on the labile nature of meanings that material possessions accrue over time. At the same time, the story underscores how these meanings exceed the capacity and intention of individual agents, for the armchair's transformation of meaning cannot but be understood in the context of the son's home, populated as it is by overt signs of corruption.

Self-realization through Objects in Chaman Nahal's "The Womb"[3]

The object of attachment in Chaman Nahal's English short story, "The Womb" (1988), is a grand ancestral house. Traditionally, homes are built for one's children and grandchildren, and to die well is to die at home, surrounded by them all, in the full knowledge of the continuity of the family line. For Lala Ram Prashad, the nonagenarian protagonist of Nahal's story, his beloved home, his ancestral haveli, is all this, and more. The story begins by underscoring how the two entities, man and mansion, interpenetrate, to a point at which talking about one also invokes the other. Thus, Ram Prashad and his haveli mirror each other's sad state of neglect and disrepair: "This illness struck Lala Ram Prashad almost every winter. In spite of modernization, the haveli was too damp. It needed a new coat of paint. It needed some better ventilation, it needed a general cleaning up, and the family did not have the money for vast scale repairs" (Nahal 2010: 129). The discovery that his sons were planning to demolish the haveli after his death, and build high-rise apartments in its place, fills the old man's heart with grief. "His demise would mean the demise of many old values in the haveli, he was certain, but that it would mean the demise of the haveli itself he had not for a second thought of." The realization "[tears] a hole through [Ram Prashad's] emaciated skeleton of a body" (Nahal 2010: 132), pointing to a recurring theme in literature about ageing, linking bodies with the spaces they inhabit, with decaying houses often standing in for decaying people (Falcus 2012: 1387). It is not just Ram Prashad's physique that finds a reflection in the structure of the haveli; it is also his personality. Slowly and carefully, and always with good taste, the haveli has accommodated the signs of modernity: "The electric bulbs were lowered into the candle stand chandeliers. The phones were hidden behind niches. The TVs were firmly encased in heavy mahogany frames" (Nahal 2010: 126). But eventually the pace of change overtakes them both. It begins to dawn on Ram Prashad that the haveli will eventually need to make way for radical change just as he himself feels pressured to make way for the new generation to take its own decisions. The realization fills the old man with terror, pushing him to think of ways to rescue the haveli from this impending fate:

[H]e could still show them a trick or two. He would simply cut them out of his will. Pass all the property and the other savings on to his grandchildren. When that seemed too protracted, he thought of adding a line to the

152 Ira Raja

existing will that for the next fifty years the haveli was not to be rebuilt or sold or mortgaged or changed in any form whatsoever.

(Nahal 2010: 133)

What follows however is a twist in the tale, with Ram Prashad's initial anxiety about the fate of the haveli starting to give ground to an unexpected insouciance: "Why bother? Let them pull it down, if they so desire it" (Nahal 2010: 136). In his description of the features common to the bourgeoisie, Paul Davies observes that the insistence on enclosing oneself, the accumulation of material surroundings, an unhealthy obsession with the achievements of one's offspring, and a preoccupation with posterity – attributes that ring especially true of Lala Ram Prashad's personality – are all signs of a fearful resistance to death (Davies 2000: 127). Indeed, the haveli has been central to Ram Prashad's identity, a mark of social status, wealth, and worldly success. It is through the haveli, which Ram Prashad had fervently hoped would outlive him, that he had sought to keep the spectre of mortality at bay. By writing his sons out of his will he had hoped to exert control over the living from beyond the grave. All this changes dramatically, however, once he dissociates himself from the haveli as a narrative of identity and selfhood: "Lala Ram Prashad was gripped with tremendous fear. He wanted someone strong near him, someone to hold him as he entered the hereafter, to soothe him and comfort him" (Nahal 2010: 137). If surrendering his social identity in the face of the unknown was a risk for which he was now paying with the great fear he felt, it was a risk different only in scale, not spirit, from the risks he is known to have taken before, such as the time when desperately sick and unable to stand on his feet, "[p]ersistently, when no one was around, in the middle of the night, he would try and get up. He would totter for a few seconds and then—fall flat, either on the bed or on the ground" (Nahal 2010: 130). His history of risk-taking notwithstanding, Ram Prashad is genuinely afraid this time, looking around for someone to hold him as he prepares to take leave of the world.

Abandoning his investment in the haveli as a sign of extended selfhood that was sure to have bestowed some form of immortality on him, howsoever provisional, however, releases the haveli to play a rather different role in his life's last act. If the haveli, to begin with, was a sign of selfhood for Ram Prashad, its grandeur a testimony to his worldly success, Ram Prashad now starts to value it more as a place in which he first arrived into the world as an infant: "In what room was he perchance born—where had the whole drama begun?" (Nahal 2010: 136). Once again, we have a story offering a remarkable illustration of how the meanings that get attached to objects are not always rooted in human intention. The haveli in "The Womb," I suggest, emerges as a lively space, its shape, form, and history responsible for meanings that one might be tempted, out of habit, to trace back to the meaning-giving subject. Indeed, as the many references to its narrow paths leading to recessive spaces within the belly, as it were, suggest, there is something about the architecture of the haveli that lends itself to being read in particular ways. Thus, on his orders, each day Ram Prashad is carried on a stretcher, through deep, dark, and constricted passages, searching for the right room. He finally dies holding in his hands the photograph of a woman he's been told is his mother:

> His mother. A bedecked and bejewelled beauty—as she always was. So infinitely precious. Such a pillar of strength. She had conceived him in her womb and shielded him until he was ready to face things on his own. Now that he seemed to falter, she offered him the protection of her womb again.
>
> *(Nahal 2010: 139)*

As Kate Medeiros observes, the master narrative of ageing as the end of one's journey values the past at the expense of the present or future. It finally underwrites the assumption that everything worthwhile is achieved in one's youth, and that old age is merely a time to reminisce about the past (Medeiros 2013: 68). "The Womb," by contrast, draws on Ram Prashad's intense attachment to his ancestral home as a means of opening up an alternative view of time so that it moves not in a linear but circular fashion: past and present fuse together as Ram Prashad seizes the image of the journey of life and turns it around so that the end of the journey brings him full circle to its beginning. No longer seeking the interim immortality that his house and children can grant him, Ram Prashad is ready to embrace death as a return to the womb, for which the haveli now stands. The haveli then emerges not as a static symbol, fixed in time, but changeable. From being a structure in need of his protection when he was young, to one that promised him a life beyond death in his later years, the haveli eventually becomes for Ram Prashad a place of refuge from a linear narrative of development and a progressive modernity in which old and decaying objects such as himself and his haveli are mere impediments to be overcome.

As I have argued elsewhere (Raja 2020: 305–320) while traditionally the house metaphor codes the body as finite, subject to loss, decay, and depletion, Chaman Nahal's short story reveals the body to be simultaneously a site of continuity and connection. Thus, even though the story repeatedly casts his malfunctioning body as interrupting his attempts to communicate with others, Ram Prashad never rebukes the body. More of a friend than enemy, it allows him to distance himself from his unpleasant family even as its dysfunctionality offers him the welcome excuse to bond with his little great-granddaughter Priya, who is then invited to intercede on his behalf with the rest of the family, carrying messages between them. Far from being

154 Ira Raja

caught up in the memories of the past, Ram Prashad trains his dim eyes on the future, beyond life, to which he may be carried by none other than his own dear mother, decrying any attempts to accommodate his desire within existing discourses of religion and spirituality. The old man does not look to "return home" to an idealized past located in an image of "the happy joint family" in which all the relationships are hierarchically arranged. Instead, the model of happiness he seems to have chosen is founded on dismantling the binaries of past and present, life and death, youth and age as testified by the intergenerational friendship between him and Priya.

Crucially, for the argument of this essay, the materiality of the haveli plays a key role in bringing Ram Prashad to this realization. His love for the haveli may have begun as attachment to a worldly possession, but the epiphanic personal journey to which this attachment leads him finally enables Ram Prashad to cross over to the other side of life, in peace. None of this would have been possible without the catalytic role played by the haveli, strong and solid, holding him like a mother in its arms. It is through the mediation of the haveli that Ram Prashad is finally able to disrupt a linear view of life as a series of inevitable stages to be gone through before one finally reaches the point of death – by offering not closure but aperture – or openness – where even death fails to usher in the sense of an ending (Randall and Kenyon 2004: 334).

In conclusion, the ageing protagonists of all three stories discussed in this chapter project their own feelings, beliefs, or parts of their self onto material objects at the same time as they take into the self, elements of these objects, in what is perhaps best described as the "dialectic of transference of energies" between people and objects (Woodward 2007: 140). More than honour a past connection, these cherished possessions help older people liaise their relationships with their loved ones in the here and now, navigate the emotional turbulence that comes with the terrain, and mediate their attempts to replace lost objects, roles, and attachments. While the contents of Granny's pillow in Chughtai's story emphatically refuse her imagined continuity and connection with the past, Chaganti's "Sunstroke" by contrast accounts for the receptive quality of an object such as the armchair with its ability to feel, absorb, and transmit emotion over time, while the haveli in Nahal's "The Womb" underscores the ancestral house's capacity for conveying both continuity and disruption. The meanings attached to particular objects in late life, that is to say, mutate over time and shifting contexts, the impetus for such changes finally traceable as much to meaning-giving individuals as to the materiality of the objects themselves.

Notes

1 Also see my discussion of attachment to material objects in late life in three short stories, one each from Hindi, Oriya and Bangla in my essay "Inessential

objects: Cherished possessions in late life in Indian fiction," *Journal of Aging Studies*, vol. 67, 2023, article number 101184. https://doi.org/10.1016/j.jaging.2023.101184

2 A *haveli* is generic term for a traditional mansion in the Indian subcontinent, usually one with historical and architectural significance.

3 My discussion of Chaman Nahal's "The Womb" draws on a previously published essay, "No Time to Die: Illness, Ageing and Death in Three Short Stories from India," pp. 305–320 in *Caring for Old Age: Perspectives from South Asia*, ed Christiane Brosius and Roberta Mandoki. The concerns of the present essay however are very different to the previously published piece.

References

Appadurai, A. "Introduction: Commodities and the Politics of Value." *The Social Life of Things: Commodities in Cultural Perspective*, edited by A. Appadurai. Cambridge University Press, 1986, pp. 285–324.

Buse, C. and J. Twigg, "Women with Dementia and their Handbags: Negotiating Identity, Privacy and 'Home' through Material Culture." *Journal of Aging Studies*, vol. 30, 2014, pp. 14–22.

Chaganti, T. "Sunstroke." *Grey Areas: An Anthology of Indian Fiction on Ageing*, edited by I. Raja and translated by Jayashree Mohanraj. Oxford University Press, 2010, pp. 109–114.

Chapman, S. A. "A 'New Materialist' Lens on Aging Well: Special Things in Later Life." *Journal of Aging Studies*, vol. 20, 2006, pp. 207–216.

Chughtai, I. "Tiny's Granny." *Grey Areas: An Anthology of Indian Fiction on Ageing*, edited by I. Raja and translated by Ralph Russell. Oxford University Press, 2010, pp. 115–125.

Coleman, T. and J. Wiles. "Being with Objects of Meaning: Cherished Possessions and Opportunities to Maintain Aging in Place." *The Gerontologist*, vol. 60, no. 1, Feb. 2020, pp. 41–49.

Davies, P. "'Womb of the Great Mother Emptiness': Beckett, the Buddha and the Goddess." *Samuel Beckett Today*, vol. 9, 2000, pp. 119–131.

Falcus, S. "Unsettling Ageing in Three Novels by Pat Barker." *Ageing & Society*, vol. 32, 2012, pp. 1382–1398.

Hepworth, M. *Stories of Ageing*. Open University Press. 2000.

Keefer, L. A., M. J. Landau, Z. K. Rothschild, and D. Sullivan. "Attachment to Objects as Compensation for Close Others' Perceived Unreliability." *Journal of Experimental Social Psychology*, vol. 48, 2012, pp. 912–917.

Kenyon, G. M., J.-E. Ruth, and W. Mader. "Elements of a Narrative Gerontology." *Handbook of Theories of Aging*, edited by V. L. Bengtson and K. W. Schaie. Springer Publishing Company, 1999, pp. 40–58.

Lamb, S. *White Saris and Sweet Mangoes: Aging Gender and Body in North India*. University of California Press. 2000.

Medeiros, K. *Narrative Gerontology in Research and Practice*. Springer Publishing Company, 2013.

Nahal, C. "The Womb." *Grey Areas: An Anthology of Contemporary Indian Fiction on Ageing*, edited by I. Raja. Oxford University Press, 2010, pp. 126–139.

Nord, C. "A Day to be Lived. Elderly Peoples' Possessions for Everyday Life in Assisted Living." *Journal of Aging Studies*, vol. 27, 2013, pp. 135–142.

Raja, I. "No Time to Die: Illness, Ageing and Death in Three Short Stories from India." *Caring for Old Age: Perspectives from South Asia*, edited by C. Brosius and R. Mandoki. Heidelberg University Press, 2020, pp. 305–320.

Randall, W. L. and G. M. Kenyon. "Time, Story, and Wisdom: Emerging Themes in Narrative Gerontology." *Canadian Journal on Aging*, vol. 23, no. 4, 2004, pp. 333–346.

Sherman, E. "Reminiscentia: Cherished Objects as Memorabilia in Late-Life Reminiscence." *International Journal of Aging and Human Development*, vol. 33, no. 2, 1991, pp. 89–100.

Turkle, S. "Introduction: The Things that Matter." *Evocative Objects: Things we think with*, edited by S. Turkle. MIT Press, 2007, pp. 3–10.

Woodward, I. *Understanding Material Culture*. Sage Publications, 2007.

9

ACTOR AS A TIME-TRAVELLER

Politics of Performing Age Onstage

Mansi Grover

Date: 19th November 2021

Time: 5 PM

Location: Atelier Theatre, Delhi

Kuljeet Singh[1], the Director of Atelier Theatre[2], is holding the script of **Kuchh Afsaaney[3]** *and is reading from Sa'adat Hasan Manto's short story, "Upar Neeche Aur Darmiyaan"[4]:*

Begum Sahiba: Lady Chatterley's Lover, ye aapne takiye ke neeche kyu rakhi hui hai? (Lady Chatterley's Lover, why have you kept it under the pillow?)

Mian Sahib: Main dekhna chahta tha ke ye kitaab kitni behuda aur wahi-yaat hai. (I wanted to see how inane and bawdy is this.)

Begum Sahiba: Main bhi aapke saath dekhungi. (Okay, I will also see this with you.)

Mian Sahib: Main jasta-jasta dekhunga, padhta jaunga. Aap bhi sunti jaiye. (From here and there, I will see; read. You also attend.)

Begum Sahiba: Bohot acha rahega. (It will be extremely good.)

Vaibhav Mishra[5], a senior actor of the group, enters through the door along with a packet of samosas. He asks Shiv Shambhu Singh[6] aka Shiv to make tea for all of us. As the aroma of ginger tea fills the room, Mansi Grover[7], another actor, panting and gasping, enters. She starts the warming-up exercises with a few basic stretches. Enter Richa Mohan[8] and Bhupi Singh[9], two of the senior actors of the group. Rupank Sharma[10] and Sachin Srivastava[11] are on their way from the carpenter.

DOI: 10.4324/9780429352560-10

They had gone to get the witness box repaired. They are waiting for Jyoti Sharma[12] as she comes from far and changes three metros to reach the studio from her workplace. They are a group of twenty-five actors who juggle between their full-time jobs and passion for theatre.
It is almost after two years that they are all set to perform again. Covid-19 is like a dent in their lives that will leave its mark forever. Theatre suffered the brunt of the pandemic to the extent that many theatre companies were forced to shut their spaces. The lockdown left many theatre artists without work and several faced serious financial trouble. They had to shut their studio space at Ghitorni[13] last year and were out of work for two years. Since the situation is recovering, they have planned to organize a two-day festival to celebrate their reopening on the 14th and 15th of January 2022.
They all start with basic body exercises followed by breathing exercises and brisk walking. They all grab a cushion for themselves and sit in a semicircle in the rehearsal room. It is a small bunch of actors who take up multiple roles and could be seen travelling in different chronotopes[14] in a single play. The discussion starts with Vaibhav, who is playing three roles in three different stories in **Kuchh Afsaaney.**

Vaibhav: I am playing three very varied roles, of different ages, in three different stories. Masood from "Dhuan"[15] is an 11-year-old boy, Sirajuddin from "Khol Do"[16] is a man in his forties, and Mian Sahib from "Upar Neeche Darmiyaan" is an old man in his sixties. That would be a lot of time-travelling for me. Since "Upar Neeche Darmiyaan" is newly added to the list of stories that we would be performing, I will have to go a notch further in ageing up from Sirajuddin to Mian Sahib. I am a little relieved to know that the sequence of stories would be such that I would be time-travelling linearly.

Mansi: I have played a 12-year-old girl, Bhoomi, in one of our productions, *Prithvi*[17]. I had a difficult time preparing for that role. It was very difficult for me to age down. Age is both internal and external. I had my costumes, a school dress, a prop, and a frog, which took care of the external. It was hard for me to get the bright-eyed truthfulness that a 12-year-old is full of. How did you prepare for the role of Masood to achieve his emotional and social age?

Vaibhav: Conviction is the key to every character. One has to convince oneself that I am going to be a kid. You have to tell yourself each day that I am an 11-year-old kid. I may look like a grown man biologically, but I am a kid. I was conscious to not delve into exaggerations of any sort. There is a fine line between playing the role of an 11-year-old and playing the role of a kid with a developmental or cognitive disability since the body that would be playing the character is of a grown-up 32-year-old man. So, the actor has to convince himself first and suspend his disbelief, only then he will be able to convince the audience. I have always been curious about how audiences would respond to these performances of age.

Mansi: What has been easier for you, ageing up or ageing down?

Vaibhav: *Dekhiye*, Mansi, for me, ageing up was easier and the biggest reason for that was my body. My body is a grown-up person's body so I was very confident when I played Sirajuddin or Mian Sahib.

Rupank: For me, ageing down is easier as I have lived that age, and I could go back and draw from my own experiences to create a character.

Mansi: But sometimes the memories may trigger the past that one does not want to recall. I did not have a pleasant childhood, and when I recollected my experiences, they impacted me adversely.

Sachin: This is one of the reasons why Stanislavski's method of emotional memory[18] is controversial. As observed among other actors too, it triggered memories from the past which were harsh.

Mansi: It was more of Mansi and less of Bhoomi, it looked self-indulgent. So, for me, I had to think objectively and borrow from others' experiences. I had to negotiate and portray Bhoomi as a carefree kid which was very different from my childhood.

Rupank: I feel this is the sign of a mature actor. A novice actor would either play it stereotypically or make it all about himself. A mature actor would know how to amalgamate subjectivity and objectivity to make an age-embodied role.

Kuljeet: As an actor, you should constantly keep exploring the processes and not take them as dogmas. Every actor should negotiate and use these methods without fossilizing them. This is what we did with you, Mansi. If you remember after the emotional recall exercise with you, I realized that it was not working for you. So, we changed the methods there as Stanislavski did too. You were given your props and were asked to go on stage and start rehearsing echoing Stanislavski's "method of physical actions." You were asked to improvise and find the moment for yourself since emotional memories could not give you that moment of truth required to play the character of a 12-year-old kid. You were able to feel the real emotions after the repetition of the character's beats, and you were able to catch the rhythm and tempo of the character. Let me read what Stanislavski has to say about this method,

With time and frequent repetition...this score becomes habitual. An actor becomes so accustomed to all his objectives and their sequence that he cannot conceive of approaching his role otherwise...Habit plays a great part in creativeness.

(Stanislavski 62)

We also did a set exercise where you were asked to be with that character at the moment given to you, how that character would do basic everyday tasks, or how that character would react in a certain situation. It was all about experimentation and making a moment more about the character than the actor. Also, the more you work on the detailing of the character, the better you would be at creating an individualized character and not a cliched one. This is true for any character that you play.

Sachin: That reminded me of something that I was advised by a friend. He told me, "Sachin, there are two ways to perform, one is obvious, and the other is the opposite. Always aim for the opposite." I always remember his advice. It has helped me a great deal to break away from stereotypical portrayals.

Mansi: Interesting. Also, the more I thought about Bhoomi I realized that Bhoomi was attaining puberty which complicates her character further. She is going through a tough phase where she comprehends her gender as intersex. Her father and her friends have broken ties with her because of her gender identity. She is playing with a frog near a pond and could relate to the frog because of its intersexuality. The more I read her silence, I could feel that she has grown up too soon. Her chronological age is 12 but she is much more mature mentally. She does not have friends to play with and spends most of her time with her pet frog. With the unpeeling of her character, I realized that she is not a stereotypical heterosexual 12-year-old. I could sense such complexities while we were playing the role of siblings in Manto's "Dhuan."

Mansi Grover as Bhoomi in Atelier Repertory Company's "Prithvi" (Karen Malpede).
Photo by Niharika Grover (Atelier Theatre, New Delhi)

Masood is an 11-year-old boy who is going through a complex phase where he begins to have incestuous feelings for his sister, while his sister has a lesbian partner. Manto as a writer has offered such varied experiences of childhood that as an actor you cannot play them stereotypically. Manto's characters are dense and I feel it is where his magnificence lies. Manto has placed his characters with utmost care to present them realistically and situate them in a set chronotope. Whether it is a kid or an old man, they are not stereotypical or archetypes for others to follow. He reveals those aspects of society that many writers would usually not delve into.

Kuljeet: (reads aloud from Manto's *Dastavez*) *"Zamaane ke jis daur se hum guzar rahe hain, agar aap usse navakif hain to mere afsaaney padhiye. Agar aap in afsaanon ko bardasht nahin kar sakte to iska matlab yeh hai ke yeh zamaana nakabil-e-bardasht hai"* ("If you are unaware of the phase of the world we are living in, read my stories. If you cannot tolerate these tales, then it means this world is intolerable").

Mansi: Kuljeet, I remember there were a few fellow actors who were in disbelief over the casting of these two characters. Did you ever think of casting child actors for the role of Masood and Bhoomi?

Kuljeet: I feel these two roles are quite complex and to understand the density of their characters, I was sure that I wanted adult actors to play these roles. Also, there is always a concern and responsibility as a director of how these roles would impact a child emotionally. I believe in age-fluid casting and I feel it is the sheer belief of playing a younger character by an older actor that matters.

I remember watching Sabitri Ma, wife of Heisnam Kanhailal, a Manipuri theatre director, playing the role of a mother bird, Pebet, in the play *Pebet*.[19] I loved her performance and she made it believable. If you look at her you would see a 70-year-old woman but with the kind of work she has put in to become a little bird, it was a sheer spectacle and you believe it. So, I had a feeling that if I am casting a 32-year-old actor to play an 11-year-old boy and a 28-year-old woman to play a 12-year-old girl, I should believe in them that they would believe in the character and age, rather than how they look in real life. What is important is how convincingly you played your characters; how believable you make your characters onstage.

Mansi: Right. Also, I remember reading about Sabitri Ma's representation of Draupadi on stage. She played the role of Draupadi in their production *Draupadi*[20] which is based on Mahasweta Devi's short story "Draupadi."[21] Sabitri Ma, a septuagenarian, bares herself and performs nude as a sign of protest against the atrocities committed by the Indian army on Manipuri women. Her nakedness became the metaphor for the sordid decaying social milieu of Manipur. It is interesting how four years later, in a serendipitous turn of events, 12 middle-aged and elderly women stripped naked in broad daylight holding placards, saying, "Indian army rape us" and "Indian army take our flesh," protesting the custodial rape and killing of a young Manipuri woman. Heisnam Kanhailal had anticipated the events that were to happen four years after the performance was first staged.

What intrigues me is how an ageing body which usually comes with a master narrative of decline and powerlessness, became a symbol of resistance and a site of protest. She was able to give a radically contradictory and shifting meaning to old age in her act of nudity on stage. Her naked body became the voice when the speech itself was unheard. Sabitri Ma and those 12 women reconceptualized the body politics of the ageing bodies and subverted these "powerless" and "feeble" bodies into hallmarks of defiance and resilience. It is remarkable how an ageing body could be turned into a fierce persona disrupting and undermining the dictates of the established power.

Kuljeet: I sense a similar streak of subversion of ageing when I see Bhupi Ma'am perform Kulwant Kaur in Manto's "Thanda Gosht."[22] Bhupi Ma'am, who is in her sixties, performs the character of Kulwant who is a ferocious woman in her mid-thirties and is poles apart from what Bhupi Ma'am personifies in real life. I wonder if a younger actor would have played Kulwant or Draupadi, would it have generated a similar radical narrative of subversion of ageing bodies or not?

Talking about Kulwant Kaur, it is the narrative of the text that became the focus for me. The narrative did not offer the age of the character and an actor's age became secondary as I have always believed in age-fluid casting. Therefore, I took the liberty to cast an older actor to play a young woman. I was more concerned about the emotion and the truth of the moment that should be attained by the actors onstage.

Kuljeet Singh as Ishar Singh and Bhupi Singh as Kulwant Kaur in Atelier Repertory Company's "Kuchh Afsaaney" (Sa'adat Hasan Manto).
Photo by Niharika Grover (Atelier Theatre, New Delhi)

Mansi: There are negative views on ageing that are shaped by prejudices, stereotypes, and discriminatory attitudes towards older people. The anxieties associated with growing old are manifestations of fear because of which older people are overlooked, omitted, and "Othered." Generally, old age connotes an "inability" to perform the functions of youth. Quite often an ageing body is seen through a decline narrative, as deficient and incompatible to perform roles of femininity and masculinity. So, the moment you place an older actor to play a character against their chronological age, it is a courageous act of redefining the body politics of an ageing body. When we talk about ageing bodies, we are *looking* at bodies that are governed by their restrictive social roles and have "fallen away" from standards of beauty set by society. These women present a theatricalized display of simultaneously aged and un-aged body bodies. The postmodern poetics of an ageing body sees ageing with all its simultaneity, contradictions, and disruptions, beyond the binaries of youth/age and life/death.

Also, the metanarrative of debility that surrounds ageing made me think about what Pierre Bourdieu calls the body capital. According to him, the physical body is also a form of capital (body capital) and can be converted into other forms of capital such as economic capital, social capital, cultural capital, and symbolic capital. I was wondering if any one of you ever felt that your body capital as an actor has declined due to your age, and because of which you are deemed unfit for a particular role.

Kuljeet: This is true for cinema, not so much when it comes to theatre. The basic difference between watching a theatrical performance and a film is that the audience is aware that it is a performance and you have the liberty to portray any role. The audience will believe you if they are convinced by your performance. In cinema, the audience comes with a different mindset and there is a shelf-life of every actor. Theatre lets you imagine and the audience is fully aware of it.

I am reminded of a wonderful example of the serpent and the rope explained by Prasanna in his text *Indian Method in Acting*. He talks about how the actor is supposed to cheat well on stage, and one does not have to bring a real snake on stage but brings out only the terror of a snake. The audience has to imagine the snake. Taking cues from the serpent and the rope, the audience will believe you even if you are 70 and playing the role of a bird as done in *Pebet*. You cannot reach the ideal but it is all about the attempt to reach there. A good actor will make that attempt and believe in the process to reach closer to the ideal with every performance. The actor must suspend his disbelief to play a role with conviction, and the same goes for the audience to be convinced.

Mansi: If we look at the literary representations of old age, there is a constant narrative of deficit and abjection. But I feel if we look more closely at the process of ageing, it may vary according to innumerable variables, depending on family background, geography, social status, income, gender, education, etc. I read a short story by R.K. Narayan some time ago, "A Willing Slave" (1943), and found the intersectionality of age, gender, and class in it as thought-provoking. But there is often a superficial reading of old age devoid of personhood and agency for older people.

Jyoti: If we talk about Begum Sahib's character from Manto's "Upar Neeche Aur Darmiyaan." I saw her old age as a social location where the institutional processes, cultural expectations, and interactional practices intersect. I was trying to explore her character as an individual taking into consideration her desires and autonomy. The character of Begum Sahib is complex as she is coy as well as bold. She is a post-menopausal woman who wishes to be sexually active with her husband but is shy at the same time as society would not expect people advancing in age to be sexually active.

But here Manto gives us a couple who desires to have sex and enjoy the act of love-making at an age while they are dealing with health issues and still trying their best at it. I had to convince myself first that people in their sixties and seventies have sexual desires, but society has made it taboo. Many myths reinforce society's belief that older people are sexless, that sexual activity for older persons is immoral, abnormal, and dirty, that sexual desires and physical capacity for sex automatically decline with age, that impotence is part of ageing, and that sex is only for the young. My perception and sensibilities about growing older and old age changed after performing Begum Sahib's role. Theatre lets an actor take up different masquerades and evolve as a person.

Mansi: Also, performances of age can transport audience members to new enactments, conceptions, embodiments, and performatives of ageing and old age.[23] This is fascinating how Manto gave us an unconventional account of old age through the characters of Begum Sahib and Mian Sahib. The story offers so much about the couple who are conflicted between their emotional age and biological age, not to forget the social expectations that force the elderly to behave as asexual. The characters reveal how their bodies betray them when they desire intimacy but are unable to do so due to their ageing bodies. The couple encounters the clash between the perceived responsibility to be a good husband or wife (symbolic capital) and the inability (body capital) to meet these expectations in old age. Manto has demystified the myths of ageing by talking about the sexual desires of the elderly.

I am reminded of the two plays by Samuel Beckett, *All That Fall*[24] (1956) and *Not I*[25] (1972), which deal with the experiences of ageing women. Richa, you also played an old woman in *Ashadh Ka Ek Din*,[26] do you feel Mohan Rakesh gave us a conventional character or did he portray it differently?

Richa: If you go by the text, you would see Ambika, Mallika's mother, as a typical older woman who is ailing and dealing with health issues. She is as protective of Mallika as any mother would be. She is like every mother who is conservative about her daughter falling in love with a man of her choice. The play starts *in media res* and in the first scene itself, one could read that she is unhappy with Mallika. Vaibhav was directing that production and he asked me to explore the physical attributes of the character and the key to that was conviction.

I did not want to play Ambika as a stereotypical mother dealing with age issues, I wanted to play her in a manner where she might be physically frail owing to her health issues, but she is a woman who would voice her concerns as a mother. Also, I could see her struggle as a widow. Her struggle as a single mother and her prudence regarding her daughter's choices is something that I explored at my end. As a widow, she has to perform the roles of woman and man in the household, albeit with limited bodily abilities. Being a widow and a single parent, though giving her autonomy and independence, also increases her responsibilities towards Mallika. I remember reading Badal Sircar's *Baro Pishima* (1959)[27] (translated in Hindi as *Badi Buajee*) to understand Ambika's demeanour as a protective parent. If given a chance to play the character of Badi Buajee, I would like to reread and reimagine her, and the same goes for Munshi Premchand's "Boodhi Kaaki."[28]

Richa Mohan as Ambika in Atelier Repertory Company's "Ashadh Ka Ek Din" (Mohan Rakesh).
Photo by Niharika Grover (Atelier Theatre, New Delhi)

Mansi: Each of us is performing our chronological age with set sociocultural expectations. Stanislavski proposes the actors find a conscious means to train the unconscious to perform a different chronological age. An actor has to consciously acquire this skill through hours of practice and instruction. The repetition of actions becomes the most important technique to develop a habit so that it becomes an actor's "second nature." To perform the age of Ambika, Richa must have consciously chosen the actions and habits of people falling under that age bracket. While we are acting out a certain age, for instance, in Richa's case Ambika, one may argue that an actor is *performing* the age of the character. We as actors are essentially attempting to create *a performance of a performance*. It is rightly suggested by Age theorist Margaret Morganroth Gullette in her work *Aged by Culture* that we need to start thinking about age as a performance.

Age theorists have borrowed the concept of performance from Judith Butler's *Gender Trouble* to substantiate age. She posits performative as a constant iteration that transforms an action into a reality. Age, as well as gender, can be viewed as performative, in that each of us performs the actions associated with a chronological age minute by minute, and that the repetition of these performances creates a so-called reality of age both for us and for those who interact with us.[29] Age, therefore, is like an everyday ritual one performs according to one's chronological age. It is an illusion created by performing repeated actions according to the socio-cultural expectations surrounding an individual based on one's chronological age bracket.

Bhupi Ma'am, have you ever felt that your identity as a woman in her sixties is coded? Do you feel that your body is "disciplined" according to your chronological and biological age?

Bhupi Ma'am: This is a very pertinent question, Mansi. There is more of a decline narrative than a progress narrative associated with old age. I feel, perhaps the most well-established myth is that mental and physical deterioration is inevitable. To some extent this is true. People do experience wear and tear as they grow older, but much of the decline in vigour in old age can largely result from people *expecting* to decline and how society perceives the role of older people. We are supposed to "act" our age. If you ask me, there is a difference between the way I look and the way I feel. There is a yearning to present a consistent, unified identity. I feel younger than my chronological age and I would not lie but there is a deep-seated longing for agelessness.

Kuljeet: *(giggling)* Bhupi Ma'am, this is my line. I connect with it a lot.

Bhupi Ma'am: *(smiling)* Turning 60 and getting a tag of a "senior citizen" has brought in a sense of alienation in me. There are times when I forget that I am 60 and the revelation of my age comes from outside and not from within. I do not accept it willingly.

Kuljeet: I feel you are echoing my thoughts. I feel I am 23 but my chronological age is 43. With my grey beard and the way I fashion myself, people assume that I am 53. Even the kind of roles I am offered in cinema would hint a lot at how we think about age in our day-to-day lives. I played Kalki Koechlin's father in *Margarita with a Straw*[30] when I was 35; however, chronologically Kalki and I have just five years of age gap. There are times people who are chronologically in my age bracket have touched my feet thinking that I am in my fifties. I have faced this on numerous occasions.

Bhupi Ma'am: *(smiling)* I understand what you are saying, Kuljeet. I keep experimenting with my looks as I love to feel free of the tag of a senior citizen. The rigid number of 60 is suffocating at times as it creates expectations and the world wants you to fit in them, "act" your age, "perform" your age well. To see 60 as a threshold age, as an age of retirement, is an oversimplified concept that labels people as old and asks them to retire. I remember when I retired from my job as a teacher, I wanted to work more. I am still working because I do not feel a need to fix myself to the stamp of a senior citizen. I see these age categories as distinct, socially structured locations, a social construct based on our chronological age that sometimes structures access to or exclusion from certain opportunities and privileges. There are a whole lot of cultural expectations associated with every age. Instead of looking at age in categories and labelling a certain age as a threshold age, age should be seen in a continuum. I am in complete awe of Sabitri Heisnam for challenging herself through her subversive theatrical acts. I feel this would help older performers create new stories and generate new meanings out of their bodies. I wonder how complex ageing would be for Sabitri Heisnam owing to her layered marginal position as an elderly woman living in Manipur. She uses her triple-fold marginalized location and underscores the status quo through her radical act.

Mansi: It is the sheer brilliance of the group, Kalakshetra, and their director, Heisnam Kanhailal, to be able to see Sabitri Ma as an actor so full of potential even in her seventies. But there are times when a playwright offers us a stereotypical ageist old character, how would an actor negotiate to create an age-embodied role that is not prejudiced against old people?

Kuljeet: Imagination is central to character development. The first thing we as actors tend to develop in the character/role given to us is the generic qualification based on how we meet and understand people around us vis-a-vis nature/attitude/traits. Most of the time, this part of the process entangles us into creating a proverbial character-next-door and prevents the possibility of finding newer interesting personas whom we never got the opportunity to explore. Grounding reality coupled with the flight of imagination (not fancy, imagination is a serious business) helps us to carve out a sketch of the character which is next door and convincing. The latter part of exploration, as I mentioned above, requires walking an extra mile and a grand sense of responsibility. For instance, I had watched Mohan Rakesh's modern classic, *Aadhe Adhure*[31] several times by different teams from India, and every time I was disillusioned with the way the central character, Savitri, is represented on the stage. I feel Rakesh's detailed delineation of the character mentioned in the text consciously or unconsciously impacts the actor who prepares for the character and this impact ends up in a textbook portrayal of similar Savitris. I wonder what would I do if I had to direct an actor to play Savitri.

Mansi: Ira Raja in her book *Grey Areas: An Anthology of Indian Fiction on Ageing* anthologized numerous writings on ageing from a range of Indian languages. The first writing that she lists is a play by Krishna Baldev Vaid, *Humari Burhiya* translated as *Our Old Woman*. The play is structured around the silent figure of an old woman who has been abandoned by her uncaring family and progresses into becoming an allegory of Mother India. I vary such allegorical construction of age. I have my doubts regarding a metaphorical reading of ageing characters. David Mitchell and Sharon Snyder, eminent disability studies scholars, gave the term "narrative prosthesis"[32] for the literary texts which read disability at a symbolic level. Taking cues from their argument, I feel such representation of ageing leads to the further perpetuation of stereotypes against ageing as some sort of deficit and decline.

In the background one could hear Kuljeet's father, an octogenarian, listening to the evening prayer and enjoying every bit of it. Meanwhile, Kuljeet's mother scolded his father over his request to have another piece of barfi, "tussi ki nyaaneyaan haar karde ho." (you are acting like a kid.)

Mansi: (*smiles*) The reason for these stereotypes and tropes is ageism that marginalizes old age and creates it as an "Other." Age theorist Anne M. Wyatt-Brown writes about ageing as a missing category in current literary theory. There have been representations of ageing and old age as motifs, metaphors, or symbols signifying something. The most famous representation of old age by Shakespeare is that of King Lear, as a self-proclaimed "poor old man / As full of grief as age; wretched in both" (Act II, scene iv, ll. 275–6). He is mistreated and discarded by his children. The concept of life as a series of "ages" or "stages" in the most famous Jaques' "All the world's a stage" speech in *As You Like It* talks about old age as "second childishness and mere oblivion, / Sans teeth, sans eyes, sans taste, sans everything" (Act II, scene vii, ll. 165–6). These reductive decline narratives see old age as frailty, debility, and weakness.

We as writers and artists should seek to find a language and perspective that does not diminish the dignity, agency, and personhood of an ageing person while still attending to the physical and socio-cultural realities of old age. The ageing characters should be moved from the periphery to the centre of the work of art to reimagine what has been termed the "social imaginary of the fourth age."[33] We should attempt to understand our "shared vulnerability"[34] with older adults and the need for "intergenerational connection and care."[35] As writers and actors, we should be able to critique and reimagine pervasive cultural narratives, tropes, and practices to create more nuanced and subjective perspectives on older age.

Rupank: How do you think one can achieve this?

Mansi: Manav Kaul, one of the very popular playwrights that we have in India today, wrote a play, *Bali Aur Shambhu* (2006).[36] I liked his writing as it is colloquial and presents old age in an unconventional way, not a reductionist perspective of old age as decrepitude. The central characters are situated in an old-age home and one could see them beyond the decline narrative. Similarly, we are experimenting with the form and content of one of our productions, *Chootiye*.[37] It is still in its nascent stage, and we are reading and archiving the lived experiences of women at various stages. It is a play about four women of different age groups. Nobody else would be writing their stories for them, they would write their own stories. I have included my grandmother as one of the writers to explicate her life from her standpoint. I would be using her reminiscences recorded in the form of oral narrative as it would empower not just her but also the audience to achieve an integrated sense of worth regarding ageing.

Some years back she had bouts of dementia due to an overdose of medication. She was behaving as if she was a young mother of my age. She used to keep a *ghunghat*, a veil when she was young and she was transposed to those times of her life. She would knit sweaters and that was one activity that she kept on doing while she was in that phase. Also, she was constantly keeping a check on her *baari*, her almirah, as that was the first iron almirah purchased by

Actor as a Time-Traveller **171**

my grandfather and it was very dear to her. It gave her a sense of belonging and identity.

There are other instances that I have listed to be included in the production. I remember my grandmother would tell my mother to remove her facial hair and my mother would ask her why she wanted to get her hair waxed now that she is almost 85. I guess, Kathleen Woodward, a famous Age theorist, is right when she writes, "An 85-year-old [. . .] will be perceived first as old and only second as a woman or man."[38]

Internalized ageism hegemonizes adulthood and perceives old age as a second childhood, devoid of implications of gender and sexuality and characterized by physical and cognitive inferiority as well as dependency. The metaphorical connection between childhood and old age leads to infantilizing practices through which the adult status, or personhood, of elderly people, becomes obscured and older people are transformed into metaphoric children. Elderly people actively regenerate their personhood as individuals, as vulnerable adults, by asserting their closeness to death, and its frailties and dependencies leading to subversion of their infantilization. Thus, we are trying to counterbalance such negative, reductive, and ultimately ageist perceptions through personal accounts suited to the creation of new cultural narratives of deep old age by including their voices and their narratives.

The leitmotif in the lives of these four women is a mirror. The four characters would explore their identities through this leading motif, and interestingly, the fourth character, the woman in her eighties is denied a mirror in her room. The mirror connects the four generations of women and symbolizes "generational identity," an identity which "has to do with feeling oneself linked, unconsciously if not consciously, to the generations ahead and behind, through the relation of caring."[39]

Though my grandmother is not with us today, I have archived these details about her life to include them in our production as I feel it is an important aspect of her life. These little anecdotes also suggest the situation many women face in old age after devoting their lives to their families as wives, mothers, homemakers, and carers. There is a need to create a discourse away from ideas of a "failed old age" to reconsider the value and personhood of people with physical and cognitive impairments and to shift the focus to person-centred care given our shared vulnerability.

Kuljeet: I can see that your writing is shaping up well. As a writer, you have a huge responsibility and it takes a lot of courage to map the lacuna in the representation of old age, in fact, any marginalized group, to bring us face to face with the truths of life. It is important to not weigh human lives as assets or liabilities. I can recall many of our discussions from disability studies and you would often talk about our bodies as ever-evolving. It is essential to understand how our bodies are always changing, and old age could be seen as a bridge between past and present, linking generations. It is pertinent to identify old age as an important component of identity and difference.

Ageing is a universal experience and should be seen as a continuum not to be seen in binaries. Age is a fluid category and a performance in itself that all of us perform daily. The marginalized older characters should be given an equal space instead of a peripheral one to reimagine and reconceptualize what we have internalized all our lives. An actor has the liberty to get into any age and understands body politics along with the socio-cultural codes that govern a body. The sheer belief of an actor to take up a masquerade of any age would create what Stanislavski calls the "magic if."[40]

Mansi distributes the costumes to all the actors for their specific roles. They change into their costumes and come back to the rehearsal room. Meanwhile, one could hear Kuljeet's voice in the background as he reads from Peter Brook's The Empty Space,

> *I can take any empty space and call it a bare stage. A man walks across this empty space whilst someone else is watching him, and this is all that is needed for an act of theatre to be engaged.*
>
> (Brook 11)

Bhupi Ma'am and Vaibhav are standing in front of a mirror, fashioning themselves according to the characters and their respective age that they would be performing. In one corner, Bhupi Ma'am, as Kulwant Kaur, is dressed in a bright pink salwar-suit with her hair tied in a braid using a paraandi.[41] She is using a hair dye stick to blacken her greys and a concealer to patch the wrinkles and fine lines around her eyes and lips. Vaibhav, dressed as Mian Sahib, is wearing a beige kurta-pajama with a white skull cap on his head. He is using white watercolour to give a sense of greys in his hair, and a contouring stick to create wrinkles and freckles around his eyes and forehead. They both then take their positions. Kulwant Kaur, with lustful eyes, is sitting on a stool waiting for Ishar Singh. Mian Sahib, with curious eyes and inhibition in his body, is sitting on a bench with a stick next to him, reading Lady Chatterley's Lover. The curtain goes up.

Notes

1 Kuljeet Singh is the director and the founder-member of Atelier Theatre. His chronological age is 42.
2 Atelier Theatre is a Delhi-based theatre group founded in 2004.
3 *Kuchh Afsaaney* is a collage of six banned short stories by Sa'adat Hasan Manto, namely "Dhuan," "Bu," "Kaali Salwar," "Thanda Gosht," "Khol Do," and "Upar Neeche aur Darmiyaan" – adapted and dramatized for stage in Hindustani.
4 "Upar Neeche Aur Darmiyaan" a short story written by Sa'adat Hasan Manto around 1950 (exact year not known) deals with a Muslim couple who are rediscovering their sexual life in their sixties.
5 Vaibhav Mishra is a senior actor in the group and has been working with the group since 2014. His chronological age is 34.
6 Shiv Shambhu Singh is the production head of *Kuchh Afsaaney*. He joined the group in 2019. His chronological age is 22.
7 Mansi Grover is an actor and researcher of the group. She started working with the group in 2017. She is also the moderator for this paper. Her chronological age is 32.
8 Richa Mohan is a senior actor in the group and has been working with the group since 2015. Her chronological age is 45.
9 Bhupi Singh is a senior actor in the group and has been working with the group since 2013. Her chronological age is 62.
10 Rupank Sharma has been working with the group since 2012. His chronological age is 25.
11 Sachin Srivastava has been working with the group since 2016. His chronological age is 26.
12 Jyoti Sharma has been working with the group since 2018. Her chronological age is 30.
13 Atelier Theatre created a three-story studio space in Ghitorni, New Delhi, in 2018. It had a cafe, a rehearsal space, and a performing space called the Magic Box. The space had to be shut down owing to the COVID-19 pandemic.
14 Chronotope is a term given by the Russian literary theorist Mikhail Bakhtin (1895–1975) to refer to the coordinates of time and space invoked by a given narrative, also known as the "setting" of a given narrative.
15 "Dhuan," published in 1941, is a short story by Sa'adat Hasan Manto, which deals with the sexual awakening of a boy named, Masood, who starts having incestuous feelings for his sister.
16 "Khol Do," published in 1948, is another by Sa'adat Hasan Manto, is a story of Sakina who gets separated from her father, Sirajuddin, in one of the incidences of violence during the Partition, and is eventually found in a refugee camp.
17 *Prithvi*, an adaptation of *Extreme Whether* by Karen Malpede, is a 60-min production by Atelier Repertory Company set in 2013 Uttarakhand and symbolically looks at climate capitalism and human-led environment catastrophe. It is the story of Prithvi, an environment activist whose father Ambar was murdered by the nexus of climate change deniers. Prithvi continues with what Ambar left until she meets her destiny. Her daughter, Bhoomi, an intersex child with a frog friend (which has six limbs because of the presence of Atrazine in the well) tells a moving tale of the current Anthropocene.
18 Emotional memory is one of the acting techniques popularized by Constantin Stanislavski, a famous Soviet and Russian theatre practitioner. It is when an actor draws from real past experiences where one felt a similar emotion required by the role that one is playing. Stanislavski introduced this method in his text, *An Actor Prepares* (1936).

19 *Pebet*, a play by Heisnam Kanhailal, is based on one of the "fireside" stories passed down over several generations in Manipur. It describes a family of the extinct Pebet birds facing extinction due to an external threat, from a cat. It is a political satire commenting on the contemporary situation of the indoctrination of Hindu culture in Manipur and its colonization of the Meitei identity.

20 *Draupadi*, a play by Heisnam Kanhailal, based on a short story of the same name by Mahasweta Devi, describes the humiliation and sexual violence suffered by Dopdi Mejhen at the hands of the Indian army. Sabitri Heisnam plays Dopdi and bares herself in the last scene protesting against the commander and embodies the spirit of resistance.

21 "Draupadi," published in 1978, is a short story by Mahasweta Devi depicting the custodial rape of Dopdi Mejhen, a tribal woman from the Santhal tribe of West Bengal. She rips off her clothes and walks towards the commander and her nakedness becomes the symbol of defiance.

22 "Thanda Gosht," published in 1950, is another short story by Sa'adat Hasan Manto that faced obscenity charges. It is a tale about brutality and violence that happened during the Partition. Ishar Singh is numb and confesses to his partner, Kulwant Kaur, about his barbaric act of raping a corpse of a woman.

23 Valerie Barnes Lipscomb and Leni Marshall, *Staging Age: The Performance of Age in Theatre, Dance, and Film* (New York, US: Palgrave Macmillan 2010), 1.

24 *All that Fall* (1956) is a one-act radio play by Samuel Beckett dealing with the relationship of Maddy Rooney, a septuagenarian, with her husband. It charts the journey of Mrs. Rooney to the train station to meet her blind husband. She meets various people on her way and her conversations with them reveal various aspects of her past life.

25 *Not I* (1972) is a short dramatic monologue written by Samuel Beckett performed in a pitch-dark space with a single light beam illuminating a mouth. It is a woman's mouth and she describes various events from her life.

26 *Ashadh Ka Ek Din* (1958) written by Mohan Rakesh is considered the first Modern Hindi play. It is a three-act play centred around the love story of poet Kalidas and Mallika, sometime between 100 BC and 400 BC.

27 *Baro Pishima* (1959), translated in Hindi as *Badi Buajee*, a comedy by Badal Sircar, one of the most influential playwrights of India, depicts the problems faced by an amateur theatre group trying to put up a performance in their colony. The rehearsals take place at Anu's house and the sudden arrival of *baro pishima* creates a huge problem for the group as she is against Anu performing in public. It is a play within a play about how the group outwits *pishima* and is finally able to put up a successful show.

28 "Boodhi Kaaki" is a short story by Munshi Premchand and depicts the life of an old woman who lives with her nephew's family. She suffers neglect at the hands of her nephew's family and is left alone to live a life of hunger and penury.

29 Valerie Barnes Lipscomb and Leni Marshall, *Staging Age: The Performance of Age in Theatre, Dance, and Film* (New York, US: Palgrave Macmillan 2010), 2.

30 *Margarita with a Straw* (2014) is a film by Shonali Bose depicting the sexual discovery of a young girl, Laila. She has cerebral palsy and is a student at a college in Delhi. She moves to the US for further studies. She is bicurious and discovers this about herself after meeting Khanum in the US.

31 *Aadhe Adhure* (1969), a play by Mohan Rakesh, depicts the story of a dysfunctional family caught in the web of destitution. It is a family of five members, husband (Mahender), wife (Savitri), elder daughter (Binny), son (Ashok), and youngest daughter (Kinni). There is constant tension among them throughout the play.

32 David T. Mitchell and Sharon L. Snyder, renowned Disability Studies scholars, develop a theory called Narrative Prosthesis that deals with the pervasive use of disability as a trope in literature and film.

33 Michaela Schrage-Früh, "Reimagining the Fourth Age: The Ageing Mother in the Poetry of Mary Dorcey and Paul Durcan." *Nordic Irish Studies*, Vol. 17, No. 1, SPECIAL ISSUE: Women and Ageing in Irish Writing, Drama and Film (2018), pp. 77–94 (Dalarna University Centre for Irish Studies), 77.

34 Schrage-Früh et al. 87.

35 Schrage-Früh et al. 78.

36 *Bali Aur Shambhu* (2006) is a play written by Manav Kaul about two men from very different spheres of life sharing a room at an old-age home. As the play unfolds, a disturbing past about their lives is revealed.

37 *Chootiye* is a production by Atelier Repertory Company which is currently in the pipeline. It is a performance probing women's sexuality through patriarchal linguistic biases, established semiotic signs, chauvinistic social norms, dominating cultural paradigms, and exploitative moral codes at different stages of women's life.

38 Kathleen Woodward, "Performing Age, Performing Gender," *NWSA Journal* 18.1 (2006): 162–189.

39 Kathleen Woodward, *Aging and Its Discontents: Freud and Other Fictions* (US: Indiana University Press, 1991) 101.

40 Constantin Stanislavski's "Magic If" describes an ability to imagine oneself in a set of fictional circumstances and to envision the consequences of finding oneself facing that situation in terms of action.

41 *Paraandi* is a hair accessory made with threads, worn by women in Punjab, India, and is used to tie hair in a braid.

Bibliography

Aadhe Adhure. By Mohan Rakesh, directed by Lillete Dubey, performance by The Primetime Theatre, 15 Dec. 2013. Little Theatre Group, New Delhi.

Ashadh Ka Ek Din. By Mohan Rakesh, directed by Vaibhav Mishra, performance by Atelier Repertory Company, 13 Sep. 2019. Safdar Studio, New Delhi.

Bali Aur Shambhu. By Kaul, Manav. Adapted and directed by Darakht, 20 Sep. 2019. Akshara Theatre, New Delhi.

Beckett, Samuel. *The Complete Dramatic Works* (2nd ed. Rev.). Faber and Faber, 1990.

Bourdieu, Pierre. "The Forms of Capital." *Handbook of Theory and Research for the Sociology of Education*, edited by J. Richardson. Greenwood, 1986, pp. 241–258.

Brook, Peter. *The Empty Space*. Penguin Modern Classics, 2008.

Butler, Judith. *Gender Trouble: Feminism and the Subversion of Identity*. Routledge, 1990.

Devi, Mahasweta. "Draupadi." *Breast Stories*, translated by Gayatri Chakravorty Spivak. Seagull Books, 2010.

Draupadi. By Mahasweta Devi, directed by Heisnam Kanhaialal, performance by Kalakshetra Manipur, 14 Apr. 2000, Imphal.

Gullette, Margaret Morganroth. *Aged by Culture*. University of Chicago Press, 2004.

Kuchh Afsaaney. Directed by Kuljeet Singh, performance by Atelier Repertory Company, 10–11 Feb. 2018. Akshara Theatre, New Delhi.

Lipscomb, Valerie Barnes. "Introduction." *Staging Age: The Performance of Age in Theatre, Dance, and Film*, edited by Valerie Barnes Lipscomb and Leni Marshall. Palgrave Macmillan, 2010, pp. 1–7.

Manto, Sa'adat Hasan. *Dastavez*. Translated and edited by Balraj Menra and Sharad Dutt. Rajkamal Prakashan, 2004.

Margarita with A Straw. Directed by Shonali Bose, performances by Kalki Koechlin, Sayani Gupta, and Revathi. Viacom18 Motion Pictures, 2014.

Mitchell, David T. and Sharon L. Snyder. *Narrative Prosthesis: Disability and the Dependencies of Discourse*. University of Michigan Press, 2003.

Narayan, R. K. "A Willing Slave." *Malgudi Days*. Indian Thought Publications, 1982.

Pebet. Directed by Heisnam Kanhaialal, performance by Kalakshetra Manipur, 2006. Shri Ram Centre for Performing Arts, New Delhi.

Prasanna. "The Serpent and the Rope." *Indian Method in Acting*. National School of Drama, 2014, pp. 78–86.

Premchand, Munshi. "Boodhi Kaki." *Boodhi Kaki*. Hind Pocket Books, 2019.

Prithvi. Directed by Kuljeet Singh, performance by Atelier Repertory Company, 12 Aug. 2018. Stein Auditorium, New Delhi.

Rossen, Janice and Anne M. Wyatt Brown. *Aging and Gender in Literature: Studies in Creativity*. University Press of Virginia, 1993.

Schrage-Früh, Michaela. "Reimagining the Fourth Age: The Ageing Mother in the Poetry of Mary Dorcey and Paul Durcan." *Women and Ageing in Irish Writing, Drama and Film*, special issue of *Nordic Irish Studies*, vol. 17, no. 1, 2018, pp. 77–94.

Shakespeare, William. *Shakespeare: Complete Works*. Edited by W. J. Craig. Oxford University Press, 1966.

Stanislavski, Constantin. *An Actor Prepares*. Translated by Elizabeth Reynolds Hapgood. New York: Routledge/Theatre Arts Book, 1989a.

———. *Creating A Role*. Translated by Elizabeth Reynolds Hapgood and Edited by Hermine I. Popper. Routledge, 1989b.

Vaid, Krishna Baldev. "Our Old Woman." *Grey Areas: An Anthology of Indian Fiction on Ageing*, edited by Ira Raja. Oxford University Press, 2010, pp. 3–22.

Woodward, Kathleen. *Aging and Its Discontents: Freud and Other Fictions*. Indiana University Press, 1991.

———. "Performing Age, Performing Gender." *NWSA Journal*, vol. 18, no. 1, 2006, pp. 162–189.

10

HIS MASTER VOICE

Amitabh Bachchan, Aural Stardom, and the Ageless Baritone

Madhuja Mukherjee

Before I embark on a detailed discussion on the stardom, subjects of ageing, and the "agelessness" of the voice of the Indian superstar Amitabh Bachchan, I wish to comment on the nature of his star persona. On 12 May 2019 Amitabh Bachchan (b.1942), one of the biggest stars of Indian cinema, completed 50 continuous years in the film industry. Writing about Bachchan, in his seminal book *Ideology of Hindi Film*, M. Madhava Prasad (1998) analyses specific films starred by him and proposes that during the 1970s–1980s Indian cinema underwent an "aesthetic of mobilization." Prasad draws attention to the dynamic correlation between the political crises of the Indian nation-state during the 1960s–1970s and the formal contours of Hindi films. He examines the complicated links between the transformations within the film industry and the on-going battle over the formation of the post-independence nation-state. Describing the Hindi films of 1960s as "feudal family romances" (Prasad 1998: 64), Prasad illustrates in what ways such films tackled the tussles over the newly formed ("secular," "democratic") republic in tandem with the persistence of pre-modern social codes and moral order.[1] In Part II of the book, Prasad explains the manner in which following the demise of India's first Prime Minister Jawaharlal Nehru, alongside the swift rise of (his daughter) Indira Gandhi, the film industry altered "formally" or industrial forms and styles changed, through a process which he describes as "aesthetics of mobilization" (Prasad 1998: 138–159). Prasad argues that popular cinema "went through a phase of uncertainty before regrouping around a figure of mobilization, a charismatic political-ideological entity embodied in the star persona of Amitabh Bachchan" (1998: 24). Briefly, Bachchan became, and continues to be, the

DOI: 10.4324/9780429352560-11

pivotal point around which the film industry – now converging with other media platforms including Television and Internet – constantly reorganizes.[2]

That Bachchan's star value is momentous to the Hindi film industry is almost commonsensical; but, the questions that I hope to raise are connected to his on-screen persona, the modes through which, despite his chronological age, 50 years on, he continues to deliver what may be described as *"one man"* or solo hits. More precisely, the objective of the chapter is to examine the mechanisms via which such stardom is produced. For instance, 2019 also recorded the release of Bachchan's film *Badla* (Sujoy Ghosh 2019), which became one of the most successful films of the year as well as of Bachchan's career. I argue that, in this film Bachchan plays his own star persona, and the film works as a key to comprehend the characteristics of his stardom. The film, in fact, has a somewhat straightforward plot in which a woman (Naina, played by Tapsee Pannu) is involved in an extramarital affair, and on her way back home, from one such sojourn, she accidentally kills a man. Eventually, the parents of the deceased person get the stench of the murder, and they plot against the couple that committed the crime. En fin, the father (Nirmal, played by Tanvir Ghani), wins Naina's trust by wearing the "prosthetics" mask of a lawyer (named Badal Gupta) and extorts her statements. In the final scene it is revealed that Badal Gupta was somehow delayed for the meeting, and it was Nirmal who had deceived Naina by wearing the mask, to obtain justice for his son. My contention is that, despite the "plot," a few thought-provoking things unfold in the film. First, Nirmal, who pretends to be the lawyer Badal Gupta, and is a wearing mask, is in actuality wearing a "Bachchan" mask in his attempt to mislead Naina and record her confessions. Secondly, and more importantly, the crux of the story, the confrontation scenes between Nirmal and Naina, are *not* played by Ghani and Pannu, respectively; in its place, Bachchan appears as his own mask. So, even when as per the plot Nirmal (Ghani) wears a mask to capture the murderer, the actor Tanvir Ghani is not made to wear any mask. Rather, Ghani does not play this part at all; instead, as elaborated earlier, it is Bachchan who performs as his own mask. The "Bachchan mask," therefore, is perhaps comparable to the Dali masks used in the TV series *Money Heist* (2017) and it functions like a floating signifier, meaning diverse things, yet, by and large, evoking a series of inter-related affect.

The problem of the film is thus, as following – if Nirmal is pretending to be Badal Gupta, what character does Bachchan play? I speculate that Bachchan does not play any character in the film; he simply plays his own audio-visual figuration, which becomes acceptable for the audience because his star persona is effortlessly identifiable. I, therefore, assert that the complication of the "narrative" is pertaining to a star text, and hence, even when plot-wise Nirmal dons the Badal Gupta mask, it is not exactly like the real Badal Gupta (a third person/actor); in fact, it appears like Amitabh Bachchan or is Amitabh Bachchan and seems somewhat appropriate. As a result, the film becomes an elaborate display of Bachchan's star power and underlines the significance of the persona that persists outside any filmic text and cinematic causality.

Consequently, it appears plausible for Bachchan fans and the general audience that Nirmal would (magically) transform into another person, that is "Amitabh Bachchan," and speak in his voice as well, as soon as he adorns the iconic mask.[3] Indeed, it may have been unacceptable, if not improbable, if Bachchan – pretending to be a mask – would have spoken in Ghani's voice. So, while in effect, Nirmal is played by both Bachchan and Ghani; there are also two types of voices which are at play in disparate scenes; and, at the point when the actual Badal Gupta (played by a third actor) arrives on the scene, his brief act is dubbed by Bachchan. Clearly, Bachchan's voice is recognizable without the body, and the dubbing done by Bachchan for his look-alike bestows logic and meaning to the act of wearing a "Bachchan" mask and speaking in his voice. As a matter of fact, this dubbing done by Bachchan may not have been pertinent if the voice of Amitabh Bachchan had not emerged as a principal constituent of his stardom. The aura of his physicality (particularly height, gait, and uses of left hand) aside, even when Bachchan has taken up multiple roles and appearances, throughout his exceptionally long career, the performances of his voice have remained unflagging – more or less.[4]

For viewers of Indian cinema and fans of Amitabh Bachchan it is not unknown that his deep baritone operates as an independent category and the recognizable voice not only subsists beyond films, it circulates autonomously outside cinematic representations through varied imitations and caricatures and is attached to multiple audio-visual texts. For example, in 2010 *Times of India* reported that Bachchan would sue a chewing tobacco brand since they used (a mimicry of) his voice for an advertisement without his approval.[5] The report added that "[y]ou're not an aspiring actor unless

FIGURE 10.1 The Bachchan mask in *Badla*.

FIGURE 10.2   Prosthetics and aging in *Gulabo Sitabo*.

you've tried your hand at an Amitabh Bachchan imitation. From radio to ads to comedy shows, good/bad/downright criminal copies of his voice and mannerisms are everywhere." More important, for this chapter and the volume, is the following query: while Bachchan, the person and the actor, has undergone natural advancement of years and physical transformations, and has performed characters which are far older than his actual age,[6] *why* and *how* does – the object of our enquiry – his baritone voice remain "ageless" and retain its vocal flexibility? By evoking Michel Chion's (1982) influential study of voice, I stress upon the acousmatic features of Amitabh Bachchan's voice as discernible in a variety of films and explore the ways in which it is fabricated, its pliability repeatedly (and mechanically) recreated, and the process through which such a voice mobilizes industrial benefits. Finally, I shift the focus of Cinema and Star studies from "image" to "voice," and stress the manner in which the changing body of the star has been substituted by a more or less stable, "ageless," and virile voice which is perhaps the basis of his continuing popularity. Briefly, I connect the densities of voice in cinema and stardom with subjects of "ageing" and "ageism" in order to examine the industrial ramifications of age-related debates.

(Visualized) Acousmêtre

This chapter revisits Indian superstar Amitabh Bachchan's enduring stardom by detouring the concept of "voice in cinema" and the problematic of "Acousmêtre" introduced by Michel Chion (1982), and consequently, rethinks Bachchan's star persona – which has been reinvented at various junctures

– through the deployment of his (variable/specific) voice. A range of writings on Bachchan and on the political contexts of India during the 1970s has focused on the significance of his star persona,[7] which has evolved via shifting textual and extra-textual registers.[8] Most of the scholarship, nonetheless, has addressed the implications of his "image," and the persona which is identifiable as a traumatized, brooding, and angry on-screen figure. As discussed elsewhere (Mukherjee 2002, 2015), the star persona of Bachchan has developed and morphed over the decades through a series of interpolated texts, and yet, it is easily comprehensible through the performances of an ambiguous tragic aura often held together by a haunting past, brooding intensity, forbidding anger, alongside an (oedipal) obsession with the mother, and a proletarian identity. By and large, during his early phase (1970s and 1980s) Bachchan performed roles of peripheral and working-class characters including small/big time smuggler, dock worker, railway porter, wronged police officer, coal mine labourer, as well as characters from religious minority communities (Muslim and Christian) and an orphan.[9] The figure recurrently faces death at closure, thereby, ironing out some of the unsettling political quandaries introduced by the text; also, the portrayal of the wounded body, and the uses of his left arm are often developed as semantic excesses. For instance, the physical bearing of the broader social anguish is palpable in *Deewar* (Yash Chopra 1975), in which his left arm is inked with the words "Mera baap chor hai" ("My father is a thief"),[10] in *Trishul* (Yash Chopra 1978), in which he wears his deceased mother's beads around his neck (like a noose), in *Kaala Patthar* (Yash Chopra 1979), in which his face is smeared with black tint and dirt, and in *Agneepath* (Yash Chopra 1990) wherein his body is coated with blood and muck.[11]

Star studies have been one of the central points of contestation within Cinema Studies, and have highlighted crucial aspects of the film industry, cultural forms, and popular cultures.[12] Prasad (1998: 141) clarifies how, "[f]rom the star's perspective, his/her body is a source of rent, since it's a principal quality, charisma, is coded as a possession that he/she is 'born with', notwithstanding the work that goes into producing it." Alternately, Mary Ann Doane (1980) draws attention to the problem of "Voice in Cinema" and "The Articulation of Body and Space." She calls attention to the dynamic relation between the "phantastic" body created by technology and the voice (recorded elsewhere and sometimes playing from elsewhere) and underscores how cinematic practices seek to marry these two disparate elements.[13] Truly, cinema brings two different kinds of aura together – that of the image and of the "disembodied" recorded voice.[14] In relation to such play between image and voice, I reconsider the specificity of "voice in cinema," theorized in the works of Michel Chion.

The editor's note (xi) to the book *Voice in Cinema* reminds us that:

[o]f course, we say, it is speech, and song, that organize movies, and then we focus attention on the words (or less often, the musical qualities of

songs) that fall from the shadows of mouths we see on the screen. *But it is the voice – not as speech, not as song, but everything that's left afterward* [italics added] that is the subject of Chion's investigation.

Chion writes about the "elusiveness" of voice or the sonic element of words. He discusses the manner in which voice in cinema becomes a "vehicle" or a "verbal signifier"; and how beyond "the speech act" and beyond words, *it is the voice* that may be studied as a discreet "medium" or carrier of feelings. He borrows from Jacques Lacan to describe the voice as the *objet (a)*, which is thus, fetishized. He shows how the notion of sync-voices is borrowed from theatre, while application of music is derived from "opera, melodrama and vaudeville; and voiceover commentary from magic lantern shows"; though, cinema has its own specific ways of manipulating these. He (5), however, underlines how:

> [i]n actual movies, for real spectators, there are not all the sounds including the human voice. There are voices, and then everything else. In other words, in every audio mix, the presence of a human voice instantly sets up a hierarchy of perception.

The materiality and the import of the voice, accordingly, is the crux of this study. Chion shifts the focus of exploration of soundtracks from its diegetic (and melodramatic) function, in order to retrieve the sound of cinema from the story. Chion elaborates on how sounds and voices in cinema "wander" on the body of the screen, and await "a place to attach to." He asserts that such deployment of sounds and voices *belongs to cinema alone*. In brief, Chion questions the primacy of the image in cinema and highlights the impact of voice. Voice, according to Chion, is the peg on which the viewer's attention is hooked. Furthermore, voice is studied as the double or the shadow of the image, which thickens and enriches the soundtrack.[15]

Elaborating on the concept and cinematic function of the "acousmatic being," he discusses in what ways voice may be heard without its cause or source "being seen," as well as about its all-pervasive quality and omnipotence. Chion (21) stresses:

> when acousmatic presence is a voice, and especially when this voice has not yet been visualized –that is, when we cannot connect it to a face – we get a special being, a kind of talking and acting shadow to which we attach the name "acousmatic being".

"Acousmêtre" is the voice that is yet to be "visualized"; however, if the (disembodied) voice is audible after the character has been presented, it is described as "visualized acousmêtre," while voiceover is defined as "commentator-acousmêtre." Note, a number of thrillers and Noir or a range of Indian films involving telephone, radio, gramophone, tapes, etc., play with this idea of the "acousmatic."[16] Chion further considers the subject of "de-acousmatization" which takes place at the point when the source of voice is revealed (see Chion's study of *Pyscho* (Hitchcock 1960)). Chion analyses the moment of revelation or the situation of "de-acousmatization" as a "symbolic act."

Additionally, Chion's (24) emphasizes that

> [t]he acousmetre, as we have noted, cannot occupy the removed position of commentator, the voice of the magic lantern show. He must, even if only slightly, have one foot in the image, in the space of the film; he must haunt the borderlands that are neither the interior of the filmic stage nor the proscenium – a place that has no name, but which the cinema forever brings into play.

The problem of "voice in cinema" becomes meaningful, as we consider a range of cases from popular Indian cinema. For instance, while we are, by and large, cognizant of the role and mass popularity of playback singers in mainstream films, and how some playback singers – such as Lata Mangeshkar and Kishore Kumar – have become legends in their own fields,[17] it must be accentuated at this juncture that other actors and professional dubbing artists regularly dub voices of renowned (female) stars. In an unpublished paper ("Voice of Sridevi/ body of Naaz") for example, I underscore the fashion in which the voice of the iconic star Sridevi was as much a construct as was her towering image, considering "Baby Naaz" aka Salma Baig, an actress from the 1950s–1960s, dubbed for a variety of her films until filmmaker and producer Yash Chopra reinvented her image and voice for the film *Chandni* (1989). By then, though, Sridevi's archetypal "child-like" voice, which was actually that of Naaz, had already become familiar to the audience. Furthermore, another exceptional star, Rekha, dubbed for Sridevi for the film *Aakhree Raasta* (K. Bhagyaraj 1986). Such doubling, consequently, compels us to think through and think about the processes of the making of a leading film star. Therefore, in relation to such studies and particularly to Chion's groundbreaking and nuanced reading of voice, I examine the phenomenon of Bachchan's voice, and its "ageless" manifestations. I ask – does the evocation of Bachchan's (autonomous and disembodied) voice in different texts make him an "acousmatic being," especially when he has "one foot in the image"? Or is the figure a "visualized acousmêtre" as well as a "commentator- acousmêtre"? I signpost a few crucial and specific aspects of Hindi popular cinemas, which enable and affect application of voices in cinema, and demonstrate the dynamics of Bachchan's on-screen persona – an ageing body/ ageless voice –, which I read as an industrial construct and requirement.

Aural Stardom

Mary Ann Doane reflects on the body and the image separation and suggests that "the body acts as an invisible support" (Doane 1985: 168). In connection to such deliberations, I study Amitabh Bachchan's voice – his body double as it were – and its *disappearance* and *(re)appearance* (or the Freudian "Fort-da game" as Chion would describe it) as evident in films like *Reshma aur Shera* (Sunil Dutt 1971), in which the character played by Bachchan is rendered voiceless, and *Shamitabh* (Balki 2015), in which he lends the unmistakable baritone to a rising young star (played by Dhanush), alongside certain films in which he performed as voiceover artist. Bachchan debuted in the film industry as a voiceover artist through the landmark Indian New Wave film *Bhuvan Shome* (Mrinal Sen 1969), followed by his character role in *Saat Hindustani*, in the same year, made by the celebrated journalist, writer, and filmmaker K.A. Abbas. Through such films, and a number of others, and specifically through a reading of a series of para-texts which include sonic albums and even comic books, I explore in what ways the distinct baritone evolved, became popular, and circulated as an independent category, and thereby, emphasize upon the ways in which it has remained "ageless" and has deepened over the decades. So, by invoking Chion (1), from his opening comments in the "Prologue: Raising the Voice," in which he defines the "strange object," I wish to stress that

> a serious theoretical elaboration of the voice as an object did become possible with Lacan, when he placed the voice-along with the gaze, the penis, the faeces, and nothingness – in the ranks of "object (a)," these part objects which may be fetishized and employed to "thingify difference."

Indeed, Bachchan's voice becomes an obscure object of desire that evolves and yet remains constant for the viewer to be recalled as a discrete thing. Likewise, in the context of age discourses, while questions of "agelessness" of (male) stars remain central, it must be noted that it is essential for the film industry to generate para-texts continually and produce a bankable star. In this regard the body of the star and his/her on-screen appearance has been seen as the key to the construction of the star image. Moreover, the body and its transformations (due to age, disease, accident, and other causes), and various stages of physical modifications, have affected both the careers as well as the well-being of many (female) stars.

In reality, even Bachchan's careergraph (which demonstrated unprecedented upward movement during the 1970s and 1980s) slid during the early 1990s. This was preceded by his serious accident during the shooting of the film *Coolie* (Manmohan Desai 1984), following which his physical appearance changed considerably (as he gained weight and the contours of his body changed); just as the types of roles shifted remarkably. Yet, the industry, heavily dependent on his star power, continued to shell out characters which were partly super-heroic (as in *Ganga Jamunaa Saraswati* [Manmohan Desai 1988], *Toofan* [Ketan Desai 1988], *Jaadugar* [Prakash Mehra 1989], *Aaj Ka Arjun* [K.C. Bokadia 1990], etc.), or were versatile character types who could perform action, comedy, and romance. During the 1990s, while the Khan-Trio rose to stardom,[18] Bachchan delivered a few solo hits like *Khuda Gawah* (1992, Mukul S. Anand), and yet, by 2000 he re-emerged on the scene by acting out "character" roles in films such as *Mohabbatein* (Aditya Chopra 2000) and *Kabhi Khushi Kabhie Gham* (Karan Johar 2001). More importantly, disparate media forms (for instance, advertisements) reinvented his star status as he shifted to television and played the host of the uninterruptedly popular TV show *Kaun Banega Crorepati*.[19] Perhaps Bachchan would have been restricted to playing what I had described as "grand patriarch" elsewhere (2002) had *Baghban* (Ravi Chopra 2003), *Bunty aur Babli* (Shaad Ali 2005), and *Cheeni Kum* (Balki 2007) not been declared as hits and *Nishabd* (Ram Gopal Varma 2007) had not presented him as a solo star and the desiring and desirable man in his "sixties" and accentuated his vocal tonalities (discussed later).

In the opening commentary to the volume *Revisiting Star Studies* Sabrina Qiong Yu (2017: 2) asks:

> when a star gets older and becomes less glamorous, is s/he still a star? When a star's face gets injured and loses his/her acclaimed beauty is s/he still a star? When a star from a past era is unscrupulously appropriated by social media users, is s/he still a star?

Sabrina Qiong Yu, as a matter of fact, interrogates any blanket understanding of stardom and the deployment of homogenous methods to study stars in disparate contexts. The volume also highlights how ageing may function as a "masquerade," and work in different ways for male and female stars. Truly, how stars attain sustainability and continue to enjoy stardom over decades is connected to the ways in which the persona is reinvented at various junctures, through intermediality and industrial conditions. For example, Lisa Purse's essay in *Revisiting Star Studies* discusses how Tom Cruise's persona as the "youthful" and "non-ageing" action hero is linked to the notion and lifestyle of "successful ageing" which are reinstated by a range of para-texts (such as magazine articles, photo-shoots, advertisements). Moreover, Aagje Swinnen (2012), in the introduction to *Aging, Performance and Stardom*, reminds us of the manner in which Susan Sontag had alerted us to the "double standards of ageing," particularly in relation to women and actors. Swinnen also brings to light in what ways consumerist culture encourages us to reject bodily changes that occur due to the passing of years, while women are particularly at a risk of being ridiculed if and when they don't perform their "age." The volume also includes a case study of the Hollywood star Goldie Hawn's career as an example of "ageless blonde."

In the context of Indian cinema studies, such debates are yet to make any dent, although a number of (male) stars who are above 50 have successfully bypassed both popular and academic age discourses, and continue to play lead roles in a number of popular films (albeit often produced by themselves). While the enigmatic actor Rekha (b. 1954) is still considered to be a personi-fication of charm and fashion, a range of other stars, including the 1908-born action heroine "fearless" Nadia persisted acting in films until she was 60, just as, the posters of the action film *Khiladi* (Homi Wadia, 1968) used a formidable picture of hers holding a gun; super star Rajnikanth (b. 1950) continues to offer successful films, although off-screen he sports a reced-ing hair line and grey beard with ease.[20] The point is that such examples elucidate how long-term stardom may not be exceptional in certain (Indian) contexts, and with regard to specific kinds of stardom; however, Bachchan's re-figuration in the 2000s as the "salt-and-pepper" man with a quintessen-tial baritone becomes our point of exploration, considering he has been able to perform both his age and remain virile too in films such as *Cheeni Kum* and *Nishabd* discussed later, although in films such as *Deewaar* (Milind Luthria 2004), *Sarkar* (Ram Gopal Verma 2005), *Last Lear* (Rituparno Ghosh 2007), *Bhuddha hoga terra baap* (Puri Jagganath 2011), *Wazir* (Bejoy Nambiar 2015), and *Pink* (Aniruddha Roy Chowdhury 2015) he plays a "senior" yet powerful character, which drives the narrative flow of the films.

It has been discussed how star personae are created through several agencies including film magazines, interviews published on audio-visual platforms, stage shows, fan clubs, and (even) gossip, which operate outside the cinematic texts.[21] Such para-texts frame stars as both "ordinary" and "extraordinary" persons (see Dyer), which may also be defined as "nor-mal" and "excessive." Nevertheless, my on-going research on film maga-zines such as *Filmfare* shows how the popular English press (particularly *Stardust*) and Bachchan had a complicated relationship from the time the state of Emergency was declared in India in 1975, and the freedom of Press was curbed, which in the long run triggered a ban on Bachchan by the Press. Recently, an e-magazine quoted him from his blog:

> [a]fter and initial period of acknowledging my work, the press went against me, because they were informed by 'sources' that I had brought on the idea of Emergency and a ban on the press!! [sic] … no, interviews, no mention or pictures, or news of mine were ever printed in any form of the media during that time. So, no Deewar, or Sharabi, or Muquaddar ki Sikander [sic] Lawaaris, Natwarlal, Bemisal, and so many many others went blank.[22]

The rift was partially mended after Bachchan suffered a near-fatal accident in 1983 during the shooting of *Coolie*. The (supposed) reciprocal ban, however, did not affect Bachchan's career in the least, and in fact, in that period he delivered hits year after year (with several big films being released in the same month). These films include his career-defining roles such as *Deewar* and *Sholay* in 1975, *Amar Akhbar Anthony* and *Parvarish* in 1977, *Trishul*, *Don*, and *Muqaddar Ka Sikandar* in 1978, *Mr. Natwarlal* in 1979, *Dostana* in 1980, *Yaarana*, *Naseeb*, and *Lawaaris* in 1981, and so on. While it is clear that he garnered a fan base, which was far wider than any star that preceded him, and that, he enjoyed a mass appeal because of such films; yet, the characteristics of his stardom, as transpiring through the above-mentioned films, provoke us to rethink certain set approaches within star studies (discussed earlier).

One of the ways of comprehending this unique condition, and gauging how he attained superstardom without the mutual support of film magazines (in the absence of commercial/satellite TV at that time), is by looking into the vernacular press publications such as *Mayapuri* (Hindi), which did cater to Bachchan's growing stardom, at least to an extent. It may also be understood by studying the growth of exhibition networks and the ways in which the industry re-organized itself by producing Amitabh Bachchan starring blockbusters,[23] as well as by making films in which he essayed "double-roles."[24] Further, something more decisive was transpiring around his aural stardom. I wish to particularly focus attention on the momentous release of the Long Playing records by Polydor, comprising sound and dialogue track of the landmark film *Sholay*. As I have analysed elsewhere (2014) *Sholay* invested heavily in the image (70 mm prints), but, specifically in sound, which included the application of stereophonic sound, making of signature tunes for the major characters, a memorable sound design for the entire film as opposed to uses of genre music (which was a regular practice in popular [Hindi] cinema). The *pre-release* contract with Polydor Music Company as narrated by Anupama Chopra (2000: 21), "G. P. Sippy [was] dreaming big ... He wanted to make a multi-starrer ... He was looking for scale and grandeur." Hence, musician Vasudeo Chakravarty created sounds on his amplified cello, which was thereafter mixed with the sound emanating from a brass pot. This eventually became the well-known tune associated with the menacing villain Gabbar Singh (Amjad Khan). The six-track sound of *Sholay*, technologically difficult at that time (and even later), transformed the soundtrack of Indian films. The sound of *Sholay* was popularized through the Polydor LP records, and audiences assembled in the theatres to listen to the "stereophonic" sound of the film. *Sholay* was not yet another dacoit film, and even when it borrowed from Indian sub-genres, it was one of the most expensive films to be ever made in India (until 1975), and it effectively

188 Madhuja Mukherjee

combined sub-cultural genres with the style of Hollywood and Spaghetti "Westerns."

While *Mother India* (Mehboob Khan 1957), *Mughal-e-Azam* (K. Asif 1960), and *Sholay* are amongst the few films which redefined industrial trends, *Sholay* is unique because the film's song/musical album and the "dialogue and sound" album were released separately, thereby becoming a pioneering film which capitalized its soundtrack. The 56-minute "sound and dialogue" album was an "extra-long playing" record with stereophonic sound and encompassed dialogues and sound from the key scenes of the film. "Side A" of the "dialogue" album included sounds and voices from: i) the scene in which Thakur Baldev Singh searches for Jai and Veeru, ii) (the comic) scene with Soorma Bhopali, iii) Jai and Veeru meet Basanti for the first time, iv) Gabbar and his men attack Ramgarh and encounter Jai and Veeru. "Side B" contained dialogues and sounds from the scenes in which i) Gabbar attacks Ramgarh during Holi, ii) Veeru and Basanti's romantic scene (in which he threatens to commit suicide), and iii) the climatic scenes in which Jai rescues Veeru and Basanti and sacrifices his own life, followed by the final "retribution." The main voices, as described by the LP back-cover, were those of "Sanjeev Kumar, Dharmendra, Hema Malini" which is followed by lesser-known stars of the period including "Amitabh Bachchan, Jaya Bhaduri" and the newcomer "Amjad [Khan]." While, the backcover of the album underscores the soundtrack stating: "selections featured in it have been derived from the original soundtrack of the film, and repro-duced" and "the dialogue as well as the sound effects and the background music is in the full splendour of the stereophony"; moreover, the LP covers draw our attention to the way in which the long-term popularity of certain scenes, dialogues, and voices were shaped through exclusive publicity and marketing.

One may speculate that the media content mentioned above generated the enduring popularity of the dialogues of *Sholay*, and made Bachchan's dis-embodied voice recognizable, acceptable, and transportable, and I suggest that he became what Chion would describe "acousmatic being" with one foot in the film.[25] This is, nevertheless, not to undermine the popularity of other actors who emerged out of the *Sholay* phenomenon (especially that of Amjad Khan); besides, this is also not to imply that the "image" of Bachchan had no significance whatsoever, particularly when his height, stature, and demeanour is part of both cinematic and extra-cinematic mythmaking.[26] However, my attempt here is to unpack the manner in which his iconic (and disembodied) voice, which remains unfaltering despite his biological age, was emphasized, and thereafter, went through a process of iconification following the *Sholay* phenomenon – which ran in a Mumbai theatre for five consecutive years, and its sound (LP records) which preceded the film's release, sold 500,000 units, and eventually became a collector's item.

By the mid-1980s Bachchan was instrumental in launching his own comic book series, with himself as the super-hero character called "Supremo." Scroll.in reports how the India Book House publisher Pammi Bakshi met Bachchan and proposed to launch a super-hero comic book for children. The famed filmmaker, writer, and poet Gulzar was roped in as the writer, and the *Amar Chitra Katha* illustrator Pratap Mullick was employed to do the design. The report states how:

> Mullick was not interested in popular cinema, and had not even watched any of Bachchan's films. Once Mullick had been persuaded, he watched Bachchan's movies and devised between eight and 10 costumes for Supremo's character. Bachchan approved one – a pink, fitting outfit with a wrap and holster and a pendent around his neck. Supremo does not have any obvious super powers, but simply happens to possess the right combination of strength and intelligence.[27]

Modelled on Bachchan's appearance, the comic book's plots and narratives borrowed heavily from the actor's erstwhile hits and dialogues – Supremo took care of two young boys named Vijay and Anthony,[28] and had a pet falcon as in *Coolie*, renamed as Shaheen. Published in both English and Hindi, the Supremo comics had a certain reach across North and West Indian territories, and I wish to propose that it culminated in the emergence of the super-heroic figure, as in films like *Shahenshah* (Tinnu Anand 1988) and other films like *Toofan* and *Jaadugar* mentioned earlier.

Will Eisner in *Comics and Sequential Art* (1985)[29] points out that comic book designs do not merely utilize imageries, frames, panels, tiers, and its sequential flow, and the "texts," in fact, also work as "images" in such art. In the Hindi version and the third edition of the Supremo comics as the aliens attack ("*Hamla*") and destroy Earth's gravity, things begin to fly across expansive landscapes. A particular tier from *Hamla* demonstrates three adjacent panels, while a large fish sketched in the background covers two panels, and also covers the gutters. On the left panel, of the tier, two young boys – Anthony and Vijay – wonder "how to put the fish (Sonali) back in the tank." In the middle panel, there is a portrait of Bachchan/Supremo, sporting large sunglasses. Supremo says – "Woh tum mujh par, chhor do" ("leave it to me"). The dialogue drawn inside the speech balloon in effect heightens Bachchan's "manner of speaking," and the stresses he usually applies in his audio-visual texts. In reality, it is likely that one (re)imagines Bachchan's voice – and lines such as "Jab tak baithne ko na kaha jaaye sharafat se khade raho" (remain standing until you are told to sit down) from *Zanjeer* – as one goes through the visualizations. The third panel presents a full figure of Bachchan and shows Supremo running (in his deep pink costume, with a wrap and a thick belt around his waist) to save the world.[30]

Additionally, I would like to venture that a third significant situation had developed prior to the *Coolie* incident, and Bachchan's return as a super-hero (in films and through comics). Arguably, following the growing recognition of Bachchan's voice and mannerisms, facilitated by the release of the *Sholay* LP records, in 1979 Bachchan was reintroduced as a "singing" star through the popular film *Mr. Natwarlal* (Rakesh Kumar). By his own admission he had sung the song "Mere Paas Aao" for children on a special request by his friend. Following this, a series of other songs became popular by means of two consecutive films, namely *Lawaaris* (Prakash Mehra) and *Silsila* (Yash Chopra), both of which were released in 1981, reinventing Bachchan as a singer. While the song "Mere angane mein" from *Lawaaris* was a big hit, *Silsila* had two popular songs – "Rang barse" and "Neela asmaan so gaaya" – which were essayed by Bachchan. Moreover, his voice/recitation of poems intercepted the famous song "Yeh kahan aa gaye hum," sung by Lata Mangeshkar.

It must be stressed at this juncture that Hindi film songs were available through gramophone records since the inception of the Talkies during the 1930s, and later, these were commonly accessible through audio-cassettes; the 1950s Hindi film songs travelled across South Asia also through radio transmissions.[31] Hence, Bachchan's distinctive voice not only became accessible through other media, following the mass acceptability of his songs and singing voice, the voice per se could be dubbed by voice-doubles and professional singers like Sudesh Bhonsle, and applied to film after film through the 2000s.[32] The exploitation of Bachchan's singing voice as in *Baghbaan* ("Chali, Chali" and "Hori khele Raghuveera"), the alternate use of playback singers like Bhonsle, for the well circulated and provocative song such as "Jumma Chumma" from the film *Hum* (Mukul S. Anand 1991), and the application of Shankar Mahadevan's (music composer and singer) voice for "Kajra Re" and "BnB" (from the film *Bunty aur Babli*), as well as for the song "Rock n Roll Soniye" (in *Kabhi Alvida Naa Kehna* [Karan Johar 2006]) are points of deliberations.

Such smooth interchangeability of Bachchan's voice with proficient and junior (in age) playback singers, who could also imitate his voice, facilitated the industry, which is hugely dependent on his stardom and therefore, milks it to collect revenue.[33] Thereby, such industrial products reinstitute the myth of Bachchan's "un-ageing" baritone. This, in effect, implies that the "Bachchan" (like) voice would remain flexible and active over the years, irrespective of the complexity of the musical composition or his physical age(ing). As a matter of fact, what "sounds" like Bachchan, *may or may not* be his own voice. Moreover, Bachchan's baritone became remarkably deeper over time and was also used in a number of films including *Satranj ki Khiladi* (Satyajit Ray 1977) and *Lagaan* (Ashutosh Gwariker 2000) as the "voiceover," which would and could introduce the problem and the plot of the film. Additionally, both *Kahaani* (Sujoy Ghosh 2012) and *Badla* used songs sung by him in the (opening) title sequences to emphasize the crux of the story.

Ageless Baritone

Besides the different ramifications – with regard to subjects of "acousmatic being" and "visualized acousmêtre" – of Bachchan's voice charted out so far, the other aspect that I wish to accentuate is the application of his voice as narrator/voice-over artist (or its function as "commentator-acousmêtre"). Consider the introductory sequences of *Bhuvan Shome*. Describing Bhuvan Shome (the character), the voice of Bachchan echoes an Awadhi accent, albeit, without any of his well-known inflections and intonations (also see *Bawarchi* 1972, for a similar rendition). The voiceover, in fact, primarily acts as the narrator and commentator across scenes and establishes the problem of the story. In the opening scenes, we see the character Bhuvan Shome (played by Utpal Dutt) riding a Tonga, and taking off. As Bachchan speaks his voice is now and then intercepted by Dutt's performative speech. This sequence also brings forth Mrinal Sen's experimental style in which he not only uses still images but also animation. Bachchan's voice critiquing the Bengali *bhadralok* goes on to say – "Bangal ... sonar [Golden] Bangal ... Mahan [the Great] Bangal ... Vichitra [variegated] Bangal," which thereafter, quickly merges with cries, shouts, and slogans recorded during contemporary political turmoil. This oration is supported by stills of Vivekananda, Rabindranath Tagore, and shots of Satyajit Ray (looking through the camera) and Ravi Shankar (playing Sitar), which are followed by shots of political movement, rallies, and the infamous strike of cinema halls that halted film production during the period. Bachchan's chaste Hindi and tonality effectively heightens the critique of the *bhadralok* that Sen seeks to foreground through the film (in which the elderly and righteous Shome develops a certain affection for a village girl when he takes a break from his taxing job and goes hunting).

If the long narration at the beginning of *Bhuvan Shome* is playful and enticing in *Shatranj ke Khiladi* – made eight years later – the voice sounds deeper and affected by Bachchan's emergent manner of speaking. The stresses and the pauses as well as his timbre and vocal range dramatize the mock battle of "Awadh" performed on the chessboard by Mir (Saeed Jaffrey) and Mirza (Sanjeev Kumar).[34] It is difficult to tell whether Satyajit Ray had cast Bachchan for his manner of speaking (voice, accent, performative quality) or Bachchan brought into the film his own intonations. However, as one listens to the credit sequence of *Shatranj ke Khiladi*, it is clear that Bachchan's vocal weight and timbre had changed remarkably from the early phase.[35] In fact, a range of other shifts become audible as we take into account Ninad Kamat's comment that,[36] Bachchan is "more nasal," and "less bass," and thereby, mull over how the voice has deepened gradually – or vacillated between baritone (mid range) and bass (low range). For instance, *Laagan* opens with Bachchan's heavy voice stating – "1893, Champaner." His diction, inflections, pauses, and rendition attach a historical aura to an otherwise fictitious tale. This notable shift from an agile narrative voice to a weighty authoritative voice sums up Bachchan's long and persisting career. During this extensive period, Bachchan's voice did not actually go hoarse or lose its flexibility with its natural maturation; rather, by and large, it modified from Baritone to Bass and not only sounded deep and sensitive but overwhelming as well.

The song "Rozana," from the film *Nishabd* for instance (in which the character is in love with his daughter's young friend and, eventually ends up separating from his wife and daughter), is performed by Bachchan and sounds like a lament, a cry, and a mode of storytelling, which is similar to a Nazm, as it were. The song acts as a narration of the socially unacceptable love between an "elderly" person and a teenage girl and also functions as a confession – laced with pain – about an impossible love and relationship, and his inability to let it go. The big close-ups of his face, the unconventional camera angles, the sharp light, and the uses of blue filters highlight the character's anguish, while the face with age-lines is juxtaposed with shots of the girl Jia (played by Jiah Khan), moving around happily and freely with a hosepipe. Although the film was a box office failure, it did reconfirm that Bachchan was still viable as a solo and (even) romantic star.

Notwithstanding the investments that went and go into the making of his stature (through the repeated emphasis on his height, his large frame, gait, and demeanour), his voice, and such soulful rendering of poems, alongside the dubbing of his voice by playback singers in the prelude to the songs such as "Jumma Chumma" (e.g., the lines "Arre oh Jumma, bahar nikal, [...] aaj ka wadah hain, dekh main aa gaya ... " [O Jumma, come out ... you had promised, see I am here]) or in the "BnB" feat in *Bunty aur Babli* create the necessary sonic mix-ups for the industry, and fantasies for the larger public. Non-technical viewers, therefore, generally speaking, need to scan the credit lists to spot who performed which song considering that disparate voices sound like Bachchan's. Similarly, more recently, a number of advertisements (in different languages) in which Bachchan uses his persona as a brand have effortlessly dubbed his voice with copy artists and have passed those on as Bachchan's "ageless" baritone to the masses.[37]

The Acousmatic/Image

While Bachchan has rarely had any chance to experiment with his image – marred by a fair number of failures as in the case of *Aag* (Ram Gopal Varma 2007), or celebrated for his performance as in *Paa* (Balki 2009) – his attempts to try and test his voice acting is even rarer. It is public knowledge that Bachchan had given a shot at altering his voice, in order to make it sound hoarse and dry (or "aged"), with less vocal flexibility, in the (now) cult film *Agneepath*. Although Bachchan eventually received the National Film Award for Best Actor for his performance in the film, *Agneepath* failed to impress Bachchan's fans and was quickly redubbed and released to recover the losses.[38] In reality even when Bachchan essayed double or triple roles, donning uncharacteristic looks (as in *Kasme Vaade* [Ramesh Bahl 1978], *Don* [Chandra Barot 1978], *Bemisal* (Hrishikesh Mukherjee 1982), *SattePeSatta* [Raj Sippy 1982], *Desh Premi* [Manmohan Desai 1982], *Mahaan* [S. Ramanathan 1983], and so on) his exemplary voice for all such characters remained identical.

In the context of the construction of Bachchan's (timeless) voice, *Agneepath* informs us about the modes of production of voice in cinema, the ways in which a film may have a "double" voice track – the resurgence of the older version (with Bachchan's "Marlon Brando" modulations) on online portals, illustrates the duality of filmic texts. In this regard, the two films, *Reshma Aur Shera* and *Shamitabh*, analysed in this chapter, function as brackets which hold his aural stardom together. For instance, in 1971 Bachchan had played a speech-impaired character in Sunil Dutt's classic *Reshma Aur Shera*. Nevertheless, in retrospect, *Reshma Aur Shera* appears like an ironic example of the "lack," and the fetishized voice Chion argues about, which becomes conspicuous through its absence. The lack of Bachchan's baritone in *Reshma Aur Shera* is almost uncanny so to speak; its nonexistence becomes a forceful reminder of the baritone. In the film Sunil Dutt (also the director) plays the protagonist, who fights a feudal order. Set in the open, barren terrain of Rajasthan, the film comments on the Rajput moral order and the tradition of honour killing. Shot expansively on location and edited at a languid pace, the film stands out as an exceptional cinematic venture of the period. It opens with Reshma (Waheeda Rahman) and Shera (Dutt) falling impossibly in love with each other. The complications intensify when Shera disobeys his father's wishes and tries to initiate an alliance between the two rival families. Shera eventually turns up at Reshma's brother's wedding armed with a transistor (which is perhaps the only sign of modernity and that of the outside). While pacts are forged and everlasting feuds are forgotten, Shera's disappointed and enraged father Jagat Singh (Naval Kumar) arrives at the site with his sons. They force Shera's younger and weaker brother Chotu (Bachchan) – who is also speech-impaired – to take up the gun and shoot Reshma's father (K.N. Singh), and her newly married brother (Ranjeet).

The wedding scene quickly turns into a ceremonial mourning, and Shera swears revenge against his own father and brothers. Later, as a social outcast Shera yearns for justice and the film turns into a scathing critique of feudal values and masculinity. In due course, Shera kills his brother Vijay (Vinod Khanna) and looks for Chotu, who takes refuge in Reshma's house to save himself from his brother's wrath. Women – Shera's mother (Sulochana Jr.), Reshma, and her widowed sister-in-law (Rakhi) – emerge as powerful figures who struggle to impede the stream of bloodbath. En fin, Reshma marries Chotu (to protect him from his brother's vengeance) and Shera is obliged to drop his gun. In the last scene, Shera drops dead on the sand dunes as does Reshma, while sand storm covers the lovers' bodies. The film ends as an extended exploration of the vast and barren landscape of Rajasthan, in which Reshma and Shera's bodies are swallowed by the sand. The film emphasizes the brutality of pre-modern cultures and practices and achieves an epic dimension in the way it frames multiple families, locked in their own ritualistic atrocities and the landscape as a silent witness to the malice that continues to influence generations.

On the one hand one may enquire about the diegetic function of Chotu's character, on the other, the role raises critical questions with regard to the star body. While it is not unusual for young entrants to be dubbed by professional voiceover artists,[39] nonetheless, the absence of Bachchan's voice in the film underscores the function of voice in manufacturing stardom. While Bachchan describes (on his blog) how he was an unknown actor when the film premiered, his co-actor K.N. Singh claims that it was he who suggested that Bachchan's voice be removed since his diction (as a Rajasthani) was not precise.[40] Likewise, in her book on the making of *Sholay*, Anupama Chopra (2000) narrates how the team contemplated until the release of the film whether they should dub Amjad Khan's voice with a voice artist or not because the tonality of his voice apparently made him sound like a weak villain. Although finally Khan's own voice was retained and his performance became a major draw for the film, such industrial deliberations accentuate the importance of voice in the making of a star. Similarly, if K.N. Singh's point is taken into account then the removal of Bachchan's (irreplaceable) voice from *Reshma aur Shera* at the shooting stage underlines the manner in which industrial parameters are instrumental in the production of aural stardom, through its many coordinates across disparate media texts, which includes the processes of image making (supported by para-texts such as print and Television media), and particularly through the circulation of sonic elements via radio, audio albums, etc. More importantly, in the context of the chapter, it shows how voices of actors are sometimes substituted by skilful voice-over artists to achieve a certain affective component.

Contrarily, the plot of the recent film *Shamitabh* is built upon Bachchan's voice, its all-pervasive features, and its omnipotence. In the film Danish (Dhanush) is a young and aspiring actor who cannot speak, and hence cannot secure film roles. Eventually he and an assistant director (Akshara Hasan) are able to convince an extraordinary yet failed actor – a drunkard living in a graveyard – to lend his voice so that Dhanush can become the star he wants to be, by the dint of an outstanding voice. After some persuasion Amitabh, the name of the character played by Bachchan, agrees to play his part and lends his voice, through what is described as "Live Voice Transfer Technology" that uses embedded micro-recorders and earpieces and empowers the voiceless to speak through a "borrowed" voice. Irrespective of the credibility of plot, what is noteworthy is the premise of the film – Bachchan's baritone wandering to find a younger body. As the film progresses Danish becomes a star with the voice of Bachchan, and Amitabh (the character) becomes increasingly aware and demanding regarding his function both within the films in which Danish performs and during his public appearances. Following a series of tussles over what comes first, the voice of the senior star or the body of the junior, finally, they become friends. Eventually, however, Danish dies, and Amitabh loses his voice in the same accident. In the final scene a broken and elderly man Amitabh (Bachchan) returns to the graveyard, and sits in front of Danish's grave mourning and making silent lip movements and gestures. Yet, the voice is actually audible, through flashback, as Amitabh hears his own deep baritone – presently more bass – emitting all Bachchan-like intonations, pauses, and the highs and the lows. The film borrows from a range of sub-texts and addresses Bachchan's acoustic stardom, its many renditions across audio-visual texts, as well as illustrates the film industry's own efforts to deploy Bachchan's star persona, despite his biological age. Moreover, Bachchan frequently modifies his voice performance in the film and appears baritone when he lends his voice to Danish, and more bass when he performs as Amitabh. Remarkably, the authority of the voice over the body and the struggle over it – its *disappearance* and *reappearance* as Chion puts its – are evident in the scenes, in which the unique baritone (re)claims its dominance over the body. In fact, right from the introduction of the characters, and through many scenes which follow, Amitabh – both the character and actor – reinforces his star charisma, and thus, discloses the strife of the industry to maintain Bachchan's (withering and wavering) stardom. In the film Amitabh/Bachchan effectively becomes a star with a virile voice without a body (as the character sleeps on an unoccupied grave), and in the long run becomes what may be ascribed as an "acousmatic" being. By describing Bachchan's voice as "voice of God" (which is actually used to describe the acousmatic voice of the voiceover artists),[41] and by emphasizing the potency of his vocal prowess, the film may also become a "fan" film, as well as an example of the struggles within the industry, and its attempts to recuperate a productive stardom.

Within the framework of the ageing bodies and performances of agelessness, as well as of aural stardom of Amitabh Bachchan, two recent films, namely *Paa* and *Gulabo Sitabo* (Shoojit Sircar 2020), in which he has altered his voice considerably, become significant. In *Paa* for instance,

Bachchan plays a 12-year-old child called Auro, who suffers from progeria which causes him to mature rapidly and unusually. The child is finally instrumental in bringing his unwedded Maa (Vidya Balan) and Paa (Abhishek Bachchan), a political leader, together at the time of his untimely death. Just as the film uses a prosthetic to de-age Bachchan,[42] the actor also reinvented his physical gestures and "de-aged" his voice by changing its tonal quality, and by making it sound thinner and younger (childlike) as his vocal pitch jumped up and down. In a way the film reaffirmed the notion of Bachchan's dynamism as the (then) 67-years-old star astoundingly played the role of the son of his own real-life son (Abhishek Bachchan). Further, in *Gulabo Sitabo* Bachchan has been (further) aged by the application of prosthetic (nose) and makeup (beard), and more importantly, he has transformed his physicality and has spoken in a voice, which sounds breathier and softer – as though emanating from a severely affected larynx. In the film Bachchan has also worked on his speech and has used slurs and sometimes inaudible utterances to heighten Mirza's (Bachchan) corporeal and social vulnerability. Such a performance of advancing years, nonetheless, reconfirms Bachchan's agility and ability since the film repeatedly suggests that Mirza is 78 years old, which is Bachchan's (then) present age, and yet, his off-screen star persona – as evident from different media platforms – upholds his vigour and currency. Briefly, scripted TV programmes such as *Kaun Banega Crorepati* (awaiting season 12 in 2020) and films like *Badla* (released in 2019) seemingly present his "actual" age and voice as fashioned through multiple media agencies for his fans and the public; whereas, *Gulabo Sitabo* apparently narrates the story of a 78-year-old elderly and weaker person. Such usages of voice and performance have political, aesthetic, and industrial functions (to borrow from Prasad, 138). In due course, and in a literal sense, Amitabh Bachchan resonates as the "industrial hero" whose stardom and its sustainability is continuously recreated through repeated revitalization as well as memorialization of the "ageless" baritone.

Notes

1 For an alternative argument also see Ranjani Mazumdar "Aviation, Tourism and Dreaming in 1960s Bombay Cinema," and Sangita Gopal *Conjugations*.
2 See Henry Jenkins' influence work *Convergence Culture*. On mainstream Hindi cinemas also see *Bollywood Reader* edited by Rajinder Dudrah and Jigna Desai, Ranjani Mazumdar's *Bombay Cinema*, as well as Rachel Dwyer and Divya Patel edited *Cinema India*.
3 Also see *Fan Cultures* by Matthew Hills and the *Framework* 58 (1–2) dossier "The Fan as Doppelganger" edited by Anupama Kapse and Meheli Sen.
4 Note, in two exceptional cases, for the film *Paa* (Balki, 2009) and for a more recent venture, *Gulabo, Sitabo* (Shoojit Sircar, 2020), Bachchan's appearance has been completely altered through prosthetics, and specifically in the latter

film, in which Bachchan ironically plays his own age (78 years), he has wilfully "aged" his voice and intonations, and delivered indistinct speech to sound "older."

5 See https://timesofindia.indiatimes.com/entertainment/hindi/bollywood/news/Big-B-to-copyright-his-voice/articleshow/6888630.cms (accessed on 25 February 2020).

6 For example, in *Black* (Sanjay Leela Bhansali, 2005), and *101 Not Out* (Umesh Shukla, 2018).

7 See for instance Sudhanva Deshpande "The consumable hero of globalised India", Ashwani Sharma "Blood, Sweat and Tears: Amitabh Bachchan, Urban Demi-God" as well as Ranjani Mazumdar's "From Subjectification to Schizophrenia: The 'Angry Man' and the 'Psychotic' Hero of Bombay Cinema."

8 On Star Studies especially see the decisive volume *Stardom, Industry of Desire* edited by Christine Gledhill, as well as *Stardom and Celebrity: A Reader* edited by Sean Redmond & Su Holmes.

9 We must also examine how star personas are constituted through a series of omissions and inclusions of the disparate roles essayed by the actors. For instance, *Zanjeer* and *Abhimaan*, *Chupke-Chupke* and *Sholay*, *Alaap* and *Amar Akbar Anthony* were successful in the same year, that is, 1973, 1975, and 1977, respectively. Moreover, we ought to take into account the number of middle-class roles Bachchan performed in the films directed by Hrishikesh Mukherjee (for instance, *Namak Karam* (1973), *Mili* (1975), *Bemisal* (1982)), as well as in Basu Chatterjee's *Manzil* (1979).

10 Note, in *Deewar* Vijay's (Bachchan) father is a Union leader, and the film is set against the famous struggles of the mill labourers of Bombay.

11 Furthermore, in *Zanjeer* (Prakash Mehra, 1973) several marginalized and dispossessed characters either aid him or become "donors" (Prasad, 144), and form a collective in Vijay's quest for (extra-legal) justice and revenge; in addition, *Deewar* (Yash Chopra, 1975) "is more accurately described as an allegorization of the history of the nation-state itself through the masochistic fantasy [...]" (Prasad, 150).

12 See Richard Dyer's (1986) landmark study on stars and society and his reading of stars as sites of ideological struggle.

13 For a feminist reading also see *The Acoustic Mirror* by Kaja Silverman.

14 Note, while Indian popular films regularly dubbed voices of the actors to eliminate location sound/noise until the early 2000s, a particular scene in *Yaarana* (Rakesh Kumar, 1981), which could not be dubbed due to technical reasons, still bears location noise, and therefore, accentuates the process. Go to 37:00: https://www.youtube.com/watch?v=lcm8f4mVm6Y

15 Writing about the "magic and power" of "acousmêtre", Chion foregrounds the moment when Greta Garbo attained cinematic voice with the arrival of the "Talkies". Also see Madhuja Mukherjee "Early Indian Talkies: Voice, Performance and Aura."

16 See Neepa Majumdar "Sound in Indian Cinema."

17 On the specific use of playback see Madhuja Mukherjee, "Popular Modes of Address and Art of Playback in Hindi Melodramas" and "Hindi Popular Cinema and Its Peripheries: Of Female Singers, Performances, and the Presence/Absence of Suraiya" by Madhuja Mukherjee, and Neepa Majumdar "The Embodied Voice."

18 The Khan-Trio signify Shah Rukh Khan, Salman Khan, and Amir Khan, the reigning stars of contemporary Bollywood. Note, all three Khans are producers as well.

19 The success of *Kaun Banega Crorepati* promoted the much-acclaimed film *Slumdog Millionaire* (Danny Boyle, 2008), which was an adaptation of a novel published in 2005.
20 See Madhava Prasad "Fan Bhakti and Subaltern Sovereignty."
21 Also see Rajinder Dudrah *Bollywood Travels: Culture, Diaspora and Border Crossings in Popular Hindi Cinema*, which focuses on Bollywood travel shows across the globe.
22 Fromhttps://www.filmibeat.com/bollywood/features/2018/when-the-media -banned-amitabh-bachchan-for-15-years-they-wanted-to-teach-him-a-lesson -273060.html (accessed on 11 March 2020)
23 See *Movie Blockbusters* by Julian Stringer.
24 Note, in Indian contexts, only a few female stars like Nargis, Hema Malini, and Sridevi have performed dual roles.
25 Also see Madhuja Mukherjee "Early Indian Talkies" on the subjects of aura, performance, "embodied" and "dis-embodied" voices.
26 Indeed, Bachchan lookalikes have acquired their own popularity. See https:// www.republicworld.com/entertainment-news/bollywood-news/amitabh-bach-chan-doppelganger-shashikant-pedwals-tiktok-video.html (accessed on 13th March 2020).
27 From:https://scroll.in/article/760969/happy-birthday-mr-amitabh-bachchan -superstar-and-comic-book-supremo (accessed on 14 February 2020).
28 While Vijay was the screen name of Bachchan in numerous films, the name Anthony was used in *Amar Akbar Anthony* (Manmohan Desai, 1977).
29 Also see Heer and Worcester edited *A Comics Studies Reader*.
30 Note, during this time, in 1984 precisely, Bachchan also became a Member of Parliament, although his political career was short-lived and controversial.
31 See Peter Manuel's groundbreaking work *Cassette Culture*, Farrell's essay on "The Early Days of the Gramophone Industry in India", Aswin Punathambekar's "AmeenSayani and Radio Ceylon" as well as Madhuja Mukherjee "The Architecture of Songs and Music."
32 See Sudesh Bhonsle perform "Jumma Chumma": https://www.youtube.com/ watch?v=-ES_SuyELv0 (accessed on 28 February 2020).
33 Also see Prasad's argument as referred to in the beginning of the chapter.
34 On *Shatranj ke Khiladi* see the following: https://theprint.in/features/reel-take /rays-shatranj-ke-khilari-asked-difficult-political-questions-is-an-election-must -watch/228189/ (accessed on 19 September 2020).
35 Also see Suresh Jindal *My Adventures with Satyajit Ray*.
36 An actor, a regular voice artist, and Bachchan's dubbing artist, particularly for advertisements in Tamil and other languages.
37 See Tata Sky ad: https://www.youtube.com/watch?v=VHL_3_Q2m04
38 See a contemporary review republished in Koimoi: https://www.koimoi.com/ bollywood-news/blast-from-the-past-agneepath-1990-review/ (accessed on 2 June 2020).
39 For instance, both Rani Mukherjee's and Deepika Padukone's voices were dubbed by Mona Ghosh for their respective first "big" ventures, to improve their performances.
40 See https://srbachchan.tumblr.com/post/28530918048 (accessed on 4 March 2020).
41 For that matter, Bachchan's voice was actually used as a heavenly voice in the film *Hello Brother* (Sohail Khan, 1999).
42 Also, the Martin Scorsese film *The Irishman* (2019) applied digital technology to de-age the Hollywood star Robert De Niro.

References

Chion, Michel. *The Voice in Cinema*. Columbia University Press, 1999.

Chopra, Anupama. *Sholay: The making of a Classic*. Penguin Books, 2000.

Deshpande, Sudhanva. "The Consumable Hero of Globalised India." *Bollyworld: Popular Indian Cinema Through a Transnational Lens*, edited by Raminder Kaur and Ajay J Sinha. Sage Publishing, 2005, pp. 186–203.

Doane, Mary Ann. "The Voice in the Cinema: The Articulation of Body and Space." *Yale French Studies*, vol. 60, 1980, pp. 33–50.

Dudrah, Rajinder. *Bollywood Travels: Culture, Diaspora and Border Crossings in Popular Hindi Cinema*. Routledge, 2012.

Dudrah, Rajinder and Jigna Desai, editors. *The Bollywood Reader*. Open University Press, 2008.

Dwyer, Rachel and Divia Patel, editors. *Cinema India: The Visual Culture of Hindi Film*. Reaktion, 2002.

Dyer, Richard. *Heavenly Bodies: Film Stars and Society*. St. Martin's Press, 1986.

Eisner, Will. *Comics and Sequential Art*. Poorhouse Press, 1985.

Gledhill, Christine, editor. *Stardom: Industry of Desire*. Routledge, 1991.

Gopal, Sangita. *Conjugations: Marriage and Form in New Bollywood Cinema*. University of Chicago Press, 2011.

Heer, Jeet and K. Worcester, editors. *A Comics Studies Reader*. University Press of Mississippi, 2009.

Hill, Mathew. *Fan Cultures*. Routledge, 2002.

Jenkins, Henry. *Convergence Culture: Where Old and New Media Collide*. New York University Press, 2006.

Majumdar, Neepa. "The Embodied Voice: Song Sequences and Stardom in Popular Hindi Cinema." *Soundtrack Available: Essays on Film and Popular Culture*, edited by Pamela Robertson Wojcik and Arthur Knight. Duke University Press, 2001, pp. 161–181.

———."Sound in Indian Cinema: Beyond the Song Sequence." *Sound and Music in Film and Visual Media*, edited by Graeme Harper, Ruth Doughty and Jochen Eisentraut. Continuum, 2009, pp. 303–324.

Manuel, Peter. *Cassette Culture: Popular Music and Technology in North India*. Chicago University Press, 1993.

Mazumdar, Ranjani. "From Subjectification to Schizophrenia: The 'Angry Man' and the 'Psychotic' Hero of Bombay Cinema." *Making Meaning in India Cinema*, edited by Ravi Vasudevan. Oxford University Press, 2000, pp. 238–266.

———. *Bombay Cinema: An Archive of the City*. University of Minnesota Press, 2007.

———."Aviation, Tourism and Dreaming in 1960s Bombay Cinema." *Bioscope*, vol. 2, no. 2, 2011, pp. 129–155.

Mukherjee, Madhuja. "Shifting Identities and Emerging Codes: Metamorphosis of the Rebel." *Deep Focus*, July–December, 2002, pp. 5–14.

———. "Early Indian Talkies: Voice, Performance and Aura." *Journal of the Moving Image*, vol. 6, 2007, pp. 39–61.

———. "Popular Modes of Address and Art of Playback in Hindi Melodramas." *South Asian Journal*, vol. 29, 2010, pp. 91–104.

———. "The Architecture of Songs and Music: Soundmarks of Bollywood, a Popular Form and Its Emergent Texts." *Screen Sound Journal*, vol. 3, 2012, pp. 9–34.

———, editor. *Aural Films, Oral Cultures, Essays on Cinema from the Early Sound Era.* Jadavpur University Press, 2012.

———. "Hindi Popular Cinema and its Peripheries: Of Female Singers, Performances, and the Presence/Absence of Suraiya." *Bollywood and its Other(s), Towards New Configurations*, edited by Vikrant Kishore, Amit Sarwal and Parichay Patra. Palgrave Macmillan, 2014, pp. 67–85.

———. "Of Recollection, Retelling and Cinephilia: Reading Gangs of Wasseypur as an Active Archive of Popular Cinema." *Journal of the Moving Image*, vol. 13, 2015, pp. 91–113.

———. "The Singing Cowboys: Sholay and the significance of (Indian) Curry Westerns within post-colonial narratives." *Transformations Journal*, vol. 24, 2014. www.transformationsjournal.org/journal/24/02.shtml.

Prasad, Madhava M. *Ideology of the Hindi Film: A Historical Construction.* Oxford University Press, 1998.

———. "Fan Bhakti Subaltern Sovereignty: Enthusiasm as a Political Factor." *Economic and Political Weekly*, vol. 44, 2009, pp. 68–76.

Punathambekar, Aswin. "Ameen Sayani and Radio Ceylon: Notes towards a History of Broadcasting and Bombay Cinema." *BioScope*, vol. 1, no. 2, 2010, pp. 189–197.

Qiong Yu, Sabrina and Guy Austin, editors. *Revisiting Star Studies.* Edinburgh University Press, 2017.

Redmond, Sean and Su Holmes, editors. *Stardom and Celebrity: A Reader.* Sage Publications, 2007.

Silverman, Kaja. *The Acoustic Mirror: The Female Voice in Psychoanalysis and Cinema.* Indiana University Press, 1988.

Swinnen, Aagje and John Stotesbury, editors. *Aging, Performance, and Stardom: Doing Age on the Stage of Consumerist Culture.* LIT, 2012.

11

"SECOND CHILDISHNESS AND MERE OBLIVION"

Indian Films on Dementia and the Idea of Ageing Differently

Nilanjana Deb

Prologue

Her loneliness increased in the years after her husband's death. Living an isolated existence in an apartment block without an elevator, and anxious about her loss of control over bodily functions, she once hesitantly told her grown-up children leading their busy lives elsewhere to put her in an old age home. She would be better off there, she said, at least she would have people like herself with whom to talk, people to take care of her. Her children were appalled. Bad people put their parents in old age homes. Such things happened in the West, not in good Indian homes. They would never let such a thing happen, it would be a shame upon the family. Maids and domestic help were paid handsomely to look after her, and she continued to remain desperately lonely. Years later, after dementia and injuries rendered her incapable of living alone, she said to her youngest daughter in a moment of lucidity, "I have become what I am today because of loneliness. Loneliness does this to you."[1]

The Epidemic of Forgetting

While some amount of memory loss with age is seen as "natural" or "normal," there is increasing concern at the rate at which various forms of dementia are being clinically diagnosed around the world. Dementia is an umbrella term for a range of degenerative illnesses including Alzheimer's disease, vascular dementia, dementia with Lewy bodies, mixed dementia, Parkinson's disease, frontotemporal dementia, Creutzfeldt-Jakob disease, Huntington's disease, and Wernicke-Korsakoff syndrome. Dementia is marked by the

DOI: 10.4324/9780429352560-12

"disturbance of multiple higher cortical functions, including memory, thinking, orientation, comprehension, calculation, learning capacity, language, and judgement... Impairments of cognitive function are commonly accompanied, and occasionally preceded, by deterioration in emotional control, social behaviour, or motivation." (WHO: 46, 2017). The total number of new cases of dementia each year worldwide is nearly 7.7 million, implying one new case every four seconds.[2] Older age or *vaardhakya* is considered the most important risk factor for dementia, with the prevalence of the disease increasing drastically after the age of 65.[3] Economic inequity across the globe has rendered this problem more complex. As the proportion of ageing populations increases across Asia in particular, the number of people with various forms of dementia is also likely to increase.[4] With increased life expectancy due to advances in medical science, the volume and degree of care required for older dementia patients will steadily increase over the years, putting pressure on economic and other resources of the family and the state. This chapter seeks to look at some of the ways in which cultural, class, and gender differences affect social and familial attitudes to dementia patients in South Asia, a region at risk on account of the increasing numbers of the elderly living in some of the most densely populated areas of the world.

More than 11% of the four billion people estimated to be living in the Asia-Pacific region in 2015 were over 60 years of age, and it is estimated that by 2050, one-fourth of the population in the Asia-Pacific region would be above the age of 60. The number of people with dementia in the region is estimated to increase from 23 million people in 2015 to 71 million people by the year 2050. The rates of dementia occurrence in India, China, South Asian, and Western Pacific regions have been found to be increasing at three times the rate of increase in high-income countries.[5] Given the history of social and cultural attitudes towards mental illness and senility in South Asia, the degree to which developing countries in the region will be able to cope with this crisis will depend on the amount of effort the state and non-governmental agencies are willing to put into raising awareness and building infrastructure for the specialized care and treatment of ageing populations.

The 2014 Report on Dementia in the Asia-Pacific Region observed a limited awareness of dementia as well as a cultural context that denies or attaches a stigma to dementia in many Asian countries, exacerbating the meagre resources available for patients and their families. Even a decade before this chapter was written there was very little representation or awareness of dementia or Alzheimer's disease in South Asian popular culture, and the few Bollywood depictions that existed were ill-informed, to say the least. A striking example of this lack of awareness is the film *Black* (2005), where the elderly teacher Debraj Sahai, played by Amitabh Bachchan, is shown confined in empty rooms devoid of furniture, or, shockingly, chained to his bed in the later stages of Alzheimer's disease.[6] Even stranger in its depiction of Alzheimer's disease is the 2008 Hindi film *U Me Aur Hum*, where Piya, played by the actress Kajol, is institutionalized after being diagnosed with Alzheimer's as early as her twenties. Miraculously, she is "healed" by the love of her husband who brings her back home from the institution. The film ends with them celebrating their anniversary on a cruise ship more than two decades later.[7] The patient shows no deterioration from the improbably early age when she was first detected with the ailment, a miracle that is pathologically and clinically not possible in such degenerative conditions. These Bollywood films from the first decade of the 21st century only reflect the lack of knowledge of South Asians about the forms of dementia proliferating across the subcontinent. The only Indian films in this decade that made an impact through the depiction of dementia were either regional or "serious" cinema. The Malayalam film *Thanmathra* (2005), directed by Blessy, was successful in Kerala, perhaps because the state, with its high literacy rate and the highest proportion of older people in India, has achieved a greater mobilization of people and organizations working for dementia awareness.[8] Ramesan Nair, played by Mohanlal, is a brilliant government officer whose life is derailed by the early onset of familial Alzheimer's disease. The film focuses on the way in which his family rallies around to support him. In the same year, Jahnu Barua directed *Maine Gandhi Ko Nahin Mara* in which Anupam Kher played Uttam Chaudhary, a former lecturer of Hindi who suffers from dementia and nurses the delusion that he killed Mahatma Gandhi.[9]

In the second decade of this century, some films have attempted to provide a more informed representation of dementia and its impact on the individual and their family. This is perhaps a result of the increasing awareness in the urban middle and upper class about the disease affecting families across the developing world, and the greater availability of medical, ethnographic, and sociological literature on the subject through the internet. However, in all the films, scriptwriters and directors choose to show the early stages of dementia, not the graphic starkness of the later stages, when incontinence, silence, and physical rigidity set in. While this might be for aesthetic reasons, the films often provide a sentimentalized, truncated representation of what is a long and dreary battle against illness. Often, in these films, the occurrence of dementia is used as a point of entry into something else, such as an analysis of family relationships, the relationship of the individual with the community or to spirituality, or the perspective of the overburdened caregiver. There is an erasure of the incontinent or degenerating body of the aged in these films, even though dementia-induced bodily changes are crucial in shaping the care routines of patients.

Maine Gandhi Ko Nahin Mara seems to have initiated a trend of depicting learned, urban, middle- or upper class *savarna* men as dementia patients: *Astu* (2015) is a Marathi film directed by Sumitra Bhave and Sunil Suktankar in which Dr. Mohan Agashe plays the role of a retired professor of Sanskrit suffering from dementia who forgets his own name and address and begins to live with the family of an elephant keeper.[10] In the Bengali film *Mayurakshi* (2017) directed by Atanu Ghosh the dementia patient is a retired professor of History living in the past.[11] The purposes behind the pattern of repeatedly creating this kind of "privileged-abject" normative patient in Indian cinema will become clearer when I discuss the effect of class and gender on the patient and their family, and the place of privilege in the third person theorizing of selfhood. Perhaps the only Indian film in recent times that substantially deals with the gendered experience of the patient and caregiver is the Hindi film *Mai* (2013) directed by Mahesh Kodiyal, in which Asha Bhonsle plays the aged mother who becomes increasingly disoriented at being shifted from her son's home to the home of her daughter.[12] It would seem that there are no poor people with dementia in India, certainly not in Indian cinema. One can gloss this emerging homogeneous subject of films on dementia through the exploration of the cultural and socio-economic matrix through which most Indians deal with ageing and the aged.

Dementia and Cultural Difference

Bhui and Bhugra in their work on mental illness in Black and Asian diasporic communities have insisted that cultural factors need to be taken into account when questions of access to medical care for dementia patients are considered.[13] Most often, the cultural assumption of South Asians is that elders should be looked after by their families, as opposed to their seeking professional care or support.[14] These beliefs prevalent in the South Asian diaspora represent attitudes towards ageing and the care of the aged in South Asia that have "travelled" overseas. As a consequence of these attitudes, the undiagnosed dementia patient and their family suffer anxiety or go into denial over the changes in ageing body and mind, unaware that the person has some form of dementia and needs professional care. There is no urgency that an aged person may have a disease needing treatment – the elderly struggling with mental and physical changes are humorously or contemptuously dismissed with terms such as *sathiyaa gayi hai* (gone over sixty), *bahattore dhorechhe* (become seventy two-ish), and *bhimroti hoyecche* (gone senile).

There is a peculiar regionalist and nationalist bias in the assertion that South Asian elders are cared for by their families while Western families "put" the aged in old age homes. Lawrence Cohen as a "westerner" noticed this peculiar bias among his interviewees. The "us and them" sentiment marks even the discipline of gerontology in postcolonial India:

> Gerontology in India is predicated upon a sense of difference that is mapped onto a polarity of India versus the West. Its originating point asserts the moral superiority of Indianness through its representation as

the inclusive and embracing family. The continual invocation of the ideal joint family subverts both external and internal discourses of the inferiorized Indian self.[15]

According to Cohen, Indian gerontology is based on a narrative of the decline of the joint family due to urbanization, modernization, industrialization, and westernization. While the West is the source of the problem, the West is also the space from which the discipline draws its vocabulary and methodology, in a colonial deference to the perceived efficacy of Western science over indigenous forms of healing and care.[16] Paradoxically, Cohen observes a feature in popular medical writing on dementia in India and Africa that arranges itself along the lines of the "west versus us" – numerous studies in these regions claim that there are fewer occurrences of dementia in the non-Western world: claims are made that the Indian brain is a "better brain" than the Western one, and there is "no authentic case" of Alzheimer's disease among Black Africans as opposed to Afro-Americans in the USA.[17] It is as if there is a double denial happening – the patient and their family, as well as the nation, refuse to accept that dementia is real and hence refuse to acknowledge the necessity of options for rationalized care that are available. There is the additional stigma attached to mental illness in general that prevents the family from taking the elderly to a doctor. Only in extreme cases of unsocial or unusual behaviour does the family label the venerable elder "mad" and seek psychiatric care.

Contrasted with the "good" modern family that looks after its elders in keeping with the values of the old joint family system is the "selfish" modern family that "neglects" the elderly, institutionalizes them and sees them as a drain on their time, money and energy. This "selfish" nuclear family is depicted in both scientific narratives and popular culture in South Asia as a negative effect of westernization and modernization on the Indian family. The formulation of the simplistic binary of "good" and "bad" family can be understood differently if we think of the term "caregiver" itself. This is a term that emerges in the West as a result of the rationalization of medical care for terminally ill patients. There is no native equivalent of this term in India. It becomes difficult for a lot of people to understand that they are not only daughter or son, they are also caregiver, a "job" requiring the acquisition of specialized skills for handling patients at different stages of the disease. The "good" versus "bad" family is actually a binary of "emotional" versus "rational" approaches to the care of the elderly. In *Mai*, the "rational" son and his wife want to put the mother in an old age home, while the "emotional" daughter fights to bring Mai to live with her own family. In keeping with South Asian stereotypes, the son is shown as a negative character and the self-sacrificing daughter as heroic in her struggle to "save" Mai. The tension between the "emotional" and the "rational" is similarly played out between the daughters of Professor Shastri in *Astu*. According to the younger daughter, a person who is "not himself," who has no sense of who he is, is a "dead" person. She feels that her elder sister's concern for her missing father is therefore unnecessary as he is no longer the person they knew, and suggests institutionalization as a practical solution. On the other hand, Ira, the more "emotional" elder daughter, is convinced by her visit to an old age home that an institution is not the place for her father.

Cultural factors determine the ways in which the elderly patient relates to the physical space of their family home. Notions of the "retreat" of the elderly from worldly life into a space of contemplation and seclusion are built into the traditional ideas of *vanaprastha* and *sannyasa* in the subcontinent. The aged are expected to become less "obstrusive" within the space of the household as their ability to earn or work decreases, to live in a separate room if space permits, or in a corner reserved for them, as the rest of the family goes about their work in the capitalist economy.[18] However, this authority becomes severely compromised when the venerable elder is found to be speaking "gibberish," losing control over bodily functions, and forgetting names, dates, and events. The onset of dementia, visible to close family from the third or fourth stage of the illness, renders the body and voice of the elderly in South Asia subaltern.[19] The old man or woman, oscillating between anxiety over diminishing faculties, "childish" and "difficult" behaviour, and an unresponsive silence, becomes like Gilbert and Gubar's madwoman in the attic, a difficult absent-presence. Another reason for the increased marginalization of the aged, indeed a psychological trigger for mental illness, can be the sense of psychological isolation due to the death of the elderly person's spouse. *Astu, Mai, Mayurakshi*, and *Maine Gandhi Ko Nahin Mara* all show dementia patients whose spouses have died – there is no one of their own generation left in the household, as it were, to understand and look out for them.

Most South Asian families construct identities for the elderly that are related to the family's projection of its core values. The dementia patient throws the self-image of the "good family" into crisis; the plaintive and "strange" behaviour of the dementia patient in front of guests or outsiders becomes a cause for anxiety as the family begins to feel that they will be judged as bad or neglectful by others. One recalls the innumerable times when one's grandmothers, both dementia patients, complained to visitors that they had not been fed when the reality was that they had forgotten that they had eaten. Particularly stressful is the patient's wandering and getting lost from home, which can be misconstrued by outsiders as the extreme carelessness of the patient's family.[20] There are scenes of the patient getting lost in *Mai, Thanmathra*, and *Astu* where the panic of the family is palpable. Mai contracts pneumonia after wandering for a long time in the rain, and her family blames itself for her subsequent premature death. In

Astu, the elder daughter leaves her father alone in her car for a few minutes, only to find that he has disappeared when she returns. Having strayed away from his daughter's car to follow an elephant passing by, Dr. Shastri can no longer remember the way back, or his own name and address. He follows the elephant, occasionally crying and holding his head in his hands because he cannot remember anything. Inevitably, the younger daughter blames her elder sister for her father's disappearance, suggesting that an old age home would have been a safer place for him.

"For Their Own Good"

The dementia patients' bodies and voices are therefore often cloistered out of the gaze and hearing of outsiders. This is not very different from the isolation of the patient in an institution in developed countries, though families in South Asia seem to think that loneliness within the home is better than loneliness in an institution. The eventual loss of language is part of the progression of the disease, but long before that, the anxiety or impatience of the family can silence the patient. This subaltern silence can often be misread, and cultural frameworks in the subcontinent do contribute to this:

> Yet the old person who was not heard might be spoken of by others as the old person who would not be heard, the latter-day forest-dweller. Silence, withdrawal, and a break in communication between young and old pointed as well to the transcendent voice of the jivanmukti, the realized in life, or in more everyday language, to an old person heard as religious, as a serious bhakt, or devotee.[21]

Like the child, the "ideal" elderly person may be "seen but not heard." The old person is repeatedly exhorted, in many South Asian homes, to turn to remembrance of the divine, so that this remembrance may be of use at the time of their dying. The elderly are told by their families to renounce the worldly attachment or unfulfilled desire that might be holding them back. The presence of the dementia patient in the home, in the advanced stages of the illness, becomes a long wait for final release. However, the "religious" approach of communities to the aged can rob the individual of agency, of voice, as people remain content to view the disintegrating outside of the person as a symbol of the transience of material things, without engaging with the complex emotional and psychological inner world of the patient.

The general lack of awareness about geriatric illnesses in the state's health care system in South Asia means that, ironically, many elderly people are misdiagnosed as having dementia when they actually need counselling for clinical depression, and vice versa. In addition, factors such as deafness and lack of mobility in old age can add to the expression of both depression and dementia. In almost all the different kinds of dementia, there are overlaps between emotional and psychological distress and clinical illness. Alzheimer's disease, the most common form of dementia, often manifests in the early stages as depressed behaviour and anxiety over the forgetting of names and events.[22] The affective aspect of the illness is often neglected in popular cultural and medical discourses when compared to the greater stress on the loss of memory. The overlaps between psychological disorders like depression and dementia are yet to be dealt with adequately. Cohen's field work in Varanasi among lower-income group families of patients affected by dementia showed that affective changes were perceived as more important markers of senility by Indian families than the loss of memory. Many of Cohen's interviewees did not count memory loss as a crucial aspect of the narrative of ageing. It was more the behavioural changes that put the family's assumptions about respect or *seva* for the aged to the test.

While the views of the family of the patient on this matter are easier to obtain, it is harder to get patients to talk about themselves. The anxiety, frustration, and emotional lability of the patient, denial and withdrawal into silence, and incoherence in later stages means that the dementia patient is often spoken for, rather than speaking for himself or herself. As Cohen puts it,

> The power of Alzheimer's as popular category lies in its expression of a structuring of social relations in which dependency is equivalent to the loss of identity... non-sense suggests a nonself. Selves, to remain selves, must account for themselves.[23]

Only physical manifestations such as weeping, shouting, hiding or rearranging things, or throwing tantrums provide some idea to others of the fast-changing inner world of the dementia patient. The subaltern patient cannot be truly understood even when he or she speaks. In *Mai*, the doctor tells the patient's family to "treat her like a baby."

In most of the films on dementia such as *Astu*, *Mayurakshi*, and *Mai*, the patient is taken by relatives to a doctor after exhibiting unusual behaviour, and put through a battery of linguistic and cognitive tests, MRIs, and diagnostic procedures. When the diagnosis of dementia is confirmed, the information is not given to the patient but to the people who are accompanying them. It is as if even in the early stages of the illness, the person's identity has become "mere oblivion." In these films on dementia, and often in real life, doctors often ignore the dementia patient even if they are sitting in front of them. Medical sociologist Renée L. Beard says that through this act of excluding them from deciding their fate, they are promptly "relegated or socially disenfranchised. And they have to work hard to... get taken as still a sentient and capable, competent person."[24]

Dementia and Class Inequality

As with other kinds of subaltern identity, the well-being and agency of the "senile" person are rendered even more precarious through the intersections of gender and class. The eliding of diversity among dementia patients on account of caste, gender, rural or urban location, class, migration and displacement, traumatic history, and ethnicity creates an undifferentiated monolithic subject in medical and social analyses of dementia in South Asia. The link between women and poverty has been long established, and poor women and impoverished communities in general often do not get the nutritional and environmental support that builds up cognitive adaptability, as it were, for later life (see Rogers 2012).

The importance of education for children in South Asia, especially neglected girl children cannot be overemphasized as a pre-emptive measure to slow down the spread of dementia across ageing populations in the subcontinent. Limited access to education or intellectual nurturing, common among girl children in South Asia, has been described as a contributing factor to increased risk of dementia in later life as it reduces the cognitive reserve of the brain. Cognitive reserve determines the way in which the brain can continue to efficiently use its resources, develop alternative strategies, and re-allocate alternative neural pathways and networks even after there is neuropathological damage in the brain. In other words, though the brain may visibly show changes as in Alzheimer's disease, the individual may not show or feel any signs of deterioration for a long time. The effort invested by the state and the family in nurturing childhood cognition, providing education in childhood, as well as training for fruitful employment contributes to building this cognitive reserve. Needless to say, girl children in South Asia and children in general from socio-economically marginalized families who are deprived of education are at greater risk of not being able to develop adequate cognitive reserve as a buffer against dementia.[25]

Class is therefore a crucial factor in determining the occurrence of dementia, as well as its treatment, determining not only the degree of awareness that the patient and caregivers have about the disease but also the expenditure that families are willing to undertake for care and treatment. The urban middle class in India is more likely to have at least a belated awareness of dementia. Outside of the bourgeoisie, coping mechanisms for dealing with "difficult old people" are not connected to any knowledge of dementia or Alzheimer's disease, and access to medical care for them is rarely considered necessary. Dementia care is indeed expensive – the expenditure in the later stages of the illness extends not only to paying hired help to relieve the primary familial caregiver but also the purchase of diapers, medicines, and so on. An entire economy of medicines, goods, and services for "seniors' care" thrives on the growing incidence of dementia in India, particularly providing services for elders whose well-to-do children live separately from them. For families that cannot afford these goods and services, the physical and mental strain upon the primary caregiver drastically increases, and the quality of life of the patient can be adversely affected: "The old woman is weak because we are weak."[26]

The normative dementia patient in cinematic representations is middle class and male; "memory loss ... tended to be as a loss experienced by middle-class families, particularly in their concern about old men."[27] In cinematic representations, the particular "loss" experienced by the privileged elderly is symbolically represented through the forgetting of "classical" texts and lyrics. In *Astu* the professor of Sanskrit becomes agitated when he cannot remember the correct textual source of a particular *shloka* he is quoting, and gets angry when his daughter corrects him. In the end, he is reduced to silence and a few words like "mother" and "hungry," though there are flashes of remembrance when he can recall entire Sanskrit *shlokas*. In *Thanmathra* the highly educated Ramesan, who knows a vast number of songs, poems, facts, and figures, becomes anxious on forgetting the lyrics of a song by Subramania Bharati that he has been asked to recall. He rushes out from his bath to jot down the lines that he suddenly remembers, but the water dripping from his head symbolically blots the words on the page. Later, as dementia sets in, he cannot express himself in complete sentences, not even to write a resignation letter or farewell speech. There is a flashback where Ramesan's son remembers his father telling him about Alzheimer's disease: "like receding waves, what we learn, everything is taken back."[28] Obviously, this loss of memory affects those who are involved in the knowledge economy or in office jobs more. In socio-economic groups where the display of knowledge and complex cognitive abilities is not a measure of the individual's personal or professional competence, dementia can go unnoticed for much longer, and is not perceived as a "great loss."

There is a growing number of non-resident Indians who maintain elderly parents in India by hiring carers as they are physically unable to look after their parents themselves. Even agencies that provide trained carers make a distinction often made between old persons who have wealthy offspring living elsewhere sending money for nurses and housemaids, and old people whose children cannot afford expensive help – the distinction between the higher-paid "nurse" and the "ayah" become important in Indian geriatric care. In *Maine Gandhi Ko Nahin Mara*, there is an elder son living abroad who sends money for the family after the elderly lecturer loses his job. *Mayurakshi* uses the "NRI connection" to create an elitist narrative about the disease, bypassing issues such as the daily drudgery of caregiving. Aryanil, the son who lives abroad pays for the care of his father by hiring two persons to look after him, and he complains about how he cannot leave his job in the USA because he has to pay for the expenses of his father and his ex-wife and child from an earlier marriage. Though deeply attached to his dementia-afflicted father, Aryanil is settled in Chicago, USA, and effectively cut off from the old man. *Mayurakshi* is about a brief visit by the son to Kolkata, where, within a five-day span of reunion, Aryanil comes to terms with his own past. At the end, he flies back to Chicago leaving his father behind. This category of expensive "long-distance" care is projected as almost inevitable in the context of the South Asian diaspora. The travel to the West (or the desire to settle there) in these films reinforces the "rational/ west" versus "emotional/east" binary that has been discussed earlier. A very different scenario is shown in *Mai*, where the son wishes to send his mother to an old age home because he has received a job offer in the USA – it is revealed later that the son had used the excuse of an "overseas job" only to get rid of his dementia-afflicted mother.

Unlike the elite and the bourgeoisie who focus on the depletion in the quality of the social and intellectual life of the patient due to memory loss, dementia is represented among lower-income groups by a notion of deprivation – the mind and body becoming "weak" due to poverty, years of hard work, poor nutrition, and lack of medical care. Even loneliness is determined by class differences, it would appear, as the size and organization of the domestic space determines the physical isolation of the patient from the rest of the family. In higher-income group families, a television set is often placed in the room or home of the dementia patient, and it is assumed that this device will adequately compensate for the lack of human touch and conversation. In most cases, families who can afford an *ayah* assume that she can provide enough company or conversation for the patient when the reality is that highly specialized training is required to address the cognitive, emotional, and psychological aspects of dementia care. The expense of hiring help often means that physical and hands-on care has to be provided by family members in lower-income group families. The "suffering" of the patient's family is both real and culturally constructed – families which have no scope for hiring help cope differently from those who can do so, and they also narrativize their caring differently. On the other hand, the refusal of dementia patients to "cooperate" or "adjust" to strangers such as *ayahs* and nurses employed by middle-class or upper-middle-class households means that close relatives even in more privileged families do have to provide physical care and cleaning of the patient themselves whenever the need arises. The dearth in South Asia of professional caregivers trained specifically to deal with dementia patients means that service providers charge high rates that very few apart from the Indian elite and Indians living abroad can afford for a long time.

In *Astu* the difference in approach to dementia care among different socio-economic strata is shown through the contrast between the professor's Brahmin upper-middle-class family and the socially marginalized elephant keeper's family. Dr. Shastri's personal care – tasks like shaving, for example – is done not undertaken by his family members, but by a student who is given free accommodation and meals. The physical presence of the professor in his daughter's home is shown to irritate the other family members so much that he is sent off to live alone, with the village youth as caregiver. When Dr. Shastri wanders off and gets lost, the poor mahout's family living on the outskirts of the town takes him in. The mahout Anta, played by Nachiket Purnapatre, is awed by the fact that the local temple priest has said that the old man is probably a learned saint and that Anta is getting an opportunity from God to serve a saint. Throughout the film, religious belief plays an important role in shaping the attitudes of the carers towards the patient: the professor's daughter feels that his mental affliction is the deserved *karma* of what she imagines to be his infidelity to his wife. Anta's family, on the other hand, believes that they are repaying the debts of a previous life by taking care of the old man. *Astu* implies that Anta and his family, in spite of their own poverty and lack of resources, still possess the quality of empathy that members of the professor's own urban, modern family have lost.

The Woman Patient and Caregiver

While dementia patients are rendered subaltern because of their behaviour and language/silence, women patients are "doubly in shadow" to use Spivak's term, because of their location within patriarchy. Their opinion is rarely taken into consideration: sons, husbands, and other relatives often take decisions on their behalf, even in matters of property and inheritance. Because of the financial insecurity that many women in South Asia suffer, one often finds that women patients often become anxious or accusatory about their real or imaginary jewellery, and hoard assorted objects – in *Mai*, for example, the old mother keeps insinuating that her things are being stolen, and collects objects from around her daughter's home to hide in her suitcase.[29] The Alzheimer's Disease International report on Women and Dementia also observed that the micropolitics of the domestic space can lead to problems for many women: "For women who develop dementia, it can be difficult for themselves and others to accept the change in their role and identity. The shift from being the main caregiver within the family to the one now needing to be cared for is a profound one that is often resisted."[30]

Since long-term memory remains for a longer time in dementia patients as compared to short-term memory, it is important to acknowledge that the experiences of living as a woman under patriarchy determine the ways in which South Asian women remember (or forget) elements of their pasts. For the elderly mother in *Mai*, her memories of being a young mother, such as recollections of taking her children to a neighbour's home in a *chawl* on

"Second Childishness and Mere Oblivion" **213**

Wednesdays to see *Chitrahaar* on television colour her present. Her traumatic long-term memory of trying to protect her daughters, and confronting a man who was harassing her and her daughters becomes so powerful that in the present, she starts hitting the bewildered taxi driver who is driving her home. In *Mai* another aspect of the impact of patriarchy on the lives of the South Asian elderly woman is revealed – Mai confesses that she is ashamed to live in the home of her married daughter – it is implied in the film that the rapid decline in her mental and physical health is due to the sudden displacement from her son's home, which is her "rightful" place.

Lawrence Cohen's story of "The Philosopher's Mother" illustrates the stark lives of many elderly and unwell women in India. Cohen narrates his visit to the Calcutta home of noted Marxist philosopher Debi Prosad Chattopadhyay during his field work on Alzheimer's disease. As Chattopadhyay holds forth on *rasayana* and senility, Cohen is haunted by the brief glimpse of the philosopher's mother, "an old woman in a white sari in a room next to the office, sitting on a bed and staring at the wall." The philosopher's office and his mother's room are on the first floor, while he and his wife live on the second floor. During his visits to Chattopadhyay's home, he hopes for some communication from her, but she is completely silent, and withdrawn, sometimes sitting up, at other times lying down on her bed, like an aged pet animal. Cohen draws a startling parallel between the elderly and animals at the end of the anecdote:

> In Varanasi old people and dogs were seen to have a lot in common: abject dependence and a voice whose desire was no longer heard, so that it became more and more desperate and repetitive in its demand: ultimately, barking.[31]

Reading the anecdote of Chattopadhyay's silent mother helps one to understand the importance of what academician Dr. Julie Banerjee Mehta has been doing to facilitate a "voice" for her dementia-afflicted mother, Dr. Anima Banerjee, in her Calcutta home. Dr. Mehta's mother is in the advanced stages of dementia, but her daughter helps her to paint: brush, canvas, and colours are placed in front of her, and she is encouraged to use them. The colours and patterns of dots in her paintings come together in unusual and beautiful ways, and a public exhibition of the paintings has been held to wide acclaim. Dr. Mehta and her husband introduce visitors to her, and even in the later stages of dementia, when she hardly speaks, Dr. Anima's eyes show a flicker of acknowledgement when people talk with her. She is not excluded from conversations in the home, unlike many patients who are automatically ignored as if they are insentient. The family rallies around Dr. Anima to help her maintain her dignity: Dr. Anima is not a "non-self."

Dr. Banerjee Mehta left her job in Canada to care for her mother in India; her example leads one to discuss the other aspect of gender and dementia – the woman as caregiver. In most developing countries where the institutionalization of dementia care has not happened, the primary caregiver is often the daughter or daughter-in-law. This is not to detract from the fact that sons and male relatives can and do look after dementia patients, taking on the emotional and physical strain of caregiving. *Thanmathra*, which deals with early onset dementia, shows the elderly father of Ramesan Nair bringing his dementia-afflicted son home to look after him after he leaves his job. Since Nair has lost his job, his old father sells off large portions of his own property to feed the family. In *Mayurakshi*, the tenderness of the son as he picks up the spectacles from his sleeping father's hands, or applies talcum powder on his father's body also breaks the gender stereotypes about caregiving. However, in *Mayurakshi*, the son returns to America within a week, leaving the long-term care of his father in the hands of Mallika, who is a paid caregiver provided by an agency. My concern in this chapter is the vast majority of women who are unpaid relatives or hired caregivers across the world. Caregiving is emotionally draining – one has to deal with the patient's mood swings without getting angry or abusive, "play along" with the patient, and cope with the pain of caring for someone who no longer recognizes the carer. It is a cultural expectation in most patriarchal Asian societies that women will assume the role of carer for the elderly in the family as part of the woman's commitment to the family. This puts great stress on most women, as they have to balance this work with their jobs and the demands of other family members such as husbands or children. The transition for a woman from being homemaker to long-term caregiver can be quite stressful, especially if the rest of the family does not cooperate with her or is resentful of the old person making so many demands on her time. Often, women caregivers have to readjust not only their daily life routines but also their job situation, working part-time or from home, or even quitting their jobs to look after the dementia patient full-time. Since women managing households full-time have little time to attend to their own needs, the mental and physical health of women caregivers is jeopardized, and the rest of the family often does not know how to provide support and relief to them, especially as the patient in their care progresses to the stage of total dependency.

In *Astu*, when the elderly Dr. Shastri, lost and far from home, involuntarily soils his clothes, the impoverished elephant-keeper's wife Channamma calmly washes and dresses Dr. Shastri, stating that she is used to cleaning up her own small children, and tells her panic-stricken husband that they can start thinking of the old man as their third "child." Dr. Shastri begins to call her "Ma" as she takes him under her wing. At the end of the film, when Channamma hands over the ailing professor to his daughter, she advises Ira to look after the old man "as if he were her baby." The invocation of motherhood in the film is a reflection of the assumptions about the relationship between "maternal instinct" and care for the elderly in South Asia. South Asian cinema in general seems to take for granted that the "natural" instinct for nurturing makes women ideally suited to take on the responsibility of looking after the patient. In *Mai* Padmini Kolhapure plays Madhu, Mai's eldest daughter, a successful working woman who has to face the resentment of her husband and daughter when she brings her mother home. The daughter complains about having to share her space with her grandmother, while the husband keeps complaining about the extra demands made on their time and finances and the disruption of their social life. Eventually, Madhu decides to leave her job to look after her mother full-time, struggling to balance her duties as caregiver with her role as homemaker. Though initially sullen and resentful, Madhu's husband comes to appreciate the extent to which his wife serves her ailing mother. In a manner typical of Bollywood melodrama, he tells Madhu's brother, who had abandoned Mai, that he should pray that a daughter might be born into his family so that he might be looked after in his old age.

Memory, Selfhood, and Dementia

Class and gender have also shaped the theorizing and aestheticization of illness in Indian cinema. As stated earlier, the focus on memory loss as a problem is because these films take educated middle-class men in the early stages of dementia as "classic cases" for the portrayal of the disease. As Cohen puts it, memory becomes a "critical sign of the self primarily within third-person discourse, in the abstract discussion of the body and its relation to the community, the state, and the cosmos."[32] The leisure of the *savarna* bourgeoisie allows for the kind of contemplation of selfhood that we see in a film like *Astu*, set apart from the materiality of failing bodily functions, food, and daily expenses. This "third person discourse" allows for questions to be raised about the loss of selfhood that seems to concern the more privileged in the developed and developing world. However, through these questions, the films do open up a space for the discussion of how the narrativization of ageing and dementia might be indigenized, extending the debate around memory loss and the loss of selfhood beyond Western philosophical paradigms.

The opening scene of *Astu* introduces the theme of memory and selfhood. The protagonist's elder daughter Ira is shown conducting a theatre workshop, in which she tells the participants to forget the markers of their identity and all their social and familial bonds. They are to forget themselves, in order that they may play other characters better. There is complete silence in the darkened room, and all the participants have their eyes closed, as they imagine becoming disconnected from everything that makes them what

216 Nilanjana Deb

they are. Suddenly, the aged Dr. Shastri barges into the class and withdraws again in a state of confusion, unsettling his daughter. The viewer does not know at this early stage of the narrative that Dr. Shastri has dementia. This initial scene of contemplation upon withdrawal from worldly attachments, however, will reverberate in the viewer's mind, as the film tracks the gradual transformation of the illustrious professor of Sanskrit into *King Lear*'s "unaccommodated man." The film asks questions that help the viewer to understand that the problems faced by the dementia patient are but a sharpening of focus on problems faced by all human beings. Who do we become when start forgetting who we were, or what we did in the past? What happens to our identities when short-term memory fails, but long-term memory remains? What implication does this have for our understanding of the "self"? The bourgeois narrativization of dementia seems to revolve around the loss of selfhood, with the recurrence of terms like "The patient has lost himself," "the patient is not herself anymore," and so on. This is consistent with the idea of the continuum of memory holding selfhood together, common in Western philosophy and literature. The loss of memory is seen as highly undesirable in many Indian cultures of the subcontinent as well, with remembrance (*zikr, simran*, or *smaran*) being described as important to the spiritual life of the individual. In Ayurveda, typically, the theorizing of memory and ageing is done through an alternative physiology of "*indriyas* (sensorium), *mana* and *atma* (soul)":

> *Atma* perceives information using *mana* (mind), *budhi* (intellect), *jnana* and *karmendriyas* (cognitive and conative sense organs). The collected information is stored by *samskara* (processing) in the form of *smriti* (memory). *Smriti* is explained as a remembrance of things directly perceived, heard, or experienced earlier, which is the property of *atma*...*Indriyas* are controlled by *mana*, and *mana* is itself under the control of *vata*. *Vata* restrains and impels mental faculties, coordinates sense faculties, and prompts speech. On aging, *vata* (body humor) gets vitiated which leads to improper functioning of mental faculties."[33]

This alternative discourse of degeneration with age trickles down to non-medical communities and results in the sentimentality about intellectual loss among the *savarna* privileged, and the lamenting of *kamzori* or weakness among the socio-economically disadvantaged.[34] The fact that the dementia patient in *Astu* is a former director of the Oriental Research Institute in Pune, well versed in Asian philosophies, is a deliberate move that allows for the privileged "third person discourse" of memory and selfhood to emerge. "Astu" or "so be it" is a Sanskrit term used frequently by Dr. Shastri. It becomes a signifier for the mental state of acceptance of things as they are in the present moment. Dr. Shastri's predicament is framed within Vedantic,

"Second Childishness and Mere Oblivion" **217**

Zen, and Taoist philosophies. The idea of living in the present in these philosophies has resonance not only with the professor's condition as he leads an uncertain existence with the elephant keeper's family but also with the experience of dementia itself, when the future is uncertain and the past rapidly fades away. Upanishadic quotations are also used in the film, in which the oneness of all things is invoked to illustrate the professor's condition as he wanders like a vagabond from one place to another, eating all kinds of food, residing in all kinds of places, dependent on other living beings for survival. The Upanishads teach that the individual is not different from the rest of existence, as in Buddhism, but base this unity on an underlying and unchangeable universal consciousness or *atman* that is not affected by changes in circumstance. His condition strips him of his *brahminical* privilege and makes real the egalitarian teaching of the Upanishads in his life.

Zen and Taoist philosophy are frequently explained by the professor in flashback scenes in *Astu*. Zen is invoked because the identity of the dementia patient, stripped of conventional social identity, often unable to recall specific names or dates, becomes a relational entity, dependent upon a web of human and nonhuman relations within which the body and mind are embedded. Because the brain and cognitive functioning is associated with selfhood in Western discourses that value the autonomy of the individual, dementia patients can be easily dismissed as "absences" or "lost selves." Apart from materialist philosophies that see the individual's identity purely as a product of historical relations, Zen can help recuperate an identity that does not depend on any cognitive or physical autonomy but acknowledges a state of being constantly in flux. It allows one to imagine a relationality of being, similar to the condition in which Dr. Shastri finds himself after losing his way home. As Hershock puts it, personhood is like a story that comprises "all the characters, all the actions, all the places and events that occur in what we refer to as 'the world.'"[35] Zen distinguishes between the conventional and ultimate reality of a person, between the assigned social identity of the scholar Dr. Shastri and the ultimate instability of a composite entity in constant flux. One's "presence" is the result of a multitude of aggregates, each of which is in a state of perpetual change due to its relationship with others, both within and without that which was conventionally referred to as "the person." This idea of selfhood can accommodate the changes that come over an individual with ageing and forms of mental and physical illness, without seeing those changes as a falling into a void, or a loss of self. Dr. Shastri achieves the state of living in the present, at peace with all forms of contingency.

While films like *Astu* allow the reader to appreciate alternative non-Western philosophical frameworks as a means of offering dignity to patients suffering from degenerative conditions like dementia, who may otherwise be viewed dismissively as "child-like" or "animal-like" by society, it must be

218 Nilanjana Deb

remembered that such philosophical concerns are "third person discourse" that does not remove the cultural ignorance of communities outside of the *savarna* middle class and elites. As I have shown in this chapter, there is as much economic, social, and psychological heterogeneity among dementia patients in South Asia as there is among humans in general. There is no one-size-fits-all discourse that can remove cultural ignorance about the disease in the region. From a sociological perspective, it might be more apt to focus, in conclusion, on the fact that the dementia patient is a living, breathing individual dealing with physical, emotional, and psychological change, like any other human being. There is no loss of self in dementia patients even if we do not explain ageing through philosophical discourses – "the only self that unravels is the social one that we impose upon them by not being tolerant of difference or not accepting that their communication or their interactions have changed."[36]

Epilogue

But she did not want to renounce everything yet, like the scriptures told her. Relatives had taken her out of school and married her off at a very young age, because "she had no father." All her life, she had struggled to be a good daughter-in-law, wife, mother, grandmother. Now, as she floated between self-awareness and forgetting, drifting from the home of one grown-up child to another, she understood that she was too old to do the things she wanted. So she imagined another life, a secret fantasy she shared only with her granddaughter. In her next life, she would not marry. She would live with parents who would let her study. She would be a professor, and have a house in Shantiniketan with a garden and rooms filled with books. Whenever she would forget what she wished for herself, her granddaughter would remind her. A smile would light up her small, wizened face. There is nothing in the universe outside of stories, they say. She had a story for her future.

Notes

1 The words in italics in the prologue and epilogue are mine. Both my grandmothers suffered from different kinds of dementia in their old age and dealt with it in different ways. The authors of the Amsterdam Study of the Elderly (Amstel) observed that "Individuals with feelings of loneliness remained 1.64 times more likely to develop clinical dementia than persons who did not feel lonely." The feeling of loneliness can become worse due to the deteriorating social skills of the dementia patient, or their reduced mobility due to age and poor health (see Campbell, 2012).
2 World Health Organization and Alzheimer's Disease International, *Dementia: A Public Health Priority*, 2012, p. 2. www.who.int/mental_health/publications/dementia_report_2012/en/ accessed on 4 April 2018.

"Second Childishness and Mere Oblivion" **219**

3 *Vaardhakya* would roughly cover two phases in Indian systems of describing age. The first phase is from 60 to 80 years, and the second covers the period from 80 years onwards, till death.
4 Alzheimer's Disease International, 'Dementia in the Asia Pacific Region', 2014, p. 18. https://www.alz.co.uk/adi/pdf/Dementia-Asia-Pacific-2014.pdf accessed on 7 April 2018.
5 Ferri *et al*, as cited in Rosie Erol, Dawn Brooker, Elizabeth Peel, 'Women and Dementia: A Global Research Review', Alzheimer's Disease International, 2015, p. 11. https://www.alz.co.uk/sites/default/files/pdfs/Women-and-Dementia.pdf accessed on 6 March 2018.
6 Sanjay Leela Bhansali, *Black*, 2005, Dancing Dolphin, DVD.
7 Ajay Devgan, *U Me Aur Hum*, 2008, Ajay Devgan Films and Eros International, DVD.
8 Blessy, *Thanmathra*, 2005, Century Films. http://www.hotstar.com/movies/thanmathra/1000160452/watch accessed on 21 March 2018.
9 Jahnu Barua, *Maine Gandhi Ko Nahin Mara*, 2005, Anupam Kher, DVD.
10 Sumitra Bhave and Sunil Suktankar, *Astu – So Be It*, 2013, Sheelaa Rao and Mohan Agashe, Amazon Prime, accessed May 2018.
11 Atanu Ghosh, *Mayurakshi*, 2017, Firdausal Hassan and Probal Halder for Friends Communication.
12 Mahesh Kodiyal, *Mai*, 2013, AMG Worldwide Entertainment, Alliance Entertainment and Rhythm D'vine Entertainment, DVD.
13 K. Bhui and D. Bhugra, 'Mental Illness in Black and Asian Ethnic Minorities: Pathways to Care and Outcomes', *Advances in Psychiatric Treatment*, 8, 2002, pp. 26–33. https://www.cambridge.org/core/journals/advances-in-psychiatric-treatment/article/mental-illness-in-black-and-asian-ethnic-minorities-pathways-to-care-and-outcomes/B44BECFA32EBBABCA9105E2792F92BF5 accessed on 2 April 2018.
14 Sara Turner, Alison Christie, Emma Haworth, 'South Asian and White Older People and Dementia: A Qualitative Study of Knowledge and Attitudes', *Diversity & Equality in Health and Care*, December 2005. http://diversityhealthcare.imedpub.com/south-asian-and-white-older-people-and-dementia-a-qualitative-study-of-knowledge-and-attitudes.php?aid=2524 accessed on 15 April 2018.
15 Lawrence Cohen, *No Aging in India: Alzheimer's, The Bad Family, and Other Modern Things*, Berkeley: University of California Press, 1998, p. 106. http://ark.cdlib.org/ark:/13030/ft658007dm/p.106 accessed on 4 February 2018.
16 Ibid.
17 Ibid., pp. 30–31.
18 *Vanaprastha* literally means retreat into the forest, and generally implies seclusion, *while sannyasa* is renunciation of all worldly desires and relationships.
19 New York University's Dr. Barry Reisberg has outlined seven major stages of Alzheimer's disease as a "Global Deterioration Scale" for measuring the progression of the disease.https://www.dementiacarecentral.com/aboutdementia/facts/stages/ accessed on 15 February 2018.
20 There are, of course, frequent cases of the actual abandonment of the aged far away from their homes by their families in both the developed and developing world.
21 Cohen, *No Aging in India*, p. 176.

220 Nilanjana Deb

22 However, there are physical markers of Alzheimer's disease, such as brain cell death that distinguish it from conditions such as clinical depression in the elderly. Rachel Nall, '10 Types of Dementia', https://www.healthline.com/health/types-dementia accessed on 17 April 2018.
23 Cohen, No Aging in India, p. 59.
24 R..L Beard, Webcast, *HealthTalk*, 2009. https://www.everydayhealth.com/alzheimers/webcasts/alzheimers-and-dementia-does-loss-of-memory-mean-loss-of-self.aspx accessed on 10 April 2018.
25 Marcus Richards and Amanda Sacker, 'Lifetime Antecedents of Cognitive Reserve', *Journal of Clinical and Experimental Neuropsychology*, 25:5, 2010, pp. 614–624, DOI: 10.1076/jcen.25.5.614.14581 accessed on 21 May 2018.
26 Cohen, No Aging in India, p. 232.
27 Ibid., p. 127.
28 Blessy, *Thanmathra*, 2005, Century Films. http://www.hotstar.com/movies/thanmathra/1000160452/watch accessed on 21 March 2018.
29 *Stri-dhan* or women's wealth was often limited to the jewelry that women received at the time of their marriage and served as their only insurance, explaining the anxiety over losing jewellery.
30 https://www.alz.co.uk/sites/default/files/.../Women-and-Dementia-Summary -Sheet.pdf accessed on 15 May 2018.
31 Cohen, *No Aging in India*, p. 188.
32 Cohen, *No Aging in India*, p. 127.
33 Prakash Mangalasseri, Seetha Chandran, 'A Brief Insight into the Pathogenesis and Management of Alzheimer's Disease in Ayurvedic Parlance', *International Journal of Green Pharmacy*, 11 (1) January–March 2017 (Suppl), p. S82.https://www.researchgate.net/publication/316170019_A_brief_insight_into_the _pathogenesis_and_management_of_Alzheimer%27s_disease_in_Ayurvedic _parlance accessed 17 June 2018.
34 Cohen, *No Aging in India*, p. 230.
35 Peter D. Hershock, 'Person as Narration: The Dissolution of "Self" and "Other" in Ch'an Buddhism', *Philosophy East & West*, vol.44, no.4, 1994, p. 691.
36 R.L. Beard, Webcast, *HealthTalk*, 2009. https://www.everydayhealth.com/alzheimers/webcasts/alzheimers-and-dementia-does-loss-of-memory-mean-loss-of-self.aspx accessed on 10 April 2018.

References

"Dementia in the Asia Pacific Region." Alzheimer's Disease International, 2014. www.alz.co.uk/adi/pdf/Dementia-Asia-Pacific-2014.pdf. Accessed 7 Apr. 2018.
Barua, Jahnu, director. *Maine Gandhi Ko Nahin Mara*, 2005. The producer was Anupam Kher, and the music was distributed by Yash Raj films.
Beard, Renee L., Webcast. "HealthTalk." 2009. www.everydayhealth.com/alzheimers/webcasts/alzheimers-and-dementia-does-loss-of-memory-mean-loss -of-self.aspx. Accessed 10 Apr. 2018.
Bhansali, Sanjay Leela, director. *Black*, 2005. It was produced by Sanjay Leela Bhnasali and distributed by Zee Motion Pictures.
Bhave, Sumitra, and Sunil Suktankar, directors. *Astu–So Be It*, 2013. It was produced by Sheelaa Rao and Mohan Agashe.
Bhui, K. and D. Bhugra. "Mental Illness in Black and Asian Ethnic Minorities: Pathways to Care and Outcomes." *Advances in Psychiatric Treatment*, vol. 8, 2002, pp. 26–33. www.cambridge.org/core/journals/advances-in-psychiatric

-treatment/article/mental-illness-in-black-and-asian-ethnic-minorities-pathways -to-care-and-outcomes/B44BECFA32EBBABCA9105E2792F92BF5. Accessed 2 Apr. 2018.

Blessy, director. *Thanmathra*. Century Films, 2005. *Hotstar*, www.hotstar.com/ movies/thanmathra/1000160452/watch.

Campbell, Dennis. "Dementia Linked to Loneliness, Study Finds." *The Guardian*, 10 Dec. 2012. www.theguardian.com/society/2012/dec/10/loneliness-dementia -link. Accessed 10 Jun. 2018.

Chandran, Seetha and Prakash Mangalasseri, "A Brief Insight into the Pathogenesis and Management of Alzheimer's Disease in Ayurvedic Parlance." *International Journal of Green Pharmacy*, vol. 11, no. 1, Jan.–Mar., 2017, p. S82. www.researchgate.net/publication/316170019_A_brief_insight_into_the _pathogenesis_and_management_of_Alzheimer%27s_disease_in_Ayurvedic _parlance. Accessed 17 Jun. 2018.

Cohen, Lawrence. *No Aging in India: Alzheimer's, The Bad Family, and Other Modern Things*. University of California Press, 1998. ark.cdlib.org/ark:/13030/ ft658007dm/p.106. Accessed 4 Feb. 2018.

Devgan, Ajay, director. *U Me Aur Hum*. Ajay Devgan Films and Eros International, 2008.

Erol, Rosie, Dawn Brooker, and Elizabeth Peel. *Women and Dementia: A Global Research Review*. Alzheimer's Disease International, 2015. www.alz.co.uk/sites/ default/files/pdfs/Women-and-Dementia.pdf. Accessed 6 Mar. 2018.

Ghosh, Atanu. *Mayurakshi*. Firdausal Hassan and Probal Halder for Friends Communication, 2017.

Hershock, Peter D. "Person as Narration: The Dissolution of 'Self' and 'Other' in Ch'an Buddhism." *Philosophy East & West*, vol. 44, no. 4, 1994, p. 691.

Mahesh, Kodiyal, director. *Mai*. AMG Worldwide Entertainment, Alliance Entertainment and Rhythm D'vine Entertainment, 2013.

Nall, Rachel. "10 Types of Dementia." *Healthline*. www.healthline.com/health/ types-dementia. Accessed 17 Apr. 2018.

Richards, Marcus and Amanda Sacker. "Lifetime Antecedents of Cognitive Reserve." *Journal of Clinical and Experimental Neuropsychology*, vol. 25, no. 5, 2010, pp. 614–624. http://10.1076/jcen.25.5.614.14581. Accessed 21 May 2018.

Rogers, Madolyn Bowman. "Dementia Numbers in Developing World Point to Global Epidemic." *Alzforum*. www.alzforum.org/news/research-news/dementia -numbers-developing-world-point-global-epidemic. Accessed 4 May 2018.

Turner, Sara, Alison Christie and Emma Haworth. "South Asian and White Older People and Dementia: A Qualitative Study of Knowledge and Attitudes." *Diversity & Equality in Health and Care*. diversityhealthcare.imedpub.com/sou th-asian-and-white-older-people-and-dementia-a-qualitative-study-of-knowled ge-and-attitudes.php?aid=2524. Accessed 15 Apr. 2018.

World Health Organisation. *The ICD-10 Classification of Mental and Behavioural Disorders*. www.who.int/classifications/icd/en/bluebook.pdf. Accessed 3 Nov. 2017.

World Health Organization and Alzheimer's Disease International. "Dementia: A Public Health Priority." 2012. https://iris.who.int/bitstream/handle/10665 /75263/9789241564458_eng.pdf?sequence=1. Accessed 12 April 2018.

12

AGEING, CARING, AND MORTALITY

V. Geetha

Around 2006–2007 I was witness to a friend, comrade, and fellow feminist, gradually retreating from the world. She turned rather quiet, her memory went into hiding, and in addition fell ill often. Around this time, her daughter and I were engaged in gathering her writings on socialism, labour, gender, and caste into a volume. Initially she was enthusiastic about the project, but soon it became evident that she was not going to be able to keep up with the task of overseeing what we were doing.

Over the next few years, she slowly transformed into another person, as Alzheimer's syndrome took hold of her. When she lost her words, we realized that we had reached a point of no easy return. Yet she was not entirely lost to herself or us. A drifting melody, certain names, children, holding her hand long enough would bring her back into an interactive moment, which lasted sometimes for minutes, at other times longer. I started reading as much as I could about Alzheimer's and one particular essay has stayed with me from that time. Authored by Gisela Webb, Professor of Religious Studies at Seton Hall University (New Jersey), it was a personal account of how she came to terms with her mother who endured Alzheimer's for 16 years.[1]

Webb wrote of what helped her understand her mother's condition as well as her role as chief caregiver. She was initially non-plussed that there was very little available by way of writing that helped her understand the gradual loss of a loved one, as you knew her, the death of memory, and the experience of time, without a sense of duration and movement. While there were explanations and studies that pointed to what one might expect to find as the condition progressed, and how one ought to prepare oneself, these did not engage with the larger and unvoiced anxiety that the disease invoked: that it was an intimation of mortality before death. Webb turned to religion to make

DOI: 10.4324/9780429352560-13

sense of it all. Buddhist and Sufi literature provided important pointers: the radical impermanence of life that Buddhism expounds helped to focus on the passage of all that we hold dear into nothingness and instilled the need, therefore, to be available to the moment, and inhabit it with compassion and responsibility. Sufism, with its invocation of a threshold that we pass through before we are delivered from mortality, helped navigate the crucial passage that connects time and death. While in that threshold moment the living are pared of all dross and come to terms with how life had been, and what it meant.

I returned to Webb's essay many years after I first read it, in the wake of the coronavirus pandemic that has more or less structured life in the year 2020. In all the news, numbers, prognosis, predictions, dire warnings, and cautionary tales which circulated around its advent, I had not found anything that helped me grasp the imminence of death. We felt sober, grave, glum, and wrenched as we let go of loved ones and rendered them to the care of the state which meanwhile had to plan for dignified burials and cremations. We worried about those vulnerable to being infected such as the elderly, those who were ill and we feared for ourselves: that we might be the bearers of the virus, or succumb to it. Yet there was something amiss. Here we were stopped short by mortality, and we appeared desperate, awkward, and mostly maudlin.

Rereading Webb I realized that we needed words, notions, and ways of being that would help us inhabit this moment with grace, and weightlessness. For, the moment was saturated with information, angst, anger, etc. and at times appeared miasmic, clothed in a cloud of unknowing. One needed to be able to hover over it, rather than be held captive to its weight and heft. I am not sure I have found what Webb managed to find, though her wise words on what she learned from Buddhism and Sufism continue to resonate with me. Staying with her sense of what religions offer in moments such as these, I offer some loud thoughts on themes that the pandemic had rendered pertinent: ageing, the labour of care, and the exceptionable moment that returns us to what we are, fragile moral beings.

***

For one who grew up with English literature, and still turns to it for making sense of the world, I realized that the ageing female body has not quite been a literary subject. It is hard to find female equivalents of Tithonous, "whom cold immortality consumes" and who is gifted with eternity but not agelessness.[2] Or of Lear, who wanders about in bitter loneliness, chafing at the winds and the world. It is not that older women do not feature in literature, but their aged body does not stand in for the mortal condition so to speak, and remains an object of disquiet, if not disgust. In fact, it is not even quite

224 V. Geetha

human. As crones and witches, hags and nags, women are preternatural, as if they had defied time but not in a way that pushes us to question the limits of life, rather they appear malevolent forces, time's own perverse creations. While in some contexts and cultures, there is the wise older woman, the female shaman, the magical spinner of life and death, the prophetess, and so on, she is again, not emblematic of what it is to be human, and is the very stuff of myth.

In contrast, men who confront their growing old with irony and anger, or wisdom and resignation, become emblematic of the human condition. Yeats' great lines that begin *The Tower* are brilliant in their evocation of old age:

> What shall I do with this absurdity —
> O heart, O troubled heart — this caricature,
> Decrepit age that has been tied to me
> As to a dog's tail
> Never had I more
> Excited, passionate, fantastical
> Imagination, nor an ear and eye
> That more expected the impossible —[3]

The rest of the poem stands as testimony to how the imagination, with utter confidence, transcends what it derides. Old age is both a condition of existence and trope and in either guise it communicates the power of what cannot be doubted: the indomitable authority the poet exercises over life and death and thereby affirms what another male poet would say of him: that his "unconstraining voice" would continue to persuade us "to rejoice."[4] In this loop that encircles death and fame and constitutes tradition, a canon is thus born, sealing human destiny as essentially one that is to be measured by men's sense of the world and time.

In contrast to the old poet who rues his age, and yet finds a way to triumph over his ironic invocation of it, are the lines Yeats reserves for women, grown old in the espousal of passionate politics. While this could be put down to his own anxieties over outspoken women, the lines that mark their physicality are rather telling: ageing women's bodies stand testimony to their minds gone awry, with the one completing the other, whereas ageing notwithstanding, men's bodies become the occasion to celebrate their ever curious minds.

> Great windows open to the south,
> Two girls in silk kimonos, both
> Beautiful, one a gazelle.
> But a raving autumn shears
> Blossom from the summer's wreath;

The older is condemned to death,
Pardoned, drags out lonely years
Conspiring among the ignorant.
I know not what the younger dreams –
Some vague Utopia – and she seems,
When withered old and skeleton-gaunt,
An image of such politics.[5]

***

There is a sense of living, ageing, and dying that may be traced back to women's everyday cultural expressions, the lullaby and the lament. In many Indian languages, the lullaby is a female genre, not only because women sing it but because it brings the newborn into real and fictive kinship contexts, thereby mimicking what women do, as they transact between households, families, and neighbourhoods. The lament is about separation and memory, about what cannot be forgotten and what will endure. And this is a poignant genre, of bearing witness to a life as well as letting go. The lullaby and lament, together, describe a wide arc, within which is held a distinctive knowledge, to do with bearing life, sustaining it, and finally memorializing it. It seems to me that this is of the time of reproduction, of being in the body and the world, simultaneously, and in that sense it speaks of the labour of care and survival, as much as it does of mortality and death.

That these are matters that cannot be easily disentangled came home to me, when I was reading two Buddhist texts: the *Therigatha* and *Manimekhalai*. Both these texts engage with questions of mortality, desire, suffering, and death, and importantly, in and through an engagement with women's lives.

The *Therigatha*, or songs of the elder nuns, features the spiritual journeys of several theris, as they came to reckon with bodily existence, conjugal burdens, and the inevitability of death, sorrow, and loss.[6] Given the social marking of the female body as essentially sensual and germinal, the theris' search for a life, not tied to craving and attachment, is particularly poignant and stark. The daughter who puts by adornment and riches, because she does not find them attractive or meaningful, the courtesan who turns her back on her sensuous life, acutely aware of how the body surrenders to decay, the wife who is finally freed from the burden of pestle and mortar, the mother who puts by grief for the death of a child, when she finds out that sorrow and loss are not hers alone, and that she must hearken to the loss of others: the renunciation of female-specific experiences, of the reproductive life, no less, makes for a gentle and unhurried understanding of mortality and suffering. In turn, this understanding opens a window onto a new world, defined by limitless compassion, with both human and non-human existences.

The Tamil epic *Manimekhalai*, authored by a man, the poet Sattanar, engages with the time and life of reproduction in a defined, urban context: the epic narrates the tales of at least half a dozen and more women who, in different ways, are caught within the bind of sensuality.[7] Claimed by love, desire, and duty, these women endure wrong and suffering until the Buddha's words reach them. The protagonist Manimekalai, as caught in a sexual narrative as the others in the story, learns from these other fates and, eventually, transcends the sexual role she is expected to play as the daughter of a courtesan. But meanwhile she escapes seduction in the city by hiding in a crystal enclosure, realizes the frangibility of all flesh by wandering through a charnel house, and intuits wisdom during a dream-like sojourn on a remote island ... Her journey towards renunciation and knowledge begins when she returns to the city from the island, bringing with her a magic bowl that will never want for food, with a mission to feed the hungry.

Significantly, she transits through these many spaces by shifting shapes, now a woman from the here and now, then a being, acutely aware of her previous birth. She serves as her friend's double, changes into male attire ... and gradually attains a state of compassionate enlightenment. The epic envisages the female body as the very form of mortality, of life that is subject to ageing, decay, and death and in and through the transformations that this body is subjected to, as it transits an array of identities, its protagonist finds equipoise.

For the theris, release from craving and sorrow represents not just spiritual and within limits, social autonomy, but also a state of knowledge: about mortality, and the need, therefore, to transcend the limits of the sensual life by attending to the life-force, the jeeva, that attends all existence, so that we don't lose ourselves in indulgent pleasure or sorrow. In a sense, this is knowledge that takes female existence out of the germinal, the birth-giving body, and links its labour of care to the fragile and existential human body, as such.

For Manimekalai, given charge of the bowl that never empties, feeding the world, especially its most abject inhabitants, becomes a mandate that is further fortified when she is tutored in the knowledge of suffering and release from it. The epic contains a dense philosophical treatise that is expounded by a Buddhist monk to his willing female pupil. Caring and compassion are thus rendered fitful adjuncts to meditative as well as logical reflections on suffering and the cessation of suffering.

These Buddhist texts foreground the virtue of *maithri*, which becomes the context in which the theris as well as Manimekhalai move away from family and kin, community, and socially mandated duty and, in their renunciation, discover revolutionary potential, to remake not only their lives, but relationship, as such.

**

It seems to me that the knowledge that emerges from within the sphere of the germinal, the time of reproduction is one that calls on us to pause, and take note of how life is tended, and equally all that thwarts us from valuing the act of tending. As feminists, we are on familiar ground here, having raised fundamental questions to do with the social value of affection and the economics of nurture. Yet, there are two concerns that we might need to rethink: one, the sexual division of labour is further segmented in that it is underwritten by caste and class and rendered as much as "service" as work. Then there is what might be called, "public" care labour. Whether this is work to do with hygiene, including medical support work, sanitation, or death, it is more or less undertaken exclusively by dalits. In these tasks, the workers labour, as women do, to sustain life and, in addition, assist with the rituals of death.

How might we hold together the unmarked labour of care that women perform in their households, and the marked and stigmatized labour that these workers carry out?

In the context of the 2020 coronavirus pandemic, the layered nature of household labour was made all too evident. Of all those who lost work during the extended months of lockdown in India, domestic workers were the ones that returned to their tasks the soonest, since households could not do without them. Also, in a context where working-class employment levels had fallen, most workers were eager to take up work as soon as it was possible to do so, never mind that their home situations were not ideal, in that children, the sick, and the elderly in their contexts too had to be cared for.

Feminist theorizing of care work, of household tasks, has pointed out that while these latter are not easy to monetize, they must, nevertheless, be accorded value. For they directly sustain the workforce and help reproduce it, and in that sense these tasks are linked to the generation of surplus and the accumulation of capital. On the other hand, as those directly involved in this process, we have also realized that these tasks possess an affective edge, that we are linked to those whom we care for, by ties of affection and duty. Also, it is evident that these tasks are life sustaining and central to how we remain connected to each other. Discussions around care, therefore, hinge on this dual understanding of the word, and it has been difficult to view care work in clear and disambiguated terms.

However, as is evident, such an understanding does not help us cognize assisted household labour, the fact that the sexual division of labour is actively mediated by caste and class and emerges as service labour of a distinctive kind. The household worker, as cook, cleaner, childminder, or house nurse is seen as "part" of the household. Since these workers' tasks require them to inhabit living spaces that are otherwise the employer's domain, caste, and class markers are temporarily suspended, just so the sick are taken care of, meals are cooked and children fed and put to sleep. While in sheer exchange terms, these tasks might (in some cases) fetch a modestly decent wage, in terms of the services rendered, the measure of their worth is given by affect, by an admixture of emotion and duty.

This ambiguity that proceeds from our complex and slippery understanding of housework as well as our unreflective sense of service labour, as such, is yet to be sorted through in feminist analyses of housework – what often eludes understanding is that in a caste economy, service is defined in rather particular ways, and not so long so, service labour, was an aspect of relationships of caste bondage, and was expected to be performed with due diligence – as *begar*, *vetti*.

With regard to public care labour, to do with sanitation, disease, and death: often such labour is taken for granted, or accorded visibility only so that it can continue to be performed, as we were witness to, during the pandemic, or indeed during moments of great natural disaster, when death and illness throng public spaces. Tragically enough, it becomes a sign of the "normal," and as such is expected to continue, even in abnormal times. And here I would like to recollect a tale from not so long ago.[8]

In the wake of Partition-related violence women from all communities were abducted, assaulted, and married against their wishes. In order to keep their national identities unsullied, governments of India and Pakistan planned and executed massive recovery operations, to restore abducted Muslim women to Pakistan and Hindu and Sikh women to India. Kamlabehn Patel, who assisted Mridula Sarabhai in this task, writes of a particularly difficult recovery that she had to oversee. A group of Hindu women and children, 600 in all, were rescued and brought to a transit camp in Lahore before they could be sent to India. Their health and hygiene situation was alarming, they were hungry and emaciated, and generally disoriented, and very soon the camp was flush with their excrement, vomit, etc. So much so that Kamlabehn had to requisition the government of Pakistan for a team of sweepers to clean the place and disinfect it.

Now, we know that in the wake of Partition, the government of Pakistan had passed a law that forbade sweepers, all dalits, and mostly Hindus from leaving their homes until further notice, since otherwise there would be no one, literally, to keep the streets and public facilities clean. In that context Kamlabehn's request assumes significance: in her otherwise nuanced, gentle narrative, where every suffering refugee is granted a human face, the sweeper becomes a sign of the "normal," of that which must continue even in exceptional times and can be counted on. By the same token, she is not granted any particular salience, whereas in terms of what she was called to do, she had to respond to an extraordinary situation. As she disappears into her task, she is kept out of history and memory.

We see this time and again, when such labour and labourers are called forth when, around them, the world has literally gone to pieces. Whether it was the tsunami that swept the south Indian coast in 2004 or periodic floods that wash over Indian cities, we are witness to work that is seldom taken note of, and literally merges into the backdrop, of what is to be cleared and cleaned. On the other hand, it is work that literally reproduces the conditions of well-being on a daily basis, even as the labouring body, literally, is sacrificed – low pay, no safety gear, caste-based and imposed – in order to ensure the public good. And here one cannot but be reminded of fables of sacrifice, where the worker has to necessarily die in order that a monument might be left standing.

The life-affirming and yet invisible and sacrificial nature of public care labour is both appalling and poignant. And while, to an extent, feminist thought has denaturalised the family and care work, we need to do more, and take on the responsibility of thinking through acts of private and public care, marked by notions of service and duty, which are implicated within an economy of service, underwritten by caste.

***

During the 1870s famine in colonial India, gangs of women workers pressed upon colonial officials to give them work, since the policy was to feed those that worked. In his account of the famine William Digby had this to say about a woman worker that he encountered on the road:

> She had taken under her motherly protection a young widow who was reduced to skin and bone from sheer want of food. She pulled her about like a child to show me her condition, and then said with a strong touch of sarcasm in her tone: "This is the kind that they refuse to employ on the relief works. If you are strong and can find work somewhere for yourself, you may be taken on; but if you go to the relief works because you have nothing to eat, they tell you are too young or too weak. In order to be employed on a relief work, you must have at least a couple of pice or a seer of grain to call your own. If you have got nothing you will get nothing ... So it happens every day. ... in these hard times we don't try to eat every day, all our efforts are bent toward getting a meal once in two days; then, when our bellies are filled, we can be at rest for a day."[9]

This staving off, of hunger, is work, in itself. And it is labour that is performed so that the labourer might continue to labour. What appeared exceptional to

230 V. Geetha

Digby is tragically not always so – and the utter precarity that marks worker existence in India is there for us to see, and which was brought home to us, during the 2020 coronavirus pandemic.

The moment the government of India announced what has been described as the world's most draconian lockdown, a tragedy of immense proportions unfolded in our cities. From around the middle of April we were witness to thousands of workers, stranded in cities without work and the assurance of shelter or care, begin their long march home, to their villages and towns. If we needed an ocular demonstration of worker alienation, here it was – the buildings that they had helped build, the tracks they had laid for our trains to run, restaurants and malls they cleaned and secured for us, as we ate and shopped, loomed silently over their frail lives.

However tragic, this walking away from places of work, signalled freedom, as much as it represented fear. Significantly enough, such "freedom" was denied public care workers, who were called upon to work even harder, even as they were subject to greater vulnerability, in terms of health.[10]

In this context, it becomes important to think of what we think and do when we "care": the understanding that inheres in the act of labouring hard to feed a hungry family, or abide by a loved one, who is waiting to pass on; or what a worker confronts and acknowledges of a day, when, yet again, she has to sort through undifferentiated and often toxic waste. Or what the sheer routine of tending a funeral or preparing a grave suggestively communicates. There is a twilight zone that such labour sketches, where life and death are not as separable as we imagine them to be, and yet we realize the importance of labouring for life, and often, as the worker on the streets knows, at tremendous cost to oneself. This ought to give us pause and push us to think of public care labour not just in terms of denuded rights, but, equally, of the existential and life-sustaining labour that it is.

***

To care then encodes a knowledge that in an existential sense may be found in the writings of women who are conscious of the germinal time of reproduction and look to take life beyond the social limits that wedge that time. Acts of caring, in this sense, are akin to practices of asceticism and compassion, and without taking away from the sheer injustice that underwrites both household and public care labour, it ought to be possible to value and valorize such acts.

Notes

1 Gisella Webb, "Intimations of the Great Unlearning: Interreligious Spirituality and the Demise of Consciousness which is Alzheimers", Crosscurrents, 52, no. 3 (2001): 324–336.

Ageing, Caring, and Mortality **231**

2 The poem can be accessed at: https://www.poetryfoundation.org/poems/45389/ tithonus; accessed on November 28, 2021.
3 W. B. Yeats, *Collected Poems*, London: Macmillan (Picador Classics), 1990, 218.
4 W. H. Auden, "In Memory of W B Yeats", New York: Vintage Books, 1979, 81.
5 W. B. Yeats, op.cit., 263.
6 The classic edition of the *Therigatha* is this: *Poems of Early Buddhist Nuns*, translated by C.A.F. Rhys Davids and K.R. Norman, Oxford: Pali Text Society, 1989.
7 For an English (prose) translation of the Manimekhalai, see Alain Danielou (translator, with the collaboration of T V Gopala Iyer), *Manimekhalai: the Dancer with the Magic Bowl*, New Delhi: Aleph, 2018.
8 See, in this context, Kamla Patel, *Torn from the Roots: A Partition Memoir*, translated by Uma Randeria, New Delhi: Women Unlimited, 2006, 83–88. Also see, Akanshka Kumar, "Locating Dalits in the Middle of Partition and Violence", *Journal of Studies in History and Culture*, 2, 2016 (http://jshc.org/wp-content /uploads/2018/08/JSHC_Issue-2_Vol-2_2016.pdf; accessed on November 28, 2021).
9 William Digby, *The Famine Campaign In Southern India (Madras and Bombay Presidencies and Province of Mysore) 1876-1878, Volume 1*, London: Longmans, Green, and Co., 1878, 277–278.
10 See, in this context, Sylvia Karpagam (with Jerald D'Souza), "Occupational Hazards in Healthcare Settings: A Study of Invisibilised Frontline Workers in Bengaluru", *Economic and Political Weekly*, April 24, 2021, 60–65.

References

Auden, W. H. *In Memory of W B Yeats*. Vintage Books, 1979.
Danielou, Alain. *Manimekhalai: The Dancer with the Magic Bowl*. Translated by Alain Danielou and T. V. Gopala Iyer. Aleph, 2018.
Davids, Rhys, et al. *Poems of Early Buddhist Nuns*. Pali Text Society, 1989.
Digby, William. *The Famine Campaign In Southern India (Madras And Bombay Presidencies And Province of Mysore) 1876–1878* (Vol. 1). Longmans, Green & Co., 1878.
Karpagam, Sylvia and Jerald D'Souza. "Occupational Hazards in Healthcare Settings: A Study of Invisibilised Frontline Workers in Bengaluru." *Economic and Political Weekly*, April 24, 2021.
Kumar, Akanshka. "Locating Dalits in the Middle of Partition and Violence." *Journal of Studies in History and Culture*, vol. 2, no. 2, 2016. http://jshc.org/wp -content/uploads/2018/08/JSHC_Issue-2_Vol-2_2016.pdf
Patel, Kamla. *Torn from the Roots: A Partition Memoir*. Translated by Uma Randeria. Women Unlimited, 2006, pp. 83–88.
Tennyson, Alfred. "Thithonus." https://www.poetryfoundation.org/poems/45389/ tithonus.
Webb, Gisella. "Intimations of the Great Unlearning: Interreligious Spirituality and the Demise of Consciousness Which Is Alzheimers." *Crosscurrents*, vol. 52, no. 3, 2001, pp. 324–336.
Yeats, W. B. *Collected Poems*. Picador Classics, 1990, p. 218.

13

LONELINESS, BELATEDNESS, AND CARE

Arriving Late Where You No Longer Are

Trina Nileena Banerjee

The Black Dog

I begin with a short piece of prose that I wrote in thinking about grief. For those who have read it, it has references to *Killing the Black Dog* by Les Murray:

> *Let us imagine that there was an appointment and you arrived late. Let us imagine he waited for you a long time. Now, here you are – on the same bench, waiting. He was someone you were desperate to see. He was someone you were afraid of meeting. When he came, he had - waiting behind him – a black dog. The dog looked at you with eyes that had all your memories in them.*
>
> *They made you want to cry out aloud. Sometimes you wanted to howl.*
> *When you sat together on that bench, there was always the black dog between you. It never left. When you two laughed, it stared at your faces in disbelief.*
> *You wanted to see him, but you feared the dog.*
> *You wanted to go, but you kept looking at the clock as it ticked, but you did not move.*
> *The clock ticked one way, stopped, looked at you, went back a bit, went the other way, hesitated, and ticked again. But you would not move.*
> *You knew he was waiting, a man you loved: breathing a bit heavier each day. But you refused to get up.*
> *The clock was timid, it played along. It told you there was time. There is always time. Tomorrow. And tomorrow. And tomorrow.*
> *You did not get up.*

DOI: 10.4324/9780429352560-14

You willingly missed the bus. You called a cab and cancelled.

The man you loved was waiting. The bench was wooden, the sky was grey, and the black dog never left his side. You could not move.

Now you are on this bench, waiting. You know he is not coming. He is never coming back. But you are waiting. Your black dog is waiting with you.

The clock is smashed. Time is a joke. Time is a slap on your sorry face.[1]

The Pandemic and Belatedness

It took me a long time to begin writing this piece because I realized at the start that I could not bring myself to write of loneliness and care merely as an academic. All that I had read and researched would not suffice to tell the truth about my experiences in the last couple of years. Loneliness, time, and care had attached themselves to each other in a strange triad in my consciousness, especially since the beginning of the pandemic in 2020.

Despite this, I could not identify, let alone theorize, the sources of certain kinds of pain. Perhaps I could not write because I was afraid. I knew all kinds of things would come tumbling out, along with the finality of the loss that I had experienced. It was a mess I could not clean up on my own because the last person who knew its true nature – that mad chaos of memories, grief, horror, laughter, love – was gone.

I lost my father to cancer in the summer of 2019. I had no other family. I needed to speak to and of this grief, of the irreversible and absolute nature of this end, and of my inability to return to a place where I was still whole, put together – not scattered in a million pieces across my past.

I wanted to write to make sense of all this. And one of the troubles seemed to be that as an academic, I had grown terrified of writing in the first person. I could not speak the "I" any longer with any degree of ease or assurance.

In 2020, the pandemic shut us all in. It has been difficult, to varying degrees, for all of us. Indeed, the fact that some of us can speak of the difficulty of being shut in is a function of our privilege. We had access to a home. After the lockdown in India, millions of our people were forced out and onto the streets. Masses of migrant workers were compelled to leave the cities where they worked. They made futile and desperate attempts to return home. Thousands were forced to migrate, without any access to resources or support or livelihood. In a way, the state had enforced upon us not just a collective isolation but also a desolation – a desperation – that was experienced collectively. It was as if in order to protect a certain class of people, another could be left without care, on the streets to starve. All collective political protests that had gathered momentum in the beginning of 2020 were effectively shut down. It was evident that the state did not care for the people on the streets. And it did not care about the more privileged as long as they were shut in, and shut up.

Shut in thus, each of us had a diverse range of experiences, some strangely unprecedented emotional journeys. My father had died on the 5th of June 2019. I went back to work on the 7th of June. I had not allowed myself the time to mourn. It was after the beginning of the lockdown that I was suddenly faced with an onslaught of memories, which I had kept in abeyance so far. Grief came to me like a flood that I did not know how to stall or resist.

But this essay is not about what happened to me and how I coped with my sudden onset of a much-delayed mourning. I want to write, rather, about how my experience of overwhelming grief led me to think about this sudden state of collection isolation in relation to time, productivity, wasting time, "living in the past" as well as giving and receiving care.

It is true that with the beginning of the pandemic we had all begun to experience time differently. For many of us, it had been slowed down perforce, while for others, it had speeded up incredibly. For example, time fled for care workers and those on the frontline. Nurses were faced with unprecedentedly long work hours and an endless battle with death. One thing seemed suddenly clear. Those occupations that we had deemed the most valuable – the jobs that were most high-profile and highly paid, those which were considered the most expensive and productive – were certainly not the ones that kept us alive. Many of us now realized that what keeps us alive as a society – as communities – is a whole lot of labour that was often not recognized as such. This included caring for those who are fragile, the terminally ill, and those who were vulnerable in different ways. This included many kinds of invisible labour within the home and processes of giving and receiving care outside day-to-day calculations of what was productive and/ or profitable.

I began to think, somewhat aimlessly, about the pandemic and what it might be teaching us. I was overwhelmed with a sense of belatedness. What was hurting me the most, I realized, was my inability to return to the time that had gone: a time that I had spent speeding from one place to another, when I could have spent it caring for that which mattered.

I watched and re-watched a couple of films that had been my father's favourites. And in those films, I found people waiting. These images kept coming back to me: a kind of waiting that was after the fact. Belated. I found people waiting when it was no longer necessary or possible to wait, when what they were waiting for had already gone. This was the most acute part of their pain, and I tried to understand this in relation to how we think of time. I thought of how I had always imagined my life as a process of getting somewhere, being someplace within a certain amount of time, as being more and more productive.

Loneliness, Belatedness, and Care **235**

I shall begin to speak of these two or three films, perhaps a novel or two, in relation to these thoughts. Perhaps there will be a political point somewhere underneath to be extracted. But I shall deliberately avoid trying to spell it out or make this essay about formulations such as that. These are my thoughts in the raw and I have not tried to theorize the politics that, perhaps inevitably, underlies all of this. I do not even hope that this essay makes sense. But I do hope that it finds *resonance* somewhere.

Are You Thinking of Ending Things?

In one of the scenes in his recent film *Are You Thinking of Ending Things?*[2] Charlie Kaufman writes something like: "We have the illusion of moving through time. But perhaps it is we who are still, and it is time that is moving through us." In *Are You Thinking of Ending Things?*, a young couple, who have been dating for a few months, make a journey through the snow in the depth of winter to visit the young man's parents in their country house. The film begins on a light, optimistic note. But as the two young people travel through the emptiness and the snow, the film's tone gets steadily darker. When they arrive at the country house, strange things begin to happen. Instead of seeing the young man's parents at a particular time in their life, we meet them at different ages. It is not quite that we, along with the young couple, have travelled back in time. Rather, it is as if all the young man's memories are now jumbled together, all coming at him (and at us) simultaneously. On this visit, he has a conversation with his parents when they are 40 and he is a mere teenager. In the very next scene, he meets them when they are very old, almost about to fade away: hardly even able to talk or whisper. His memories, instead of following a linear motion that he can make sense of, fall at him at the same time. He begins to grow more and more confused.

At one point late in the film, we realize that this young man, his girlfriend, and his parents are all characters in an unwritten novel. They are images in the mind of another character whom we have not yet met. This is our unseen protagonist: an ageing janitor trapped in a sprawling school building alone during a harsh winter. The school building is empty, everything is snowed up and even the roads are blocked with snow. The janitor's white hair resembles the snow, as he dutifully cleans the empty school corridors, fruitlessly, every day. The school seems to have been closed for months now, the students far away and the janitor shut into this vast, sprawling building with a bleak and desolate landscape shining outside. He seems to be the only human alive – in fact, the only living thing – not only in this enormous building but perhaps in the whole wide world. As he cleans the endless, empty corridors of the school, the janitor thinks about his own life. He imagines he is writing a novel about his youth. We realize that what we have been travelling through from the beginning of the film is a novel that

236 Trina Nileena Banerjee

was never written. In his mind, the janitor is writing a script of his own loneliness. He wishes to make sense of all his memories, to record them in their chaotic simultaneity. But it is, in fact, too late to write. Even at the end, he is unable to leave a note that can communicate his desolation to the world. The weight of the memories that run him to the ground remains his alone.

Are You Thinking of Ending Things? begins like a chirpy little love story on a note of brightness. Like many of Kaufman's films, it ends with a desperately lonely character who encounters the unbearable heaviness of time on his own. Facing death, the janitor does not see himself at the end point of a line that he has been walking through all his life. Rather, he seems to be waiting for some sort of closure to the scattered confetti[3] of events and memories that seem to fall around him in random sequences all the time. He wishes only to gather them together into some kind of order and meaning. He fails. The film ends with a fantasy of the young man (perhaps the janitor's younger self) winning an award. Perhaps, in a sense, an award would be a closure: a kind of reward for having lived a life that was so difficult. But there is no one left to hand out this award. His parents are gone. His lover is absent. Even the schoolchildren, who barely ever looked at him, are now gone. So, in the middle of the winter holidays, the old janitor, an insignificant character even in his own novel, dies, locked in his car in the frozen schoolyard. He freezes to death, alone and naked, having written nothing.

Two ideas strike us here with remarkable force.

First, the sense of memory is chaotically simultaneous. Memories do not come at you with any semblance of piecemeal progression so that there might be some hope of digesting them. Rather they come from all directions, from all parts of your life at the same time, till you are in the middle of this vortex that pulls you in different directions. It is this terrifying simultaneity that the janitor is unable to grapple with.

Second, there is a sense of belatedness. One is always-already too late, not just to make amends but even to communicate one's desperation to another soul in the world. At the end of the film, the novel does not get written. But we have somehow entered the mind of a man who wanted to write a novel about his life and failed.

Throughout the film, he waits for someone to arrive. Stuck in the abandoned school building in the middle of a snowstorm, he hopes that *someone* will come. They could be one or two of the school children (now grown up), who had once studied here, on a nostalgia trip. He fantasizes about their arrival.

From the beginning of the film, as spectators, we have the sense that the two young people are being watched by somebody, somebody that we cannot see. As the couple drives through the night, the desolation of the frozen winter road is broken by another reality. Flashes of someone looking out from a window, a curtain parting, a floodlit corridor, a snowed-up yard, a point-of-view shot of the road.

There is a voyeur. Is it us? Is he sinister? Are we? Why does he stalk these young people? Why do *we*?

We do not clearly see the janitor till the last half hour.

We begin to wonder what Kaufman is doing with the idea of time here. How is it that he sees journeys and waiting? Who is waiting for whom?

Soon the desolate and seemingly interminable winter roads begin to resemble nightmare landscapes and what had begun as a love story starts to border on the edge of turning into a horror film. This is reminiscent of Kaufman's well-known style: his deliberate, playful, and sometimes diabolical mixing of genres from the time of his early classic *Adaptation* (2002). In sum, released in the year of the pandemic, *Are You Thinking of Ending Things?* (2020) brings together the themes of isolation, interminable time, and care in a baffling set of puzzles that tell us more about ourselves than the story at hand.

What is loneliness but the lack of care?

Like Someone in Love

Abbas Kiarostami's *Like Someone in Love* was a French-Japanese production that was made in 2012.[4] It is not one of Kiarostami's best-known films but is unique in being set in Tokyo and not somewhere in Iran. The film's protagonist Akiko is a young girl who is a student by day and a high-end sex worker by night. She has left behind her life in the village as well as her family in order to make a life in Tokyo. On the day that the film begins, Akiko is hired by a retired college professor to spend the evening with him. It is unclear why he has done so: it becomes evident at the very beginning of their meeting that he is completely uninterested in a sexual encounter. He appears lonely. He seems to want a conversation. They talk. Akiko sleeps. On the next day, the old man, whose name we find out is Takashi, drops her to college. At the college, Noriyaki, Akiko's jealous and possessive boyfriend, appears and assumes that Takashi is her grandfather. Takashi does not correct him. Noriyaki tells Takashi that he wants to marry Akiko. Takashi patiently explains to him that perhaps he is not mature enough to be married. He does everything he thinks that a real grandfather would have done in his place. Almost incredibly, two strangers connected to each other through a girl they both think they know (girlfriend/sex worker) have a conversation about marriage. Takashi keeps playacting to protect Akiko. Slowly, a strange, almost familial, tenderness develops between the old man and the young girl. Later the same day, Takashi receives a panicked phone call from Akiko. He drives back to the bookstore where he had dropped her. He finds Akiko with a bleeding lip, evidently Noriyaki has hit her on the face. Takashi takes her back to his place, where she stays till Noriyaki arrives screaming and throws something heavy at the window. We neither see Noriyaki nor the object he throws, but we see Takashi get hurt and fall down. The film ends with the camera resting unsteadily on the empty room. It ends before we know what has happened to Takashi. All through its curious storyline, *Like Someone in Love*[5] seems to be asking questions about what love is. What constitutes loving and caring for someone? How does someone who loves behave?

However, beyond the primary narrative trajectory of the film and these three main characters (Akiko, Takashi, and Noriyaki), there is another character who appears in passing in one scene of the film. It is perhaps one of the most significant scenes in the film, but it appears, at first glance, to be peripheral to the main action. As Akiko travels in the taxi towards her client's address, she receives a call from her grandmother in the village. She tells Akiko that she has not seen her in a long time and is coming to Tokyo this evening to meet her. She will wait under the big statue on the main square outside the station for Akiko to arrive. Akiko asks the taxi to drive by the station. At this point, we do not know what she intends to do. From Akiko's point of view, we see her grandmother waiting just as she had said she would: a tiny old woman at the foot of an enormous statue. She is hopeful, and she is waiting. Akiko asks the taxi driver to circle around the statue. She watches her grandmother from a distance but does not stop. She circles one more time and then the taxi drives away. Akiko leaves without stopping. Her grandmother continues to wait at the foot of the statue, trusting that Akiko will arrive.

In many ways, the scene encapsulates the quiet agony that lies at the heart of this film. We can find many possible subtexts for why Akiko does not stop. It is true that she has become a person that her grandmother no longer knows and that much of her experience in the city cannot be shared with the people she comes from. What has Akiko left behind? What is she trying to escape? What about her own self does she find impossible to present to those who wait for her? She looks, with strange longing, out of the cab window at the old woman whose face we cannot see. The audience, too, waits for her to stop. Unlike her grandmother, they know that she is here. She came. In a remarkable affective echo, this waiting without resolution is replicated at the end of the film, when Noriyaki hits Takashi through the window. Takashi falls and the frame is suddenly empty. Akiko does not move, inside the frame or anywhere else. The camera does not move either: holding the empty room in place like a bated breath. The film ends before we know what has happened to Takashi. Perhaps we remember at this point that we do not know either what happened to Akiko's grandmother. Did she return to her village? How long did she wait? Is she alright?

Waiting is replicated, unresolved, many times throughout the film.

Perhaps we also find ourselves wondering what happens to Akiko after this. She has places to go, classes to attend, work to do, and clients to visit. She moves from place to place every day. But there are other characters in the film who are stationary, who do not move: people who evidently have nowhere to go. These are people who are waiting. An old man waits in his apartment. An old woman travels a long way from the village to the city simply in order to wait.

Once again, there are two ways in which time functions here. In the first, it is filled with things to be done. In the second, time is filled with waiting. Waiting for what? Perhaps just to sit next to someone. Most often, that someone does not arrive. On the terms that Akiko's life is lived, this second is wasted time.

Reflecting on the two ways in which time functions in the film got me thinking about the relationship between loneliness and time. I came upon the idea that loneliness is a missed encounter. You wait for each other; it is just that you wait at different times. Time is wasted waiting for someone who does not arrive. And again, time is dedicated to waiting for someone who can no longer arrive. Such is the scene: you are waiting, and a train goes by. Or a taxi goes by. Someone passes you by, but you do not meet them. Imagine that the taxi keeps going by without the encounter ever taking place. Is this what loneliness is? A repeated missed encounter where your mind finds itself imprisoned? Scholars will think of many things here: Freud's distinction between "mourning" and "melancholia,"[6] for example. Where does one end and the other begin? How many of these missed encounters do we struggle with in our conscious minds? How much of it moves towards a fractured resolution and acceptance that we can live with? How much of it do we internalize? How does what is never articulated, even to ourselves, keep us imprisoned in a single moment of looped time? Do you find yourself asking, repeatedly, "what if"?

What if Akiko had stopped? What if she had got out of the taxi?

What does loneliness have to do with time and what does time have to do with care? It is a cliché that time stretches out to infinity when we are lonely. While this might be true, that is not all of it.

I am interested here in the inseverable connection we have established between time and productivity: the idea that you are meant to *use* time to produce something, get somewhere, and achieve something. We are eternally afraid of wasting time. What if you are merely waiting? Has time stopped? Are we subjects who have the capacity to waste time? *Are we in charge of time?* Am I an actor who wastes the time that is meant to be used? When can we stop thinking of time as capital: something that is spent, wasted or saved? For example, why is "living in the past" a waste? We say this to each other all the time: "stop wasting time, live in the present." As if we could waste time if we wanted to, as if we were really that big? To return to Kaufman, what if we were standing still, and it was time that was moving through us? What if we were caught in the illusion that we were progressing, going from point to point, while in truth we were, like Akiko, circling eternally across a place at which we do not have the courage to stop?

We think we are getting somewhere. Instead of the woman from the village bearing gifts, we end up meeting an old man who is just as lonely. Like the woman in the public square, he is waiting for someone to sit beside him.

"Mrs. Dalloway said she would buy the flowers herself."

Virginia Woolf's *Mrs. Dalloway* (1925) begins with an ecstatic sense of motion. Those of us who know the novel well, know this: Clarissa Dalloway is always busy. She is organizing a party, she has things to do, places to visit, and flowers to buy. As soon as the novel begins, we find her amidst the chaos of the London streets. She walks briskly down the street. It is summer in London.

> *Mrs. Dalloway said she would buy the flowers herself.*
>
> *For Lucy had her work cut out for her. The doors would be taken off their hinges; Rumpelmayer's men were coming. And then, thought Clarissa Dalloway, what a morning – fresh as if issued to children on a beach.*
>
> *What a lark! What a plunge! For so it had always seemed to her, when, with a little squeak of the hinges, which she could hear now, she had burst open the French windows and plunged at Bourton into the open air. How fresh, how calm, stiller than this of course, the air was in the early morning; like the flap of a wave; the kiss of a wave; chill and sharp and yet (for a girl of eighteen as she then was) solemn, feeling as she did, standing there at the open window, that something awful was about to happen; [...]*
>
> *For having lived in Westminster – how many years now? Over twenty – one feels, even in the midst of the traffic, or waking at night, Clarissa was positive, a particular hush, or solemnity; an indescribable pause; a suspense (but that might be her heart, affected, they said, by influenza) before Big Ben strikes. There! Out it boomed. First a warning, musical; then the hour, irrevocable. The leaden circles dissolved in the air. Such fools we are, she thought, crossing Victoria Street. For Heaven only knows why one loves it so, how one sees it so, making it up, building it round one, tumbling it, creating it every moment afresh; but the veriest frumps, the most dejected of miseries sitting on doorsteps (drink their downfall) do the same; can't be dealt with, she felt positive, by Acts of Parliament for that very reason: they love life. In people's eyes, in the swing, tramp, and trudge; in the bellow and the uproar; the carriages, motor cars, omnibuses, vans, sandwich men shuffling and swinging; brass bands; barrel organs; in the triumph and the jingle and the*

strange high singing of some aeroplane overhead was what she loved; life; London; this moment of June.[7]

Soon after this, we meet Septimus. Septimus is a soldier who has returned from the First World War. He is what in those days would be called a victim of "shellshock." In these days, he might have been diagnosed with "Post-Traumatic Stress Disorder" or PTSD. In short, Septimus can no longer make sense of his own life. His life has, for all practical purposes, stopped. He no longer has anywhere else to go. Time seems to have condensed with a strange heaviness around Septimus. As we move from Clarissa's mind to Septimus', time changes its gait for us.

> *"K ... R ..." said the nursemaid, and Septimus heard her say "Kay Arr" close to his ear, deeply, softly, like a mellow organ, but with a roughness in her voice like a grasshopper's, which rasped his spine deliciously and sent running up into his brain waves of sound which, concussing, broke. A marvellous discovery indeed – that the human voice in certain atmospheric conditions (for one must be scientific, above all scientific) can quicken trees into life! Happily, Rezia put her hand with a tremendous weight on his knee so that he was weighted down, transfixed, or the excitement of the elm trees rising and falling, rising and falling with all their leaves alight and the colour thinning and thickening from blue to the green of a hollow wave, like plumes on horses' heads, feathers on ladies', so proudly they rose and fell, so superbly, would have sent him mad. But he would not go mad. He would shut his eyes; he would see no more.*
>
> *But they beckoned; leaves were alive; trees were alive. And the leaves being connected by millions of fibres with his own body, there on the seat, fanned it up and down; when the branch stretched, he, too, made that statement. The sparrows fluttering, rising, and falling in jagged fountains were part of the pattern; the white and blue, barred with black branches. Sounds made harmonies with premeditation; the spaces between them were as significant as the sounds. A child cried. Rightly far away a horn sounded. All taken together meant the birth of a new religion –* [8]

Septimus is sitting on the same morning on a park bench with his wife Lucrezia. He is unable to speak, relate to others, to remember things clearly. It seems that he has begun to hallucinate. Once again, we have two people on opposite sides of time. We have a woman who has things to do, and we have a man who can no longer attend to the present. Having lost touch with life, Septimus is no longer in attendance. Clarissa is going somewhere. She is constantly going everywhere. For Septimus, on the other hand, time has stopped. People do not make sense to him anymore. He feels in his bones

242 Trina Nileena Banerjee

that the trees are alive. He is viscerally embedded in another time, which no one else, not even his wife, can see or hear or feel. He is active in that time, and that time is alive around him, even as he sits quite still on the park bench. The leaves of the trees above him seem alive, they seem to be speaking to each other. You could say he is hallucinating. He has failed to be present, to live in the moment, and to attend to life. Irrevocably delayed by his shellshock, he has not managed to arrive in the present.

But what about Clarissa? Mrs. Dalloway runs endlessly from shop to street and back again because she refuses to encounter the emptiness of the present. She cannot pause, because pausing would be too much like death. By running, she avoids being present.

But when the news of Septimus' death arrives at her party, she stops. He was a young man she did not know. Yet the world suddenly grinds to a halt for Clarissa.

> Then (she had felt it only this morning) there was the terror; the overwhelming incapacity, one's parents giving it into one's hands, this life, to be lived to the end, to be walked with serenely; there was in the depths of her heart an awful fear. Even now, quite often if Richard had not been there reading the Times, so that she could crouch like a bird and gradually revive, send roaring up that immeasurable delight, rubbing stick to stick, one thing with another, she must have perished. But that young man had killed himself.
>
> Somehow it was her disaster – her disgrace. It was her punishment to see sink and disappear here a man, there a woman, in this profound darkness, and she forced to stand here in her evening dress. She had schemed; she had pilfered. She was never wholly admirable. She had wanted success. Lady Bexborough and the rest of it. And once she had walked on the terrace at Bourton.[9]

Is Clarissa lonely? It is too late to meet Septimus, to know who he was. He is gone. But is Clarissa still alone? Or will she be waiting for something that is no longer possible?

From its very first page onwards, the novel juxtaposes external and internal motion. Septimus sits still as a rock. But he is eternally connected, even in his hallucinations, to the trees above – their leaves, the sap running inside them – all of which seem to be in constant motion, speaking to each other in voices he can almost decipher. And is Clarissa constantly running in order that she may not come face to face with the stillness, the silence of the present moment?

The Edge of Heaven

Fateh Akin's 2007 film *The Edge of Heaven* is a Turkish-German production that tells the story of three pairs of parents and children: two mothers and daughters, and one father and son. It is too complex and involves a plot to lay down in full here. I will focus only on the final section of the film.

A woman arrives in Istanbul after her only daughter has been shot in a chance encounter amidst political turmoil and a student uprising. She has come from Bremen after having received news of her daughter's death. She can no longer meet her daughter. In the hotel, she decides to stay in the room where her daughter had stayed. There is a strange density with which the objects in the room surround her: objects which her daughter had once touched. As she touches them, they seem to almost assault her in the emptiness in which she finds herself. She finds herself unable to return to her life in Bremen. She is compelled to stay. She rents the room above the bookshop where her daughter worked and begins, belatedly, to live the life her daughter lived. Now, when it is too late, she begins, a little, to understand who her daughter was.

Of the other pairs, a son, a now unemployed professor of Literature, arrives in a small Turkish fishing village in search of his long-estranged father. Having learnt that his father has gone out fishing, he arrives on the beach and sits down on the sand to wait for his father. The film ends as he is looking at the incoming waves, waiting for his father's boat to come back.

Just like in Kiarostami's film, we do not know at the end what happened to Takashi, or the old woman lost in the city, here, too, we do not know when the boat is coming back, or if it is coming back at all. The film ends in a frame where the young man sits with his back to the camera on the beach and we look at the waves with him, waiting as he does, for his father to return.

The film has, just as in *Like Someone in Love*, tricked us into waiting for someone who may not return. Akin begins the film with this trip to the fishing village, and we only know the end of that journey when everything is already over. Time loops back to the past jaggedly between these two scenes from the son's trip, and there is a sense of belatedness even before the film has properly begun. The whole film trips us up with missed encounters, one piling up on top of the other, and it seems to have been always-already too late, from the start.

"Pray, do not mock me."
In the way that we live, our time is constantly structured to escape loneliness, to escape the one who is waiting. Yet it is also structured to constantly, generationally produce more and more of it. More and more waiting. More and more loneliness. The pandemic has alerted us to the critical importance of care work. We have begun to talk about it so much more over the last few years. Such brilliant work has been produced in this respect by so many scholars, especially social reproduction theorists.[10]

But what exactly are the limits of care work? Is sitting beside someone on a park bench care? Does it constitute work? You could argue that is an absolute waste of time. It produces nothing more than more empty time. So, we do not sit. And because we do not sit, there is always someone waiting. For a while it is others: children with arms reaching out, waiting to giggle. The old with heads nodding off. A woman desperately in love. And then, one day, it is us: us, waiting with a black dog on the bench. The doctor says we hallucinate. Alzheimer's has taken reality and language from us, taken away the forward-moving lurch of jagged time. But it has given us the leaves of trees talking with desperate urgency to each other, *now*. Because it can no longer wait:

> *Pray, do not mock me. /I am a very foolish fond old man, /Fourscore and upward, not an hour more nor less. / And to deal plainly/ I fear I am not in my perfect mind.*

You arrived late; he was gone. You did not have time to stop. And now, time refuses to stop and turn for you. What is loneliness? It is the absence of care. But more devastatingly, it is waiting for a time that will not return.

Sorry, We Missed You[11]

An interlocutor asked me if we could think of "care-work" as a kind of "productive intimacy." Perhaps there is a way to uncouple care and work, I thought. Perhaps there is a way to stop thinking of time as a resource that we must spend, save, waste, use badly or well. It is absolute importance to raise the demand for care, long-invisibilized and devalued in our world as work. This has also been the political push of social reproduction theorists in academia. And it is undeniably important politically, especially at this moment.

But to say at this moment that we must also reflect on the value of that which non-work might seem a manifestation of privilege in the present contingency. Does having "excessive time," more time than we need to produce what we need to produce, allow us the "luxury" of waste? What are we doing when we sit next to someone on a park bench: doing nothing at all, not even speaking, for all practical purposes, *wasting* the time that is afforded to us? Who hands out time? How do we win it? How much labour or privilege can win us what amount of time? How do we settle these accounts? Or is it time to throw away these calculations? Why would I want to think of intimacy as productive in the first place? Is not intimacy the very opposite of productivity? What does it produce but more, useless intimacy? Can we allow it to find us a moment outside the logic of productivity, perhaps (daringly) outside a teleological logic altogether? Why must we think of something as productive in order to see it as valuable? Care must be recognized as work, and valued as work. *But care is much more than work.*

In Ken Loach's most recent film *"Sorry We Missed You"*, one of the main characters is a care-worker who takes care of old people in their homes. These elders live alone, usually with no one to take care of them, or even visit them. In a very Loach-like way, we see, in very great detail, the minutiae of this woman's labour as a care-worker. We begin to understand what she actually does – the dirty bedclothes, the washing, the bathing, the clothing, the feeding. Loach's most effective political and visual strategy here is forcefully visualizing what is often made invisible. We hardly ever see such work on screen: it is too mundane, too dreary, too disgustingly physical to darken our spectacular screen games. But Loach gives it all to us, dirt, sweat, and grime. In one of the houses the care-worker visits, the patient wants her to brush her hair. This often delays the care-worker, but she always complies. Technically, this does not qualify as part of her work: this slow, tender brushing of long white hair. The patient is not disabled, capable of doing this bit by herself. Yet this tiny excess *defines* their relationship. We realize that the old woman's daughter used to brush her hair, a daughter who is now absent. The care-worker brushes another mother's hair, even as she misses her own children whom she has left at home. She does not have enough time for them. Yet she does this in excess of what she is meant to do as a care-worker. She gives it *tenderness*.

Who is this woman whose hair is being brushed? She is one of those who have been declared useless and unfit to produce by the state, the economy, by every infrastructure of power that exists. What is the logic of "herd immunity" after all? That *some people can be spared*. Those who are more vulnerable, and more fragile can, in fact, be allowed to die. What was the logic of the lockdown in India? Did it not see some people as excessive? Fit to be left alone? Not deserving of care? It was clear that some people would be protected at the cost of others; that some lives are more necessary than others.

In *Sorry, We Missed You*, this totally unnecessary moment of hair-brushing is lingered upon by Loach with a strange kind of tenderness. Nothing is productive or useful in this action. Yet it creates a moment of intimacy that holds a relationship together. It is not work. Yet it might be at the core of what sustains and keeps alive an old woman. Both women, perhaps.

How do we begin to talk about this? Perhaps this excess is crucial. That waiting on the beach, that slow brushing of the hair, that extra turn around the square: are these really the things we do in our "spare" time? *Or are they at the core of how we survive?*

What Happens to Akiko?

Since I saw Kiarostami's film for the first time, I have often wondered what happens to Akiko after the end of the film. I have wondered about Akiko's loneliness. How would Akiko survive coming back to that square for the rest of her life? That is perhaps the "belatedness" I am talking about. I began with a black dog. What does Akiko see on the bench beside her grandmother? The quietly raging black dog of their two-fold loneliness? She does not stop, but she is drawn to her grandmother. This *ambivalence* is at the core of her loneliness. She circles, but she cannot stop. As spectators, we know for sure that the old woman is waiting. But what is Akiko doing? What we miss, perhaps, is that Akiko is also waiting. She wants to prolong the moment in that circling cab as long as possible, she wants to be able to look at her grandmother for as long as she can afford to. She wants to linger on and on, without stopping. The vision of her grandmother waiting sustains her: this missed encounter around which her mind loops again and again. There will also be a moment when Akiko begins her waiting after the fact. How will she then return to this square? This is the terrifying belatedness I am talking about. *We wait for each other, but at different times.*

Notes

1 Les Murray, *Killing the Black Dog* (Collingwood: Black Inc., 2009).
2 Charlie Kaufman, *Are You Thinking of Ending Things?* (Netflix, 2020), 134 minutes. Based on a novel by Iain Reid. [Iain Reid, *I'm Thinking of Ending Things* (New York: Simon & Schuster, 2016)].
3 The reference to memories and time as confetti scattering randomly around you is to be found in another Netflix series, *The Haunting of Hill House*. It appears in a speech by a character called Nell, who is the youngest of five children. [Mike Flanagan, *The Haunting of Hill House* (Netflix, 2018)].
4 Abbas Kiarostami, *Like Someone in Love* (The Criterion Collection: Japan-France, 2012), 109 minutes.
5 "Like Someone in Love" was a song composed by Jimmy Van Heusen in 1944. The lyrics were by Johnny Burke. Bing Crosby made it a hit in March 1945. It is a jazz standard. The lyrics were:
   "This change I feel puzzles me.
   It's strange, a real mystery.
   Maybe you see it.
   If you do see it
   What on earth can it be?
   Lately I find myself out gazing at stars,
   Hearing guitars like someone in love.
   Sometimes the things I do astound me,
   Mostly whenever you're around me.
   Lately I seem to walk as though I had wings,
   Bump into things like someone in love.
   Each time I look at you I'm limp as a glove
   And feeling like someone in love.
   Lately I find myself out gazing at stars,
   Hearing guitars like someone in love.
   Sometimes the things I do astound me,
   Mostly whenever you're around me.
   Lately I seem to walk as though I had wings,
   Bump into things like someone in love.
   Each time I look at you I'm limp as a glove

And feeling like someone in love."

6 Freud, Sigmund. "Mourning and Melancholia", in *The Standard Edition of the Complete Psychological Works of Sigmund Freud*, Volume XIV (1914–16) (London: The Hogarth Press and the Institute of Psychoanalysis, 1957), pp. 243–258.
7 Virginia Woolf, *Mrs. Dalloway* in *The Collected Novels of Virginia Woolf* (ed. Stella McNichol, London: Macmillan, 1992), pp. 35–36.
8 Ibid., pp. 48–49.
9 Ibid., p. 169.
10 Tithi Bhattacharya, *Social Reproduction Theory: Remapping Class, Recentering Oppression* (London: Pluto Press, 2017).
11 Ken Loach, *Sorry, We Missed You* (United Kingdom, 2019), 101 minutes.

References

Bhattacharya, Tithi. *Social Reproduction Theory: Remapping Class, Recentring Oppression*. Pluto Press, 2017.
Flanagan, Mike. *The Haunting of Hill House*. Netflix, 2018.
Kaufman, Charlie. *Are You Thinking of Ending Things?* Netflix, 2020.
Kiarostami, Abbas. *Like Someone in Love*. The Criterion Collection, 2012.
Loach, Ken. *Sorry, We Missed You*. United Kingdom, 2019.
Murray, Les. *Killing the Black Dog*. Black Inc., 2009.
Reid, Iain. *I'm Thinking of Ending Things*. Simon & Schuster, 2016.
Woolf, Virginia. *Mrs. Dalloway, The Collected Novels of Virginia Woolf*. Macmillan, 1992.

INDEX

Italic page references indicate figures

Aag (Ram Gopal Varma 2007) 192
Abbas, K.A. 184
Abhinaya Darpana 128
Abrams, M.H. 120
Adaptation (2002) 237
"affordance," concept of 146
age differentials 82
ageing bodies 2, 3; of bodybuilders and
  dancers 10; *see also* bodybuilding;
  and performances of agelessness *see*
  Bachchan, Amitabh; physical exercise
  104; site of protest 162; symbol of
  resistance 162
ageing female body 223–225
Ageing in Contemporary India (Suhas
  Kumar Biswas 1987) 6
ageism 42, 44, 49, 67, 68, 139, 169, 171,
  180; in China 14; cosmetic industry
  3; defined 2; in Europe 14; in Indian
  classical dancer *see* Indian classical
  dancer, ageing for; in Japan 14
aging and elderly population:
  abandonment by kin members
  43; care roles and dependencies
  81; conceptualize care and
  companionship 41; contextualizing
  ageing 75–76; cultural narratives
  of 171; cultural understandings of
  personhood 37; decision-making
  within family 36; discourse of

6; discrimination 39; economic
inequity 202; emotional ties 37;
fear, anxiety, and inevitability of
death 36; Indian classical dancer
see Indian classical dancer, ageing
for; joint family principle 41; legal
determinism 39; living conditions 37;
National Policy for Senior Citizens
2011 38–39; negative stereotyping
of 2; normative family 76–78; in
nuclear middle class urban family
79; onstage performance *see* onstage
performance, age-related politics;
performers and athletes 120; physical
and cognitive impairments 171;
practitioners 118; queering aged care
practices 97–98; Section 125 CrPC
37; social and cultural construction
of 4; in social context 76; social
reality of sons 36; social security 39,
43–46; social understanding of 76;
sociological research 35; specialized
care and treatment of 202; violence
against 83; voice, in cinema *see*
voice, in cinema
Ahmed, Mona 52
Ahmed, Sara 55
Aich, Manohar 104, 106–108, 115
AIDS Bhedbhav Virodhi Andolan
  (ABVA) 50

250 Index

Akiko 245–246
Akin, Fateh 240–244
All That Fall (1956) 165
Alter, Joseph S. 106
Alzheimer's disease 202–203
Ambedkar 26
Anjali (1957) 130
Antentas, J. M. 4
Anthropocene 5–6
anti-ageing creams and serums 3
anti-ageing medicines 5
anti-CAA movement 31
anti-CAA protest sites 11
Are You Thinking of Ending Things?
    (2020) 235–237
Aristotle 13
Asif, K. 131
Atelier Theatre 157, 173
Atwood, Margaret 74
authoritarianism 9
Ayurveda 216

Bachchan, Amitabh 10, 202; accident
    187; acousmatic features of 180;
    acousmatic/image 192–196;
    advertisements 192; *Badla* (Sujoy
    Ghosh 2019) 178, *179*; *Baghban*
    (Ravi Chopra 2003) 185; *Bbuddha
    hoga terra baap* (Puri Jagganath
    2011) 186; career-defining roles
    187; character and actor 195;
    Coolie (Manmohan Desai 1984)
    184; criminal copies, of voice and
    mannerisms 179–180; critique of
    bhadralok 191; *Deewaar* (Milind
    Luthria 2004) 186; *Deewar* (Yash
    Chopra 1975) 181; Indian cinema
    and fans of 179; *Kaala Patthar* (Yash
    Chopra 1979) 181; *Kabhi Khushi
    Kabhie Gham* (Karan Johar 2001)
    185; *Khuda Gawah* (Mukul S. Anand
    1992) 185; *Last Lear* (Rituparno
    Ghosh 2007) 186; *Mohabbatein*
    (Aditya Chopra 2000) 185; multiple
    roles and appearances 179; National
    Film Award for Best Actor 193;
    on-screen persona 182; *Paa and
    Gulabo Sitabo* (Shoojit Sircar 2020)
    180, 195–196; peripheral and
    working-class characters 181; physical
    modifications 184; *Pink* (Aniruddha
    Roy Chowdhury 2015) 186; political
    contexts 181; powerful character
    role 186; *Reshma aur Shera* (Sunil
    Dutt 1971) 184; "salt-and-pepper"
    look 186; *Sarkar* (Ram Gopal Verma
    2005) 186; *Shamitabh* (Balki 2015)
    184; *Sholay* 188; "singing" star 190;
    star power 179; state of Emergency
    186; Supremo comics 189; *Trishul*
    (Yash Chopra 1978) 181; TV show
    Kaun Banega Crorepati 185; vocal
    weight and timbre 191; *Wazir* (Bejoy
    Nambiar 2015) 186
Bakshi, Kaustav 7
Balasaraswati, Tanjore 135–136
Bali, Arun 6
Bali, Vyjayanthimala 139
Banerjee, Trina Nileena 7
Bano, Bilquis 27
Barker, Meg 93
Baro Pishima (1959) 166
Barrett, Michelle 42
Barua, Jahnu 203
Beard, Renée L. 208
Beckett, Samuel 165
belatedness, sense of 233–235
Benhabib, Seyla 61
Benjamin, Walter 141
Bergson, Henri 120
Bhattacharya, Nikhilesh 108
Bhave, Sumitra 203
Bhonsle, Sudesh 190
Bhuvan Shome 184
Bichat, Xavier 5
bio-technology 4, 6
Biswas, Ranjita 7
Biswas, Suhas Kumar 6
Black (2005) 202
bodybuilding: aesthetic perfection
    112; ancient sculptures 110–111;
    embodied archive 118, 119;
    embodied knowledge 116–119;
    preferred styles of posing 113
Bolt, Usain 121
Bourdieu, Pierre 109, 163
Brooks, John Ellingham 65, 66
Buddhism 223, 225, 226
Butler, Judith 100, 167
Butler, Robert N. 2

Calasanti, Toni 3
capitalism 99
Capote, Truman 66
care 3, 233–234; collaborative care
    97, 98; and companionship 44, 46;

of elderly population *see* aging and elderly population; heteronormative care practices 96; heteronormative structure 100; institutional care 39; and intimacy 79–83; loneliness and 233, 237; paid care givers 101; and parent–child relationship 78–79; queer care practices 96; social organization 91, 92
caregivers 95–96
care work/workers 94–97, 243–245
caring and compassion 226
Cashel Byron's Profession 120
Castro, Fidel 30
Chakravarti, Paromita 10
Chakravarty, Vasudeo 187
Chandralekha 140
Chandrasekhar, C.V. 129
Chapman, David L. 111
Chattopadhay, Suman 34
Chifney, Ron 113
Chion, Michel 180–183
Chopra, Anupama 187, 194
Chowdhury, Bhaskar Roy 138
Chowdhury, Buda 132
Chowdhury, Indira 108
36 Chowringhee Lane 41–42
Citizenship Amendment Act (2019) 15–19
class inequality 209–212
Cohen, Lawrence 3, 205
collaborative care 97, 98
Comaneci, Nadia 121
Comics and Sequential Art (1985) 189
community solidarity 66
consumer capitalism 50
consumer products 45
consumptive labour 51
corporeal schema 118, 119
Counsel Club 70, 71
COVID 1, 4, 223, 227; lockdown experience 2–3; old and young populations 2; pandemic and belatedness 233–235
Cruise, Tom 185
Culture, Context and Aging of Older Indians: Narratives from India and Beyond (Jagriti Gangopadhyay 2021) 6

"daadis" (paternal grandmothers) movement: anti-CAA protesters 28–29; anti-CAA protests 10;

CAA and Shaheen Bagh protest 15–19; dominating daadis (dabang daddis) 26–30; history and nation 22–26; intergenerational cross-learning 20; political activism 19; political community 28; political establishment 19; right to equal citizenship of India 15; vulnerability analysis 26–30
Dahan 42
Daly, M. 61
Das, Adiguru Pankaj Charan 138
Das, Dayanidhi 132
Das, Deba Prasad 132, 138
Das, Kumkum 132
Das, Pankaj Charan 132
Das, Veena 44
Datta, Biswanath 104, 106, 108–110, *112*, 115, 120
Dave, Naisargi 51
Davies, Paul 152
Deb, Nilanjana 7, 8
Deewar (Yash Chopra 1975) 181
Deleuze, Gilles 102
dementia, Indian films in: 2014 Report on Dementia in the Asia-Pacific Region 202; analysis of family relationships 203; Asia-Pacific region 202; *Astu* (2015) 203; and class inequality 209–212; and cultural difference 204–207; *Mai* (2013) 204; *Maine Gandhi Ko Nahin Mara* 203; *Mayurakshi* (2017) 204; memory and selfhood 215–218; risk factor for 202; scriptwriters and directors 203; social and familial attitudes 202; woman patient and caregiver 212–215
D'Emilio, John 50
De Senectute 13
Dev, Sitara 130
Dhall, Pawan 52, 56
Digby, William 229
Dikshithar, Muthuswami 140
disability movements 82
Discobolus 110
discrimination, against older people 2
Doane, Mary Ann 184
Dostana/Friendship (2008) 50
D'Souza, Dominique 52, 55
Dutta, Aniruddha 70
Dutta, Raghunath 132
Dying Gladiator statue 110

252 Index

The Edge of Heaven (2007) 240–244
Eisner, Will 189
elderly males 13
elderly women 37; anti-CAA protests
10; bodily privations of 27; living
alone 37
Eng, David L. 51
Enter the Dangal (Rudraneil Sengupta
2016) 106
ethical ageing 48
Europe, ageing economies of 14
Evans, David 56

family 101; economic dependence,
of parents 81; girl children 83;
heteronormative family 75;
heterosexual kinships and queer
friendships 89–92; normative family
76–78; parent–child relationship
78–79
Farnese Hercules statue 110
Federer, Roger 121
Federici, Silvia 21, 31
Fineman, Martha 27, 28
Foucault, Michel 64, 70, 91, 94
Freeman, Elizabeth 48
*Friendship as Social Justice
Activism* 67

Gandhi, Indira 177
Gangopadhyay, Jagriti 6
Gautam, Siddharth 52
Geetha, V. 7
gender and age 77
Gender Trouble 167
genetic engineering 4, 6
gerontocracy 35
gerontological theory 148
Ghani, Tanvir 177
Ghosh, Atanu 204
Ghosh, Bishnu Charan 111
Ghosh, Rituparno 42
Gohil, Manvendra Singh 52
Gopal, Meena 44
Gopal, Ram 138
Gopinath 138
Govind, Priyadarshini 129
Greece 88
Greene, Graham 66
*Grey Areas: An Anthology of Indian
Fiction on Ageing* 169
Grover, Mansi 10
Guattari, Felix 102

Guha, Gobar 108–110
Gullette, Margaret Morganroth 167
Gupta, Abhijit 108
Gupta, Keshub Chandra Sen 111
Gupta, Sunil 52
Gursahani, Roop 69
Guruswamy, Menaka 64

Halberstam, Judith 48
Harari, Y. N. 4
Harrison, Robert Pogue 128
Hawn, Goldie 186
*Health Status of the Urban Elderly: A
Medico-social Study* (S. Siva Raju
2002) 6
hegemonic heterosexuality 100
heteronormative marriage 89
heteronormativity 98
Hochschild, Arlie 101
Hogeveen, Bryan 117
hug buddies/professionals cuddlers 102
Humari Burhiya 169

Ideology of Hindi Film 177
Indian classical dancer, ageing for:
acutely image-conscious 139;
Balasaraswati's performance
135–136; Bharatanatyam 134,
137, 138; Chandralekha's life 141;
Dev, Sitara 130, 131; Devadasi
Abolition Bill 137; experience of
aging 134; gender difference 138;
gender stereotypes 137; hegemonic
gender–ageist discourses 139;
intensification and acceleration of
127; Kelubabu's performance 132–
134; life experiences to abhinaya
135; masculinity, representations
of 138; Navtej's appearance 140;
Odissi dancers 132; performance
and age 128; performer's self
138–139; physical decline and social
marginalization 127; postures and
gestures 128; retirement age 127;
self-presentation in performance
130; social constraints 127; stage
presence 129; Vyjayanthimala's
daily routine 139–140
India politics 14
intergenerational kinships 89
intimacy: and care 79–83; daily living
of 92; queer intimacies 83–85;
understanding and living of 92

Isherwood, Christopher 66
Italy 1

James, Henry 66
Javalis 129
Jehangir, Cowasji 130
Johar, Navtej Singh 52, 139, 140
joint family principle 41
Joshi, Arvind 44

Kahaani (Sujoy Ghosh 2012) 191
Kalam, Abdul 26
Katju, Arundhati 64
Katz, S. 4
Kavi, Ashok Row 52
Keats, John 121
Khakhar, Bhupen 52
Khatun, Asma 23
Kher, Anupam 203
Khiladi (Homi Wadia, 1968) 186
Khokar, Ashish Mohan 138
Kiarostami, Abbas 237
Kidwai, Saleem 52
Kingston, Mark 91
kinship-based support systems 9
Kodiyal, Mahesh 204
Kolkata 33–34
Krishna, Gopi 131
Kuchh Afsaaney 157, 158, 173
Kumar, Kishore 182
Kumar, Pushpendra 127–128

Lacan, Jacques 182
Lacchu Maharaj 131
Lagaan (Ashutosh Gwariker 2000) 190
Lamb, Sarah 36–37
Levrini, O. 4
LGBTIQ+ community 49, 53
LGBTIQ+ movement 48, 54, 56
Liederman, Earle E. 111
Like Someone in Love 237–242
"The Living Statue" (S. Bose) *114*
Loach, Ken 244–245
loneliness 42, 49, 65, 68, 83, 89, 207, 211, 233, 236, 239, 245, 246
Lowen, Sharon 133

Mahanagar 41
Mahapatra, Kelucharan 132
Maharaj, Birju 132, 140
Maharaj, Kishan 137
Maharaj, Shambhu 131
Mahatma Gandhi 26, 30, 203

Maine Gandhi Ko Nahin Mara 203
maintenance, of parents 40
Maintenance and Welfare of Parents and Senior Citizens Act 39, 43
Maintenance Tribunal 40
Majee, Shantanu 10
male gerontocracy 14
Managed Elder Care 45
Mandal, Saptarshi 63–64
Mander, Harsh 25
Mangeshkar, Lata 182
Manimekhalai 225, 226
Mansukhani, Tarun 50
Manusmriti 31
marriage 89; adjustment with parents-in-law 36; ageing and 63; and blood relations 77, 84; and friendships 69; heteronormative marriage 76; heterosexual marriage 55, 62, 63; and sexuality 65; Special Marriage Act 100
material culture studies: absence of deference and care 149; attachment to object 150; circumstances 146; concept of "affordance" 146; detachment and withdrawal 145; developments in 146; discourses of religion and spirituality 154; gerontological theory 148; material possessions 150; material poverty 149; material surroundings 152; mutuality and co-dependence 146; physical objects 149; self-realization 151–154; sense of self 149; social lives 146; social trajectory 148; "Sunstroke" (Tulasi Chaganti 1977) 149–151; "The Womb" (Chaman Nahal 1988) 151–154; "Tiny's Granny" (Ismat Chughtai 1954) 147–149
Maugham, William Somerset 65
Mbembe, Achille 1
Medeiros, Kate 153
Merleau-Ponty, Maurice 106, 116–118
Messi, Lionel 121
Mishra, Loknath 132
Mishra, Sanjukta 132
Mitchell, David 169
Modi, Narendra 20
Mohapatra, Kelucharan 132, 138, 139
Moitra, Shefali 99, 102
Money Heist (2017) 177
monogamous couplehood 101

254 Index

monogamous heterosexuality 101
Montero, Barbara 120
mortality 152, 223, 226
Mortals and Immortals 110
Mother India (Mehboob Khan 1957)
  130, 188
Mrs. Dalloway (1925) 240
Mughal-e-Azam (K. Asif 1960)
  131, 188
Mukherjee, Madhuja 10
Mukherjee, Sujaan 10
Mullick, Pratap 189
Muslim women 15

Naidu, Sarojini 130
Najan, Nala 138
Najma (1943) 130
Narayan, R.K. 164
National AIDS Control Programme
  (NACP-I) 55
National Family Health Survey (NHFS)
  data 37
National Policy for Older Persons 38
National Policy for Senior Citizens
  38–39
necropolitics 1
Nehru, Jawaharlal 25, 177
Neil Thompson (1998) 36
Nichomachean Ethics 13
*No Ageing in India: Alzheimer's, the
  Bad Family, and Other Modern
  Things* (Cohen 2000) 3, 6
non-monogamous homosexuality 101
normative family 76–78
Not I (1972) 165
nritta 128

oldage homes 41, 43, 89
older males 14, 139
onstage performance, age-related
  politics: characters onstage 161;
  childhood and old age 171;
  chronological age 165–166;
  conviction 158–159; discriminatory
  attitudes 163; emotional and social
  age 158; emotional memory 159;
  emotion and truth of moment
  162; experimentation 160; *vs* film
  164; imagination 168; internalized
  ageism 171; literary representations
  164; physical and socio-cultural
  realities of 170; physical attributes,
  of character 165; prejudices and

stereotypes 163; representation of
  ageing 169, 171; restrictive social
  roles 163; sexual desires 165; site of
  protest 162; social expectations 165;
  sociocultural expectations 166, 168;
  stereotypical ageist old character
  168; stereotypical portrayals
  160–161; subjectivity and objectivity
  159; symbol of resistance 162

Paa (Balki 2009) 192
paid care givers 101
Pakeezah (1972) 131
Pallum, W.A. 112
Panigrahi, Sanjukta 132
"The Panther on a Lion" (S. Bose) *113*
Parekh, Amritlal 137
parent–child relationship 78–79, 82
parents: maintenance of 40; parenting
  of 82
paternal grandmothers *see* "daadis"
  (paternal grandmothers) movement
Patnaik, D. N. 132
Patnaik, Kali Charan 132
patriarchalism 35
Phoenix, Cassandra 104, 115
physical ability 118
physical activity 121
Piku 43
Pillai, K. N. Dhandayuthapani 139
Pillai, K. P. Kittappa 139
Pillai, Meenakshi Sundaram 138
Pillai, Muthukumaran 138
Pillai, Vazhuvoor Ramiah 139
Plato 13
political hierarchies 20
political protest 15
polyamory 93, 101
polysexuality 94
Prasad, M. Madhava 177
Prashad, Lala Ram 151
Pratchett, Terry 74
Puar, Jasbir 2
public care labour 228, 229
Purse, Lisa 185
Purser, Aimie 117

queer communities 89, 92, 101
queer-identified women 88
queering chrononormativity: absence
  of ageing queer individuals 62–64;
  challenges of 57–59; ethical ageing
  59–62; HIV-AIDS prevention

measures 56; homosexual relationality 65; LGBTIQ+ community 49, 53; LGBTIQ+ movement 48, 54, 56; male sexual and reproductive health 53; non-heteronormative sexual identities 54; physical and mental degeneration 52; protection of transgender persons' rights 52; queer bodies and queer intimacies 51; queer intimacies 55; Seenagers GupShup group 67–70; social scrutiny 55
queer intimacies 83–85

Rahman, Indrani 132
Raja, Ira 7, 8
Rajnikanth 186
Raju, S. Siva 6
Ramanan, Sumana 130
Rao, US Krishna 138
Rasikas 132
Raut, Mayadhar 132, 138
Ray, Deeptanil 108
Ray, Satyajit 41, 135, 191
Reddy, Radha 132
Reddy, Raja 132
religious affiliations 21
Ricoeur, Paul 7
Roseneil, Sasha 91
Rosselli, John 108
Roti (1942) 130
Roy, Sandip 54, 56–57
Rubin, Gayle 40

Saat Hindustani 184
Sandow, Eugen 108, 110, 111
Sandow's Magazine of Physical Culture (1897–1907) 110–111
Sangeetaratnakara 128
Sappho for Equality 88
Sarabhai, Mallika 134, 135
Sarabhai, Revanta 134
Satranj ki Khiladi (Satyajit Ray 1977) 190
satyagraha 30
Scranton, Roy 5
Sec. 377 of the Indian Penal Code 49–50
Section 125 Criminal Procedure Code (CrPC) 37
Seemabaddho 41
Seenagers GupShup group 67–70
Segal, L. 34, 46

Sen, Aparna 41
Sen, Rukmini 7
Sen, Saswati 132
Sengupta, Rudraneil 106
"Senior Privilege Account," for senior citizens 45
sexual desire 84, 91
sexual division of labour 227
sexual indiscipline: and affective relationalities 92–94; of queer lives 93–94
sexual violence 44
Shah, A. M. 36
Shah, Chayanika 7
Shaheen Bagh protest 15–19
Shakespeare 169
Shamitabh 194
Shankar, Uday 138
Sharif, Nawaz 20
Sharma, Anupam Joya 58
Shaw, George Bernard 120
Shivram, Anand 138
Showalter, Elaine 58
Singh, Amobi 138
Singh, Atombi 138
Singh, Bentu 52
Singh, Bipin 138
Singh, K.N. 194
Sinha, Mrinalini 108
Sircar, Badal 166
Sircar, Shoojit 43
Situating the Self (1992) 61
Snyder, Sharon 169
social autonomy 226
social constructionists, account of ageing 134
social gerontology 145, 146
social lives 146
social marginalization 127
social organization, of care 91, 92
social reality 44
social security and ageing, in India: business of caregiving 45; care and companionship-based discourses 44; fine and imprisonment for abandoning parents 43; "Senior Privilege Account" for senior citizens 45
social stratification systems 35
social trajectory 148
social value: of affection 227; cultural richness and 71
" *Sorry We Missed You*" 244–245
South Kolkata 33

Special Marriage Act 100
Spencer, Herbert 120
Spender, Stephen 66
Still Alice (2015) 45
subaltern narratives 108
SubramaniaIyer, Patnam 129
Subramanyam, Malavika A. 58
Sufism 223
Suktankar, Sunil 203
Sunder, Yog 138
Sunderland Daily Echo and Shipping Gazette 108
"Sunstroke" (Tulasi Chaganti 1977) 149–151
Swinnen, Aagje 185

Tagore, Rabindranath 130
The Temple 66
Thadani, Giti 52
Thanmathra (2005) 203
Therigatha 225
Thompson, Neil 36
time, person's relationship with 75
Time Binds: Queer Temporalities, Queer Histories (2010) 48
"Tiny's Granny" (Ismat Chughtai 1954) 147–149
traditional authority 35
Transgender Persons (Protection of Rights) Act 2019 99
transgender women 70
tribal communities 79
Trishul (Yash Chopra 1978) 181
Tulle, Emmanuelle 108, 115
Tulsidas 130
Turner, Bryan S. 35, 38, 39

U Me Aur Hum (2003) 203
Understanding Greying People of India (Arun Bali 1999) 6

United Nations 3
urban India 102

Vaardhakya 219
Vaid, Krishna Baldev 169
Vaidyanathan, Rama 142
Vanita, Ruth 52
Vatsyayan, Kapila 126
Vidal, Gore 66
Vincent, J. A. 5
violence 83; hate and 84; Partition-related violence women 228
Vionnet, Claire 118
voice, in cinema: Bachchan's voice 180, 183, 184, 189, 190, 192, 194, 195; carrier of feelings 182; commentator-acousmêtre 183; de-acousmatization 183; materiality and import of 182; problem of 183; sounds and 182; visualized acousmêtre 182
vulnerability analysis 26–30

Wacquant, Loic 106
Wadia, Riyad 52
Watt, Carey 111
Webb, Gisela 222
Weber, Max 35
Weeks, Jeffery 61
Wilde, Oscar 66
Williams, Tennessee 66
"The Womb" (Chaman Nahal 1988) 151–154
women: age and gender hierarchies 81; caregivers 214; from dominant caste and upper class backgrounds 80; education and work 80; queer-identified women 88
Wyatt-Brown, Anne M. 169

Zen 217

Printed in the USA
CPSIA information can be obtained
at www.ICGtesting.com
LVHW021126170924
791293LV00002B/425